SALISBURY: THE MAN AND HIS POLICIES

Salisbury

The Man and his Policies

Edited by

Lord Blake
Provost of The Queen's College, Oxford

and

Hugh Cecil
Lecturer in History, University of Leeds

**MACMILLAN
PRESS**

First published in 1987

Published by
THE MACMILLAN PRESS LTD
Houndmills, Basingstoke, Hampshire RG21 2XS
and London
Companies and representatives
throughout the world

Typeset by Wessex Typesetters
(Division of The Eastern Press Ltd)
Frome, Somerset

Printed in Hong Kong

British Library Cataloguing in Publication Data
Salisbury: the man and his policies
1. Salisbury, Robert Arthur Talbot
Gascoyne-Cecil, *Marquess of*   2. Prime
ministers – Great Britain – Biography
I. Blake, Robert Blake, *Baron*   II. Cecil,
Hugh
941.081'092'4   DA564.S2
ISBN 0–333–36876–2

Contents

Contents

Preface

A hundred years ago, Robert, third Marquis of Salisbury, formed his first majority government. Since then, he has been the subject of one major biography and several importance monographs. This volume offers a wide range of Salisbury studies, presenting fresh insights, much new research and a variety of interpretations.

After the Introduction (Ch. 1), which outlines his career, the next three essays deal with aspects of his personality. J. F. A. Mason gives us a portrait of the man and his interests, drawing on a uniquely broad knowledge of the Salisbury archives (Ch. 2). The sketch 'Lord Salisbury in Private Life' by Lady Gwendolen Cecil (Ch. 3) was found recently among her papers and contains details not used in her four-volume work on her father; her biographical approach, her unusual character and Salisbury's home life are discussed in the explanatory essay that follows (Ch. 4). The other six essays are on Salisbury's politics. R. M. Stewart looks anew at the combative young Tory at the outset of his public life and the early political journalism (Ch. 5). E. D. Steele considers Salisbury's record as India Secretary in its entirety, giving close attention for the first time to his concern for the domestic as well as the external affairs of the Indian sub-continent (Ch. 6). A. N. Porter reviews Salisbury's foreign policy and seeks to bridge the historiographical divide between those historians who have looked at the 'realities behind diplomacy' and those who have studied the subject from a traditional 'pure diplomacy' angle (Ch. 7). Dr Steele, on the Anglican Church, demonstrates the central place of religion in Salisbury's political life, using Lambeth records and the imperfectly explored sources in the Hatfield collection (Ch. 8). John France takes the themes of Conservative leadership and the perplexing relationship between the third Marquis and the Liberal Unionists which was a vital factor in his party's success at the end of the nineteenth century (Ch. 9). Finally, F. M. L. Thompson employs hitherto untouched Hatfield estate papers to compare Salisbury's record of improvement on his own properties with his well-publicised pronouncements favouring housing-reforms on a national scale (Ch. 10).

It was never supposed that a collection of this kind could be comprehensive; Ireland, for example, is not the subject of a separate essay (though it has received attention in two essays), because the scholars approached were otherwise engaged; essays on other topics were offered but had to be withdrawn because of serious illness; treatment of Salisbury's foreign policy in a 'traditional' manner was passed over in favour of its examination from a less familiar viewpoint. Nor is this a 'commemorative' volume, conceived of in a devotional spirit. If Salisbury emerges, none the less, with credit, this is the result of independent judgement. Besides the presentation of his personality, our concern is that the disinterested research on his politics, embodied here, shall illuminate key aspects of his career for the reader and ease the burden of a future biographer struggling through the vast mass of documents in the Hatfield House Muniment Room.

We are much indebted to the present Marquis of Salisbury for permitting the contributors to quote from material in the Salisbury papers and for his interest and generous hospitality. We are also deeply grateful to the Hatfield Librarian, Robin Harcourt Williams, who has given so much of his time and expert advice. We should like to record our warm thanks to Professor L. P. Curtis, Dr Roy Foster, the late Viscount Macmillan of Ovenden, Mr David Tweedie and Professor John Vincent for help and ideas, to Leeds University for financial assistance towards research, and to Mrs Ann Dale, Mrs E. D. Steele, Mrs Margaret Walkington and Mrs Lorraine Winter for all the typing-work they have done on this volume.

ROBERT BLAKE
HUGH CECIL

Notes on the Contributors

Lord Blake is Provost of The Queen's College, Oxford. His writings include *Disraeli* (1966) and *The Conservative Party from Peel to Thatcher* (1985).

Lady Gwendolen Cecil (1860–1945) was the younger daughter and biographer of the third Marquis of Salisbury.

Hugh Cecil is a Lecturer in History at the University of Leeds. He wrote his doctoral thesis on Lord Robert Cecil during the First World War and at the Peace Conference of Paris.

John France wrote his doctoral thesis (Cantab.) on 'Personalities and Politics in the Formation of the Unionist Alliance, 1885–1895'.

J. F. A. Mason is the Librarian of Christ Church, Oxford. He was the custodian and cataloguer of the papers of the third Marquis of Salisbury during the twenty-five years they were housed at Christ Church (up to 1975).

A. N. Porter is a Reader in History at King's College, London. His writings include *The Origins of the South African War: Joseph Chamberlain and the Diplomacy of Imperialism* (1980) and *Victorian Shipping, Business and Imperial Policy: Donald Currie, the Castle Line and Southern Africa* (forthcoming).

E. D. Steele is a Senior Lecturer in History at the University of Leeds. His writings include *Irish Land and British Politics: Tenant-Right and Nationality, 1865–70* (1974).

Robert Stewart holds a history doctorate from Oxford University. His writings include *The Foundation of the Conservative Party 1830–1867* (1978) and *Henry Brougham, 1778–1868: His Public Career* (1986).

Professor F. M. L. Thompson is the Director of the Institute of Historical Research, University of London. His works include *English Landed Society in the Nineteenth Century* (1963) and *Hampstead: Building a Borough, 1650–1969* (1974).

1
Introduction

LORD BLAKE

Robert Gascoyne-Cecil, third Marquis of Salisbury, was born at Hatfield, the family seat, on 3 February 1830. He died on 22 August 1903. Electorally he was the most successful of all Conservative leaders. He was Prime Minister 1885–6, 1886–92 and 1895–1902. He led his party in five general elections, three of which – 1886, 1895 and 1900 – he won with conclusive majorities. Of the two that he lost, the election of 1885 was a short-lived Gladstonian victory soon reversed, and the election of 1892 was a temporary hiccup in the long run of Conservative success from 1886 to 1905. It did little harm to his party and little good to his opponents.

Cecil was the third son of his father. The second died in infancy. The eldest, who was eight when Robert was born, suffered from a disease of the nerves which caused blindness and death before he was fifty. He never married and his younger brother was therefore, from childhood onwards, the probable but by no means certain heir to the title and its great estates. The nomenclature of the British aristocracy is notoriously confusing. I shall refer to him as Lord Robert Cecil or Cecil till the death of his brother on 14 June 1865, when he becomes Viscount Cranborne, the courtesy title of the heir to the marquisate. He becomes Lord Salisbury with the death of his father on 21 April 1868.

The Cecils were and are one of the oldest and grandest of English families. The originator of their eminence was Lord Burghley, minister of Queen Elizabeth I. He was married twice and had a son by each wife. From the elder son descends the peerage which became the marquisate of Exeter. In August 1853 Lord Robert Cecil obtained his parliamentary seat, the borough of Stamford in Lincolnshire, from his distant cousin, the current Lord Exeter, in whose gift it was. There was no contest then or at any subsequent election during the fifteen years before Lord Robert succeeded his father in the peerage. Burghley's younger son, Robert – a name which has latterly, with one exception, been appropriated in the family for the heir-apparent – followed his father as minister to Queen Elizabeth and then to James I. He was rewarded by being created Earl of Salisbury. But the genes which are supposed to produce brain power seem to have receded in his descendants. Of them Lady Gwendolen Cecil, daughter and biographer of the third Marquis, writes, 'during more than a century and a half the general mediocrity of intelligence which the family displayed was only varied by instances of quite exceptional stupidity'.

This state of affairs was changed by two marriages. The seventh Earl in the latter years of the eighteenth century married Lady Emily Hill, daughter of the first Marquis of Downshire. She was a woman of vivacity, wit and energy. She made her husband's town house in Arlington Street the leading Tory salon of her day, and William Pitt showed his appreciation of her support by giving the Earl a step up in the peerage. She outlived her husband by many years, dying tragically in the fire which destroyed a wing of Hatfield in 1835. Their son, the second Marquis, made an even better, if less aristocratic, marriage than his father. His wife, Frances Gascoyne, belonged to the *haute bourgeoisie*. Sole heiress of her father, Bamber Gascoyne, she brought not only brains but wealth into the family, for she inherited large estates in Lancashire and Essex. This asset was given recognition in the family name by the prefixing of 'Gascoyne' to 'Cecil'. She, like the Dowager Marchioness, was a deeply committed Tory, but she died at forty, when Lord Robert was only ten, and therefore cannot have had much influence on his outlook. Her husband was an able and intelligent man who served in Lord Derby's cabinets of 1852 and 1858–9, but his primary interest was not political. What concerned him far more was the management of his property and his position as a Hertfordshire grandee.

Lord Robert had an unhappy childhood. He had little *rapport* with his father, and his mother's early death was a bitter blow. His life at his private school and Eton was miserable. Tall, thin, myopic and stooping, he was the inevitable victim of bullying at a time when schools were barbaric to a degree inconceivable today. Being extremely clever, he was put into classes with an average age three years above his – which made his situation even worse. When he was fifteen his father removed him to be educated by a private tutor, significantly putting his youngest son down for Harrow. Years later Cecil was asked why he had acquired such a remarkable familiarity with the byways, passages and alleys of London. His reply was that this was how he avoided the risk of meeting an Etonian contemporary in the broader streets.[1]

He fared better at Christ Church, Oxford, where he matriculated in December 1847 after two happy years at Hatfield. He was Secretary and Treasurer of the Union and he read papers to the Pythic Club, that exclusive and supposedly secret society which still exists in Christ Church today, though less for intellectual than for gastronomic pleasures. But illness, nervous and physical, obliged him to go down after two years with an 'honorary fourth class'. He prepared for the Bar but was never called. In 1851 on medical advice he took a long sea voyage, which lasted two years, to South Africa, Australia and New Zealand. In August 1853 he was returned to Parliament for Stamford, and in October he competed for, and won, a Fellowship at All Souls' College, one of Oxford's most notable academic 'plums'.

Four years later he took one of the wisest decisions in his life. He married Georgina Alderson, daughter of Baron Alderson, a judge of the Court of Exchequer, who hailed from Norfolk. She was of the same High Church persuasion as he was. Religion played a vital part in both their lives. She also had a similar sense of humour. But unlike Cecil she was sociable, gregarious and extrovert. She was highly intelligent and ready to talk about all the topics of the day; she suffered from none of the nervousness, the introspection, the shyness which afflicted him in his youth, but which evaporated to a great extent as their married life went by. She was his prop and invaluable support for forty-two years till she died in 1899. The marriage did not meet with the approval of her father-in-law. Money was the reason. She had very little, and Lord Robert only had the interest on £10,000 made over from his mother's fortune and an allowance of £100 a year from his father, which the latter firmly declined to increase. He supplemented a joint income of about £700 a year by an occasional directorship and very frequent journalism – over 600 pieces for the *Saturday Review*. In the early 1860s he was earning at least £300 a year by his pen – a useful addition to his resources. These articles and some thirty-three for the *Quarterly Review* between 1860 and 1883 were anonymous, but they reveal to posterity the 'philosophy' of a Conservative leader with a degree of detail and candour to which there is no parallel.[2] He did not write for pleasure. With the death of his brother in 1865 and his own accession as heir to Hatfield he received a substantially increased allowance from the second Marquis, and the need to write for money vanished.

Derby did not offer him as was expected a post in the Conservative Government of 1858–9, but over the next seven years he attracted more and more notice as a pungent, sarcastic, mordant Tory, though somewhat quirky and heterodox. He did not trust Disraeli and in April 1860 attacked him in the *Quarterly*[3] with such vigour as to draw a reproof from the heads of both branches of the Cecil family. However, Disraeli was the last man to care. By 1866 Cranborne, as Lord Robert now was, had become an obvious runner for the Cabinet, and Derby made him Secretary of State for India in July. By March next year he was out, resigning along with Lord Carnarvon and General Peel because he considered that he had been double-crossed by Derby and Disraeli over the safeguards which he had understood would be inserted in their Reform Bill in order to limit its democratic effect. He was very bitter in print and speech at the time but later decided that the *volte-face* was the result of muddle, confusion and expediency rather than a Machiavellian plot – which was probably true. Nevertheless he was most reluctant to accept Disraeli's offer of the same post in 1874 and he only did so under strong pressure from friends, who were just as doubtful about the Prime Minister as he was.

The interval between his two terms of office saw his accession in 1868 to the marquisate and the estates which went with it and in which he took a far greater interest than one might have expected from his aversion to country pursuits. It also saw his election as Chancellor of Oxford University in 1869 in succession to Lord Derby. From this vantage point he endeavoured to push the modernisation of education particularly in the physical sciences, of which he was a keen amateur practitioner. In 1876 he was to promote a Bill to set up a Royal Commission on Oxford. In the winter of 1867–8 he somewhat surprisingly took on the post of temporary chairman of the Great Eastern Railway and held it till 1872 with notable success.

His second term at the India Office was marked by a considerable closing of the gap between him and Disraeli. They never became intimate, but on the central issue during Disraeli's premiership, the Eastern Question of 1876–8, culminating in the Congress of Berlin, they took the same view at the moment of crisis. Alarmed at the vacillation and indecision of the fifteenth Earl of Derby, his Foreign Secretary, Disraeli had for some time been taking Salisbury into his confidence on foreign affairs and indeed had sent him as an emissary to the Porte in 1876. When Derby finally resigned, on 27 March 1878, the succession almost inevitably went to Salisbury, who in fact was to do all the real work at the Congress.[4] Salisbury thus began his career in the office from which his reputation as a statesman mainly derives. His first term ended in 1880 with the fall of the Conservatives. He doubled the Foreign Office with the premiership in 1885–6, again in 1887–92 and 1895–1900, the only person to have done so apart from Ramsay MacDonald briefly in 1924. There was no reason to take this unusual course – at any rate for so long – unless he regarded foreign affairs with consuming interest, for the Conservative Party was not so destitute of talent as to be incapable of producing reputable candidates.

When Disraeli died in 1881, Salisbury became Conservative leader in the House of Lords, while Sir Stafford Northcote remained leader of the Commons. One of them was certain to be the next Conservative prime minister. The activities of Lord Randolph Churchill and the Fourth Party together with his own deficiencies ensured that it would not be Northcote. When Gladstone resigned in the summer of 1885, the Queen sent for Salisbury. The Conservative prospects did not seem very good. Most people expected a Liberal victory at the next election and another five or six years of Liberal rule. The Liberals did indeed win the 1885 election, but Gladstone's espousal of Irish Home Rule split his party and opened the way to a Conservative breakthrough which, apart from a brief interval, saw out Salisbury's time. Thus he owed his ascendancy largely to Gladstone. This did not worry him at all. He used to maintain, so Lady Gwendolen tells us, 'that Mr. Gladstone's existence was the greatest source of strength which the Conservative party possessed. . . . He did not shrink from facing the fact that according to his view the success of his own party was dependent on the existence of the other; "I rank myself no higher in the scheme of things than a policeman – whose utility would disappear if there were no criminals." '[5]

Salisbury was deeply devout in matters of religion, which he always regarded as far more important than politics. This piety did not preclude – indeed, why should it? – a certain cool, realistic and rather sombre pessimism in the affairs of this world. It was not cynicism, at least not in Oscar Wilde's definition, but it could sound like cynicism. Salisbury was a very unconventional Conservative. He did not embrace positive Conservative 'causes' with any particular enthusiasm, nor did he have any great attachment to the ancient institutions of the country on grounds of emotion, romance or history. He was the least sentimental of Conservatives. But he dreaded the march of democracy, which he regarded as productive of nothing but ill. He was brought up on memories of the Reign of Terror. The Paris Commune, whose ferocious suppression in 1871 gave him much relief, was a reminder of the egalitarian lava which might suddenly yet again erupt from a seemingly extinct volcano. He valued the Conservative Party and the institutions that it cherished for reasons of a sort of inverted Utilitarianism. They were useful to check changes which, far from producing, as Bentham believed, the greatest good of the greatest number, would have exactly the opposite result.

He had a semi-Marxist concept of class, but as with his Utilitarianism he drew the opposite conclusions from the originator of the faith. Class conflict might indeed be a major factor in history, but this was no reason for the possessing classes to surrender. On the contrary, they should resist by every means in their power. He hoped, long before it happened, for an alliance of Conservatives and moderate Liberals united by a desire to preserve the position of the propertied class to which they both belonged. Events, by no means wholly in his control, brought about just such a union. The split in the Liberal Party over Irish Home Rule, which was an issue of property as well as of race, religion and nationalism, ensured his political ascendancy whether independently supported by the Liberal Unionists or in actual coalition with them.

Inside the Conservative Party Salisbury's position was unchallenged after the end of 1886. When he returned to the India Office it had been by no means clear that he would reach the top. Apart from Disraeli himself there was Derby, son of a famous father and an aspirant for the premiership even in 1874, Gathorne Hardy, Stafford Northcote and perhaps some nominal figure such as the Duke of Richmond. By 1885 all of them were out of court. But there was a new star in the firmament, Lord Randolph Churchill, who had engineered the eclipse of Northcote in favour of Salisbury, though with motives anything but altruistic; he had a popular appeal which potentially threatened Salisbury, who nevertheless felt obliged to make him in 1886 both Chancellor of the Exchequer and Leader of the House of Commons – a dual position which could well be a menace to a peer prime minister of relatively recent appointment. But Churchill was reckless and only half-balanced mentally. His

resignation in December on an issue from which he could not hope
to make any political capital was readily accepted, and he sank with
little more than a ripple in the stream of politics. All attempts at a
rapprochement failed. 'Did you ever know of a man who having got
rid of a boil on the back of his neck wants it back again?' So Salisbury
is said to have replied to some well-meaning peacemaker.[6] Salisbury
was safe, but it is interesting to notice that he never again appointed
someone to double the Treasury with the leadership of the House.
Goschen, a Liberal, became Chancellor, and W. H. Smith succeeded
as Leader. When the latter died in 1891, Salisbury appointed his
own nephew Arthur Balfour, whose private correspondence had
done much to enlighten him about the aims of Churchill and the
Fourth Party.

It is easy in retrospect to regard the sixteen years of Conservative
ascendancy under Salisbury after 1886 as more securely based than
it really was – or, at any rate, than it seemed at the time. The
apparently conclusive victory of that year depended for subsequent
success on Liberal Unionist support, which required continuous
vigilance and management. At an early stage by-elections began to
go against the Government, and the 1892 election was a defeat,
albeit marginal. The Liberals, however, bedevilled by personal
feuds, made mistake after mistake and the 1895 election turned out
to be an easy win for Salisbury, though he worked hard for it and
took much trouble in oiling the party machine. This time the Liberal
Unionists formally joined in a coalition government. Once again,
however, the electoral fortunes of the Conservatives slumped and
they lost by-elections with monotonous regularity until the Boer
War broke out, dividing the Liberals and uniting 'patriotic' support
for the Government. Salisbury dissolved Parliament in the autumn
of 1900 well before there was any need to do so and won easily – the
first example of the electoral opportunism which we take for granted
today. He resigned in 1902, handing over the leadership to Balfour.
He did not live to see the debacle that ensued four years later.

Salisbury was in electoral terms the most successful leader the
Conservative Party has so far had. Yet he has never occupied the
position that one might have expected in the Conservative hall of
fame. Peel and Disraeli and Winston Churchill, each of whom won
only a single general election, are, for differing reasons, much better
remembered. There is perhaps some justice in this discrimination. It
would be hard to argue that the Conservative ascendancy from 1886
onwards owed any specific debt to its leader, whose real metier was

in foreign policy – not a field in which elections are at all often won or lost. The break-up of the Liberal Party over Ireland and the slow movement of the more prosperous elements of the middle class away from Liberal nonconformity into Tory Anglicanism were not events within Salisbury's control. The most one could say is that he made the best of the opportunities presented to him and that he did not muff his chances. This is certainly something and not all politicians achieve it, but it is not the basis for a hero-worshipping posterity.

Moreover Salisbury, though respected by his followers, was not really understood by them. His Conservatism was impeccable. He could never be accused, as both Peel and Disraeli were, of 'betraying his party'. When he carried measures of a 'liberal' tendency, his followers appreciated that he was only doing so to forestall similar legislation which would be much more damaging to Conservative interests if shaped by Liberal hands. Yet, although his Tory orthodoxy was not in doubt, his reasons for upholding it, and indeed his whole mental outlook, were different from those of the party faithful. He was very much of an intellectual, arguably the most intellectual of all Conservative leaders. He was also in secular matters a profound pessimist and believed that the state of politics was getting worse. But this did not preclude him from doing all he could to slow down the process, and even those who found his outlook puzzling and perhaps uncongenial could not deny that in the course of nearly fourteen years as Prime Minister he was remarkably successful in doing so.

NOTES

1. Lady Gwendolen Cecil, *Life of Robert Marquis of Salisbury*, I (London, 1921) p. 15.
2. There are two excellent books on Salisbury's intellectual attitude: Michael Pinto-Duschinsky, *The Political Thought of Lord Salisbury, 1854–1868* (London 1967); and *Lord Salisbury on Politics: A Selection from his Articles in the Quarterly Review, 1860–1883*, ed. Paul Smith (Cambridge, 1972), which reprints seven of Salisbury's articles in the *Quarterly*.
3. 'The Budget and the Reform Bill', *Quarterly Review*, Apr 1860; repr. in *Lord Salisbury on Politics*, pp. 115–18.
4. The situation was slightly embarrassing, as Derby had married Salisbury's stepmother.

5. Lady Gwendolen Cecil, *Biographical Studies of the Life and Political Character of Robert Third Marquis of Salisbury* (London, 1949), p. 84.
6. Quoted in Robert Rhodes James, *Lord Randolph Churchill* (London, 1959) p. 311.

2

Lord Salisbury: A Librarian's View

J. F. A. MASON

Robert, third Marquis of Salisbury, sat in the legislature of his country for fifty consecutive years: from 1853 to 1868, first as Lord Robert Cecil and then as Viscount Cranborne, he sat in the Commons as the Conservative member for Stamford on the interest of his kinsman Lord Exeter, until in 1868 he succeeded to his father's peerage. During those fifty years he changed in appearance from a spare young man who had only recently acquired good health to the massive, high-domed figure of the caricaturists; but he always remained a reluctant legislator, pessimistically convinced that man could not be perfected by Act of Parliament. Lord Exeter warned him to expect office in a Conservative government if one was formed at the end of 1855, when Cecil was not quite twenty-six; as it was, he was thirty-six when he first held office, by promotion direct from the back benches to the Cabinet. When, in 1902, he resigned the office of Prime Minister, he had held high office for twenty of the intervening thirty-six years, as Secretary of State for India for eight months under Lord Derby until his resignation over the Second Reform Bill, and for four years under Disraeli; as Secretary of State for Foreign Affairs for two years under Disraeli; and as Prime Minister for thirteen of the seventeen years between 1885 and 1902, doubling this with the Foreign Office except for two periods which amounted to a little over two years. His private papers, in about 200 volumes and over 400 boxes, could, placed side by side, stretch most of the way round the Upper Library of Christ Church, and on a morning in high summer in 1975 they did. The thoughts that follow derive mainly from the fact that the papers were my responsibility for most of the period during which they were in the custody of Christ Church until their return to Hatfield in July 1975. I must speak as a mere librarian: Salisbury is to me in the first instance a man who

10

received and wrote letters. I propose to look at four aspects of his career: his connection with Oxford, his qualifications for high office, his secretariat, and the attitudes revealed by his work at his desk.

Lord Robert Cecil came up to Christ Church as a Gentleman Commoner in Janury 1848, and resided for six terms. Some notion of what sort of place it was may be gathered from a letter written by another Etonian, Lord Dufferin, to a friend two years earlier:

> There is an immense deal of formality and etiquette mixed with the manners of a school; so that it is hard to conduct yourself decently. . . . In winter chapel is at 8 (during summer at 7) after chapel we breakfast. At 9 one has some lecture or other to go to. At 2 men begin to turn out for exercise, at 5 we dine, directly after dinner wine parties are given and about eleven or twelve we go to bed. . . . There are two lectures a day and they last an hour each. . . . There are numerous clubs, some literary, others convivial. . . . These wine parties last a couple or sometimes 3 hours. After wine we amuse ourselves at chess, whist, music or reading as we fancy. . . . I had no idea until I came to Oxford how far Tractarian principles had spread. . . . You know Pusey is a canon of Christ Church. He is a most miserable man to look at, has miserable health, and has lost many children. The dean Gaisford has got a very bad name for incivility, but I do not think he is so bad as he is reported . . . there are college examinations at the end of every term. If a man has been irregular and boisterous without having committed any extraordinary breach of discipline these examinations are made a handle of and he is ejected.[1]

Matters cannot have been much different when Cecil arrived. His tutor was the Senior Censor (the executive officer of the Students – i.e. Fellows – of Christ Church), Osborne Gordon, formerly of Bridgnorth School, 'a pearl among tutors', as Sir Keith Feiling called him, and one of the greatest censors and tutors in the history of Christ Church – and perhaps the only one ever alleged in print by a pupil (a Mitford) to have been seen the worse for drink at Paddington Station.

As was thought proper under Gaisford for one of Cecil's birth, he did not read for Honours: the first of his termly reports runs as follows: 'three plays of Sophocles, *valde bene*; Horace, Odes and Epistles, *satis bene*; Translation, *satis bene*; Greek, *valde bene*; Theology, *bene*, Trigonometry, *optime*'. (He would not have been able to do Trigonometry at all if he had not been removed from Eton at sixteen.) So he went on, with five or six subjects each term, and very good marks in each. Two things are obvious about his academic record: first, this is not the reading of a pass man, for it offends against the basic principle that, if too much matter is crammed into certain kinds of head, an equivalent amount will be ejected; secondly, the marks themselves are much above a pass man's level – at the end he was given an 'Honorary Fourth' in mathematics.

Cecil in 1853 won a Fellowship at All Souls', and by the convention of those times took his name off the books of Christ Church. But he was not forgotten there: in 1865 he was among those considered as an arbiter in the struggle for power between the Canons and the Students of his old College, and late in 1869 his nomination as Chancellor of the University was widely supported by members of Christ Church. Salisbury became Chancellor without any real opposition not because Convocation wished to make sure of a future Prime Minister – on the four previous occasions the University had elected someone who already was or had been Prime Minister – but to secure the best available opponent of the moves to abolish the remaining religious Tests.[2] Among Salisbury's backers for the chancellorship was Dr Pusey; alas, within a few months the new Chancellor was in trouble with the occupant of the South-West Lodgings: he proposed for honorary degrees at his Encaenia three men whose private conduct Pusey thought was improper. Pusey sent the Chancellor what Salisbury (no mean judge) thought 'an intemperate letter'; it was typical of Pusey that he gave it to Dean Liddell, the Vice-Chancellor, to hand over. The Marquis thought that as the University had honoured Lord Palmerston it ought not to object to his nominations of men whose errors were neither well-evidenced nor likely; but he withdrew the names, and Pusey had struck one more blow – though for what, as can happen in such cases, is none too clear. The two were soon on good terms again and deep in correspondence on the Second Commission.

As his sons grew up, Lord Salisbury faced a difficulty about Christ Church, as a result of which he sent four of his sons to University College. Kenneth Rose has cited three reasons: recollections of the aristocratic dissipation of his own undergraduate days, the matrimonial designs of Mrs Liddell for what are described as the three younger sisters of her famous daughter, Alice, and disquiet about unorthodox instruction at Christ Church.[3] The story of Mrs Liddell's matrimonial plans is, no doubt, good for a laugh; but Rose has failed to notice that the Liddells had not three unmarried daughters but two: for Edith (who in any case was seven years older than Salisbury's eldest son) they could make no plans, for she had died, much mourned, in 1876 and had been commemorated by an anguished inscription in Christ Church Cathedral ('Ave dulcissima, dilectissima Ave'). Moreover, it does not seem to me axiomatic that the second cousins of Henry Liddell, Earl of Ravensworth, would be thought unworthy of the sons of Robert, Marquis of Salisbury, and the daughter of a Tractarian judge. It is the received tradition here that the young Cecils were diverted to University College because Lord Salisbury could not risk their being affected by one particular influence in Christ Church. It had elected a Tutor in Ancient History: his name was R. W. Macan. In 1877 Macan had published a book entitled *The Resurrection of Jesus Christ* which the Master of Selwyn has described as 'radical enough'. Pusey and Salisbury thought it unsound. The book is not in Christ Church library. In 1881 Macan committed a further imprudence: he married, and thus had to be re-elected to his studentship and tutorship. In the early 1950s, older men at Christ Church who had known survivors from that time of turmoil could still point out to a new arrival the place where seventy years before, on 15 June 1882, Dr Pusey had stood when, after struggling for the last time from his lodgings, he addressed the Governing Body with all the weight of his eighty-two years, the solemn utterance of a dying man and, perhaps, a frenzy induced by many past failures to stem the tide of secularism, and urged that Macan be not re-elected. This time Pusey won, by sixteen votes to eleven, with one abstention; Macan was not re-elected, Christ Church was divided for some years, and the young Cecils continued to go to University College.[4] The first two went there in 1880 and January 1882, and the third twelve months later. But planning is not an exact science: in 1884 University College elected a new Fellow and Tutor in Ancient History – his name was R. W. Macan. However, Salisbury sent his son Hugh to University College in 1887, and none of his sons came to any harm there. University College did not teach Lord Hugh Cecil better manners in the House of Commons, but perhaps Christ Church could not have done that either.[5]

This story does not figure in Liddon's *Life* of Pusey, which merely says that 'although wearied by his effort to attend a meeting of the Governing Body in the previous day'[6] he left the next day for Ascot – I mean, of course, his house there – where he died three months

later. Dr Macan became Master of University College and died, full
of honours, as recently as 1941, aged ninety-three. It must be added
that after 1882 he stuck to the safer ground of Herodotus and
translations of the Collects into Latin verse. His last surviving child
died in 1976 aged ninety-one.

I have dwelt on the Macan episode because the facts seem to me
not to accord with Lady Gwendolen Cecil's picture in her biography
of her father: she stresses that Lord Salisbury encouraged the
growth of a spirit of free inquiry in his children.[7] Yet no explanation
that has been given of his sons' move to University College assumes
that they had any choice in one of the most important decisions of
their lives, or shows their father as anything but a heavy Victorian
parent.

After Pusey's death, it was in Salisbury's house at 20 Arlington
Street, with his encouragement, that was launched the project we
know as Pusey House.[8] Salisbury remained in touch with other
Christ Church friends, notably Dr Liddon (Pusey's ally in the Macan
debate) and C. L. Dodgson (Lewis Carroll). Dodgson first met the
Marquis through Liddon and photographed him at the chancellorial
Encaenia in 1870; he dined at the Cecils' London house a fortnight
later, and from then on he was an occasional visitor to Hatfield. It
has not been noticed that Dodgson occupied rooms in Christ
Church which had also been Salisbury's. From time to time he
favoured Salisbury with letters on a strange variety of subjects:
vivisection, 'proportionate representation', a proposal for a series of
look-out points in London to watch for fires, the desirability of a visit
by the Queen to Dublin in 1897 (she did go, in 1900), and what
Dodgson called 'the transmigration' of the inhabitants of Tristan da
Cunha. The suggestion about watch-towers (made the day after a
serious fire at the Criterion Restaurant) appealed to Salisbury's love
of gadgetry; and he actually tried to do something about the
transmigration of the Tristanians – a cause dear to Dodgson because
his brother was chaplain in that remote and windswept archipelago.

Christ Church eventually elected Salisbury to an honorary
studentship, the highest dignity it can confer, but not until 1894. He
was the first Christ Church prime minister to receive this dignity
after his accession to the highest office; but this of course is a mere
accident of chronology, for Honorary Students were not made in
Christ Church between the foundation and 1858, when Gladstone
(in recognition of his services during the first phase of Univeristy
reform) and nine others were so honoured. In 1878 Christ Church

honoured both William Stubbs and S. R. Gardiner in this way: both
had overcome obstacles, for Gardiner had once been an Irvingite
(had indeed married Edward Irving's daughter), and had in
consequence been removed from the roll of Students by Dean
Gaisford; Stubbs (who when he was honoured was Regius Professor
of Modern History) had not even been a commoner, but had been a
Servitor (with free rooms and lecture fees paid) living in an attic in
the Peckwater Quadrangle of Christ Church. After 1878 the college
made no new Honorary Student for fourteen years until it honoured
Liddell, after his retirement; then, in 1894, on the same day Lord
Rosebery and Lord Salisbury received this distinction – the 'dark
horse in the loose box', who had been Prime Minister for three
months, and the greatest active statesman of his day, who had been
Prime Minister for most of the previous nine years. One may safely
deduce an impasse between opposed political groups in that
Governing Body: those who wanted Rosebery had to stomach
Salisbury. Five years later, when Dr A. T. Carter, long afterwards a
generous benefactor, proposed the renegade Liberal Lord Dufferin
for the same distinction, to be beaten by twenty votes to six, it was
very hard treatment for a man who had been Ambassador in St
Petersburg, Rome and Paris, Governor General of Canada and
Viceroy of India; but his name had been involved in a financial
scandal.[9]

To Lord Salisbury as Prime Minister Christ Church owes several
canons and two of its deans: in 1891 he named Paget as Dean and in
1901 T. B. Strong. This was before the casual institution of the
process of informal consultation the origins of which had been
described by Sir John Masterman: Paget was strongly pushed by Sir
John Mowbray, a member of the House and MP for the University;
Strong was recommended by Paget and by Sir Michael Hicks Beach,
who was at Christ Church in Liddell's early days, and wrote a brisk
letter surveying the field, ending with a brief clear message of the
kind which Salisbury liked: 'No answer required. I advise Strong.'
And Strong it was, for nineteen successful years.

Salisbury was Chancellor of Oxford for longer than anyone else
has ever been: the convention of the time did not require him to
come there much, though he came on certain grand occasions – for
instance an appeal on behalf of the Radcliffe Infirmary (1 March
1893) – and his correspondence was mostly routine except when
chancellorial permission was sought by those who wished to
migrate from one college to another. These included Arnold

Toynbee, who went from Pembroke to Balliol. In the 1870s, as Oxford's Chancellor in the Cabinet, Salisbury played a crucial role in the passage of the Oxford and Cambridge Bills. His letters to Disraeli show that he attached no sanctity ('finality' was not a word he liked) to the position reached by the Oxford Act of 1854, and that he correctly divined the new situation: that both Conservatives and Liberals in Oxford were afraid of losing revenues 'to Colleges in the North' (by which he meant those many miles north of Keble). As the present Chancellor, Lord Stockton, reminded Oxonians not long ago, if you want a reform the first thing to do is to get hold of someone else's property.

In considering Salisbury's preparation for high office, to which I now turn, his position in Oxford has some place, not merely because any experience of disputatious quarrelsome men such as dons must be useful in dealing with similar men who are politicians, but also because both his election as Chancellor and his conduct in that office show something of an ability to attract support on other than straight party grounds. As Lord Blake has said, he was certainly no stereotype. He clearly lacked some of the gifts necessary for full social intercourse with some, at any rate, of his class and party. He could not see too well and was not to be found on the grouse moors. He did not enjoy being on a horse, and as time went on a horse would not much have enjoyed it either. He disliked horse-racing: after his accession he cancelled permission for the Hertfordshire Yeomanry races to be held in Hatfield Park, because they had come to be frequented by 'large numbers of the worst part of the population of London' and produced 'disorder and demoralisation'. However, it is satisfactory to note that he once allowed a visiting party into the Park with the proviso 'That they must not interfere with the cricket'. He gloomily accepted the regular effects of the racing-calendar on the political one, but he fully shared the view that from August to October ministers were entitled to travel: thus in 1888 Baron de Worms, whose mind was always on sugar, was told sharply on 25 August from the Second Empire surroundings of Royat, 'till the end of October it will not be possible to get at the Cabinet'. Salisbury did not much enjoy the clubs: according to his secretary he 'found the Athenaeum and the two Carltons more than enough', though he felt he had to join the Prince of Wales's Marlborough Club, which was 'free from political bores and [where] the food was particularly good', and he belonged to smaller, more select institutions. Even at the Athenaeum he had his troubles: in

1901 Curzon in India was regaled with the news that Salisbury had to give up lunching there because his umbrella was always being stolen. Salisbury himself apparently had no doubt about the culprits: 'It's the Bishops', he said. The point is that he did lunch *there*, thus avoiding the boredom but also the political benefits of the two Carltons; after all, he had become a member by ordinary, not extraordinary, election as far back as 1858.

In some respects he was unique among our prime ministers and in a few he remains unique now. He is, so far, the only prime minister who has ever been a Fellow of All Souls' after examination; this may tell us something about other prime ministers – perhaps also something about All Souls', though he was in fact founder's kin. He was the first prime minister who had travelled round the world: in 1851–3, for the sake of his health and on the advice of Dr Acland, he visited Cape Colony, South Australia, Victoria, New South Wales, Van Diemen's Land and New Zealand before returning round the Horn. The next future prime minister to go round the world was his nephew Balfour, in 1875–6, and then Ramsay Macdonald in 1906. Except for Wellington's passage to the Cape and India, Disraeli's and Gladstone's Mediterranean visits and Derby's trip to America, Salisbury's predecessors' journeys had been only to Europe. In South Africa Salisbury thought the Kaffirs 'a singular instance of a tribe totally without the idea of God', and the Boers 'as degraded a set of savages as any white man in the world'; he found South Australia 'the youngest and most Yankee of the colonies', described with great humour and some condescension the goldfields further east,[10] but liked New Zealand, favourable references to which crop up in his writings. Salisbury has another qualification for ruling men: it cannot be said that he had known poverty, but he had certainly known adversity – his father had much disliked his marriage to Georgina Alderson, and for some years the younger Cecil was somewhat straitened in means, living in Mansfield Street, which lay north of Wigmore Street and was therefore unfashionable. His father thought that Miss Alderson's family contained unreliable members, and he may have been right: Georgina's brother E. P. Alderson (his middle name was Pakenham) certainly led Salisbury into some unwise ventures. It was lack of means which led Salisbury to become the most prolific working journalist among prime ministers: he wrote for the *Quarterly Review* and the *Saturday Review* because he needed the money to augment the £400 a year which he received in parental allowances. For the

Quarterly he wrote twenty-four articles at up to 15,000 words a time between 1860 and 1866, and a further nine between 1867 and 1883 – a total of over 370,000 words; for the *Saturday* he wrote perhaps 1,250,000 words over a period of ten years (1856–66). From the *Saturday* alone he doubled his income in the early 1860s. In all this vast output – the equivalent of 20 volumes for the Oxford Historical Monograph series or over three volumes of *EHR* – he never descended to mere padding, but read the books he reviewed, cracked jokes, and stated his extreme views, without wasting a word. He never drooled, and showed an ability not common among journalists to get facts right. Like his Christ Church report, his record in journalism shows a capacity for consistently regular application.

The need for journalism faded when Cecil's elder brother died in 1865, and he became his father's heir. Next year, and again eight years later, he went to the India Office. He is the only secretary of state for India who ever became prime minister, but he never visited India (which no prime minister between Wellington and Macdonald visited). Only two points need to be made about his tenure. First, the affairs of India touched the domestic affairs of Britain at several points, notably its military establishment and manufacturing districts. Secondly, the Secretary of State for India had one function which no other Cabinet minister performed and which was good training for the highest office: at this time he chose bishops. The see of Calcutta fell vacant in 1866, and the task of filling it distracted Salisbury during the next two months. There were at least twenty-three candidates, though five, each of whom had recommended himself (one of them three times), stood no chance; and there were several refusals. Even his final success may have taught him something: he finally got an acceptance from one of his own relations, Robert Milman, Lady Salisbury's first cousin. (I am not going to talk about the Hotel Cecil, except to report an apt comment by Salisbury's younger brother Eustace on the new government of 1895: 'It is too much to expect that everybody should be satisfied – but everybody (including the Family) is – I think – fully represented'.) In 1876 Salisbury was again at the India Office when Milman died, and the Secretary of State had to go through the process again, though this time the answer emerged more quickly.

In the interval between his resignation in March 1866 and his succession to his father, Salisbury widened his experience still further. He was badly hit by the City crash of Overend Gurney just before he went to the India Office, but his first employment after his India Office was not due to a wish for financial gain. In January 1868 he became Chairman of the Great Eastern Railway for four crucial years in the history of that line, now recalled to us only by the names of some East Anglian hotels. No other prime minister has ever run a railway, though Gladstone in the 1840s worked hard on complex railway legislation, and Harold Wilson wrote a thesis on railway finance which was stolen by an undiscriminating and we must hope disappointed thief. In July 1867 the Great Eastern had been put in the hands of the Receiver, and at an interview in Scotland the chairmanship had been offered to and refused by Sir Edward Watkin, a Liberal MP who was already chairman of other companies. Watkin, by his own account, promised to find a substitute: this was Salisbury, whom he had long admired. Characteristically, Sailsbury answered Watkin's eventual letter by return of post.

Salisbury's papers contain about 2000 letters received by him as Chairman of the Great Eastern; 800 of them (about two every three days) were from the General Manager, Swarbrick. I am grateful to my friend Professor Theo Barker of the London School of Economics for an early sight of his study of this material.[11] Again, the impression is of a man with a remarkable capacity for mastering new matter and for the efficient dispatch of complex business. A week after his election he introduced a new arrangement by which individual directors took responsibility for the company's six major functions (traffic, ways and works, stores, locomotion, finance, and steamboats); he himself took the chair at all meetings of the committees concerned. The chairmanship also involved negotiations with foreign powers – in this case the chairmen of the other railway companies, men like Richard Moon who behaved like petty kings in their own domain. The famous circular which Salisbury later sent out when Foreign Secretary after four hours work one night was not the first great circular which he despatched; he sent one to his fellow railway chairmen in 1869, and put Moon in his place when he was supercilious about it.

When Salisbury took over the Great Eastern some of its locomotives ran wearing notices that they were the property of certain specified creditors as security for debts – there is apparently one of these informative objects in the Wisbech Museum. In July 1868 the Official Receiver was discharged and next year the Great Eastern paid a dividend again: the cash necessary for re-expansion had been advanced following a conference between Watkin, Rothschild, two other bankers and Salisbury. The Great Eastern got remarkable value for the Chairman's salary of £700 a year, not all of which Salisbury received. Salisbury got an acquaintance with the world of business, further confirmation that he could master any brief (as befitted a member of the Royal Statistical Society, he quickly appreciated the value of high load factors on his line) and, as I shall remark later, further evidence that the experts were not to be trusted.

Three months after Salisbury took over the Great Eastern his father died. The Salisbury property was by no means exclusively rural: it included urban property in Ilford and Hatfield, and over 1000 acres at Childwall in Liverpool. Salisbury did not much enjoy the routine aspects of running a great estate during the years 1872–4 and 1880–5 when he had most time for them: he was interested rather in electric light for Hatfield House. But it may be argued that his position in Hertfordshire was important in the second of the three critical periods in Salisbury's life.

In the first, in the 1850s, he was saved from ill-health by Dr Acland and the world tour, and from self-doubt and unhappiness by Georgina Alderson. (His mother had died in 1839, and he missed her much.) The second period was a briefer one, beginning with his resignation in March 1867. Up to this time and later his judgement was suspect; he wrote so many sharp things about Disraeli (though he did not write all those attributed to him) that his return to office might have been difficult – perhaps, like Henry I with Anselm, he was banking on the older man's early death. After Disraeli's defeat in 1868 he wrote in the *Saturday* an article entitled 'How the Old Tories Look at the Elections'; does the adjective suggest that he intended to form a corps as inward-looking as the Old Whigs of a century before? He would have been foolish to do so: whether or not he had schoolboy intimations of future greatness, such intimations crowded on him after his resignation: Lord Exeter hoped that Salisbury or General Peel would form a Conservative government – though as to Peel the dream was futile; more important, Sir Philip Rose, the Principal Agent of the party in the 1850s and Disraeli's 'man of business', wrote the day after the resignation to say that 'nothing will ever shake my convictions as to the future of your political career'. Rose was perhaps hedging his bets. What emerge from Salisbury's papers are the practical demands of his position. Between 1866 and 1874 he had plenty of time to become convinced

of the necessity of co-operation with others: for most of the time he
had to chair meetings, first of his Council at the India Office, then of
the Great Eastern, and from 1868 on his county. It was perhaps in his
own county of Hertford that Salisbury came to recognise that there
could be no future in standing aside from his party. He refused
point-blank to help the Hertfordshire Conservatives in the general
election of 1868 – and was not displeased that the Great Eastern was
accused of showing favour to both sides in that contest. His
increasing participation in county politics, in a cause which could
only assist Disraeli, can be traced in his correspondence during the
next few years with the squires of Hertfordshire (whom, of course,
he met on county business) – R. W. Gaussen, Abel Smith, Colonel
Smith-Dorrien and the Dimsdales. Service as MP for the borough of
Stamford was not a good apprenticeship for politics after the Second
Reform Act, for Stamford had not taken too much notice of the
First;[12] in Hertfordshire there was for a time a Conservative
Registration Society, linked with a Central Conservative
Registration Association in London, and Salisbury aided it. At the
local level Salisbury was thoroughly involved with the
Hertfordshire Conservatives: on 12 February 1874 one of the squires
acknowledged receipt of some 'handsome enclosures' (he did not
mean birds) in meeting the election expenses; on the 16th Disraeli
wrote to suggest a meeting, and Salisbury entered the Government.

I turn now to Salisbury's secretariat. Until he was thirty-eight he
had no private secretary, though of course he had an official one
when at the India Office. For whatever reasons, very few letters *to*
him survive for the years before 1866: no doubt the move to and
from Mansfield Street explains this dearth. Until 1868 he kept no
copies of his out letters, though his relatives kept the letters sent
from the Antipodes, and of course some survive in other collections.
For some years before 1868, no such copies survive in his own
papers, and this want of material for half his life, including the first
of the three most critical periods, has deterred at least one
biographer. In 1868, after his father's death, he acquired a very
efficient and tidy private secretary in R. T. Gunton, who outlived
him. Gunton saw many official papers and wrote or typed letters at
Hatfield on political business, though not normally those to more
important correspondents or those on more important topics. For
instance, it is a fair reflection of Salisbury's views on Imperial
Federation that it was Gunton who typed letters on that subject.
Above all Gunton started and kept letter-books for his master: from

May 1868 he recorded copies of nearly 500 letters in the 'Secretary's Note-books', as they were called.

I need not dwell on the merits of the staff which Salisbury enjoyed as Foreign Secretary, for they have been well marshalled for us by the formidable researches of Dr Zara Steiner:[13] Thomas Sanderson, whose powers of drafting matched Salisbury's own, Julian Pauncefote, Philip Currie and the Foreign Secretary's own private secretary, Eric Barrington, a stickler for dress and an arrant snob. It was Barrington's task to produce the file copies of Salisbury's out letters, and in the 140 volumes of private Foreign Office correspondence which are now at Hatfield there are copies of nearly 1500 letters so entered; these are additional to those in official custody. Those 1500 copies are of course the main source for Lady Gwendolen Cecil's account of her father's diplomacy; she has been critised for not casting her net wider, but her knowledge of her father's papers was enormous: there was no section of them in which one might not find annotations in that spidery hand – written, improperly, in ink.

As Prime Minister Salisbury's first private secretary was Henry Manners, later Marquess of Granby and Duke of Rutland. One can easily be misled, but he creates no impression of great efficiency; he was to develop into the forbidding figure who gave the young Duff Cooper such a chilly reception at their well-known meeting in the First World War. In 1888 Manners was succeeded by Schomberg McDonnell, brother of the Earl of Antrim, then aged twenty-seven and so a contemporary of Salisbury's children. McDonnell (always known as Pom) was, like Manners, one of the 'souls' who gathered round Curzon, and a man at home in the clubs who was able for that reason to remedy any deficiencies in Salisbury's own knowledge of society and intrigue. Above all, he was discreet and efficient, clearing business through with great rapidity; moreover he could look after himself, and in dealings with Sir Ellis Ashmead-Bartlett he had to.[14] He stayed with Salisbury until the end, apart from the period out of office, when he worked in the Conservative Central Office, and a year at the Boer War. McDonnell served his master particularly well on three important topics which had to be put before him: bishoprics, lord-lieutenancies and honours.

The correspondence on vacant sees is extensive, and the more so where the bishoprics at issue were in most eyes the least desirable – the Welsh sees. Salisbury sometimes sought advice on clerical preferment, but got a good deal which was unsolicited. His Christ

Church acquaintance Lord Harrowby advanced the claims of Low Churchmen in near-illegible handwriting; Salisbury's brother-in-law Beresford Hope pushed the claims of the High Church, as did Lord Beauchamp (like Harrowby, another contemporary at Christ Church), who was never content to move one cleric if he could possibly move two. Salisbury once gave deep offence to Beauchamp by filling up a canonry of Worcester (Beauchamp's own country) without consultation. However, on another occasion Salisbury had to admit that he had given a promise about a canonry of Chichester to the Duke of Richmond, who at Goodwood House took a natural interest in such a matter. It is well known that the clergy themselves exasperated Salisbury by their hesitations and refusals – though no such reproach can be brought against the two deans of Christ Church whom he made: Paget accepted the offer on the day it was made, and Strong on the day after. (This, of course, was before the Post Office had applied its mind to delaying the mails.)

Lord-lieutenancies took up less space – there were many more counties than dioceses, but Lord Lieutenancies lasted longer, indeed were meant to: Shropshire enjoyed into the second half of the twentieth century the nominal and absentee sway of a descendant of Robert Clive nominated by Salisbury as far back as 1896. McDonnell's dockets are a short guide to the relative standing, financial difficulties (and sometimes the marital problems) of Unionist and Liberal Unionist aspirants and nominees in the counties which happened to fall vacant. Again it was the fish in the smallest ponds who caused the most agitation: what seems to us excessive correspondence was generated by the need to find lords lieutenant for such distant and minute satrapies as Bute and Nairn. The office was important because its holder had the nomination of justices of the peace.

The number of honours awarded reached a new peak under Salisbury, because the two jubilees and still more the Coronation increased not only the zest for honours but also the willingness of the Crown to grant them. McDonnell organised the papers and kept a register; on this matter he had to work closely with two other invaluable servants of Lord Salisbury, the Chief Whip, Aretas Akers-Douglas, and the Chief Party Agent from 1885 to 1903, 'Captain' Richard Middleton, known as 'The Skipper', both of them from Kent, where Douglas owned 15,000 acres. Salisbury once paid Middleton a compliment which he never paid McDonnell: he substituted a paragraph by Middleton for one drafted by himself.

The value of their partnership has been shown in the biography of Akers-Douglas, written by his grandson Lord Chilston.[15] Liaison with them was the task of the Prime Minister's private secretary, and only Lord Chilston's book gives any idea in detail of McDonnell's role as the link between Leader and Whip and Agent. No such position applied in 1905. McDonnell deserves a separate study: he will emerge as an essential cog which never slipped.

With all his merits, McDonnell did not keep letter-books; accordingly, when Lady Gwendolen Cecil came to write the biography of her father, she set out to collect from the recipients or their heirs copies of as many letters by him as possible. For the period up to 1892 she collected as many as 3200 from nearly 100 recipients; a third of these were written to the Queen and Disraeli, and another third to Hardy, Lady John Manners, Churchill, Smith, Lytton, Carnarvon and Knutsford. Her biography was written without the aid of many or any letters to his one-time Home Secretary, Matthews (whom Salisbury ought to have sacked), Harrowby, her cousin Balfour, Cross, Richmond, Ridley or Ritchie. She also had available the letters Salisbury had written as Foreign Secretary, and the 500 preserved in the Secretary's Note-books, and entered in the later books of the Secretary of State for India. To these can now be added many further copies made at Christ Church from various drafts scattered throughout the papers.[16]

Anyone who uses Salisbury's papers must marvel at his power of lucid rapid extempore composition in any subject whatever; the replies he wrote on the backs of letters contain hardly an erasure. He possessed this same facility, as it seems to me, in the French language. At times he lamented the lack of equal clarity in others: thus he wrote in 1888, 'After my experience with Lord Wolseley I have some doubt of my capacity for translating so difficult a language as English.' Salisbury was a master of the brusque and categorical denial: those who wrote to inquire whether he really had said something which he had not, or followed some policy on his estate which he did not, received short shrift; what most annoyed Salisbury was the attribution to him in such 'impudent fabrications' of a stupidity of which he could never have been guilty. He answered such accusations if received through the post; hostile allegations in the newspapers he usually ignored, unless the perversion of truth was too 'monstrous' to be tolerated. He was of course capable of indiscretion: it is difficult to forget his description of French possessions in North Africa as 'light sandy soil', or his 'provident Somali' (also long in print) who once confused the diplomats by picking up a flag on the coast of Somaliland. His intelligence was too lively always to be discreet, and this was probably one reason why he disliked receiving deputations unless he had to: the solemnity of such occasions bored him, and he probably did not trust himself to utter the anodyne formulae dictated by prudence. On paper he knew how to say 'No', particularly to those who maintained (wrongly) that he had once given some promise of an honour, or (sometimes correctly) that some other Conservative had done so.

One them which recurs constantly in his drafts is his distrust of experts: by and large he does not cite them. It is true that there were some matters into which he felt he could not enter, such as Bimetallism or the complex question of whether there were two earls of Mar. His distaste for experts went back a long way: he was long haunted by the memory of what he regarded as a failure in 1866 of the Indian Government, i.e. the experts, to take any necessary action against a coming famine, when he was the responsible Minister of the India Office.[17] In the middle of 1868 he could write that six months at the Great Eastern had convinced him of the unreliability of engineers, who were (of course) proffering opinions about the Channel Tunnel. The most trenchant instance of his view of experts which I recall came later: it was necessary, for the purposes of creating suffragan bishoprics, for the Law Officers to decide whether Kensington, Stepney and other populous places in London were localities or 'towns'. They ruled that they were 'localities'; this was too much, and Salisbury minuted, 'Ignore the opinion of the Law Officers. It is obviously absurd.'

None of us, I think, would have liked a dismissive letter from him. Dean Liddell as Vice-Chancellor once received one; he had conveyed a resolution of Hebdomadal Council to stop payment of a salary to the Chancellor's secretary: Salisbury thanked him formally and ended, 'I have no remark to offer upon the Resolution except to say that I regret it.'

If at this stage you ask, what use did Salisbury make of all these assets, I can only refer you to the works of those able, as I am not, to put Salisbury's work in a wider context. The books of Professor John Grenville on Salisbury's foreign policy, of Dr Rose Greaves on his policy in Persia, of Lord Chilston on his Chief Whip, of Dr Perry Curtis on his coercion and conciliation in Ireland,[18] and of many others – I name only some of those who seem to me to have shown the widest acquaintance with Lord Salisbury's private papers – have not, I think, diminished Lord Salisbury's stature in public affairs. Yet a recent study, by Dr Southgate, does seek to diminish him.[19] His conception of a man who missed opportunities, and was weak as Prime Minister, is not one readily to be accepted, unless his circumstances are ignored, and the value of a valiant effort to keep the peace underestimated. My last quotations from the Salisbury Papers are from letters to two men not in politics; the first, in particular, well describes Salisbury's own view of his position, the second expresses some basic elements in his outlook. The Bishop of Rochester in 1901 wanted Salisbury to take action on the Church question: Salisbury told him it was impossible, for 'we are a Coalition government'. The Conservatives had a clear majority in the House of Commons elected in 1895, but there were Liberals in the Cabinet: 'any reliance on our assumed majority' was 'simply futile' and 'the strongest Ministry of modern times' was 'one of the most foolish cant phrases that ever obtained currency'.

In August 1902, after his resignation, Salisbury wrote to Lord Northcote, Governor of Bombay – who incidentally never seems to have taken the critical view of Salisbury's treatment of his father, Lord Iddesleigh, which some moderns take – and explained his departure. He had resigned, he said, because successive attacks of influenza had weakened his powers of work:

> especially as since the death of the late Queen politics have lost their zest for me. . . . Being in the House of Commons gives him [Balfour] an advantage which I have sadly missed. . . . In this age of the world, the fate of nations depends on the life of individuals. The Pope, the Sultan, the Emperor of Austria, have all three in their hands, by the simple process of dying, the power to throw the world into confusion. Let us hope that for sometime yet they will abstain from exercising this prerogative.

The last sentence points to a man who knew where he was with long-lasting individuals abroad, but never felt secure with the House of Commons. His distrust of this body was formed, it must be remembered, in the period when every House of Commons had overturned at least one government; it had not been aided by the advent of the Irish Question.

It is highly appropriate that this letter (one of Salisbury's last on politics) should contain a reference to the Queen. He admired her, respected and used her great knowledge, was indeed caught out by her occasionally. Her successor he thought trivial: above all the Prince, quite apart from his indulgences, could not do what Salisbury and the Queen could do so well – he could not concentrate. The Prince had given Salisbury trouble on and off for over twenty years, from the time when, making arrangements for the Prince's visit to India in the 1870s, Salisbury had expressed to the Viceroy the Queen's fears of 'zenanas being escaladed by ladders of rope'. The Prince was probably by that time physically unsuited to that kind of escalation, and preferred more convenient and semi-official arrangements; but the Queen was thinking of some of the Prince's associates, who long compounded his problems. The Prince's family did not help: the love of Prince Eddy for Princess Hélène of Orleans in 1890 caused much agitation to Salisbury, Balfour and Halsbury. In 1891 Salisbury found irksome his inevitable involvement in the affair of the Prince, Lord Charles Beresford and Beresford's wife, particularly as he had to pronounce on the letters to be exchanged. To Beresford he wrote, 'The acquaintance of *no* illustrious person is necessary for one's happiness; . . . my advice is to sit still and do nothing.' Unfortunately, Charlie B. did not. With the King's accession came the wearisome business of Coronation honours, which Salisbury found more distasteful than ever. One of his worst shocks was the Prince's request for peerages for Sir Ernest Cassell and Sir Thomas Lipton. Ten years before, Salisbury had thought knighthood 'impossible' for a man who made money as a bookmaker and brewer. It was time to go.

Thus the last great crisis of his life reached its peak: in 1898 he had been ill, at the end of 1899 his wife died, in 1900 Sir Henry Acland died, and at the beginning of 1901 the Queen died and he could not shake off influenza. This time none could help him, and he gave up. He had worked too hard for fifty years, foreign travel was no use, and in little over a year he was dead.

Lord Salisbury was one of a succession of young men from the propertied classes who came to Christ Church before serving the state as John Fell in 1660 intended they should: of those who distinguished themselves as undergraduates and politicians, one must rank him with Peel and Gladstone, though the conditions in which Salisbury, Peel and Gladstone worked at Christ Church, under a bullying dean, a bad dean, a remote dean, differed much.

In discussing Salisbury's qualifications, his servants, and his

mastery of the English language as a tool of government, I hope to
have shown that he was a complex, fascinating and likable man.
When I gave the lecture on which this essay is based, I had been
preceded in the same series by five colleagues writing on other
eminent Christ Church figures – Locke, Shelburne, Holland,
Gaisford and Pusey. That choice of personalities at least made my
concluding sentence easy for me: of the six scholars and statesmen
on the list, Lord Salisbury alone was at the same time in intellect and
attitude a scholar, and in achievement a statesman.

NOTES

In its original form this essay was delivered late in the Michaelmas term of
1977 as one in a series of lectures at Christ Church, Oxford, entitled 'Christ
Church Scholars and Statesmen'. It is based on notes made while the
Salisbury archive was housed at that college. Unless otherwise stated, the
documents quoted are from the 'Salisbury Papers' (the simple form of
citation then used) and no reference for these is given.

1. Christ Church MS 594 (photocopy), Sotheby's 6th sale, 1973, lot 263. I
   wish to thank the Marquis of Dufferin and Ava for permission to quote.
2. J. F. A. Mason, 'The Election of Lord Salisbury as Chancellor of the
   University of Oxford', *Oxoniensia*, xxix–xxx (1964–5).
3. Kenneth Rose, *The Later Cecils* (London, 1975) p. 63.
4. See Viscount Cecil of Chelwood, *All the Way* (London, 1949) Ch. 1.
5. For the children of Lord Salisbury, see below, Ch. 3.
6. H. P. Liddon, *Life of Edward Bouverie Pusey*, 4 vols (London, 1894–8).
7. Lady Gwendolen Cecil, *Life of Robert Marquis of Salisbury*, iii (London,
   1931) ch. 1.
8. College of clergy at Oxford, to promote theological study and religious
   life within the University. The proposal was accepted at the meeting in
   Arlington Street on 16 November 1882 and the sum of £50,000 was
   raised to purchase and house Pusey's library.
9. 'The Great Pacific Scandal': following allegations of fraud by Sir Hugh
   Allan, the contractor for the Canadian Pacific Railway, the Canadian
   Parliament was prorogued and the Conservative Prime Minister
   resigned. Dufferin, the Governor-General, was not a guilty party and
   did much to restore morale.
10. See *Lord Robert Cecil's Goldfields Diary*, introduction and notes by E. Scott
    (Melbourne, 1935). (Part of diary only.)
11. T. C. Barker, 'Lord Salisbury: Chairman of the Great Eastern Railway,
    1868–72', in Sheila Marriner (ed.), *Business and Businessmen* (Liverpool,
    1978).
12. On the Cecil pocket borough of Stamford, see J. M. Lee, 'Modern
    Stamford', in Alan Rogers (ed.), *The Making of Stamford* (Leicester,
    1965).

13. Zara Steiner, *The Foreign Office and Foreign Policy, 1898–1914* (Cambridge, 1969), esp. pp. 22–3.
14. Sir Ellis Ashmead-Bartlett (1849–1902), ambitious, exhibitionistic, grandiloquent, hard-working, over-spending Conservative politician of American extraction.
15. Eric Alexander Akers-Douglas, third Viscount Chilston, *Chief Whip: the Political Life and Times of Aretas Akers-Douglas, 1st Viscount Chilston* (London, 1961).
16. For Lady Gwendolen's working methods see below, Ch. 4.
17. See below, Ch. 6.
18. J. A. S. Grenville, *Lord Salisbury and Foreign Policy: The Close of the Nineteenth Century* (London, 1964); Rose Greaves, *Persia and the Defence of India, 1884–1892: A Study in the Foreign Policy of the Third Marquis of Salisbury* (London, 1959); L. P. Curtis, *Coercion and Conciliation in Ireland, 1880–1892: A Study in Conservative Unionism* (Princeton, NJ, 1963).
19. Donald Southgate, 'From Disraeli to Law', in Lord Butler (ed.), *The Conservatives: A History from the Origins to 1965* (London, 1977) p. 224.

3
Lord Salisbury in Private Life

LADY GWENDOLEN CECIL
(edited by Hugh Cecil)

This essay was one of four written by Lady Gwendolen Cecil between 1906 and 1911. These were 'studies' for the life of her father which she completed after the First World War. They were intended only to be read by members of the family. In October 1948, three years after Lady Gwendolen's death, three of these essays – on Salisbury and home affairs, as leader and at the Foreign Office – went to press in a book of 128 pages with the title *Biographical Studies of the Life and Political Career of Robert, Third Marquis of Salisbury.* This was a private edition, issued in 1949 for limited circulation only, because it was felt that some of Salisbury's remarks – about democracy in particular – might arouse unwelcome criticism at that time. Members of the family, principally Lady Gwendolen's brother and sister-in-law, Lord and Lady Cecil of Chelwood, had edited the manuscript for the volume. 120 copies were printed at a cost of £160, attractively produced on handmade paper, with white cloth covers.

These were distributed to the relations of Lord Salisbury, to the libraries of the House of Commons, of the Foreign and Cabinet Office and of Eton College – among other institutions – as well as to various individuals, including Guy Burgess, John Foster Dulles, Harold Macmillan and Adlai Stevenson.[1] In one of the most significant works on Salisbury published since that date, the author has paid tribute to 'the very frank and valuable appraisal of her father's outlook' that Lady Gwendolen gave in these essays.[2]

The fourth essay, on Salisbury's private life, which is printed here, was not included in that edition. To judge by the correspondence, the reason was probably its 'intimate' nature. Though there is nothing here to shock, there is less of general political interest than in the other studies and it is by far the most personal account of Salisbury written by his daughter. It comes nearer to hero worship than any of her other accounts. Many of the observations made in this essay appear in Lady Gwendolen's analysis of Salisbury's religious beliefs in the first volume of the *Life,*[3] for which she used his early diaries, notes and letters, as well as her own recollections. However, this study contains information not found elsewhere – for example, on Salisbury's choice of reading and on his views about the religious commentators of his day.

The text has needed very little editing. This editor has followed most of the minor changes suggested by Lord and Lady Cecil. For example, they recommended that, where Lady Gwendolen had put 'S', 'Salisbury' should be substituted. Other alterations are indicated in the notes at the end. Lady Gwendolen's life and work are explained later in this volume.

My thanks are due to Lady Gwendolen's literary executors for permission to publish this essay.

Lord Salisbury had a great many interests in life but very few pleasures. He was wont to say of himself that the only pleasure which he found entirely satisfying was that of sleep. Those of society he did not enjoy. I have already spoken of his incapacity for establishing any bond of promiscuous or general sympathy with those into whose company he might be thrown.[4] This incapacity was probably one result of a more fundamental impediment to social enjoyment from which he suffered. He could not believe that he himself, his concerns or his opinions, could be of any interest to others outside the circle of those who were bound to him by the ties of close affection. When he found himself sitting next to a stranger or an acquaintance, his first reflection was 'How bored they will be' – with the inevitably resulting conviction of how bored he himself would be. He often protested on the grounds of compassion against the issue of a proposed invitation: 'Poor man, what has he done that you should ask him? – He will feel himself bound to accept and he will be so bored.' Conversational enjoyment was all but impossible under such circumstances. It was a pity, for though he could never have earned the reputation of being a great talker, his conversational gifts were of a high order. Those who were resolved to find pleasure in his society, and succeeded in compelling him to recognise their capacity for doing so, had their reward. He was never loquacious; no man was easier to reduce to silence, and without a deliberate effort towards reticence on the part of companions more talkative than himself there was always a risk of this happening. His reading was wide and all that he had read, or at least all that he remembered of what he had read, was mentally digested and transformed into food for thought. The process was one of very pronounced activity; the opinions which he drew from books if not opposed to those of the authors studied were generally divergent from them. This constantly critical attitude effectually barred him from being overweighted with his own learning. Upon certain subjects, – and they covered a large field of human thought and interest, – it was almost impossible to catch him tripping, to discover in him any lacuna of knowledge. Yet he never for an instant gave the impression of lecturing, or of consciously imparting information. This was also partly due to the fact that he always – and in apparent sincerity – began by assuming an equal store of knowledge on the part of his interlocutor. In spite of all lamentable experience to the contrary he persisted in regarding all his children when young as reincarnations of Macaulay's schoolboy.[5] When, as often happened, in response to some assumption of the kind rather more overwhelming than usual he was met by a blunt assertion of ignorance he would receive the declaration with a somewhat pained but always new surprise. What must be described as the instructive aspect of his conversation, – only that the expression seems so entirely unsuitable to the form which it took, – had one unfortunate effect. It acted as an actual deterrent to habits of reading in those around him. It was so much easier and pleasanter, where intellectual curiosity was aroused, to obtain information by word of mouth than by the study of books; especially when the former method was accompanied as it was in this case by a running comment of the most suggestive criticism and allusion. I must not, however, be taken as indicating that the subjects of his conversational choice were all of a high intellectual order. Quite the contrary; he could discuss the plot of the last 'shilling shocker' that he had read, or the latest development in the progress of the youngest grandchild, or some trivial incident which had struck his sense of humour in the day's interviews, with as fresh an interest if not so profound a one as he would display in questioning the bearing of a new scientific discovery, reflecting upon an observed tendency in the field of larger politics, or seeking out the causes of some historical event or contemporary theological aberration. He was not fond of argument and I do not think that he argued well. His professional habits were too strong upon him; he was too keen to win, too prone to the methods of debate. Sometimes, where his real interest in the subject was sufficiently strong, he could pass from discussion to argument without ceasing to seek seriously for added light upon the point at issue. But not often. There were times indeed when he became possessed by a spirit of sheer mischief and contradiction; – refusing to see his opponent's points and bewildering him with a word-play which though quite unanswerable was unconvincing and not intended to convince. In discussion, which was not argument, none of this was so. Then he would seize a point almost before it was expressed; and it was seldom that the subject closed without larger issues or deeper foundations coming into view than had[6] been realised at the outset.

But in the memory of those who enjoyed his talk, when it was at its best, the substance is almost obscured by the brilliancy of the clothing. He hardly ever told a good story; a finished epigram or a word-play that could bear repetition was of rare occurrence; but the flashes of wit were as incessant as they were spontaneous. Even in discussions upon the most serious subjects an unexpected turn of ironic phrase, – an allusive metaphor, – a passing thrust at some object of popular worship, – an epithet whose audacity conveyed a volume of unexpressed criticism, – followed each other rapidly, claiming neither notice nor reply, past as soon as uttered. He seldom excited laughter, – an involuntary twitching of the lips or an answering gleam of the eyes were the outward response elicited. But I think that his listeners felt that every faculty they possessed of perception and comprehension was stimulated into highest activity while in his company. And there was also a sense of constant artistic satisfaction; every phrase was happy, every sentence, – even those dealing with the most trivial subjects, – had a polish and distinction of its own. I am describing him at his best, and perhaps he was never seen completely at his best except in the circle of his closest intimacy. Indeed from one point of view intimacy was absolutely necessary for correct appreciation. You had to be possessed of the key to the cypher. No man when he chose could say exactly what he meant with greater clearness and accuracy; but in social as distinct from business conversation, when he was entirely at his ease and in company where he knew that misapprehension was impossible, his true meaning was very seldom contained in the exact grammatical interpretation of his words. He would protest against such interpretation being applied. When hampered by the fear of it, his sparkle became restrained beneath a flow of careful and rather saltless courtesy, – unless indeed, as occasionally happened, that spirit of mischief to which I have alluded seized upon him. Then to the consternation of his friends he would surpass himself in what they knew could only be regarded as outrageous improprieties of sentiment; when afterwards remonstrated with, he would show his

malice prepense by impenitent assertions that he had said nothing
that was not 'highly proper', and supporting the contention by
mock serious paraphrases of his recent utterances.

His own manners were unfailingly courteous though sometimes a
little absent-minded, and he was fastidiously critical of the manners
of others, – particularly of those of women, or of men when in the
society of women. That he should have noticed, as he did in this
connection, any failure of delicacy on the one part or of due respect
on the other, was in curious contrast to his quite peculiarly
unobservant habit in nearly every other direction. In no way were
the results of this habit more striking than in his incapacity for
recognising faces. One day, – it was while the ministry of '86–'92
was in power, – he was present at a man's breakfast party. He sat at
the right hand of his host and in the course of the meal asked him in
an undertone who it was who was seated on his – the host's – left. It
was Mr W. H. Smith who had been his own colleague for years, who
was at that moment the second man in his Ministry, and in almost
daily business communication with himself. The only plea that he
could urge in excuse of this wonderful blunder was that he always
sat opposite to Mr Smith in Cabinet and had therefore never learnt
what his profile looked like. This was no doubt an extreme instance
of his failing, – but there were many others almost as bad. His sons,
if they came upon him unexpectedly or where the light was not very
good, had frequently to speak to him before he would recognise
them. His shortness of sight was no doubt, both directly and
indirectly, largely responsible for these lapses. It was not very acute;
but the defect had probably increased a natural tendency towards
the contemplation of inward rather than of outward objects of
vision.

Such pleasure in the theatre as he might have had was limited by
two impediments; he suffered physically from the bad air and
mentally from an extreme fastidiousness of taste, both as regards
the substance of the plays performed and the manner of their
performance. In his later years he rarely went to the theatre,[7] – only,
so far as I can recollect, when one of Shakespeare's plays was on the
boards. In his younger days he was fond of the French comic opera
of Offenbach; and to the end of his life he enjoyed the Italian music
of his youth and used to lament its gradual decay in the public taste.
To have it played or sung to him in his own house was one of the
most indubitable pleasures that he had; but even in this case his
desire to hear it was seldom keen enough to draw him to the opera

house. It is fair to add, both as regards the theatre and the opera, that for the last twenty years of his life he was as a rule working at too high a pressure to have either the time or the physical energy for their enjoyment. He was quite impervious to the charms of classical music and could never be persuaded to believe that anything but a respect for orthodoxy accounted for its attraction for others. He cared little for pictures or sculpture and always proclaimed himself in matters of art a philistine. His indifference to artistic surroundings was certainly shown in his choice of the furniture and decorations of his own rooms. They were saved indeed from aggressive ugliness by their very lack of pretension towards any standard of appearance whatever – as far removed from the philistinism of Tottenham Court Road[8] as they were from all other aesthetic ideals. You felt when you entered them that you were in a world where the very existence of outward form was unrecognised. The furniture was selected and arranged with an entire disregard to shape or character. Beautiful pieces left there by his ancestors were placed side by side with the crudest fittings of a modern office, or with ingenious devices of his own carried out with a fine simplicity by the house carpenter; and, except for these last, hardly any of the articles present were being used for the purpose for which they had been originally designed. Utility and convenience were the ideals exclusively aimed at, and themselves were apprehended after an entirely unconventional fashion. Where he was left to follow his own wishes, his choice of dress showed the same notes of originality in his conception of comfort and his total indifference to appearance.

There was one form of beauty however which always appealed to him strongly, – that of nature; and its hold upon him increased with age. His taste in this matter grew more catholic as he grew older. In his younger days he would scarcely admit the existence of natural beauty apart from great distances and rugged outlines. But in his old age, though he would still maintain the superiority of more majestic scenery, he enjoyed to the full the shaded greens and changing lights which belong to the restricted horizons of his own home. He had however no more taste for other pleasures proper to the country than he had for those of the town. His father, accepting the county gentleman's ideal of life as the only one possible, had had him taught to shoot and ride in his boyhood; but education proved powerless to overcome natural distaste and inaptitude. He followed both pursuits in moderation in his youth; abandoned them on the ground of expense during his early married life – but without any painful sense of sacrifice; and resumed them only fitfully in later years. A horse was never more to him than an animated and very badly regulated machine. His only object when he got on its back was to make it take him as quickly as possible from one place to another. With this view he would urge it forward at full speed, entirely disregarding both the character of the ground and the steepness of the gradients traversed; and the result was not without peril to both horseman and animal. Increasing age and weight soon made riding, thus understood, an impossibility. When he could no longer take the walking exercise by which he had been wont to keep himself in health, his doctors in vain urged the resumption of riding. A compromise was effected through the invention of the safety tricycle. He learned to ride one and he rode it almost daily till within a few weeks of his death. He would go out annually for a day or two's rabbit shooting; but I never knew him indulge in any more adventurous or more elaborate form of sport. There were however two interests connected with country life which touched him on other and more sympathetic sides of his character – that of botany which he had studied almost from his boyhood and which appealed to his love of science, and that of farming, evolved comparatively late in life as the result of circumstances which induced him to take it up as an occupation.[9]

It is indeed rather to his occupations than to his amusements that one must look for the recreations of his leisure hours. He had many intellectual interests but it was noticeable in him that even these were to a great degree translated into occupations. There was a constant aversion from inaction; the stirring of the intelligence seemed to rouse the will, the mental processes to be bound up with the voluntary ones. An exception to this might be claimed for his interest in literature, and, so far as this existed in a pure and undiluted form, the exception would have to be allowed. But an enjoyment of literature simply for itself was not strongly marked in him. He was keenly appreciative of beauties and felicities in writing, clear and unhesitating in his preference or dislike for different styles; he had the artist's value for the art which he himself exercised: but, in his choice of reading, the matter was considered at least as much as the manner. A bit of merely 'pretty writing', as he called it, bored him. Without being a voluminous novel reader he read a good many novels; but his choice in them could not be said to have been determined by their literary quality. He read them when he was tired, and like most other hard-worked men preferred those which intrinsically, or from long familiarity, made the least demand on his mental energies. In modern productions, a good story was all that he asked for; though he would occasionally growl at the appalling character of the English in which some of them were clothed. At one time he was a great reader of French novels, but like many others he lived to lament their modern decay in quality. He unhesitatingly declared his preference for studying serious questions in a direct fashion and eschewed almost entirely the novel about religious or ethical problems. Among classical novelists his affections were chiefly given to Scott and Miss Austen. The wit of the latter was a source of unfailing delight to him, and he read and re-read her books to the end of his life. The '*morale*' of both these authors was an undoubted attraction to him; he shrank from any note of moral ugliness or bitterness. Thackeray was wholly repellent to him, and, though he read and admired Dickens, he was not a worshipper. The appeal which poetry made to him was neither wide nor deep, though it had a more real existence than he himself would allow. He started with a conviction of his inability to appreciate it which was hardly warranted by the facts. Late in life he made more than one discovery of his power to take pleasure in poetry, which up till then he had never attempted to read. This was, so I recall, with some of Shelley's shorter poems and some of Milton's. There were other poets who were really life-long and familiar companions to him. Goethe's Faust he always spoke of with sustained enthusiasm. Volumes of certain small pocket editions of poetry accompanied him on every holiday that he took. They included the works of Shakespeare, Horace and Euripides – more rarely Virgil, and I think Aeschylus. In that later period, when the French novel of today had ceased to satisfy, he would lay down some specimen that had been recommended for his reading and through which, as he would complain, he had been wearily following the analysis of a most uninteresting young woman's sensations, and say with a sigh of relief: 'I have done my so many pages – and I think I may now go back to Horace!' or whichever of his favourites happened to be in his pocket at the moment. Why the classical poets mentioned should have been cherished above others must be left to those who are acquainted with them to determine.[10] Whatever may have first fixed his attachment to them, its exclusive continuance was no doubt largely the result of familiarity. Among more modern poets he was fond of Byron, cared little for Tennyson, and would not read Wordsworth. He had a keen delight in Pope's exquisite phrasing and rhythm, and was intimately acquainted with Dryden's political satires; but I doubt whether in either of these cases the poetic[11] quality in the authors had much to do with his admiration of them.

When one turns to the serious prose reading which more prominently occupied his leisure hours, one is struck at once by his preference for subjects connected with the effectual activities of life and thought. He was curious, it is true, for knowledge in itself, apart from any immediate practical use which might be made of it. But it was knowledge bearing upon the actual world in which he lived, its material nature on the one hand, its intellectual and spiritual life on the other. History, science and theology almost exclusively composed his serious reading.[12]

He was an omnivorous reader of history and managed in spite of his work to keep abreast of its modern output. But he disliked the type of history which is becoming increasingly common and popular; that in which the facts are gathered round some central idea or ideas of the author, and wherein their effect in supporting or in throwing doubt upon his theories is the aspect in which they are almost exclusively considered. 'I want to know what happened, not what the man thinks', would be his irritable comment. There were two classes of history which appealed to him. One was the picturesque narrative of events, of which the writings of Macaulay and Froude are the pre-eminent examples, and which, with less perfection of charm but perhaps greater capacity to convince, is represented in the works of the late Dr Creighton and Professor Hodgkin.[13] The other was the simple record drawn from original documents and presented largely in their language, with little comment and with no deduced generalisations. If the former class appealed to his imagination and sense of literature, the latter satisfied his hunger for material on which his own mind could work, unfretted by the intrusion of other men's opinions and theories. There were few periods or subjects of history which failed to interest him, but the subject which had the most constant fascination for him was that of the French Revolution. He collected a considerable mass of literature relating to it, both among contemporary newspapers and periodicals and among historians and memoirs of subsequent publication; a column of his library was filled with the results. The attraction which this subject had for him was very comprehensible; there is a point of view from which the Reign of Terror may be looked upon as the supreme historical Nemesis of Optimism; – whether of that displayed by the amiable theorists who hailed its approach, or that owned by the imbeciles in authority who never saw the storm coming till it was bursting over their heads.

Lord Salisbury's interest in science was fundamental to his nature. Indeed many of the intellectual traits which characterised him in his profession might be identified as belonging to the scientific order of mind. The form in which his interest was displayed exemplified in a striking manner that constant impulse towards action to which I have alluded. He read science; the shelves of his private library were furnished with the newest scientific books and papers. But his rooms were also filled with scientific instruments and apparatus; he was perpetually trying experiments of his own, taking notes of them, drawing conclusions, checking results. It was all on a minute scale; but for the moment the object of investigation was pursued with an earnestness, an absorption of mind, and an attention to detail as great as that which any professional scientist brings to the achievement of a discovery of first class magnitude. It might be only a fragment of his time that he could give, the attention of an already tired brain; but the gift such as it was was without reserve. In intention and spirit, he was never an amateur.

In the same way his interest in a new invention could not find satisfaction in simply paying to have it supplied to him. Incandescent electric lighting had just become practicable when he went out of office in '80, and the idea of installing it at Hatfield was seized upon as a welcome occupation for his leisure. It never occurred to him to put the work into the hands of experts. He drew out his plans and had them carried out under his own eyes by the half-trained and wholly untrained workmen in his own employment. The results were not immediately successful. There were some years of transition marked by dinners eaten in the light of bed-candles; by occasional storms of miniature lightning alternating with abysmal darkness; by minor conflagrations and explosions. But the master of the house regarded these incidents only as welcome evidence as to the rival merits of 'series' or 'parallels' and as to the most desirable thickness of wire to be employed or number of lamps to be used.[14] Without such failures, the interest of lighting his house could hardly have been maintained until Mr Gladstone's Home Rule Bill was introduced.

It was during the same period that the prevailing depression of agriculture left him with one or two farms upon his hands. As has been already indicated he had no natural taste for outdoor country life, and – as a science – farming had hitherto remained a closed book to him. But, since it had to be undertaken, had set about it in the same characteristic fashion. With ordnance map in hand he trudged from field to field, discussed the cropping of each, present and future, with his bailiffs and filled notebooks with elaborate statistics and carefully calculated averages of cost and profit. I do not know that he made it pay; but the work gave him an interest in his agricultural property which the fact of receiving rents from it had never produced.[15]

In the same way theology may be said to have appealed to Lord Salisbury more on its human than on its philosophic side; in its connection both past and present with the lives of men rather than in its purely intellectual aspect. He had studied and had a wide knowledge of the various phases of thought which have coloured men's acceptance of Christianity or their rejection of it from the earliest times. There was a certain detachment in his attitude towards the questions involved, as interesting him more in their bearing on the faith of others than in any possible influence they could have upon his own. But, in the former connection, such problems and the solutions which they have received did have for him an interest commensurate with what he held to be the importance of their results.

I should not venture to say how many of the Fathers he had read; – their study in the original had formed his principal occupation during the eighteen months voyage round the world which he undertook for his health in his youth. It would have been difficult to puzzle him about any of the Greek heresies of the fourth and fifth centuries, – he could define the subtleties of their divisions and sub-divisions, tell of the Councils which condemned them and of the personalities who preached or denounced them. He would discuss the Schoolmen of the thirteenth century and the sides which they took in the metaphysical controversies of their time: and his knowledge of the different shades of doctrine preached by the innumerable sects, which divided Christendom during and just after the Reformation, was full. Among questions having a nearer interest to our own day he was naturally well acquainted with the controversies which were stirred by the Tractarian movement,[16] both with regard to the Roman and the Protestant sides of the question, and with the writings of many of its leaders. He had probably read everything that Newman[17] wrote and had the greatest reverence for his genius. He would I think have preferred him as a writer above all rivals for his complete mastery of English and for the exquisite charm which characterised his use of it. But, at least in later life, Lord Salisbury was no whole-hearted admirer of the man himself. Newman's ego occupied too large a space upon his mental horizon for him to become the hero of one who at times seemed hardly conscious of the existence of his own.

Lord Salisbury's interest in the larger problems which involve the basis upon which revealed religion rests was limited by what amounted to an aversion from the science of metaphysics. To his mind the greater part of abstract philosophy was but an attempt to define the undefinable, to assume the existence of an external standpoint of observation which in the nature of things no human mind can occupy in analysing the laws of its own being. He saw lines of reasoning cut across by chasms upon whose borders the intellectually sincere were forced to pause and admit defeat; but which professors of the science had too often attempted to bridge by phrases which were but an involuntary confession of their inability to sound the depths beneath them. When such questions were brought before him as matters of interest in themselves, he would generally turn from them with an almost impatient assertion of his inability to understand the importance which other men attached to them.[18]

The only work on philosophy which I have heard him speak of with complete admiration, and recommend to the reading of others, was Butler's *Analogy*.[19] He had read it himself before he was eighteen. I believe that his was not the only case in which that work had attracted the interest of minds to whom the great mass of metaphysical philosophy, is as a closed book, but his knowledge of such literature was not profound. On the subject of Biblical criticism he was more in his element. He followed the early discussions on the authorship of the New Testament, was in this connection a great admirer of Lightfoot,[20] and from a literary point of view of Renan also.[21] It happened that soon after the publication of *Lux Mundi*[22] he went out of office, and he at once started upon a work by Wellhausen[23] for his holiday reading. His conversation at the time became a running commentary on the book. He was not struck by its argumentative power and declared it to be a prolonged begging of the questions at issue. In the light of this reading, and of the study of other books bearing on the same subject with which he followed it up, he took great exception to the phrase in the preface of *Lux Mundi* which foreshadowed in connection with those difficulties a possible crisis in the Church similar to that associated with the name of Galileo.[24] To compare a series of literary and historical theories, founded upon a wholly inconclusive and unscientific chain of reasoning, with Galileo's discovery of the Earth's movement round the sun, seemed to him a noticeable piece of exaggeration. It is fair to add that if he minimised, and he undoubtedly did, the importance of the whole of this controversy, it was partly because it hardly touched the position which he had himself always occupied on these questions. He had never accepted the extreme views of verbal inspiration, nor regarded the Old Testament as claiming any authority on matters of history or science.

The practical influence which religious belief has exerted and still exerts upon human history was constantly present to his mind. Indeed, I think that he would have maintained that it is impossible to read history in any wide sense without realising the importance of even the driest and subtlest theological controversy in so far as it embodies the religious opinions and the religious emotions of the period and which gave rise to it. He was never weary of quoting the dictum that the only really powerful influences upon the actions of men, taken in the mass, are religion and hunger. As regards the importance of this influence in the history of Christendom, this view was of necessity deepened and strengthened by the direction of his own religious beliefs. There the power at work has been that of a faith which he held to be unique in its eternal truth and divine origin. I remember some utterances of his in[25] the course of a discussion on French politics at a time when the Government of France, sustained apparently by popular approval was showing symptoms of engaging upon a frankly hostile attack on Christianity. He quoted Professor Clifford's[26] charge against that religion that it had destroyed two civilisations and had only just failed in destroying a third, – and quoted it with agreement. What had been, would be. The result was contained in the inherent nature of things, and was independent of any conscious action of purpose on the part of believers. Christianity could know no neutrality, was incapable of co-existing permanently with a civilisation which it did not inspire; and how much more so[27] with a civilisation which had been formed under its auspices and which had subsequently rejected it. Such a society if it persisted in the rejection must inevitably perish: and he spoke with gloomy and impressive earnestness of the human suffering necessarily involved in such a catastrophe. Not only did he regard all political action as of infinitely small importance as compared with this question of Christianising or of maintaining the Christianity of our civilisation but he would scarcely allow any competing value to other forms of social or philanthropic effect for the spread of culture or the elevation of mankind. He would speak · of them as being the luxuries of philanthropy and having little right to consideration while the necessities of the spiritual life were still unprovided for. He would never acquiesce in the clergy giving such work a prominent place in their ministry, nor was he himself often willing to support it. 'They are asking for bread and you are offering them a stone'[28] was his answer to an appeal for assistance for some social work carried on by the Church in a poor district of London. While full of pity for the material needs and sufferings of mankind, he was curiously little moved by the cry of intellectual destitution. This was no doubt partly due to the fact that, as I have suggested, it was always an impulse towards action or the contemplation of it which stirred his own mental interest rather than any pursuit of intellectual enjoyment for its own sake. But any attempt to reach the moral or spiritual side of man except through the Gospel aroused him to actual antagonism. His attitude on this point in its uncomprising directness might have stood comparison with that of an eighteenth century follower of John Wesley.

The conditions which surrounded his own acceptance of Christianity did not admit of his being placed in any of the categories in which it is sometimes sought to classify believers. More than one allusion has been made to the essential scepticism of his temperament. It would be difficult to lay too heavy an emphasis upon his instinctive claim to the right of free thought, upon his habitual rejection of external authority in matters of opinion. He was assuredly not among those whose religious belief is founded upon a natural impulse towards submission or credulity. Neither did his faith originate in a passive acquiescence in habits of thought instilled in childhood. So far as can be known the religious influences which surrounded him in early youth were not powerful, nor did they belong to the school of thought which chiefly coloured his creed in maturity. His mother died when he was nine years old; with his father, a man of temperament wholly different from his own, he was never intimate. In its religious atmosphere his home was typical of scores of others of the same social class at that period, scarcely touched by the wave of evangelical revival, and not yet recognising the existence of other spiritual forces – forces which from one direction or another were even then preparing to break so roughly upon the religious slumber of a century and a half's duration. When in 1845 – the year of Newman's secession to Rome and of culminating crisis in the history of the High Church movement – Lady Mildred Cecil, Salisbury's eldest sister, was married to Mr Beresford Hope – the bridegroom was rallied in his brother-in-law's presence for being a Puseyite, and the lad wondered to what the phrase referred. He had never yet heard it nor of the system of doctrine which it then represented in the public eye. He was then fifteen; six years later he left Oxford a devout Tractarian. The intellectual character of his creed, the form which his religious convictions finally assumed was certainly self-taught, the product of conclusions deliberately and independently arrived at after he had attained the age of reason.[29] And enough has already been said to show that he was not safeguarded from disturbance to his faith by any indifference. There was no inertness of mind on the subject of religion, no ignoring of the existence of conflicting opinions, no lack of curiosity in becoming acquainted with the causes that have produced them, or with the arguments by which they are defended.

And yet as a matter of fact his faith never was disturbed; nor does he even appear to have passed through any period of religious doubt, in spite of the fact that during several years in his youth his thoughts were mainly concentrated upon religious questions. This statement is no surmise, though those who knew him well would anyhow find it easy of acceptance. I can recall at least one categoric declaration.[30] In the course of a discussion as to the effectiveness, – looked upon as an argument for the truth of revelation, – of the appeal of Christian ethics to the moral sense of mankind, Lord Salisbury disputed its value. Pressed by those who differed from him he quoted his own experience. He declared that he had never known what it was to doubt the truth of Christian doctrine, while all his life he had found a difficulty in accepting the moral teaching of the Gospels. He added that, in fact, he did accept that teaching only as a matter of faith and on account of the divine authority upon which it rested. This conversation had a curious sequel. One of those who had taken part in it was present shortly afterwards at a meeting held for the open discussion of religious questions in one of the poor districts of London. A man in the audience – a dock labourer – rose in the course of the meeting to declare himself an atheist, giving as the reason for his disbelief in God the impossibility which he felt of accepting the teaching of the Sermon on the Mount. His auditor, who had been confident of the singularity of Lord Salisbury's view, was struck by its being so soon corroborated, though with a wholly different result upon the speaker's opinions, from the very other end of the social scale.

Lord Salisbury's attitude towards the issues which mainly divide English Churchmen among themselves cannot with entire accuracy be labelled with any of the party names ordinarily in use. His opinions were founded upon Tractarian teaching; in the matter of Sacramental doctrine, certainly with regard to that of the Holy Communion, he accepted the High Church position. He would define a Low Churchman as being only an uninstructed High Churchman. But he would hardly have given to questions of Church government and discipline the importance assigned to them by some of the followers of the Oxford movement, though perhaps the practical outcome of his opinions was not very different from that of theirs. If he hesitated to claim episcopal ordination as an essential condition for the true ministry of the Sacraments; if he regarded the fact of an apostolic succession exclusively through bishops as wanting in absolute proof; if he would on occasions grumble at some Roman or Anglican pronouncement as attributing too much of what he would call the 'chemical' element to ministerial ordination,[31] he would not on that ground have admitted the possibility of himself communicating in a non-episcopal church, or of encouraging others to do the same. Indeed as a matter of fact when the opportunity of doing so was presented to him he steadfastly rejected it.[32] He would undoubtedly have regarded such an action as making light of very holy things – the rule which the Church has received and holds as having at least the greatest probability of being in accordance with the Divine Will must in all things govern the practice of her members. But at the same time he extended a very large measure of sympathy and respect to other bodies of Christians. He was extremely averse from all wholesale anathemas or confident erection of limits to the operation of Divine grace. Perhaps partly on that account he had none of that nervous anxiety as to whether his own Church had maintained herself within those limits, had preserved the 'notes of Catholicity', which troubled the earlier Tractarians. He did not feel the necessity for personal agreement on matters of doctrine with the bulk of his fellow-churchmen, or with their representative leaders. Its absence did not distress him, nor could he be brought to understand the distress which in their own case it caused to Newman, Manning and their contemporaries. 'If I myself am satisfied that I believe what is true, what can it matter what others worshipping beside me believe?'[33]

But in all these matters a limitation of degree must be understood. There were items of the Christian creed for which he claimed an absoluteness of respect and acceptance which was reserved for them alone. He never consented to the mental habit of treating all variations of opinion from Roman Catholicism to Unitarianism, or to the vaguest form of Pantheism, as a continuous grading of religious thought. He drew a sharp line between those who accepted and those who denied the doctrine of Our Lord's Divinity. On one side of that line all differences were to a degree relative, temporary, superficial. With those who stood on the other side no compromise, no basis even of common action, was possible.

His aversion from the subtility of metaphysical analysis showed itself in his whole attitude towards the problems of Christian theology. I have heard him say that the foundation upon which he would still prefer to rest Christian apologetics was the old one of the historical evidence of the Resurrection. That is not the same thing as saying that Christian faith can be evolved simply by a rational process starting from a historical fact. The opinion must rather be taken as one among many indications of the limits which he placed to the legitimate action of the purely rationalising faculties of mankind. They were fitted to deal with the evidences of an event which claims to have occurred within the domain of sense appreciation; they were not fitted to bring to the test of their decision the possibilities or probabilities of Divine action, whether in things material or in things moral, to say that this or that miracle, this or that article of the Christian creed was on *a priori* grounds impossible.[34] Nor was it within their province to subject to their essentially coarse method of definition those fragmentary portions of the super-sensual world which have been directly revealed to man's spiritual nature. How far this attitude separated him from all sympathy with members of the modern broad church party needs no further emphasis; it also differentiated his habit of religious thought if not the substantial conclusions at which he arrived from that of more orthodox believers. He was a devout and frequent communicant; the Holy Sacrament occupied in his life of worship a supreme and unique position; he accepted in their simplest and most direct meaning the words of its institution. But he shrank almost with repulsion from all doctrinal formulae connected with it, from all attempts logically to define its nature, whether they proceeded from sources ancient or, Roman or Anglican. 'Why can't people talk about things that they *can* understand?'[35] he would complain when such definitions were discussed in his presence. He could hardly be brought to treat seriously the argument of Roman controversialists that there is an *a priori* probability of God's having appointed a permanent head to His Church on earth. And all arguments of a similar character from whatever quarter they proceeded were treated with a like contempt. 'What do they know about it?' The element in the Roman system to which he used most frequently to refer as being hopelessly antagonistic to his own religious ideals was that which he would speak of as its rationalising aspect; its constant tendency to subtilize, to over define, or – to use his own phrase – 'to pigeon-hole the mysteries of faith'.[36] This stress on the limits of reason[37] was unaccompanied by any effort to ignore the difficulties which its voice in isolated expression suggests. There was indeed a certain sternness of emphasis, almost a note of defiance with which at times he would face them. He never minimised the claims of reason where it acts within the scope of its own powers; he refused to ignore those claims by pretending comprehension where he had it not; but he regarded any expectation of full comprehension in such matters as an act, not only of presumption, but of intellectual self-delusion.

I have spoken of his having been himself an artist in literature and I do not think that though his output was small and in form fragmentary the title can be denied to him. He had the instinct for selection and rejection, a command of his instrument with a reverence for it which never allowed him to disregard or override the limitations which it imposes, a fastidiousness of taste which would not be content unless both ear and brain were satisfied, and above all a sure recognition of the subtlest shades of difference not only in meaning but in suggestion which an alternative choice of words contains. He corrected a good deal, and the sense of the corrected phrase often differed so slightly from that which it replaced as almost to defy verbal analysis. I am speaking of the only writing upon which I have ever seen him engaged – that of private and business correspondence. His published compositions were nearly all achieved in his youth and early manhood, and both with regard to them, and to the one or two articles which he wrote in later years, he had a peculiar sensitiveness of reserve which forbade all discussion of them and indeed all allusion to them in his presence.[38] His wife was the only person with whom this reserve was broken through; she corrected his proofs and used to help him both with her advice and criticism. She would speak of his writings to her children, but always with the warning that they must on no account mention the subject to their father, and by himself they never heard it referred to. She always professed herself unable to account for his almost morbid reserve on this point, and its explanation must be a matter for surmise only. Some of it may have been simply the result of habit. He belonged to a generation accustomed to greater reticence upon such subjects than is the present one; by far the greater number of his contributions to periodic literature were made before the magazine of signed articles had come into existence. And some of them could hardly have been published except under the veil of anonymity. It was a veil which soon became transparent, but he clung for many years to his belief in its opacity. He was extremely indignant at the public reference made to his authorship of the last article which he wrote for the *Quarterly* – the one on 'Disintegration' (October 1883). His original motive for writing was simply to earn money which he much needed at the time; later on he became anxious to impress certain facts upon the public mind and he would have held, whether rightly or wrongly, that an unsigned article was the most efficacious for that purpose. In early days the suppression of his signature saved him no doubt from many annoyances. I have seen a letter written to him by his father in the early sixties. The latter mentions a rumour that credited his son with the authorship of a *Quarterly* article attacking the then Conservative leaders; remonstrates with him on the subject, and – with a surprising absence of insight into his character – intimates that as his election and Parliamentary expenses are paid for he had no right to publish criticisms unacceptable to those who pay them. In reply the son recalls the anonymity of the article, refuses either to acknowledge or to deny its authorship, but at the same time offers at once to resign his seat rather than admit for a moment the right of anyone to interfere with his fullest liberty of utterance.[39] The offer was not accepted and in '67, when the attacks were resumed with a greatly increased ferocity, father and son were happily in accord on the issue which provoked them. This and similar experiences may have imbued him with an habitual anxiety to guard his secret. But such a reason cannot by itself account for the whole of his reserve. When in later life he did publish one or two signed articles he maintained in conversation the same absolute silence with regard to them. I do not suppose that his case is an isolated one; it must be left for those who have experienced the same shyness of authorship to understand the feeling in him. In conclusion I may observe that I believe the extent of his writing for the newspaper press to have been a good deal exaggerated. He was for some years on the staff of the *Saturday Review* for the purpose of writing a fortnightly criticism on German literature which was then a feature of that paper. During that time he wrote two or three leading articles for it and one 'middle' which was not successful. He may have written occasional articles elsewhere but I have not been able to find any evidence of the fact. On the other hand he was for seven years – from 1860 to 1866 – a regular contributor to the *Quarterly Review*, writing an article for nearly every number issued within those dates; and he wrote for it on several occasions subsequently.[40]

In his youth Lord Salisbury's health was feeble, and throughout his life the physical machine was delicately balanced, the slightest disturbance sufficing to throw it out of order. It was kept in later years under an almost continuous pressure of work. So long as he was at the Foreign Office the work practically never stopped; – Sundays or week-days, abroad or at home, in sickness or in health. During an attack of influenza, even while the fever was upon him, he rarely got more than a day or two of complete rest. Before he was well enough to leave his bed the work would begin again. It was I believe the absence of rest which told upon him rather than the actual severity of his application while he was at work. His nervous system was what is usually called highly-strung; the body and mind reacting strongly upon one another. Many months after the sudden death of Lord Iddesleigh[41] which took place in his presence, he referred a failure of strength from which he was then suffering to the mental shock he had received on that occasion; and he always attributed in part the final breakdown of his health to the double loss he suffered first in his wife's death and then in that of the late Queen for whom he cherished feelings of the warmest personal attachment. When he was unwell, even the character of the political news that he received would have perceptible effects for good or evil upon his condition. He was subject all his life to attacks of high nerve-tension combined with great mental depression. They were apparently physical in character and yet were often immediately occasioned by some subject of mental worry or distress. These 'nerve storms' as he called them became rarer as he grew older; in his youth, he suffered from them very acutely. They were then accompanied with sleep-walking and became at one time a source of real anxiety to his wife.

In another of the many senses in which that rather overburdened word is used his nerves were strong. I can recall only one thing which had power to produce in him any feeling of physical fear. He could not bear to stand near the brink of any height. The dread was admitted to be quite irrational and was felt even more for others than for himself. Those who walked with him along a cliff path had always to keep to landward of him if they wished to avoid causing him real distress. His way of life did not often bring him into the presence of danger. He met with a rather large proportion of carriage accidents which he could never be brought to regard except from a humorous point of view. His total ignorance of everything connected with the stables made perfect arrangements there impossible; his constant insistence on a reckless speed in driving and his indifference to catastrophes when they did occur no doubt largely accounted for their frequency. The occasion on which he was probably in the most real danger was when a lunatic once got into his compartment at King's Cross and travelled down along with him to Hatfield. Lord Salisbury suspected nothing during the journey, and when on arriving at Hatfield the stranger still clung to his company, he assumed him to be a guest whom he had failed to recognise and invited him into his own brougham. During the short drive up to the house, however, the man's insanity revealed itself – I do not know in what form. Lord Salisbury was in no way disturbed; on arriving at the house he went to his room, rang the bell and told the rather bewildered servant who answered it that he had left a madman in the front hall who had better be got out of the house as soon as possible. Then without further remark he settled quietly down to his work. The authorities of Scotland Yard when the matter came to their knowledge did not treat it so calmly, and precautions were taken from that time to ensure that no unauthorised person became Lord Salisbury's travelling companion on the railway.[42]

It was not however only in a steadiness of physical nerve that his courage consisted; that could but partly account for the deliberate fearlessness of death which he owned. I have heard him say that he could not understand the dread of it: 'One might as well be afraid of going to sleep.' He was possessed of another form of courage which is perhaps rarer among men than that of simple fearlessness – the courage of endurance. When he was ill his doctors would aver that his refusal to complain, his constant effort to minimise every form of pain or discomfort from which he suffered constituted, until they were recognised and taken into account, a real difficulty in the way of correct diagnosis. He was not an easy patient to deal with. In the conflict with weakness and disease, he fought every inch of the ground, resisted to the last the surrender of every habit of health, and would be conquered only by sheer physical incapacity. It is fair to add that, though his friends would remonstrate with him on this attitude, those best qualified to judge refused to condemn it wholly. When his doctor was appealed to to place an absolute prohibition upon some such imprudent strain of strength he declined on the ground that the spirit which inspired the effort was far too valuable an ally to be lightly discouraged. A typical example recurs to me, though one in which no doubt other motives were involved than a simple defiance of weakness. Lord Salisbury had always been in the habit before breakfast of attending daily prayers in the chapel at Hatfield. During his last illness the exhaustion produced by this ten or fifteen minutes service was so great that he would fall into heavy sleep in the chair that awaited him actually at the chapel door. He had to be left there sleeping for half an hour or longer before he could recover the strength enough to eat his breakfast. But when he was urged to abandon this attendance at prayers he drew himself up and with a slight shake of the head and half a smile on his lips answered at once 'No, no, – that would be mean.' This struggle with disability was far more marked during his last illness when he knew full recovery to be hopeless than during earlier failures of health. Then he accepted the paramount necessity of getting well as quickly as possible and, except for a constant craving after his work, would be submissive on the whole to the doctor's directions.

That Lord Salisbury was courageous is a fact whose statement would hardly cause surprise. A trait that would perhaps be less expected in him by general opinion was his capacity for pity, his sensitive sympathy for suffering of all kinds. Yet as a matter of fact on more than one occasion his softness of heart in this respect went far to overbalance his judgement. During the Boer War, his distress at what seemed to him the unnecessary loss of life involved in some of its minor incidents led him to urge remonstrances with an insistence which some at least of his military advisers deprecated as very unwise.[43] Even in the field of foreign affairs he has been known – I will not say to modify his policy – but in pity for the grief and anxiety of a single individual to take stronger action in the direction already favoured than he otherwise would have done. When the Mansion House Relief Fund was started in 1885 to meet the exceptional distress of that year, he was one of its chief supporters. The results which have followed from it have not been altogether happy and there were anxious economists who doubted its advisability from the first. But when their views were urged upon Lord Salisbury he only asked impatiently 'What was the use of such talking when people were actually starving?' I am not suggesting that this state of mind was normal in him; he recognised fully the inevitability of human suffering, the evils which may flow from unwise efforts for its removal. But there were undoubtedly occasions such as have been mentioned when the passion of pity in him and the hatred of suffering proved too strong for his reason to control.

The formation of a ministry was to Lord Salisbury a period of prolonged and acute mental suffering. The necessity which it involved of disappointing hopes and of wounding feelings cost him, especially in his first experience of such work, an almost intolerable pain. 'I feel sore all over' he exclaimed after a day of Cabinet making. His powers of compassion stretched beyond the limits of his general sympathies. On the evening following that of the murder of Lord Frederick Cavendish in Dublin[44] that tragedy and the circumstances connected with it were being discussed at the dinner table in Arlington Street – as was probably the case in every English household to which the news had reached that night. Party feeling was running very high at the time; Lord Salisbury had been making several speeches in fierce denunciation of Mr Gladstone and of his government, and he was engaged to address a public meeting for the same purpose that very week. Lord Frederick, as is known, had been connected with Mr Gladstone by close ties of relationship and personal association, and when Lord Salisbury observed that he had already postponed the meeting in question, one of those at the table remarked approvingly 'that it would not do to attack the old man just now'. Lord Salisbury acquiesced, – and then in a tone audible only to his nearest neighbour and with an indescribable expression of distress on his face, he added 'and besides I could not do it'.[45]

His affections were strong and deep and his nature felt acutely the need of their return. During his childhood this side of his character had been to a great degree starved, but assuredly from the date of his marriage nothing was wanting to him in this respect. It is difficult to exaggerate the value of the friend who then entered his life. In her fertility of resource, in her energy of action, in her brilliant rapidity of thought and comprehension she was capable of full companionship with him on the intellectual and active sides of his life. Inspired by the same faith as himself, following the same spiritual ideal, supplying with her strong physical vitality and her ubiquitous human sympathy the defects of his own character, she gave him this above all – the wholehearted devotion of a nature singularly gifted in its capacity for absorbing, uncompromising affection. She always frankly admitted that she cared nothing for his politics apart from himself, and had some scorn for women who pretended to a more independent intellectual position. This attitude in her was certainly not the result of any mental incapacity for comprehending the points at issue. But in every direction humanity appealed to her principally in its individual aspects. She found persons far more interesting than either the causes which inspire them or the laws which govern them. And this general interest in persons became, in the case of the few upon whom her deepest affections were concentrated, an entire devotion.

She understood her husband and could act as his interpreter with others – a function rendered important by his all but total incapacity for emotional self-expression. His affections shared to the full in that quality of selflessness which marked his character throughout. He was incapable of jealousy and would never compromise in his condemnation of that vice.[46] He offered everything and he exacted nothing, placing himself wholly at the mercy of those he loved. He had all the minor unselfishness of a woman and much of that delicacy of sympathy which is generally attributed to her sex. Small conspiracies of silence or of innocent deception were constantly needed to save him from sacrificing his convenience or comfort to what he believed to be those of others. Schoolboys had to volunteer to run his messages or he would have undertaken them himself, and even so he would apologise to them for the trouble he was giving. Conscious of his own dislike of social pleasures, he was always troubled lest the younger members of the family should thereby be deprived of them, and would take the initiative in insisting upon entertainments being provided for them in spite of the weariness which he thereby inflicted upon himself. One of the motives which impelled him during his last illness to that minimising of his sufferings and concealment of his weakness, to which I have alluded, was undoubtedly his constant anxiety lest his failing health should shadow the lives of those around him. As his children grew up, his sympathies would follow them into all the details of their professional or active life. In the midst of his own fullest occupation in public affairs he would turn aside to discuss with them their work, their plans, the object of their pursuits. Nay, he seemed to place these things first in his interest, and there was always a danger – the egotism of youth showing itself but too prone to accept the situation which he created – lest the trivialities of their lives should absorb attention to the exclusion of the great things which filled his own.

There was a traditional knowledge among his family of the passionate temper which had characterised him in youth;[47] there were moments when they could detect traces of its existence roused by others and pressing almost awfully against the iron restraint under which it was kept; but never once was it displayed towards themselves. Rebuke was very rare for him, remonstrance only occasional, and then generally conveyed in the form of a jest whose intention was however well understood. But he never snubbed, never intentionally spoke a word which could wound the susceptible vanity of youth. The acuteness of his powers of observation where his affections were concerned was in striking contrast to their dullness in some other directions. He could live in a room for a fortnight without noticing some fundamental change in its furniture or decoration, but he would at once detect unavowed trouble, physical or mental in those he loved. No absorption on public affairs seemed to have the power of deadening this faculty or of limiting his anxiety to find a remedy. Where he suspected soreness of spirit there was a fine reticence in his sympathy; no overt allusion was attempted but there was a peculiar attentiveness, an active concentration of all his powers for the purpose of cheering and soothing.[48] In earlier days one of the few things which would produce from him words of really grave remonstrance was any display of careless brutality in language among the young community by whom he was surrounded.

We have been treading on sacred ground, and beyond lies ground holier still upon which one shrinks from setting foot. His religion has been spoken of, but its innermost sanctuary has not been entered. The subject cannot be dwelt upon but it cannot be ignored. The blood in a man's veins is hidden from view, but a portrait which failed to recognise its existence, however faithfully it might delineate the features or define the anatomy, would be but the portrait of a corpse.[49] Lord Salisbury's philosophy of life, as it has been hitherto indicated, cannot easily be accommodated to his conduct. The picture as it stands is hardly convincing. The motions are inadequate to the performance. He was sceptical towards ideals, indifferent to the rewards of ambition, habitually expectant of failure as the probable outcome of his efforts. He was inspired neither to the achievement of great results nor to the satisfaction of a personal success. It is true that his natural impulse was towards activity, that it is difficult to conceive of him as in a state of habitual inaction. But an activity that was motiveless, merely constitutional, would have shown itself mechanical or spasmodic without energy, without fire, without perseverance, the very force of its compulsion, combined with its conscious aimlessness, bringing with it the bitterness of spirit from which a more languid and passive nature would have been free. Yet he showed throughout his life a persistence of effort, a fervent and sustained zeal as great as the most confident of enthusiasts could have displayed – a zeal which was never wearied, which no opposition could check and no failure quench. And though both the strength and the sensitiveness of his nature brought inevitable suffering there appeared in him a spirit of fundamental content which makes it impossible for anyone who knew him to describe him as an unhappy, still less an embittered man. It is in the absoluteness of his religious faith and devotion and above all in the personal character of their objective that the secret of these important contradictions is to be found. The private soldier neither understands, nor expects to understand, the ultimate objects towards which his action is directed; its immediate and apparent failure neither surprises him, nor has power permanently to depress him. Obedience is his motive force, and where that obedience is claimed by a leader to whom he is bound by a perfect love and trust, it can inspire in him an entire devotion of service. Such was the inspiration of Lord Salisbury's life and the source of his content. He needed none other.

NOTES

References to papers in the Hatfield House Archive are prefixed 'HHM' (Hatfield House Muniments). In details of correspondence Lady Gwendolen Cecil is referred to as 'Gwendolen', and her sister, the Countess of Selborne, as 'Maud'. 'CHE' designates changes recommended by Lord and Lady Cecil of Chelwood and adopted in the above text. Lady Gwendolen's *Life of Robert Marquis of Salisbury*, 4 vols (London, 1921–32), is referred to as *Life*. All references to the *Life* in these notes are to volumes I (1921) and III (1931).

1. See HHM/GW [Gwendolen Cecil], papers and letters relating to Lady Gwendolen's effects after her death. The fourth essay is with these.
2. See J. A. S Grenville, *Lord Salisbury and Foreign Policy: The Close of the Nineteenth Century*, paperback edn (London, 1970) p. 5, n. 1.
3. For a churchman's estimate of this skilful section of the *Life*, see HHM/GW, Edward Lyttleton to Gwendolen, 6 Dec 1921.
4. See Lady Gwendolen Cecil, *Biographical Studies of the Life and Political Career of Robert, Third Marquis of Salisbury* (London, 1949), 'As a Leader': 'These limitations in him which made the establishment of any bond of personal sympathy between himself and those who followed him almost impossible, had their effect on the character which marked his leadership' (p. 12); 'his disdain for the personal element in politics was a constant source of grievance' (p. 24).
5. Thomas Babington Macaulay, 'Lord Clive' (review, Jan. 1840), in F. C. Montague (ed.), *Critical and Historical Essays Contributed to the Edinburgh Review* (London, 1903): 'Every schoolboy knows who imprisoned Montezuma, and who strangled Atahualpa.'
6. Between 'than' and 'had' the words 'those whose existence' cut (CHE).
7. After 'theatre' the words 'at all' cut (CHE).
8. This presumably refers to the illustrious firm of Maples, long established as a supplier of carpets and furniture, particularly to large hotels.
9. During the agricultural depression in the 1880s, in particular, while he was out of office (1880–5).
10. Gwendolen was not so acquainted; she confessed, after writing of his taste for Horace, that she had never read a word of him. It is characteristic that she felt guilt at this slight omission in her researches.
11. That is, aesthetic.
12. Between 'theology' and 'almost' the words 'were the three subjects which' cut (CHE).
13. See Mandell Creighton, *History of the Papacy during the Period of the Reformation*, 5 vols (London, 1892–4), a work showing deep religious convictions combined with a sceptical, ironical outlook; and Thomas Hodgkin, *Italy and her Invaders*, 8 vols (Oxford 1880–99), which Creighton, a friend of Hodgkin, greatly admired.
14. See *Life*, III, 3–7. I am indebted to Dr Brian Bowers of the Science Museum, South Kensington, for the following information in a letter dated 3 Oct 1985:

> Nowadays our electric lighting (and other electrical equipment) is connected in parallel to the two wires that bring the supply. The supply voltage is maintained constant and the current varied according to the number of lamps connected. In the beginning it was not obvious that one should do that. The alternative is to connect all the lamps in series, design the supply to provide a constant current,

instead of a constant voltage, and vary the voltage according to the number of lamps connected. Some early lighting installations were designed on that basis. There were also hybrid arrangements.

I suggest that Lady Gwendolen overheard discussion about different circuit arrangements, and also about the wires. Higher currents require a thicker conductor in the wire. If it is too thin it will get hot, and waste power, so the optimum thickness is a matter of economics. Higher voltages require thicker insulation, or greater spacing if the conductors are bare.

In 1881, Salisbury's experiments claimed one victim, a twenty-two year old gardener, William Dimmock, who touched an uninsulated portion of the wires connecting the saw-mills, which produced the power, with the house (*The Electrician,* 17 Dec. 1881).

15. See *Life*, III, 8–9.
16. The High Church movement, whose members reaffirmed the doctrine of the apostolic succession and the sacramental mission of the Church. Salisbury felt close affinity with their views, though not sharing all of them.
17. John Henry (later Cardinal) Newman (1801–90), author of the controversial Tract 90, arguing that the Thirty-Nine Articles did not signify a true break with Rome. Joined Roman Church 1845. See *Life*, I, 24.
18. See ibid., p. 106.
19. *The Analogy of Religion, Natural and Revealed to the Constitution and Course of Nature* (1736); Bishop Butler's outlook was strongly spiritual but he distrusted 'enthusiasm' and sentiment; he argued for the truths of Christianity on reasoned and empirical grounds. See *Life*, I, 100.
20. Joseph Lightfoot, Bishop of Durham, Greek scholar and biblical commentator, worked on a joint revision of the New Testament between 1870 and 1880. In contrast with some contemporaries' elaborate theories, he believed the clue to the obscurities of St Paul's Epistles lay in an exact investigation of the Greek grammar and vocabulary used by the saint, on the assumption that Paul knew what he was talking about and could speak the Greek of his period with precision. Lightfoot's approach, both disciplined and commonsensical, strongly appealed to Salisbury.
21. Earnest Renan trained as a priest, but abandoned traditional Christianity as a result of his study of the Hebrew language and German criticism. Best known for his *Vie de Jesus* (1863), he combined meticulous scholarship with a lucid and attractive style.
22. A controversial restatement of the meaning and claims of the Church and 'Catholic' creed in an 'epoch of profound transformation', by a group of younger 'modern' High Church clergy. Since the book's appearance in 1889, according to Dean Inge in 'Bishop Gore and the Church of England', 'High Church clergy have been able without fear to avow their belief in the scientific theories associated with Darwin's name, and their rejection of the rigid doctrines of verbal inspiration'. The editor of *Lux Mundi*, Charles Gore (1853–1932), contributed to it a controversial study which suggested that the conflict between Christ's

own views on the authorship of – for example – Psalm 110 and the convincing contrary evidence of recent scholarly commentators could partly be explained by the proposition that the Saviour, as an incarnate being, had 'willed so to restrain the beams of Deity as to observe the limits of the science of His age'. This suggestion that Christ's knowledge had mortal limitations scandalised many, notably High Churchmen such as the eminent Canon Liddon, who corresponded often with Salisbury. See *Life*, I, 106–7.

23. An influential rationalistic biblical scholar; his widely read *History of Israel* appeared in English translation in 1885. Gore later denied that Wellhausen's radical questionings had been an influence on his own views in *Lux Mundi*. See Gore's Preface to *Lux Mundi*, 10th edn (1890).

24. See Gore, Preface to *Lux Mundi*, 1st edn (1889), and, more specifically, ch. 3 ('The Holy Spirit and Inspiration'): 'we are being asked to make considerable changes in our literary conception of the Scriptures, but not greater than were involved in the acceptance of the heliocentric astronomy'.
    Salisbury's choice of Gore as Bishop of Worcester in 1901 was controversial. The Low Church party, which regarded Gore as practically a Catholic, was enraged. So were those of Gore's fellow High Churchmen who disliked his 'modern' outlook on Bible criticism and his political radicalism. Salisbury shared this distaste, while acknowledging Gore's saintliness. But he thought him far too important a Church leader to remain on the sidelines, as Pusey and Liddon had done in the past, with disruptive results.

25. Between 'his' and 'in' the word 'spoken' cut (CHE).

26. W. K. Clifford (1845–79), mathematician and metaphysician, Professor of Applied Mathematics, University College, London. He held the theory that consciousness is built out of atoms of 'mind stuff'. See *Life*, I, 108.

27. Here 'less' has been changed to 'more' (CHE).

28. See *Life*, I, 120.

29. Ibid., p. 24.

30. After 'declaration', the words 'of his own' cut (CHE).

31. This was the expression that he used to apply to his son Hugh's views on the matter. See *Life*, I, 117.

32. For example, though he did not believe that a member of the Church of Scotland should be barred from communicating in an English church, when staying at the Balfour family home at Whittingehame he used, according to Lady Gwendolen, to 'go into Edinburgh in gloomy solitude for the week and solely in order to attend the episcopal church there'. Later the building of a chapel on the estate spared him this ordeal. (HHM/GW, Gwendolen to Lady Frances Balfour, 1910.)

33. See *Life*, I, 117.

34. See Ibid., pp. 115–16.

35. Ibid., p. 116.

36. Ibid.

37. Originally 'This humility of reason', which may be a typing error. 'This stress on the limits of reason' has been substituted. (Ed.)

38. See *Life*, I, 71.
39. Ibid., pp. 95–7, letter from Lord Robert Cecil (later third Marquis) to second Marquis of Salisbury, 24 July 1860.
40. See J. F. A. Mason, 'The Third Marquis of Salisbury and the *Saturday Review*', *Bulletin of the Institute of Historical Research*, xxxiv (1961). 607 articles are listed between 1856 and 1866.
41. In 1887 Salisbury took over the Foreign Office from his colleague Lord Iddesleigh. Owing to a press leak, Iddesleigh heard the news of the change not from his chief but from a newspaper. Salisbury called him to London to explain matters to him, but Iddesleigh died in the Prime Minister's anteroom before the explanation could be given. See HHM/3M [third Marquis]/E, memo by Lord Robert Cecil, 19 Jan 1887, as to the circumstances of Lord Iddlesleigh's retirement and death.
42. Another example can be given. Returning this essay to her sister after reading it, Maud Selborne described Salisbury's behaviour in the winter of 1876–7: 'As an instance of his personal fearlessness & and also his love of mischief, I quite remember when we were at Constantinople he was always trying to give his secretary the slip & go out walking by himself although he had been warned that feeling against Europeans, especially members of the Congress was so strong, that a fanatic might at any time attack him . . .' (HHM/GW, Maud to Gwendolen, 14 Oct [c. 1910]).
43. Ibid. Lady Selborne questioned Gwendolen's evidence for this statement. Even if it is correct, Salisbury's remonstrances were certainly not carried out in public, where he backed the generals' actions.
44. 6 May 1882.
45. See *Life*, III, 50.
46. Ibid., p. 27.
47. See HHM/GW, Gwendolen to Maud, 17 Mar 1910.
48. If he sensed low spirits in a person, he would commonly, unasked, direct that the sufferer be given a glass of port (information from Lord David Cecil).
49. See *Life*, I, 122.

4
Lady Gwendolen Cecil: Salisbury's Biographer

HUGH CECIL

There is a photograph of Lady Gwendolen Cecil at the age of seventy showing an elderly woman in an untidy, shapeless coat and an equally shapeless black hat, on her knees, before a snowman. She is putting the finishing touches to the lower part of its body. She is preoccupied with her task; oblivious of the bitter cold, of her age, of the camera, she is thinking only of the children she is entertaining. The photograph does not of course reveal anything about her intellectual abilities, but it gives us a succinct clue to the character of this talented and scholarly woman.[1]

Her papers in the Cecil family archives at Hatfield House furnish ample proof of her acute perception, her imagination and her breadth of learning on political matters. In her biography of her father, Robert, third Marquis of Salisbury, her vigorous intelligence can be seen at its finest. Though not the last word on him now, simply because of the progress that has since been made in late nineteenth-century historical research, the biography still stands as a master work.

Nobody who outlived Lord Salisbury understood and knew as intimately as she did the workings of his mind. It was not a simple one; its mysteries baffled many of his contemporaries. The fact that she possessed the key to so much of it is what makes her book so vivid, and so valuable to the historian. She was also a natural scholar. Though insufficiently trained, as will be seen, to perform her task with ease, she was diligent, if not detached, in seeking to establish a true picture.

The tale of her scholarly labours has its comic side. Her troubles in committing her father's portrait to paper were unending and frequently of her own making. The book was for forty years – until her death at eighty-five – a source of agonising guilt and worry for its author, though this shows little in its old-fashioned, slow-moving style.

Gwendolen, known to her family as 'Titi' or 'Tim', was born in 1860. She was the second daughter. Most of Salisbury's children had distinguished careers: 'Jem' (James, 1861–1947), the eldest son, was to be a leading and influential member of the Conservative Party; 'Fish' (William, 1863–1936) became Bishop of Exeter, 'Nigs' (Edward, 1867–1918) the financial adviser to the Egyptian Government, 'Bob' (Robert, 1864–1958) a founder of the League of Nations, and 'Linky' (Hugh, 1869–1956) a leading champion of the Church of England and a brilliant parliamentary orator; her sister, Maud (1858–1950), married a future South African proconsul, Lord Selborne. It was a family steeped in Tory tradition: aristocratic, devoted to the Crown; above all things, the Anglican Church dominated their conduct and imagination.[2]

Lord Salisbury, whose boyhood relations with his own father, the second Marquis, had been distant, was a fond and attentive parent; and his wife, Georgina, was a woman of determination and vitality who proved well up to the task of launching her husband on his political career, and of bringing up their children, first in relative poverty, and later in the palatial and demanding family domain at Hatfield House. The family was extremely close-knit – a source of political weakness and personal strength for Salisbury's sons in later years. Their later political ideas were often far more an expression of a 'Hatfield' view than of the current opinions of the Conservative Party.

Not that they were always in perfect agreement – and throughout her life, Gwendolen herself frequently found fault with her brothers' judgement: with Robert in 1930 over the Kellogg Pact[3] and his tendency to resign repeatedly on principle; with William over the reform of the Prayer Book:[4] with Hugh on his extreme views on the virtues of poverty for the poor.[5] Gwendolen's niece Lady Manners recalls in a memoir the ferocity with which she could turn on her family in the course of a drawing-room debate on politics:

She had a pugnacious side. I can remember the scene at Hatfield. The Uncles and Aunts collected, some sprawling in chairs, others swaying to and fro on their feet. Aunt T. T. walking up and down the room, her head bent, her hands clasped behind her back, musing on the conversation. Something would rouse her and she would break into the most vitriolic denunciation. Her chin out, her face slowly reddening, she would address the member of the family who provoked her in unmeasured terms of displeasure – so suddenly as to be disconcerting and in such volume that the culprit would be unable to intervene to excuse himself.[6]

Smoking and arguing, she liked to spend half the day over the newspapers with her family whenever they were gathered at the big house. If alone, she would often pore over the journals until late into the night, rocking back and forth on her knees. She was once aroused from her absorption to find that she had rocked too close to the fire and that her hair combs were smouldering.[7]

Her intellectual agility at the age of ten impressed Canon Dodgson (Lewis Carroll) when Salisbury visited Oxford with his family in his capacity as Chancellor of the University. Dodgson seems to have singled her out as a favourite. He arranged picnics on her birthdays, took her to the theatre and gave her at various times ciphers and mathematical puzzles. Later, when she reached the age at which girls, for him, ceased to be interesting and became dangerous, he paid her less attention, though he sent her in her twenties a pamphlet he had written on electoral reform.[8]

Notwithstanding any fears felt by Canon Dodgson, it was a widely held verdict that little was done at home to develop 'feminine' traits in Gwendolen. 'Il n'y a que les hommes dans cette famille-là', remarked a critical French visitor, after meeting Gwendolen and Maud.[9]

Such opinions could be disputed. Disraeli did not share them. Undeterred by the young girls' already craggy looks, he praised the two sisters for their 'wild grace'. 'Lord Beaconsfield', he wrote, 'has rarely met more intelligent and agreeable women.'[10] He conducted an effusive correspondence with Gwendolen and conferred on her and Maud his 'order of the bee' – a brooch with a bee on it – reserved for those he thought outstanding in charm and intelligence.[11]

A strikingly eccentric figure, Gwendolen inspired great affection. Her efforts with her appearance were sporadic and self-defeating. Her niece, Lady Harlech, has recalled her personality:

We all adored her. . . . She had the most extraordinary mind but was absolutely unselfish. She had very odd clothes. At [my brother] Bobbetty's wedding she had a grand brown velvet dress trimmed with fur. It was very expensive, and when she found out how much it cost, she decided she mustn't spend any more, and

so wore her ordinary brown felt hat, which did look very peculiar.
. . . I went over one *very* hot afternoon by car, and found her
sitting in the garden, reading a book, and on the table by her were
her false teeth. She saw me staring at them, and said, 'I've taken
them out, one is much cooler without them.'[12]

A family rumour has it that at one time Gwendolen received the
attentions of the fifteenth Duke of Norfolk, the head of England's
leading Catholic family and Salisbury's Postmaster general in his
1895–1900 administration. There is certainly a note of tenderness in
the surviving letters from him at a time when both his sister and her
mother were dangerously ill.[13] Whatever his feelings, religion stood
in the way of a marriage. His sister, Lady Margaret Howard, urged
Gwendolen to consider becoming a Roman Catholic; she pressed
medallions and madonnas on her, which were adamantly, but
tactfully, refused. Peggy Howard, though already in her thirties,
addressed her friend in almost schoolgirlish tones of persuasive
admiration and affection: 'No Catholic can love anyone outside the
Church as much as I love you without intensely wishing that that
person may be led to the Truth.' The Cecils' Anglican tradition
proved too strong, and Peggy's persistent efforts to gain a sister-in-
law, if such they were, were brought to an end by her early death, in
1899.[14]

Gwendolen's own religious views are recorded in many of her
letters and appear among pages full of political news and humorous
domestic gossip, showing how closely they were woven into the
fabric of her life. She was able to give her readers the detailed and
understanding picture of her father's religious life in her book
because her faith was similar to his, in nature, if not always in the
way that it was expressed. In both, Christian belief had more to do
with faith than with reasoned deduction or an ethical code, and
more to do with a practical facing of inescapable realities than with
seeking to change them by soliciting divine intervention or relying
on the efforts of the human spirit to do so – hence her extreme dislike
of Christian Science.[15] While she considered Pusey morbidly
gloomy,[16] she was also irritated by any hint of forced religious
uplift. For example, she found the Revd Winnington Ingram (later
Bishop of London), at Oxford House, Bethnal Green, 'oppressively
full of "holy joy" '.[17] Throughout her life, too, she remained
unsympathetic to what she regarded as the 'mariolatry' of the
Roman Church.[18] The pronouncements of her historian cousin

Algernon, a Catholic convert, aroused her combative side.[19] She
even disliked having a Catholic cook.[20]

For the first forty-three years of her life she lived with her parents,
and accompanied them on many of their trips abroad, including
those to the family chalet at Puys in Normandy, and later to their
large estate, La Bastide, at Beaulieu in southern France. An
exception was Salisbury's journey with most of his family to
Constantinople in 1876 for the Conference on the Eastern Question.
Gwendolen stayed behind to keep an eye on the younger children;
but she wrote eagerly for news of the Conference and the various
foreign delegates: '*Do* write and tell me what Ignatieff's like', she
implored her parents.[21]

Salisbury replied on 12 December 1876 – the only surviving letter
from him to her during this period:

I write you a hasty line – don't cavil at my calligraphy – to thank
you for your letter & to say that we are all getting on as well as can
be expected. I was presented to the Sultan on Sunday. . . . A very
comical proceeding it was. The Sultan is a poor frightened man,
with a very long nose & short, thread paper body. Fortunately
they don't have doors in a Turkish palace – otherwise an
incautious slam would certainly have blown him away. We are all
presented by a great fat man called the Dragoman of the Porte &
afterwards. . . . I had a conversation with H. M. through the
medium of the said fat man. He was all the time in a ridiculous
terror. Every time he began a sentence of any kind, he made a
grotesque reverence which consisted of three movements – first
bending down as though to scoop up ashes, then punching
himself in the stomach & then pouring the ashes over his head: &
he went through this & through all his sentences with gestures
betraying the most unaffected terror. He wriggled, perspired,
panted, gasped – in fact made such an image of himself, that I had
the greatest difficulty in getting out my sentences for laughing. In
the time of the late Sultan (who was rather a dangerous man) this
poor fat creature used to get so frightened that Sir Henry Eliot has
seen a pool of perspiration on the floor after a long audience. The
Sultan has a beautiful palace & an exquisite view over the
Bosphorus. But I do not know how long he will enjoy it. There is a
conspiracy on an average about twice a week – & neither the

French nor the Russian Ambassadors continue to keep their children here. So we may have to run for it.

The Conference (preliminary) meets every day in a stuffy room: & the great difficulty in my duties that I find is to prevent myself going to sleep during their discussions. General Ignatieff is an amusing, joking man without regard for the truth with a Calmuck face, & an inordinate vanity which our Embassy takes every opportunity of wounding. . . .[22]

Gwendolen's mother sent her detailed reports throughout the Conference period which show that Gwendolen, at sixteen, was already equal to receiving an advanced commentary on the political situation.[23] Salisbury does not seem to have written again; and practically nothing else that he wrote to her now exists. Apparently she destroyed a number of his letters at the time of his death.[24]

Among her papers, however, Lady Gwendolen did preserve some vivid impressions of her father, during the years of his leadership. In 1888, for example, she kept a diary describing political discussions at Hatfield and visits to the House of Commons.

The most memorable passage in this journal is the one in which she describes her father's reactions – which she later incorporated in the *Life* – to the news that the German Emperor Frederick was fatally ill. His wife, the eldest daughter of Queen Victoria, was firmly wedded to constitutional and anti-militarist ideas, in stark contrast to her son William, who shortly must inherit. Salisbury was warned that she might try to dismiss Bismarck and reverse the strongly nationalist trend in German foreign policy; he was afraid that this would certainly be attributed to British influence and would soon bring a violently anti-British reaction:

S. described his state of mind this morning on the subject by saying that he felt as if we were just leaving harbour, – this was the shock of that first great wave on the bar. I asked him if he meant that he did not yet know what kind of weather he should find outside, – 'Oh no,' he said, shaking his head, 'I can see the sea covered with white horses.'[25]

When she grew up, Gwendolen worked as a kind of unpaid permanent private secretary to her father. Her duties were partly political – in the capacity of a go-between – and partly social – often the protection of her father from unwanted guests. The sinister Princess Radziwill, who later cheated Cecil Rhodes out of large sums of money, once invited herself for the day to Hatfield, to Lord Salisbury's horror: 'under his direction', wrote Gwendolen, 'I wrote her such a dramatic account of the terrors of an English Bank Holiday, that she never appeared'.[26]

Social functions could wreak havoc with Salisbury's delicate nerves. When Lord and Lady Jersey were asked to stay at Hatfield, Gwendolen found she had to drop plans to invite others to entertain them:

> My father was sunk in such depths of gloom when he heard what we had done & said so pathetically that he *had* hoped for a little quiet & rest at Whitsuntide that I don't think I had better go any further. What he dreads above all are the dinners, & keeping the party as small as it is now, we shall be able to make the conversation general and remove from him the necessity of small talk.[27]

The Prime Minister's energies had to be carefully preserved, particularly towards the end of his life. Gwendolen had to tend him in the absence of Lady Salisbury, who herself was ailing. She recorded an exhausting time, just after Salisbury's return from a health cure in Germany in October 1898, when she had been on duty at home:

> Telegrams came by telephone from Münster, & during that week which began with Omdurman, went on through the Cretan riot & ended with the Empress of Austria, the poor man who received all my father's messages fainted away on one occasion from exhaustion. My father has become keen on exercise, takes daily walks before 8 a.m., & . . . has ordered himself a tricycle! It has not come yet & I have some hopes of his finding it too much for his muscles, as otherwise we shall see him scorching down the North Avenue with an inevitably hopeless smash among the lime trees at the bottom.[28]

Though she was subsequently anxious not to write her father's life as a personal memoir, such memories were the foundation of many of her historical judgements. For example, she had seen enough of Joseph Chamberlain on his visit to Hatfield to be able to explain, at least in part, his surprisingly easy relationship with his political chief, when she came to write her fifth, unpublished volume:

> Since his succession to the Commons' leadership of the Liberal Unionists in 1892, his intercourse with Lord Salisbury had become fuller and it had run so smoothly that their relations glided into those of colleagueship without any noticeable impression of novelty to themselves. There were, indeed, points of personal contact between them which were absent with Hartington, the preceding Liberal Unionist leader, in spite of the ease begotten of identical traditions of class and upbringing. Though Mr. Chamberlain's circle of outside friendship was larger than Lord Salisbury's, his social life was concentrated quite as narrowly upon his home. His intimacy with his children, his devotion to his wife, were the same. Nor must *her* personality be left out of account in identifying the causes which contributed to the ease of this collaboration. On its social side it transformed Lord Salisbury's acquiescence into an active complaisance. His taste was acutely fastidious where women were concerned and the young New England bride whom Mr Chamberlain brought to London at the close of the eighties, gratified that fastidiousness to the full. He gave her the sobriquet of 'the Puritan maiden', and if, at some pompous dinner or week-end party, the wife of his Colonial Secretary could be chosen for his companionship, the gloom of the otherwise anathematised function would be immediately lightened.

Gwendolen's work for her mother – as a kind of unofficial lady-in-waiting – was even more taxing than looking after her father. Lady Salisbury was, as Lady Gwendolen put it, 'impervious to fatigue',[29] and required constant assistance in her energetic social duties. Lady Gwendolen's very accessibility, true to the Victorian pattern of the unmarried daughter who stayed at home, made her an easy prey to the demands of both her parents. And her good nature, coupled with her lack of any sense of priorities, meant that she was an ever-willing victim. According to Lady Robert Cecil, Gwendolen's sister-in-law, this was disastrous to Gwendolen's work habits and was ultimately the chief cause of her difficulty in finishing her biography. Lady Salisbury, she recorded,

was very unpunctual herself. It one had an appointment to drive with her one would wait ages in the Armoury till she appeared. She would talk at dinner dressing-time and come down very late for dinner. . . . If she wanted one, nothing else must interfere. She was very absorbing. I delighted in her and she spoiled me very much and was a perfect companion. But if I had wanted to write a book, or be concentrated on any object for any length of time I don't how it would have been done. . . .[30]

In consequence, Gwendolen herself became a byword for unpunctuality. She would appear for dinner at 11.30 at night, not altogether sure whether she was expecting breakfast or lunch. She would sit up all night reading; then, realising with embarrassment in the morning that the maid might come at any minute to call and find her still dressed in her evening clothes, she would get hastily into bed without even taking off her shoes.[31]

Despite the mental stimulus from the endless political talk, only Lord Salisbury and his wife could actually get anything done at Hatfield. Whereas he always brought his work home with him when he could, the children needed, during their mother's lifetime, to get away to achieve very much. And this was very difficult to do, for Lady Salisbury did all she could to keep her children around her; not even marriage was regarded as an excuse from constant attendance. Lady Robert Cecil wrote of Hatfield in the 1890s that:

It really was a demoralising house. . . . Dinner generally well after 8.30 and quite often lasting until nearly 10.00. I fancy her Ladyship, being considerably deaf in those latter years, liked having people sitting close by and was in no hurry to break up. It was no doubt very bad for our digestions – one went on nibbling things just to fill up the time – and went to bed very tired and woke up the same. In London nearly every night we went out to dine at Arlington Street, and it was quite a job to get home with all the family starting to discuss things at the last moment. Very amusing – and sometimes very exasperating – that was Tim's daily life – there was nothing to force her to do a thing at a certain time – or to finish at a certain time.[32]

Lady Salisbury died in November 1899. Gwendolen took charge of the household until her father's death in September 1903, which, as Gwendolen recalled, 'was preceded by a gradual failing of the heart showing itself in his ulcered legs and sore feet. When I asked

Douglas Powell [Salisbury's doctor] near the end what he was dying of, he said it was just that the machine was worn out.'[33]

Contemporaries recognised Gwendolen's special relationship with her father. 'To you personally the loss will be irreparable and intense', wrote Lord Goschen. 'He filled so large a place in your life & you devoted it to him with such faithful and loving service.'[34]

It was the fourth Marquis of Salisbury who chose Gwendolen to write the official life of their father the Prime Minister.[35] She began work in 1906. The following year, needing seclusion, she took up residence in the keeper's lodge, a handsome seventeenth-century brick house in a wooded part of the Park, near the North Gate. It was to be her home for the rest of her life, and there, directed by an inspired gardener with advanced tuberculosis, whom she had characteristically employed out of kindness, she created a charming garden with brick paths, pergolas and a mass of flowers among which white lilies and roses predominated in the summer months.[36] The interior of the house was neither austere nor over-prettified.[37] It was decorated carefully to match the style and period of the building. The Lodge House was a restful and cheerful place for working on a biography, though Gwendolen's capacity for disorder did much to counteract its calm.

Her main task to begin with was to gather together Salisbury's voluminous correspondence with colleagues and friends. Advertisements in the national press, as well as personal requests, brought a rich harvest. The papers were housed in a basement room in Hatfield House, where she subsequently in fact conducted much of her study. By late August 1906 she could see what a mammoth labour lay ahead: 'The room is so full of cases, cupboards, etc.,' she told her sister, 'that it is only after practice that you can tread a circuitous passage from one side of the labyrinth to the other. . . .'[38] With the help of the Hatfield librarian, R. T. Gunton, these letters were copied before being returned to their owners – over 2000 in the year 1906–7 alone. Eric Barrington, Salisbury's former private secretary at the Foreign Office, furnished additionally copies of Salisbury's out letters from that department. She did not arrange the papers systematically, however, until 1921, and in consequence wasted many hours having to rewrite her manuscript each time an overlooked document was discovered.[39] But this task was never properly completed. When 'Lady Gwendolen's room' in Hatfield

House was opened at her death (not without difficulty – the key, characteristically, had been lost) the scene presented was disorderly – enough, indeed, to discourage anyone from an attempt to round off her final volume of the biography.[40]

In addition to accumulating the letters, Gwendolen also corresponded over the years with her father's former colleagues and associates, including Lord Goschen and Lord St Aldwyn. The letters between Gwendolen and Lord St Aldwyn in 1913 and 1914 throw light on her own problems and attitudes as a writer. She asked St Aldwyn, the surviving colleague who had known him longest, for his personal memories of Salisbury as he had appeared in the Cabinet. 'It is an aspect of him which naturally was not seen by his family, & which is witnessed to inadequately in his correspondence. Nearly all the most important Cabinet work is carried on in personal intercourse.'[41]

St Aldwyn's long reply is in many ways a valuable document on Salisbury's political character.[42] It furnished some information new to Gwendolen; but in her eyes its chief value was as confirmatory evidence; evidently she accepted St Aldwyn's generous and tactful tribute at its face value, despite knowledge of his differences with Salisbury:

> I do not know if there is anything new to me in the sense of revealing qualities of which I was not already conscious. In fact, since I have read letters & collected information I have come more and more to the conviction that no surprises of that kind await me. It was because I felt that at the beginning, because I believed that I *did* know him thoroughly, that I was willing to undertake the work which on other grounds might have been better done by others. But the same qualities seen from another point of view are more vividly realised – & besides it is very supporting to find one's own judgement corroborated by someone like yourself. I have received so many hints that a daughter's biography must necessarily be worthless as a true picture of character that I became nervous.[43]

Some were less helpful: Lord Carnarvon's widow, though she allowed Gwendolen to see Salisbury's letters to his former close colleague, was fussy and difficult about their use;[44] while Salisbury's younger brother, Lord Eustace Cecil (1834–1921), was an unsatisfactory source. An intelligent man with a good business head, he had pursued a worthy, rather than notable, political career as a Conservative MP for South and West Essex from 1865 to 1885. He had little to do with Salisbury either socially or politically. In his seventies, when consulted, his memory of the past had deteriorated. The difference in character between the brothers was the reason, Gwendolen believed, why they lived such separate existences. '. . . all through their lives evidently they were complete strangers to each other', she wrote.[45] 'I hope Uncle Eustace's qualities are not the "dominants" of the Cecil family & that we must look for their inevitable reappearance in the coming generation! He's quite nice – but a breed of him would be trying.'

The steady accumulation of information took time, as did the task of toiling through the relevant debates in *Hansard*, all of which she read conscientiously in the years that followed.[46] She began making notes on Salisbury's early life and the story of his marriage, in 1906, reliving with passion the story of his unhappy quarrel with his father and his efforts to earn money from journalism during his impecunious first years of marriage. She repeated to her sister – inaccurately – his poignant words to his wife: 'I've been writing till my arm aches and my heart is sick.'[47]

Meanwhile she started work, at the same time on the series of 'pilot studies' – based on personal recollection rather than research – which have been described above in the headnote to Chapter 3. These biographical essays were intended for a critical readership of close friends and members of the family.[48] Gwendolen's sister and brothers approved, but suggested alterations. Robert strongly advised her to let her father speak for himself more, through his letters.[49]

This presented a problem, as Gwendolen explained to Maud in 1910, when she began the first careful sifting of his correspondence:

> They are, of course, very easy reading, but biographically leave [much] to desire, as I feared. For one thing he never – or hardly ever – wrote a letter without some practical object in view, – & never with the object of self-expression. Therefore all the arguments he uses & the considerations he dwells on are selected with a view to his correspondent's personality and not his own.[50]

The Beaconsfield–Salisbury correspondence was a good example; and here she made an observation which her successors would be wise to note: 'if a stranger was to read them & them only he would be

convinced that the only grounds whichever [*sic*] moved my father to
action were the fate of the next division or the next bye-election'.[51]
She was persuaded, however, that a liberal use of quotations would
improve the *Life*; though, individually, few of Salisbury's letters
stood out, 'taken together they give impressions which in my own
writing I feel I missed'.[52]

Lady Gwendolen's approach to her work and the tone she aimed
at were governed partly by a mistrust of 'fine writing'. She believed
that serious historians must concern themselves with truth and
clarity rather than style. She disliked Lytton Strachey's books when
she came to read them later, linking the literary flourishes with the
distorted facts.[53] (She was unlikely to be sympathetic towards a
writer who depicted her hero General Gordon as a drunken
egomaniac.) Though very appreciative of a successful biography of
William Cowper by her nephew Lord David Cecil, she was to
describe it as 'a little *too* brilliant for my taste'.[54]

Fortunately she had a natural vigour of expression; although not
always fluent, her style compares favourably with that of many
other scholars, in her time and after. It is never banal and is often
striking. The historian J. L. Hammond, reviewing the *Life*, spoke of
its 'quiet distinction – a quality specially suitable to its subject'.[55]

Yet she had been very daunted by the task of composition, as she
explained to Lady Frances Balfour in 1910,[56] when she began
writing the first chapters of the *Life*:

> I feel nervous as to my being able to achieve the results I'm aiming
> at; – I've never tried narrative writing, & writing deliberately for
> publication, with all the audience of fools, & critics, & opponents
> in one's mind's eye, – with the rival claims of truth, and good
> taste, & prudence, to consider – the necessity of being interesting
> & the necessity of being accurate – & above all of not allowing
> these things to draw off one's attention from the supreme end of
> making a portrait which shall be living and genuine in its entirety
> – all these things make the task a very different one from the
> straightforward record and analysis written only for those who
> already knew him, which is all I have hitherto attempted.[57]

Sometimes she carried caution to excess. She might struggle for a
whole day to find the right word, and, in the name of accuracy,
would overload a sentence with parentheses and subordinate
clauses. Her desire to maintain a scholarly tone led to an almost

obsessive impersonality. None of Salisbury's children were mentioned by name, or even as 'my brother' or 'my sister'. Gwendolen herself eventually appeared in the book simply as 'a girl of fifteen',[58] and her brother Edward as 'a long-legged subaltern'.[59]

Her reticence derived also from the Cecil family's dislike of self-revelation, which had been carried to a neurotic extreme by Salisbury himself. When Gwendolen had offered her story 'The Closed Cabinet' to *Blackwood's Magazine*, for example, she insisted on using a pseudonym, despite the offer of a higher payment if she let her own name be printed.[60] The family was more than normally discreet in the protection of its members, dead or alive; Maud Selborne subsequently expressed the view that Gwendolen's unpublished 'pilot studies' were 'too intimate' to be printed in the public press;[61] this was in 1948, after four volumes of Gwendolen's biography had already appeared! Such inhibiting influences as well as her self-imposed high standards were crucial in slowing the progress of her work.

Though her papers offer no conclusive evidence about the historiographical and stylistic models she used, or the course of her literary development, it can be seen from her essay printed as Chapter 3 of this volume that she was familiar with Macaulay and that Froude, Creighton and Hodgkin were held up at Hatfield as examples of skill. Her early short stories give no hint of her later abilities: 'The Little Ray' (*Pall Mall Magazine*, Aug 1894), was in the Ouida vein – an interesting sidelight on her emotional life, but confusing to a student of her historical art.

Conscious of the need for the right location to begin her task, Gwendolen chose her father's holiday home at La Bastide, Beaulieu, which he had left her; she told Maud, 'this place is to me so peculiarly haunted by him that I made up my mind some time ago to make the start here. My tiresome health while it has delayed my coming, has been another reason for it – the climate suits me like no other I have ever tried.'[62]

Most of all she needed to escape from Hatfield.[63] The distractions there were innumerable: and she was far too enthralled to keep her nose firmly in her manuscript. Public and family dramas absorbed her. Not least disruptive were her domestic problems. She found her menage as difficult to organise as her work; running Hatfield House after her mother's death does not appear to have done much to ground her in household management. Her employees' misbehaviour in 1908 proved to be a particularly severe ordeal for her. In a few weeks 'the stone deaf' cook developed 'anaemic hysteria',[64] partly as a result of conflicts with the two maids, threw Gwendolen downstairs and was sent, after other acts of violence, to an asylum.[65]

Gwendolen's brothers and sisters often entrusted their children to her care and supervision. This absorbed much of her energy. She followed the careers of her nephews and nieces with the closest attention, particularly the budding literary career of Maud's son Bobby,[66] who was then at Winchester. She also helped her brother James design tenants' cottages, many of which were due at the time for renovation or replacement. She put a great deal of thought into this, as her notebooks show; the neatness and precision of her designs make a strange contrast with the chaos of her daily life.[67] Her sturdy and compact architecture can be seen all over the Hatfield and Cranborne estates to this day. She and her brother were much influenced by the ideas of Octavia Hill, the pioneer housing reformer. The Cecils' Liverpool properties were restored according to her theories, rather than demolished and rebuilt. Octavia Hill praised one of Gwendolen's cottage designs at the 1905 Cheap Cottages Exhibition and, as one of the judges, tried – unsuccessfully – to secure it a first prize.[68]

Other local activities included her contributions to the parish magazine, to which, as well as improving short stories, she contributed, in several parts, a scholarly history of the estate.[69] Most important to her, however, were her philanthropic activities: for example, the care of the poorest old women on the estate, and the creation of a small sanatorium with four or five beds, for consumptives, personally designed by her, with large windows and balconies to reduce the patients' feelings of imprisonment.[70] The same imaginative sympathy went into her design of a block of flats for old ladies which her brother let to them at very low rents. It went also into her continuous efforts to help out the unfortunate: 'You don't know of anyone who would like a scullery maid who is mentally deficient but *likes* working 12 hours a day?' was a typical question fired off to her sister Maud.[71]

The Hatfield estate thus had on its grounds an unofficial social worker of exceptional sympathy and generosity. An abiding concern was unmarried mothers; on Sundays she would have numbers of them back for a meal; at one time, Lady Manners remembered, she was looking after the interests of 'an old woman, legless and without fits, and her daughter with legs and fits and an illegitimate baby'.[72]

Gwendolen herself lacked her mother's rude health, though her fifty cigarettes a day, irregular hours and ceaseless worry about finishing the biography did not stop her from living to be eighty-five. Illness, 'face aches' and accidents,[73] though they sometimes gave her an excuse to keep away visitors, tended to interrupt her studies. She had little trust in the medical profession; her dentist, she reported: 'is just like Lloyd George – crossed I find with the Bp of London, & the combination doesn't inspire me with great confidence'.[74]

British public affairs were also a major distraction; as an avid spectator of the political scene in which her relations were closely involved, Gwendolen filled her letters with cogent analyses of current events: the Tariff Reform controversy, the 1906 general election, women's suffrage (which she supported), the Irish Question, the Lords crisis. Her critical comments on Arthur Balfour's leadership are particularly valuable.[75] Most interesting of all are her remarks on the outbreak of war, which show a civilised sanity and detachment all too uncommon at that emotionally fraught moment of history:

> I feel a sneaking pity for the Germans. Having made that fatal blunder in annexing the provinces [of Alsace-Lorraine] there was no way out for them. The inevitable pressure of the growing half barbarous Europe to East of them could have been faced alone – but not with the enduring enmity to West, & when they ask how they be expected to wait till the two were strong enough & for them to choose their own time for the attack, I don't feel I can answer them.[76]

It goes without saying that the events of the war itself did much to divert her from her biographical task. 'I won't discuss the news', she told her sister on one occasion very early in the war when German troops destroyed many of the ancient buildings and the library of Louvain, 'the Oxford of the Low Countries'. 'I have already wasted more than one hour of time in passing up and down my garden in an ungovernable fury about Louvain. It doesn't bear speaking of.'[77] In September 1917, she made an effort to get away and stay with friends in the country. '3 or 4 days a week concentrated work is more than I've ever done yet', she confessed.[78]

To cope with her labours she employed during the war a full-time secretary; Miss Marshall, 'a little shaking woman in a large hat', was one of nature's victims – a class of person most calculated to inveigle Gwendolen away from her work. Exasperated, but interested, she listened to her secretary's tales of wrongs, real and imaginary, though she was often forced to work at night to avoid her interruptions.[79] Miss Marshall's serious neuroses had inevitably brought her in contact with the mental health authorities. The picture she painted of the plight of mental patients horrified her employer, always moved to fury by tales of mindless bureaucracy.[80] Gwendolen immediately embarked on an enlightened campaign which preoccupied her throughout the rest of her active career – to try to reduce the number of inmates of mental homes in the neighbourhood, on the grounds that long confinement led to deterioration, and often was quite unnecessary.[81] Much later, with the aid of Miss Marshall, and her sister Lily, a small home, 'The Hospice', was, for a brief period, set up to look after ex-patients for whom Gwendolen had successfully secured decertification and whose families could not or would not take responsibility for them.[82]

Against this distracting background, four volumes of the biography achieved publication. By 1919 Gwendolen had done most of the work for the first two. In February she stayed with Lady Robert Cecil at her house, Gale, in Sussex, bringing her manuscripts with her. Lady Robert, whose husband at the time was British League of Nations and economic representative at the Paris Peace Conference, sent him a running commentary of Gwendolen's visit:[83]

                                                                    3 February
Tim said she was coming Wednesday – then she discovered a meeting on the Lunacy Laws which she said she *must* go to because they were going to abolish all Lunatic Asylums which she approves – so she settled on Friday & carefully selected a train. . . . Last night she explained rather apologetically, that after all she had decided not to come till Monday. The reason was that she always liked to come two days later than the one originally decided on! Quite mad![84]

The visit did not take place finally until 27 February. Gwendolen was plainly exhausted and needed a rest. She attributed her poor health to cheap Turkish cigarettes. Lady Robert saw it as being far more the results of overstrain from ministering to the unending needs of an indigent Hatfield family, the latest in a very long series of lame ducks whom she had adopted.[85] Later she reported:

> *Ash Wednesday*
> Tim is settling down nicely to your writing table which is covered with papers tied up in white tape. Whether any work results I cannot say.[86]

> *3 March*
> Tim looks better. I hope she will stay a long time. She seems exhausted with living in an ice house & looking after other peoples' troubles. There's no doubt Mrs. L. Darwin's old lady's receipt for a prosperous life is the right one – 'Avoid the unfortunate!'[87]

Her work habits bewildered the household at Gale:

> *11 March*
> Tim is very good on the whole and catches up the meals before they are quite done, with occasional lapses when she has a 'train of thought', translated by Reed as 'her Ladyship's watch stopped' – you should see Reed's face when Tim starts talking just as she hands her something. After a while she rams the plate into her![88]

> *March, later*
> I have read Tim's three Eastern Question chapters. I wish she would print some of the stuff at once. I have urged her to get the proofs of her Ms for purposes of correction – perhaps if she saw them she would take the plunge. I believe she dreads it![89]

The work continued laboriously during the next two years. In March 1921 Gwendolen rounded off the chapter on Salisbury's religious views (vol. I, 4) while bedridden with influenza.[90] After the over-hasty completion, in September, of her chapter on Salisbury as India Secretary, her work on the first two volumes was finished.

They finally appeared at the end of the year; Hodder and Stoughton, the publishers, had given her a very handsome advance – of £5000.[91] The enthusiastic press reaction seemed to justify the payment. Sir Ernest Hodder-Williams was delighted. 'We hope you are seeing all the wonderful reviews', he told her. 'I do not ever remember a more remarkable reception.'[92] The first two volumes sold well; it was the long delay over the next two which was fatal to the financial success of the work as a whole. They did not come out until 1931 and 1932; much impact was lost and later sales were poor. All in all, however, the book made an excellent impression.

It is now over forty years since the last volume of Lord Salisbury's life was published. Looked at today, how does Lady Gwendolen's work strike us? First, and most important, it has presented readers with an acute and intimate personal portrait of the third Marquis of Salisbury to which every student of his career must still turn to first. 'So fine is Lady Gwendolen Cecil's biographical art', wrote the reviewer of her third volume in *Punch*, 'That . . . I have throughout felt that I was gazing over her father's shoulder and watching him at his work'.[93]

We must be grateful too, in this first important study of his career, for her revision of a popular idea of her father widely held in the first two decades of this century – namely, that he was an 'isolationist' in foreign policy. Salisbury's opinions about 'splendid isolation' she made quite clear: 'the words [in his Guildhall speech of November 1896] have been used again and again as proof and embodiment in boastful form of a principle in his policy for which no other evidence exists. Isolation, in fact, is always referred to in these [his] letters as an ultimate disaster.'[94] It was a point that still had to be pressed. Only a few years before the appearance of her fourth volume, no less a work than *British Documents on the Origins of the War*, edited by Gooch and Temperley, had carried the old view about Salisbury's foreign policy;[95] while her cousin Algernon Cecil's *British Foreign Secretaries*, which came out in 1927, had spoken of Salisbury's 'strong preference for isolation'.[96]

She impressed readers, too, with her demonstration of Salisbury's importance in shaping Britain's African policy in the closing years of the century. She told her nephew Victor in 1932,

> I suspected – in which several comments have shown me I was right – that it will be new to most of my readers. His habitual averseness from occupying the front – or indeed any prominent position on the stage, was assisted in this instance by the dramatic quality of some of the other personalities involved – Cecil Rhodes, – Goldie – Baring – the adventurers – with the result that history

was in danger of being permanently falsified by the ignoring of his pervading central direction in the background, . . . my documents brought bit by bit accumulating proof of his ubiquitous initiative and the unanimous acceptance of his predominance by all the continental statesmen engaged.[97]

The book received a number of significant criticisms at the time, some of which still hold good today. Most serious was that of Lord George Hamilton, Salisbury's former Secretary of State for India. As Gwendolen told her sister, 'he demurs to my neglect of the Indian side – "the greatest Indian Secretary that ever lived", – also criticises my having spoken of him as "not an ideal Chief". He gives me two or three instances of his achievement at the India Office, but in one or two of these certainly the credit would have to be shared with the Viceroy's.'[98] In her brief half-chapter on his India-secretaryship, Lady Gwendolen erroneously states that a detailed account of Salisbury's departmental work 'would scarcely be remunerative biographically', on the ground that he left most of the initiative on Indian affairs – except those, such as the Afghan crisis, which were of imperial concern – with the Viceroy's government.[99] It was certainly also the need to hurry on with the completion of the second volume which prompted brevity on this part of Salisbury's career. Lady Gwendolen admitted afterwards that she had not treated the Indian events adequately: 'to have given a balanced analysis of his own part in them would have been a long business. But I think with another three months I could have done that part better. Something had to go.'[100] At all events, in keeping this section short, she missed a chance of giving extracts from more than a few letters in a collection which includes some of Salisbury's best – some, happily, quoted in the present volume.[101]

More recently, Professor J. A. S. Grenville in his *Salisbury and Foreign Policy* (1964), while praising her 'brilliant work', has pointed out that she was wrong in believing that Salisbury generally ignored the machinery of the Foreign Office in formulating his policies: Grenville's own findings show that, though the final decision had to rest with Salisbury, he did consult officials first. Gwendolen had decided not to read the official Foreign Office records:

at an early stage of my work I gave up the idea. . . . I found an amount of material already at my disposal so large as to make me frankly shrink from adding to it. . . . The neglect . . . appeared the more justifiable because I soon became convinced that they would add little or nothing to the elucidation of Lord Salisbury's own personality and policy.[102]

Grenville has disproved this contention. One fears, however, that, if she had studied the many thousands of telegrams and despatches with the same thoroughness, she might have added another ten years to her life's work! Apart from this, Grenville has not called her scholarship into question. Her views on Salisbury's foreign policy can in some cases be questioned, he argues, because more recently available documentation has suggested different conclusions.[103]

Her interpretations, however, can fruitfully be examined side by side with later accounts of the events of the period. The *Life* is not, unfortunately, as fully footnoted as she or later scholars could have desired – here she had to follow the publishers' wishes.[104]

There remains the problem of bias: this is the chief ground on which those who have chosen to dismiss her book have done so. Her brother Hugh had warned her not to fill it with 'unrelieved panegyric'.[105] But this was hard for her to avoid completely: she had spent the first forty-three years of her life under the spell of Salisbury's formidable and wide learning, embracing science, politics, religion and history. With his eminence in the world, his majestic though untidy appearance, tall, massive, bearded, his slow deep voice contrasting strangely with the lightning wit which would suddenly emerge from his long silences, it was small wonder that his daughter revered him almost as a god and believed unreservedly in his goodness and all-powerful wisdom.

One popularly held view which she was keen to refute was that he was hard and inhuman.[106] Her portrayal of him as a devoted family man, as a magnanimous spirit who refused to attack Gladstone's Irish policy publicly during the week following Lord Frederick Cavendish's murder, and as a political chief who was reluctant to press his colleagues too much, might be taken as a convincing refutation of the conventional picture. Inevitably, however, later historians see limitations in her portrait. Is it possible, even, that she deliberately ignored facets of Salisbury's character which were at variance with the high-minded and, in some ways, unworldly figure she depicted? Can he not also be shown to be a cunning political tactician, a warrior in the defence of property and class interest, and, at times, a ruthless beheader of leading rivals?

Professor John Vincent has pointed out in discussion the 'corpses' littering his path to the supremacy over his party: Derby, Iddesleigh, Churchill.[107] Some modern studies have on such grounds presented a rather different angle on his personality.[108] On the whole, Salisbury's stock has risen in recent years, but it is his intellectually tough and ironical outlook and his skill as a manager, more than his compassionate and 'supra-political' sides, that are increasingly the objects of interest.[109]

That Gwendolen suppressed some evidence, we know from her letters. Her motives were characteristic: the preparation of her chapter in volume III on Salisbury's relations with Queen Victoria had particularly worried her – as a loyal daughter as much as a loyal subject, some censorship seemed justifiable. The Queen respected Salisbury's judgement even more highly than that of Disraeli and was deeply dependent on him. But she gave him trouble: 'I've deliberately left out a series [of letters] dealing with her demand to have the Duke of Connaught made Comr. in Chief in India', Gwendolen admitted privately; 'They don't show her to advantage & my father was annoyed at her persistence.' She added that the incident was covered in Winston Churchill's biography of his father, Lord Randolph, and that Lord Salisbury 'was so fond of her that I'd rather leave it out.'[110]

She worried continually about how her relations would react to the *Life*: when volume IV appeared she told her sister, 'There are one or two sentiments which Willy [Lord Selborne] will quarrel with, – notably food taxes & H[ouse] of L[ords] reforms. In fact on looking through it again as a whole, I find that Jem is the only one of my relations who won't find something to quarrel with – & he will, I think, be a little shocked at some of the references to Colonials – & would be more so if I hadn't carefully bowdlerised them!'[111] Her family however were well satisfied by her pains to avoid embarassing revelations: 'You take me behind the scenes without being in the least indiscreet – or impolite', wrote Lady Robert Cecil, reading part of the manuscript before it was completed.[112]

It was not only problems of composition, her decertified mental patients and political events involving her brothers[113] which were responsible for the writing-delays of Gwendolen's later years: new documentary sources released after the war assisted her task but slowed her progress. With only a slight knowledge of German she embarked on the forty-volume *Die grosser Politik der europäischen Kabinette (1871–1914)* – 'spelt out painfully, with the aid of a dictionary'[114] – though Edgar Dugdale's four-volume translation and selection, which appeared in 1929, subsequently lightened her load. The papers of Igor Igorovitch de Staal, Russian Ambassador to London from 1884 to 1902, became available for study after 1921 (they were published in 1929). Gooch and Temperley's edited *British Documents on the Origins of the War* came out in 1926.

This meant that she could not simply write from the knowledge she had accumulated since 1906, but had to absorb a vast amount of new information. Increasingly she began to find the task of combining a close biographical study with an authoritative work on diplomacy an almost impossible one. The eleven chapters of her final unfinished volume show symptoms of her difficulties. They are full of memorable passages and excellent quotations, but the effect is at times diffuse. She ran into difficulties with keeping her chapters on the Eastern Question (1895–7) down to manageable proportions. This particular section, she complained unhappily to Maud in August 1935,

> haunted me for months; – I have cut it about, transposed it, rewritten it till I was sick of it, & put it away as hopeless. But you are quite right; – it is out of proportion, – as a whole and in parts & will never be satisfactory without drastic lopping and condensation. I am already visualising a stern concentration on the purely biographical elements – which are really not unmanageably long – and leaving Armenian history and circumstance to take care of itself.[115]

There was an additional reason why she devoted so much attention to these 'Turkish' chapters – Salisbury's friendship and close co-operation with the British Ambassador in Turkey, Sir Philip Currie: 'A further temptation in the same direction came from my father's relations with Philip Currie. I don't think it is any exaggeration to say that he wrote *ten* letters to him for every one that he wrote to other ambassadors – so that one was drowned under the flood of detail.'[116]

Had the last volume appeared within a year or two of the third and fourth, it would have provided a solid conclusion to her life's work. But by the time of her death, in 1945, she still had five years of her father's career to describe, including the highly important months of the Fashoda crisis and the Boer War. In 1953, Hodder and Stoughton wrongly concluded that it would not be worth publishing a completed version of the final volume.[117] One problem was that, although there were some notes indicating what her selection of material would have been, these would only have helped to compile a chapter or two. In good hands, however, a workable volume could certainly have been achieved at that time.

Today, the publication of her manuscript would still be worthwhile, though the interest of the book would be chiefly to the academic historian. Like Lady Gwendolen's earlier volumes, her last chapters belong to the older school of diplomatic history – now out of fashion – which tends to concentrate on the activities of national leaders and foreign offices rather than on the internal conditions and pressures among the states concerned. But it would be a great mistake to dismiss them altogether as 'out of date'. For example, her views on Salisbury's attitude over the future of the Turkish Empire in 1895–6 are still worth considering with respect, though they must be qualified. Throughout there is a very interesting selection of his letters and speeches. Her assessment of Bismarck is subtle and seemingly accurate.[118] So too is her highly original analysis of Chamberlain's political outlook. The work has the same individuality and much of the vigour of the earlier volumes.

As the years went by, Gwendolen was often ill and her eyes increasingly bothered her. By 1944 her memory was no longer good enough for her to hold together the complicated strands of her biographical narrative and she did nothing more on it in the year before she died.

She left very little money; nearly all of it had gone on charitable causes and Miss Marshall and other individuals. For many years she had kept open a special account at her bank for charitable purposes. She had been generous to the point of prodigality, and several times had been rescued from debt by her brother, Salisbury. Her extravagance used to worry her – she constantly used an ashtray appropriated from a railway carriage which had the virtue of concealing the cigarette butts as they were stubbed out. She was thus spared from seeing how much she had smoked.[119] Finance was a mystery to her: 'I have never been able to understand what "going off the gold standard" really means', she confessed to Maud

Selborne.[120] When she decided to sell La Bastide she chose a time when the franc had fallen steeply in value; the whole estate only realised £5000.[121] Today it would go for a price which would daunt many millionaires.[122]

It would be easy to paint a picture of Gwendolen Cecil which dwelt chiefly on her startling eccentricity and unworldliness. It would not be fair to do so, because her life and character were far from absurd, even though there was something unfulfilled, as Lady Cecil of Chelwood and, more dismissively, Rebecca West have both observed. At any rate, if she was 'depleted',[123] she was certainly not lacking in the finer human qualities of intellect and compassion.

No scholarly book is the worse for being composed slowly. But her extreme inefficiency meant that she wasted much of the time she spent on her writing. Evidence of her working-methods can be seen in her notebooks. Interspersed with her main subject are jottings on estate matters, on political questions, on religion. 'It would take her hours of re-reading to find what she wanted', her niece wrote.[124] These were the erratic wanderings, not of a butterfly mind, but of a powerful one which could not resist a deep plunge if something captured the imagination. Lady Robert Cecil believed that a university education would have kept her more on course.[125] It is unlikely; the disorganisation was deeply rooted in her character, although a break from the fascinating tyranny of home life between the ages of nineteen and twenty-two might have benefited her in other ways.

Whatever the ultimate causes of her disorganisation, the fact was that the life of a scholar, purely and simply, could not satisfy her whole nature; the instincts, not the temperament, for scholarship were there. But one can exaggerate the slowness of her achievement: she finished four masterly volumes on a figure of major political importance; many scholars have done less, even in forty years.

NOTES

I am grateful to the British Academy for financial assistance; to Mrs Ann Dale, Mrs Marion McCormick and Mrs Margaret Walkington for typing, to the following for advice and information (in addition to those acknowledged in the notes): Mr Robin Behar, Lady Anne Brewis, Dr Roy Bridge, Mrs Mirabel Cecil, Mr Frederick A. de Marwicz (of Beaulieu-sur-Mer); Mr Robin Harcourt Williams (Hatfield House Librarian), Professor

John Grenville, Professor W. N. Medlicott, the Marquis and Marchioness of Salisbury, Dr David Steele, Professor John Vincent and Mr Christopher Wall (Disraeli Archive, Hughenden). For permission to quote from copyright material I am grateful to Professor Anne Lambton (Cecil of Chelwood papers); Mary, Lady Manners; the Hon. Mrs Dorothy Palmer and Mr Robert Palmer (Gwendolen Cecil papers); and the Marquis of Salisbury (papers of third Marquis).

My principal documentary source has been the Hatfield House Archive. Papers cited from this source are identified by the prefix 'HHM' (Hatfield House Muniments) and classified 'CHE' (Cecil of Chelwood papers), 'GW' (Gwendolen Cecil papers) or '3M' (papers of third Marquis). In details of correspondence and other papers, Lady Gwendolen is referred to below as 'Gwendolen'; her sister, the Countess of Selborne, as 'Maud'; her father, the third Marquis of Salisbury, as 'Salisbury'; and her mother, the third Marchioness, as 'Lady Salisbury'. Lady Gwendolen's *Life of Robert Marquis of Salisbury*, I (London, 1921), II (London, 1921), III (London, 1931) and IV (London, 1932), is referred to as *Life*. Quotations from the incomplete and unpublished volume V are from the Hatfield manuscript (classified HHM/3M/CC) and are not separately referenced.

1. There are three published accounts of Lady Gwendolen: Mary, Lady Manners (daughter of Lord William Cecil, Bishop of Exeter), *Gwendolen Cecil* (privately printed, Jan 1946); Kenneth Rose, *The Later Cecils* (London, 1975) ch. 10; and Lord David Cecil, *The Cecils of Hatfield House* (London, 1973).
2. See Lord David Cecil, *The Cecils of Hatfield House*, pt III; and Viscountess Milner, *My Picture Gallery, 1886–1901* (London, 1951) pp. 81–2.
3. HHM/GW, Gwendolen to Maud, 5 Oct 1930.
4. HHM/GW, Gwendolen to Maud, 30 Mar 1928.
5. HHM/GW, Gwendolen to Maud, Mar 1925.
6. Manners, *Gwendolen Cecil*, pp. 10–11.
7. Ibid., p. 18; and Mary, Duchess of Devonshire, to whom my thanks are due for this and other information in this paper.
8. See *The Letters of Lewis Carroll*, ed. Morton Cohen, with the assistance of Roger Lancelyn Green, I *ca, 1837–1885* (London, 1979) p. 554, C. L. Dodgson to third Marquis of Salisbury, 2 Nov 1884. Also see J. N. S. Davis, 'The Salisbury Correspondence', *Jaberwocky: The Journal of the Lewis Carroll Society*, 4, no. 3 (Summer 1975), 59–65.
9. Lord David Cecil, *The Cecils of Hatfield House*, p. 286.
10. HHM/GW, extract of letter from Lord Beaconsfield to Queen Victoria, 24 Apr 1878, enclosed in letter from Lord Stamfordham to Gwendolen, 2 Aug 1923.
11. Manners, *Gwendolen Cecil*, p. 19; and see HHM/GW, Beaconsfield to Gwendolen, 20 Sep 1879.
12. Beatrice, Lady Harlech, to author, 10 Nov 1976.
13. See HHM/GW, fifteenth Duke of Norfolk to Gwendolen, 23 July 1899.
14. HHM/GW, Lady Margaret Howard to Gwendolen, 1 Dec 1893, and other letters.

15. See, for example, HHM/GW, Gwendolen to Maud, 2 July 1925, and, in general, Manners, *Gwendolen Cecil*, p. 20.
16. HHM/GW, Gwendolen to Maud, 12 Nov 1923.
17. HHM/3M Lady Salisbury/Box 3.1, Gwendolen to Lady Salisbury, 'Tuesday' [undated, c. 1889]. For Ingram, see n. 74.
18. HHM/GW, Gwendolen to Maud, 12 Nov 1923.
19. HHM/TW, Gwendolen to Maud, 21 Jan 1937.
20. I am indebted to Mary, Lady Manners, for her recollections about Lady Gwendolen, here and elsewhere in this paper.
21. HHM/3M Lady Salisbury/Box 3.1, Gwendolen to Lady Salisbury, 29 Nov 1876. Nikolai Pavlovich Ignatiev (1832–1908), soldier and diplomat; Ambassador, Constantinople, 1864–77.
22. HHM/GW, Salisbury to Gwendolen, 12 Dec 1876.
23. HHM/GW, Lady Salisbury to Gwendolen, letters Nov 1876–Jan 1877.
24. Mary, Duchess of Devonshire, information.
25. HHM/GW, Gwendolen Diary, 9 Mar 1888. The passage continues in a code (probably a book code) which has so far defied experts.
26. HHM/3M/Lady Salisbury/Box 3.1, Gwendolen to Lady Salisbury, 7 Jan [?1890s]. On 9 September 1901, several years later, McDonnell, Salisbury's secretary warned him, 'In case Princess Radziwill should endeavour to reopen communications with Y[our] L[ordship], I think you should know that she has forged Rhodes' name to bills for £3,000 and £10,000' (HHM/3M).
27. HHM/3M/Lady Salisbury/Box 3.1, Gwendolen to Lady Salisbury [?1888].
28. HHM/GW, Gwendolen to Alice Balfour, 8 Oct 1898. Kitchener's decisive victory over the Khalifa at Omdurman took place on 2 September 1898; Muslim refugees rioted at Candia, Crete, killing the British vice-consul and some British sailors; 800 Christians were massacred and the town pillaged by Turkish troops on 6 September; on 10 September, the Austrian Empress was assassinated in Geneva.
29. *Life*, iii, 29.
30. Lady Robert Cecil to Lady Manners, 14 Jan 1946. Copy in possession of Lord David Cecil.
31. Manners, *Gwendolen Cecil*, p. 13: 'After her death it was found she had noted the time of going to bed every night in her engagement book. The times varied very much. One entry was 7 a.m. Church 8.'
32. Lady Robert Cecil to Lady Manners, 14 Jan 1946. See n. 30.
33. HHM/GW, Gwendolen to Maud, 23 June 1936. Sir Richard Douglas Powell (1842–1925) was physician in ordinary to Queen Victoria from 1899.
34. HHM/GW, Lord Goschen to Gwendolen, 14 Sep 1903.
35. HHM/GW, fourth Marquis of Salisbury to Gwendolen, 27 July 1906.
36. Manners, *Gwendolen Cecil*, p. 8.
37. I am indebted to Lord David Cecil for information here and elsewhere.
38. HHM/GW, Gwendolen to Maud, 24 Aug 1906.
39. HHM/CHE/53/73, Gwendolen to Lady Robert Cecil, 16 Feb 1922. For Gunton and Barrington's work see HHM/GW, Gwendolen to Maud, 24 Aug 1906 and 19 July 1907.

40. HHM/GW, fifth Marquis of Salisbury to Lewis Palmer, 10 Dec 1947; and fifth Marquis of Salisbury to Lord David Cecil, 16 Sep 1947 (Lord David Cecil papers).
41. Gloucester County Record Office, Hicks Beach Papers, PCC/69, Gwendolen to Lord St Aldwyn, 16 Dec 1913.
42. Ibid., copy of St Aldwyn's account of Salisbury.
43. Ibid., Gwendolen to St Aldwyn, 23 June 1914.
44. HHM/GW, Gwendolen to Maud, 19 July 1907.
45. HHM/GW, Gwendolen to Maud, 20 Sep 1907.
46. HHM/GW, Gwendolen to Maud, 11 Apr 1921.
47. HHM/GW, Gwendolen to Maud, 3 Aug 1906.
48. See HHM/GW, Gwendolen to Maud, 21 Feb 1908.
49. HHM/GW, Gwendolen to Maud, 17 Mar 1910.
50. HHM/GW, Gwendolen to Maud, 29 Feb 1910.
51. Ibid.
52. HHM/GW, Gwendolen to Maud, 17 Mar 1910.
53. HHM/GW, Gwendolen to Maud, 11 Dec 1929.
54. Ibid.
55. HHM/GW, J. L. Hammond in *Manchester Guardian*, 1931, cutting.
56. Lady Frances Balfour, daughter of the Duke of Argyll and sister-in-law of A. J. Balfour; a prominent political hostess and gossip, she bore a facial resemblance to Queen Elizabeth I. More amusing than reliable, she wrote a memoir entitled *Ne Obliviscaris: Dinna Forget*, 2 vols (London 1930). Lord Hugh Cecil once said he would like it stated in his will, 'Nothing said about me by Mrs Asquith or Lady Frances Balfour is to be believed' (Lord David Cecil, information).
57. HHM/GW, Gwendolen to Lady Frances Balfour, 2 Dec 1910.
58. *Life*, III, 21.
59. Ibid., p. 28.
60. HHM/GW, William Blackwood to Gwendolen, 25 June 1894.
61. HHM/GW, Maud to fourth Marquis of Salisbury, 15 Oct 1945, and to fifth Marquis, 18 Jan 1948.
62. HHM/GW, Gwendolen to Lady Frances Balfour, 2 Dec 1910.
63. HHM/GW, Gwendolen to Maud, 3 Apr 1908.
64. HHM/GW, Gwendolen to Maud, 10 Apr 1908.
65. HHM/GW, Gwendolen to Maud, 8 May 1908.
66. HHM/GW, Gwendolen to Maud, 6 July 1906.
67. HHM/GW, plans of cottages and flats at Hatfield by Gwendolen.
68. HHM/GW, Gwendolen to Maud, 17 Aug 1905.
69. HHM/GW, misc. Hatfield Papers.
70. See, for example, Manners, *Gwendolen Cecil*, p. 17; also HHM/GW, Gwendolen to Maud, May 1925.
71. HHM/GW, Gwendolen to Maud, 12 Aug 1928.
72. Mary, Lady Manners, information.
73. See HHM/GW, Gwendolen to Maud, Apr 1910.
74. HHM/GW, Gwendolen to Maud, 12 Nov 1910. Manners, *Gwendolen Cecil*, p. 9: 'If ill, she blamed the doctor.' Arthur Foley Winnington Ingram (1858–1946), head of Oxford House, Bethnal Green, 1889; rector, Bethnal Green, 1895; Bishop of London 1901–39; known as

'Sunny Jim' or 'Chuckles'; effective and popular bishop, offered Broad Church, sentimental religious uplift.
75. See, for example, HHM/GW, Gwendolen to Maud, 9 Feb 1906 ('We are rather depressed about Arthur . . .'), and Gwendolen to Maud, 18 Nov 1936 (summing up of Balfour's career).
76. HHM/GW, Gwendolen to Maud, 5 Aug 1914.
77. HHM/GW, Gwendolen to Maud, 29 Aug 1914.
78. HHM/GW, Gwendolen to Maud, 17 Sep 1917.
79. Mary, Lady Manners, information; and see, for example, HHM/GW, Gwendolen to Maud, Mar 1925, and Gwendolen to Lady Laura Ridding (Lolly), 19 Jan 1920 and 10 Aug 1922.
80. See HHM/GW, Gwendolen to Maud [30 Jan 1930], regarding education of bargees' children.
81. See HHM/GW, Gwendolen to Maud, 3 July 1931.
82. See HHM/GW, Gwendolen to Maud [1936]: 'We have got one epileptic & a senile old lady to go on with'; and 5 Apr, 23 Apr, 24 May and 21 June 1936.
83. See in HHM/CHE 18/1–199, Lady Robert Cecil to Lord Robert Cecil (hereinafter, 'Nellie to Bob'), 7 Jan 1919 *et seq.*
84. HHM/CHE 18/14, Nellie to Bob, 3 Feb 1919.
85. HHM/CHE 18/26, Nellie to Bob, 28 Feb 1919.
86. HHM/CHE 18/27, Nellie to Bob, Ash Wednesday 1919.
87. HHM/CHE 18/29, Nellie to Bob, 3 Mar 1919.
88. HHM/CHE 18/32, Nellie to Bob, 11 Mar 1919.
89. HHM/CHE 18/40, Nellie to Bob, 30 Mar 1919.
90. HHM/GW, Gwendolen to Maud, 2 Mar 1921.
91. HHM/GW, Lewis Palmer to fourth Marquis of Salisbury, 4 Dec 1945.
92. HHM/GW, Sir Ernest Hodder-Williams to Gwendolen, 30 Nov 1921.
93. HHM/GW, *Punch*, 13 Jan 1932, cutting.
94. *Life*, IV, 86.
95. G. P. Gooch and H. W. V. Temperley (eds), *British Documents on the Origins of the War, 1898–1914*, 11 vols in 13 (London, 1926–38).
96. Algernon Cecil, *British Foreign Secretaries, 1807–1916: Studies in Personality, and Policy* (London 1927) p. 303.
97. Gwendolen to Victor Cecil (son of Lord William Cecil), 24 Feb 1932, in author's possession.
98. HHM/GW, Gwendolen to Maud, 6 Dec 1921 and 2 Jan 1922.
99. *Life*, II, 65.
100. HHM/GW, Gwendolen to Maud, 6 Dec 1921.
101. See also Lord Middleton's view that she included too little of Salisbury's humour: HHM/GW, Gwendolen to Maud, 2 Jan 1922.
102. *Life*, III, prefatory note (p. vii).
103. See J. A. S. Grenville, *Lord Salisbury and Foreign Policy: The Close of the Nineteenth Century*, paperback edn (London 1970) pp. 14–15; also Agatha Ramm, 'Lord Salisbury and the Foreign Office', in Roger Bullen (ed.), *The Foreign Office 1782–1982* (Frederick, Md, 1984). Neither of these authors has intended to imply that Salisbury's frequent absence from the Foreign Office meant that he lacked detailed knowledge of many of the cases he left in FO hands, and

readers should avoid forming any such conclusion. Ramm demonstrates, however, that, while the coherent shaping of his overall foreign policy was wholly his domain, he was ready to delegate other business.

104. HHM/GW, Sir Ernest Hodder-Williams to Gwendolen, 8 July 1921.
105. HHM/GW, Lord Hugh Cecil to Gwendolen, 5 Aug 1908.
106. HHM/GW, Gwendolen to Lady Laura Ridding, 23 Nov 1921.
107. Professor John Vincent, at a Victorian Colloquium held in Bristol University, 21 Mar 1979.
108. See, for example, Ch. 9 below; and works by R. F. Foster and P. T. Marsh cited there and elsewhere in this volume; Maurice Cowling, *Religion and Public Doctrine in Modern England* (Cambridge, 1980). Cowling has been illuminating on Salisbury's understanding of his opponents intellectual case.
109. For an 'above politics' view of Salisbury, see *Monthly Review*, Oct 1903, p. 1 – article by Lord Robert Cecil, who tried to live according to this estimate of his father.
110. HHM/GW, Gwendolen to Maud, 21 Apr 1926.
111. HHM/GW, Gwendolen to Maud 4 Dec 1931.
112. HHM/GW, Lady Robert Cecil to Gwendolen, 30 Mar 1919.
113. HHM/GW, Gwendolen to Maud, 18 Aug 1935: 'My pacifist brother is in high spirits at the prospect of seeing the League come to close quarters with its enemies at last under English leadership.'
114. Gwendolen to Victor Cecil, 24 Feb 1932, in author's possession.
115. HHM/GW, Gwendolen to Maud, 18 Aug 1935.
116. Ibid.
117. HHM/GW, Ralph Hodder-Williams to fifth Marquis of Salisbury, 30 June 1953.
118. Professor W. N. Medlicott to the author, 23 May 1980.
119. Mary, Lady Manners, and Lord David Cecil, information; and HHM/GW, Mrs J. M. Main (secretary to fourth, fifth and sixth Marquises, 1938–1974) to J. O. Floyd (Frere Cholmely and Nicholson, solicitors) regarding £42 11s. 0d. left in Gwendolen's charity account.
120. HHM/GW, Gwendolen to Maud, 23 June 1933.
121. Mary, Duchess of Devonshire, information.
122. R. N. Behar (of Le Schuylkill, Monte Carlo) to author, 9 Dec 1978.
123. Dame Rebecca West in *Sunday Telegraph*, 6 July 1975.
124. Manners, *Gwendolen Cecil*, p. 12.
125. Lady Robert Cecil to Lady Manners, 14 Jan 1946. See n. 30. For Lord Salisbury's views on women's education see below, Ch. 10.

5

'The Conservative Reaction': Lord Robert Cecil and Party Politics

ROBERT STEWART

Lord Robert Cecil's unopposed election for the borough of Stamford, a Conservative seat in the gift of his cousin, the Marquis of Exeter, brought him into the House of Commons in 1853 as the successor to the retiring member, Sir John Herries, a stolid representative of the protectionist, High Anglican Toryism which had held firm against Sir Robert Peel in 1846 and preserved in the nation's politics a party dedicated to the defence of the landed interest and the constitution in Church and state. The Conservative electors of Stamford had no reason to complain of the new member chosen for them: the frailty of his health was as nothing when set against the vigour and fertility of his intellect. As a backbencher in the House of Commons, Cecil was for twelve years a loyal, though disenchanted, upholder of his party's cause in the division lobbies. Yet it was not by his parliamentary performances that he impressed himself upon his generation, and the study of them does not get us very far towards understanding his youthful Toryism. 'There is no greater fallacy', he wrote at the end of his backbench career, 'than to estimate the store which any man sets by any particular cause, or the value of the aid he gives it, by the isolated votes that he records. By the votes a man gives he simply bears witness to the convictions of his constituency; by the party he supports he gives effect to his own.'[1] Men, in other words, not measures, governed the life of Parliament. It was outside Parliament, in his political journalism, that Cecil revealed the fundaments of his Tory convictions and rendered his chief service to his party.

There are dangers in taking opinions expressed in the public prints at face value. Cecil himself excused the abrasiveness of his remarks against Disraeli in *Bentley's Quarterly Review* in 1859 by pointing out to his father, Disraeli's Cabinet colleague, that writing for money compelled the use of language more pointed than would be appropriate in conversation: 'I must write in the style that is most likely to attract, and therefore to sell'.[2] Political journalism, being part propaganda and part wishful thinking, is especially suspect, as Cecil knew. 'So little of exact reasoning and so much of *ad captandum* declamation is employed in political discussions', he wrote once in the *Quarterly Review*, 'that words are of much more importance in it than thoughts. The man who can discover a phrase by which the desired argument or assertion is hinted, without being formally laid down, does more for his cause than the keenest reasoner.'[3] As a prophet Cecil at times appears foolish to posterity, as when he announced in 1860, after the Palmerston government's defeat on its Bill to abolish the excise duties on paper, that Gladstone's political future was permanently eclipsed and that, in contrast to the Radicals of the Manchester school, who were 'weak in all but bluster', the House of Lords had rediscovered that it possessed 'a living power, wielded freely by themselves, and recognised instinctively by the people'.[4] But such statements were intended, not so much as measured judgements, more as rallying-cries to the Tory supporters in the shires. Attention to personalities, unconcealed glee at the discomfiture of political opponents, the lively use of metaphor and the frequent recourse to an apocalyptic tone give Cecil's essays an engaging raciness. Yet much of the glitter was gold. As a reviewer remarked after Lord Salisbury's death, the essays, which rarely stopped short of 20,000 words, 'more truly portray the man than anything he said or did within the cramping limitations of parliamentary procedure or under the restraining influence of party and ministerial responsibility'.[5]

Cecil's first article, 'The Faction-Fights', was published in *Bentley's Quarterly Review* in 1859. It was a prodigious debut. For a young Conservative backbencher, even writing anonymously, to pour unqualified scorn on the tactics and political character of the leader of his party in the House of Commons was startling and, although the essay did not have the sensational public impact of Macaulay's first appearance in the *Edinburgh Review* twenty-five years earlier, Cecil was at once taken up by the Tory *Quarterly Review* (which had never quite reconciled itself to Disraeli's leadership) as its chief political contributor. The public was rewarded with a run of essays which set forth with remarkable candour Cecil's view of the course of party politics since 1846 and the present discontents of the Conservative Party.

Between 1846 and 1866 the Conservatives held office for only slightly more than two years, during Lord Derby's minority administrations of 1852 and 1858–9. Cecil nevertheless believed that throughout that period there was a conservative majority in the country and that the preponderance of opinion within the electorate was decidedly inimical to radical innovations in the country's affairs. That view was widely held. Sir William Jolliffe, about to become the party's chief whip, told Lord Derby at the beginning of 1854 that as far as he could remember 'there never was a more real Conservative feeling in the Country at large, or in our Party generally, than exists at the present time'.[6] Throughout the decade of Palmerston's ascendancy, from 1855 to 1865, almost everyone except the militant Dissenters, the Radicals of the Manchester school and the rump of die-hard Tories was content to describe himself as a liberal conservative or a conservative liberal. 'In recent years', Cecil put the point in one of his most famous epigrams, 'the Whig idea of a model political system has been this – that the Whigs should furnish the placemen, the Radicals should furnish the votes, and the Conservatives should furnish the policy.'[7]

That Cecil laid much of the blame for the Conservatives' malaise on Disraeli is notorious. By constantly seeking an alliance with any section of the Radicals which would secure a temporary anti-Whig majority in the House of Commons, Disraeli discredited himself and his party. He ought, Cecil thought, to have been taught a lesson in 1852, when, despite holding out tax 'bribes' to the Irish – his 'old game of talking Green in the House and Orange in the lobby'[8] – and the Radicals, his budget, and with it Derby's first government, was thrown out. Instead, he repeated the error in 1858–9, casting aside traditional party policy by admitting the Jews to Parliament and introducing a Bill for parliamentary reform. The result was the same: the Conservatives were ejected from office by a coalition of all the other elements in the House of Commons. The Conservative Reform Bill, though its proposal to equalise the county and borough franchises hinted at a future disfranchisement of the smaller boroughs, was clothed round with 'fancy franchises' to increase the electoral weight of the educated and propertied classes and failed to seduce the Radicals. In the following year the Whigs brought in a more extensive Bill of their own. To Cecil the moral was clear. 'As might have been expected, the Whigs declined to be outflanked. If the Conservatives chose to move in the democratic direction, it was not their part to remain behind. The positive position of political parties must change from age to age; but the relative position towards each other must be unalterable.' Thus, 'the net result of the whole transaction to the Conservatives was simply this – that, as a party, they were no nearer to power, but that democracy had advanced a stride nearer to its triumph'.[9] When, seven years later, the great 'leap in the dark' took place, it was neither 'an isolated error' nor an 'accidental weakness', but 'the culmination of a policy that has been sturdily pursued for twenty years', the policy of attempting to outbid the Whigs for Radical support.[10]

Cecil's criticism of Disraeli in 1859 was unsparing. Members, who remembered or had learned that in Peel's day he was a lively speaker, pretended to find him lively still, though he was 'perpetually rounding off and diluting his sentences, and beating out his statements with all the energy of a goldbeater, so that three minutes' worth of information shall stretch over a quarter of an hour of speaking, lest at any time his oratory should stray into the unstatesmanlike vice of brevity'.[11] The true connection between the Disraeli of 1859 and the Disraeli of 1846 was quite different. It was that he had become the exponent of that very 'organised hypocrisy' for which he had once censured Peel. Disraeli's ruling flaw was his blindness to the value of a public character, a blindness that had 'haunted him and hindered him throughout his whole career'.[12] The policy of the Conservative Government in 1859 was 'suicidal', not because of what it contained, but on account of its disclosure of the moral bankruptcy of the party's leaders. 'For in this country a reputation for sincerity is worth far more, perhaps because it is far more rare, than any amount of parliamentary cleverness or brilliancy of eloquence.'[13] In a letter of 1867 Cecil (or Lord Cranborne, as he was by then) described his allegiance to the Conservative Party as 'purely one of principle', for, he went on to his correspondent, 'as you know, I have no feelings of attachment to either of the leaders'.[14] That in 1859 he exempted Lord Derby from the tarring he so readily gave to Disraeli suggests that, like most of his contemporaries, Cecil mistakenly supposed Derby's command of the party to be more nominal than actual.

In his dismay at the Conservative Government's behaviour in 1859, Cecil went so far as to assert that the political leaders were alone accountable for the relaxation of party discipline and the abeyance of the party warfare which characterised the Palmerston era. The ceasefire had 'been attributed to any and every cause except the right one – the insincerity of the leaders whom public apathy suffers to reign, and the consequent distrust and disaffection of their followers'.[15] The country was as hostile to democratic change as it had been in the days when Peel's Conservative Government commanded a majority of ninety in the House of Commons; now the party was in a minority of forty and the reason was that men were driven away from the Conservative lobby by their 'perfect abhorrence of Mr Disraeli'.[16] A fusion of moderate Whigs and Conservatives would produce an accurate parliamentary expression of the real feelings of the electorate. Cecil professed to see only one obstacle in the way:

> We believe the solution of the difficulty is a simple one. Mr Disraeli is in the proud position of being the grain of dirt that clogs the whole machine. . . . Of the benefit to the country of such a fusion, all who love steady progress without a violent transfer of power, can hardly speak too warmly. It is the only safe bulwark against revolutionary change: it is the only hope of restoring that stability of government which in these tempestuous days the national security demands. But the condition precedent to any such happy union is the disappearance – or the miraculous conversion – of that soldier of fortune, with whom, it is now proved, not one of the leading statesmen in the House of Commons will condescend to coalesce.[17]

How far Cecil's outspoken condemnation of Disraeli reflected discontent on the Tory backbenches it is difficult to say. After the apostasy of 1867, he denied disgruntled Tories the right to deal in recrimination against Disraeli, whose shifting tactics they had never repudiated. On the contrary, they had throughout given him 'a steady, often a jubilant, support'.[18] At the time, however, he attempted to mollify Lord Exeter, who was disquieted by the severe tone of Cecil's writings, by saying that he had 'merely put into print what all the country gentlemen were saying in private'.[19] He allowed that his language was provocative, but 'readers in this rapid age are too hasty and too thoughtless to give much heed to strictures which are not flavoured with the relish of a personal application'; and he claimed to be doing Disraeli a service 'by plainly speaking out what every one was saying of him in private, and no one would say in public'. It was 'no kindness to a statesman to persist in assuring him that he is keeping the right road, when he is marching straight into a bog'.[20]

There was a small coterie of dissidents in the party, led by the member for Norfolk West, George Bentinck. In the early 1860s they would have been happy to see Disraeli replaced, but they never numbered more than a couple of dozen (Lord Derby's figure in 1857 was only five[21]) and they failed to attract the support of any leading members of the party (Joseph Henley and Spencer Walpole, who resigned from Derby's second government in protest at the 1859 Reform Bill, were too prudent to commit themselves to a cabal). Part of their weakness lay in having no candidate of sufficient stature – General Peel was their favourite choice – to mount a serious action against Disraeli. Edward Stanley, as critical as they of Disraeli, but from a liberal standpoint and therefore himself unacceptable to the bulk of the party, counted Cecil a member of the Bentinck cave, but he remarked that Cecil's ardour was 'mollified by hopes of office'.[22] Cecil was, indeed, a frequent attender at small meetings, rather like those of a modern shadow Cabinet, which discussed party policy; and he appears to have had little more than a bare acquaintance with Bentinck. In 1866 Bentinck began a letter to him in terms that do not suggest intimacy: 'Our casual meeting in the streets a year ago entailed on you an infliction of a letter of mine, and at the risk of your wishing that we may never meet again, I must send you another.'[23] There was no breach with Disraeli, who looked kindly upon the exuberance of youthful journalism, and Cecil assured Lord Exeter that, 'though, in common with many Conservatives, I cannot in private quite approve of many things Mr D'Israeli has said & done, I have never had any other intention than to give the Govt. all the support in my power in the H. of C.'.[24]

That purpose was stiffened by the events of 1860: the Liberal Government was forced to abandon its Reform Bill, the repeal of the paper duties was defeated by the House of Lords, and for the first time in a decade the majority in the House of Commons in favour of abolishing Church rates was in single figures. Here at last was the Conservative reaction and it seemed to work the 'miraculous conversion' in Disraeli, who came forward in public speeches as the unwavering champion of the Established Church and the forthright opponent of the Liberation Society and all its demands. Stanley found in Disraeli's Churchmanship merely a fresh specimen of his charlatanry. 'How', he asked, 'can I reconcile his open ridicule, in private, of all religions, with his preaching up of a new church-and-state agitation? or how can I help seeing that glory and power, rather than the public good, have been his objects?'[25] Cecil, however, wished to make the most of Disraeli's new attitude. During the session of 1860 Disraeli had acted in consistent opposition to the Liberal Government and its Radical supporters, the financial reformers of the Manchester school and the Dissenters. Cecil applauded him in the *Quarterly Review*:

> He has shown no inclination to flinch from the assertion of Conservative principles; he has made no attempts to boil them down to suit the palates of Radical allies. Mr Bright's ferocious denunciations betray his misgiving that the reckless ambition on which he once hoped to climb to power will serve him no more. We have a right to assume that the change is permanent, and that Mr Disraeli has abandoned for ever the 'unholy alliances' and the trimming tactics of which events have proved the hollowness and the sham.

Outsiders who recommended that the Conservative Party find a new leader in the House of Commons were given a sharp lesson in how the party minded its business. 'The "Times" has been over-hasty in arguing as if any question of change of leadership were in agitation among the ranks of its opponents. The Conservative party applies its own principles to its own internal government. It loves not depositions and revolutions more within its own body than in the world outside.'[26]

Disraeli's leadership had always been one of the stumbling-blocks in the way of reunion between the Peelite and Protectionist sections of the post-1846 Conservative Party. He also stood in the way of a fusion with moderate Whigs. But the possibility of a Conservative reconciliation, which in reality meant the return of Gladstone to his old party, had ended. By 1860 Gladstone was rightly looked upon as the captive of the forward movement within Liberalism, in financial and religious reform stepped in too far to return. As for the Whigs, they had no impulse to fusion so long as Palmerston's restraining grip on the advanced wing of his supporters remained firm. To get rid of Disraeli, therefore, when the objects of his dismissal were unattainable, was idle trifling.

Cecil knew, at any rate, that Disraeli was not the cause of the Conservatives' parliamentary weakness; Disraeli's behaviour, rather, was symptomatic of the degeneracy into which party politics had fallen since 1846. The split which had then taken place in the Conservative Party left it with a majority in the country, but without one in Parliament. Had the two wings of the party been able to bury their differences, all would have been well, but reconciliation was found to be impossible, and future historians were warned by Cecil that they would misrepresent the political history of the 1850s if they understated the vindictive spirit in which the feud was perpetuated year after year. By the early 1850s the protectionist wing of the party, numerically by far the more powerful, emerged as the bearer of the party's tradition and its organisation; but it had no policy. Disraeli's budget of 1852 accepted free trade as a *fait accompli*, and the cry of the Church or the constitution in danger had no force, since the Whig-Peelite majority in Parliament had designs on neither. Politics was thereby reduced to a naked scramble for place, with both parties bidding for the votes of the Radicals.

The tacit unanimity with which this generation has laid aside the ingenious network of political first principles which the industry of three centuries of theorists had woven, is one of the most remarkable phenomena in the history of thought. In politics at least the old antithesis of principle and expediency is absolutely forgotten: expediency is the only principle to which allegiance is paid.[27]

For a brief moment during the Conservative Government of 1858–9 Cecil would have had his readers believe that party itself was an outworn institution, surviving only because the Conservatives, having no *casus belli*, retained an army of well-drilled troops, especially in the constituencies, where electoral organisation was so firmly rooted that society, as Henry Drummond had put it, was no longer priest-ridden, but attorney-ridden. 'The misfortune is, that party is not dead, but only dying. Its life and its bloom are withered, but its unwieldy trunk still cumbers the ground.'[28] There is no reason to suppose that Cecil believed that sentence. He did not imagine that party was actually dying. It was suffering from a debilitating disease, but the illness was curable and the cure was a return to principles. Peel had been justly punished. 'To accept an agency or representative position of any kind upon the undertaking that you will use it to promote the views of the person from whom you accept it, and then to use it against him, is in every other sphere of action treated as the greatest crime. In law it is punished as dishonesty. In society it is scouted as dishonour.'[29] Not that Cecil was a political puritan. He was, true enough, tempted by the argument, as at various times were Wellington and Derby, that the Conservatives answered their purposes best by remaining in opposition. A strong Conservative opposition, checking the ambitions of a Liberal Government, he wrote to a friend some years later, 'is undoubtedly the condition of things under which the wearing away of the Constitution is most nearly suspended'.[30] But he was not squeamish about the public position which it profited Conservatives to adopt. 'Hostility to Radicalism, incessant, implacable hostility, is the essential definition of Conservatism. The fear that the Radicals may triumph is the only final cause that the Conservative party can plead for their own existence.'[31] After the 1852 defeat the Conservatives were bereft of principles and frontbench talent, but time would repair the deficiencies. Rather than attempt to outflank their opponents, Conservatives should hide themselves for a season, 'trusting that they should secrete new principles, as lobsters who have been maimed secrete new claws' and remembering that, 'if a considerable party will only wait, it is certain to gather leaders for itself'.[32] In the meantime the Radicals were bound to blunder into excesses and indiscretions and do part of the Conservatives' work for them.

So it happened, Cecil believed, in 1860. Bright's violent speeches on parliamentary reform, with their hints of civil disorder if it were not conceded, awakened the propertied classes from their torpor. William Forster's indiscreet admission to the Lords' select committee that the movement to abolish Church rates was but a first step towards disestablishment and disendowment rallied the friends of the Church to its defence. And Gladstone's attempt to abolish the paper duty revived the self-confidence of the House of Lords and emboldened it to throw out an important piece of Government legislation. The 'Conservative reaction' which those Liberal setbacks signalled would avail little, however, unless Conservatives understood the principles for which they were contending and resolved to make them prevail. No politician was clearer in his mind or more forthright in his statements than Cecil as to the nature of Conservative principles and the grounds of the political battle in the 1860s. From time to time he may have succumbed to the banalities of political utterance. 'The Conservative party', he wrote in 1866, 'exists to secure the balance of all interests; and it must disappear before the exclusive domination of a single class.'[33] In his franker moods (and in the 1860s they were customary) he did not shirk the issue. 'The classes that represent civilisation, the holders of accumulated capital and accumulated thought, have a right to require securities to protect them from being overwhelmed by hordes who have neither knowledge to guide them nor stake in the Commonwealth to control them.'[34] In an essay which appeared in the *Quarterly Review* in 1860 he raised the barricades against democracy in a passage of breath-taking honesty:

The issue between the conflicting forces of society is becoming narrower and more distinct. The mists of political theory are clearing away, and the true character of the battle-ground, and the real nature of the prize that is at stake, are standing out more and more distinctly every year. It galls the classes who barely sustain themselves by their labour that others should sit by and enjoy more than they do, and yet work little or not at all. Benighted enthusiasts in other lands, or other times, may have struggled for idle theories of liberty, or impalpable phantoms of nationality, but the 'enlightened selfishness' of the modern artisan now fully understands that political power, like everything else, is to be taken to the dearest market. He cares little enough for democracy unless it will adjust the inequalities of wealth. The struggle between the English constitution on the one hand, and the democratic forces that are labouring to subvert it on the other, is now, in reality, when reduced to its simplest elements and stated in its most prosaic form, a struggle between those who have, to keep what they have got, and those who have not, to get it.[35]

Cecil argued that a long period in English history was drawing to a close, a period which he called 'the epoch of ecclesiastical politics', initiated when 'the smiles of Anne Boleyn suggested theological doubts to Henry's mind' and carried on down to the day when Gladstone rallied the rabble by leading them, in 1869, to 'the rich and easy conquest of the Irish Establishment'.[36] Between those two events every important political conflict had taken religious passion either as its motive power or, at least, as its avowed cause. By the time that the Irish Church was disestablished (and the last major grievance of the Roman Catholics thereby redressed), religious zeal had faded away into class envy and politics had returned to 'the great primeval subject-matter of all human conflict',[37] the conflict over the ownership of property. Religious quarrels had blended antagonistic classes into one army and effaced the dividing-line between the haves and the have-nots: 'henceforth it seems likely that classes will have to meet each other face to face, with far less of common feelings to break the shock'.[38] The tone of Cecil's articles left little room for his readers to imagine that he regretted the change. Its potential consequences were alluring. The removal of religious distractions offered an opportunity to those owners of property who, divided by their ties to Dissent on the one hand and to the Anglican Church on the other, found themselves ranged as Whigs and Conservatives against each other, to discard their traditional political differences and join forces in the war to preserve property. In the 1860s that war was being waged on three fronts: fiscal, constitutional and (as the *dénouement* of the dying epoch) ecclesiastical.

The ancient quarrel between Dissent and the Church fixed, in the mid-nineteenth century, on the campaign mounted by the Liberation Society to abolish Church rates. Even before his undergraduate days Cecil had read Church history with an absorbing interest, and a deep attachment to the place of the Establishment in the national life was one of the earliest marks of his Conservatism. In the mid-1860s Stanley referred to High Churchmen and Tories 'of the bitter intolerant school – Robert Cecil's',[39] but his language was extravagant, for Cecil was no more than an orthodox representative of the High Church position within Anglicanism. He disdained equally the Low Church, the Broad Church and the extreme, Anglo-Catholic Puseyite tendency. The Broad Churchmen, wishing to have Christian morality without its creed, were like men who would have oak trees to cut down without having to plant them first. 'To most Churchmen, it will be a matter of less interest to inquire how this school is to be refuted than how it is to be repelled. The impossibility and self-contradiction of a religion without dogma is a fact that to most minds does not need formal proof.'[40] As for the Puseyites, when he discovered on his trip to South Africa in 1851 that their doctrines prevailed in the colony, he wrote home that 'Antichrist has penetrated even here'.[41] In the Low Church he found nothing but 'haziness & undefinedness'; the various views of Low Churchmen were 'either verbal quarrels or errors in doctrine'.[42] Nor did he share the bigoted anti-Catholicism of the 'No-Popery' section of the Conservative Party, who, in the 1850s, continued to make impotent protests against the annual parliamentary grant to the Roman Catholic seminary at Maynooth: when he first stood for election at Stamford, in 1853, he sent his election address for approval to Lord Exeter and, on being returned an edited version, was forced to tone down some of his patron's 'Protestant emendations'.[43]

The Church played a part in the 'Conservative reaction', not simply because the defence of the Establishment had been a cardinal element in Toryism for generations, but because the privileges of the Church were the object of renewed and spirited assault from the Liberation Society in the late 1850s. When, at the elections of 1859, the Society for the first time undertook to raise a systematic electoral organisation in the constituencies, Disraeli suddenly came out in his Church colours. 'The fact is', he wrote to Lord Malmesbury in 1861, 'in internal politics there is only one question now, the maintenance of the Church. There can be no refraining or false Liberalism on such a subject. They are both out of fashion, too.'[44] To defend the Church – its endowments, its tithes, its local rates – was to uphold the constitution and private wealth against the Radicals and their Dissenting allies. The Church could not befriend the Liberal Party, Cecil wrote in 1865, because, 'whatever may be the theoretic value of a democratic Christianity, the practical fact is, that whenever the Liberals triumph, the extreme Dissenters triumph also'.[45] Gladstone's recent career pointed the moral. The zeal for reform and for reduced tariffs which had brought him into combination with Bright had undermined his High Churchmanship and induced him to vote, against all his earlier opinions, for the abolition of Church rates. His migration to Liberalism had landed him in the embrace of the Dissenters. Liberal Anglicans who cared more for duty-free goods than the endowments of the Church might not recoil from the embrace. 'But there are other persons who think a good deal more of religious Establishments and religious teaching than they do of tariffs. And that any of these should still give their confidence to Mr Gladstone, and should be willing to quarrel with the Conservative party in order to uphold him, is one of the political puzzles of the day.'[46]

Church defence was thus a potential means of tempting moderate Whigs away from the Radical-tainted Liberal Party. It was so all the more because the Dissenters' quarrel with the Establishment was at heart not religious, but economic. The 'impulse of covetousness' inspired the Dissenter, although it was 'mingled with and sometimes masked by hostile religious zeal'.[47] The campaign to abolish compulsory Church rates was, in Cecil's view, part of a general strategy to rob the rich. The Dissenters maintained that their object was merely to relieve non-Anglicans of the burden of contributing to a local tax for the upkeep of a Church in which they did not worship. Even that argument, since the rate was voted by the vestry, comprising the whole of the parish, not just Anglican communicants, was shallow, and the proposed remedy, voluntary exemption from payment, was at odds with the fundamental justification of all taxation. As well might a rich man claim exemption from the poor-rate, or a pacifist from the proportion of his taxes which was appropriated to military spending, as a Dissenter from the Church rate:

> The whole theory of a common fund is at an end if each individual who contributes to that fund is entitled to a veto on its application. And the veto is not one whit the less noxious because the objection which it expresses is a very strong one, even to the extent of being founded on religious feeling. But what is vaguely termed a 'conscientious objection' – as if all objections on secular grounds were unconscientious – is scarcely urged at the present day. It belongs to an earlier phase of the dispute.[48]

Voluntary exemption, though Dissenters still appealed to it, no longer satisfied the cupidity of the Liberationists. Behind the attack on Church rates lay the broader design on tithes and the very Establishment of the Church. Those Dissenters who restricted themselves to the narrow issue were Girondins paving the way for the Jacobins:

> The Church of England is too massive a fortress, her bulwarks are grounded too deeply in the affections of the nation, to be carried off by storm at a single blow. Nor are the affections of the people in this case her only defence. The particular measures, advocated by her antagonists for the purpose of destroying her, outrage a set of feelings more sensitive and more widely spread than any ecclesiastical allegiance. Projects of spoliation alarm other classes besides the friends of the Church; for landed proprietors have an instinctive aversion to see landed property violently transferred. Proposals for annihilating one of the estates of the realm have an interest which is something more than ecclesiastical.[49]

Whether Cecil was right to apply a kind of 'domino theory' to religious issues is open to question. From hindsight it appears that the successive yielding to the Dissenters' demands, including the refusal to extend the Establishment to the colonies, the abolition of the compulsory Church rate in 1868 and the admission of Dissenters to the ancient universities in 1871, rendered disendowment and disestablishment more, not less, remote. For the rest of the century interest in ecclesiastical questions steadily waned.[50]

Cecil was on better ground in treating the Church-rate issue as merely one of the signs of the gathering assault on property. His remedy for ending the Liberation Society's agitation breathed a youthful Tory confidence. That agitation, conducted through the vestry meetings, disturbed the peace of the country and, more important, set the law at nought by making it virtually impossible for parishes to collect a rate which Parliament made it their duty to collect. Since, in Cecil's view, giving in to the agitation by relinquishing the rate would simply encourage the Dissenters to press more diligently towards their more fundamental objects, the solution was to reform the constitution of the vestry. As matters stood, every occupier in the parish was entitled to vote in the vestry, regardless of whether he was rich enough to pay the rate, a state of affairs which Cecil declared to be 'anomalous and indefensible'.[51] Rid the occupiers of their power by confining the vestry to the owners of property (the majority of whom were Anglicans and, when they were not, anti-Radical) and the agitation would disappear because it would have no field of operation.

So Cecil turned on its head James Otis' famous principle, 'no taxation without representation'. 'No representation without taxation' became the watchword with which he sought to rally the owners of property, the repository of the conservative sentiments which he believed the majority of the electorate to hold, to the defence of the existing electoral system. He would restrict the franchise to those men rich enough to pay the income and property tax. Each man, Cecil argued, possessed two fundamental rights: the one to do what he wished with his own body (so long as his exercise of the right did not trespass on another man's identical right) and the other to do what he wished with his own property (subject to the same qualification). Since every man's share of the first right was equal, each man might claim an equal share in government. The snag was that property was not equally apportioned among the population, and, since the chief end of government was the protection of property – 'with the protection of life and limb Parliament has not now very much to do' – parliamentary representation should reflect the inequality of property ownership.[52] There had been in the history of the world only one experiment of 'a democratic legislature, sovereign, uncontrolled, in the midst of an aristocratic society',[53] and it was the constituent assembly which met in Paris in 1789. Its wild pranks were not likely to be imitated in England, but its purpose, to transfer property to the have-nots, was the purpose of the English Radicals. Wherever democracy prevailed, the state power was used 'to plunder the well-to-do classes for the benefit of the poor'.[54] Hence Bright's repeated declaration that a Reform Bill would be useless unless it produced a change in the fiscal system. 'The first consequences, in his mind, of a measure that shall confer all political power on the poor, is the transfer of all taxation to the shoulders of the rich.'[55] The method was already being tried most flagrantly in Gladstone's budget of 1860. It was to replace indirect taxation by direct taxation. That was the form that 'democratic confiscation' took in England. Gladstone intended to substitute for the remission of the paper duty an extra penny on the income tax. The precedent was fraught with danger. 'Once admitted that a direct tax may be laid on for the purpose of taking off an indirect tax . . . and there is no reason that the process should not be repeated *ad infinitum*. Inasmuch as all classes alike pay indirect taxation, while only those who do not receive weekly wages pay the income-tax, this change is a direct and simple transfer of taxes from one class of the community to another.'[56]

Cecil's argument was consistent with orthodox nineteenth-century apologies for the income tax. The tax was defended as a necessary evil (originally introduced as a wartime expedient and intended to be temporary) whose purpose was solely to raise revenue. It was not an instrument for redistributing wealth. Neither Pitt, who first levied the tax, nor Peel, who revived it, had ever so conceived its function, and Gladstone, in invoking their names to support his massive reductions of indirect taxation in the 1860 budget, was maligning their financial stewardship. Peel's free-trade budgets of the 1840s, by abolishing or greatly reducing import duties on essential raw materials, had been intended to stimulate industry by lowering costs and increasing consumption at home and abroad. Gladstone, as the list of items from which the tariff was to be removed by his measures – wine, silk, gloves, watches, plate –

showed, had no such purpose. True, the taxes on those items were paid by the rich, but that merely disclosed a sinister motive, or at least a sinister consequence, of Liberal finance. 'That the tariff might be simplified, all the duties upon the luxuries of the rich have been repealed, and all the duties upon the luxuries of the poor have been retained. If there had been a wilful desire to make the most popular form of tax unpopular, it could not have been attempted with a better will.'[57]

Cecil wished to spread taxation as widely as possible over the whole of the population. But if property were to supply the membership of the House of Commons, was it not equitable that it should supply also the revenue of the government? The principle that taxation follows upon representation was embedded deep in English constitutional history, in the demand of the mediaeval barons that the redress of grievances must precede the granting of supply to the Crown. 'This question of the incidence of taxation is in truth the vital question of modern politics', Cecil wrote in 1860. 'It is the field upon which the contending classes of this generation will do battle.'[58] It had always been so, as Cecil himself, despite his description of the preceding three centuries as the ecclesiastical epoch, did not gainsay:

> If all that business were to be withdrawn from Parliament which directly or indirectly affects the distribution of property, its occupation would be gone. If it were not for the complex interests which the existence of property creates, the machine of civilised government would be far too cumbrous for its work. If it were not for the guard which those who own property must keep over their possessions, representative assemblies would scarcely be needed, and assuredly no one would dispute over their composition.[59]

Yet it is beside the point to chide Cecil for his inconsistency in arguing that property should predominate in Parliament and indirect taxation provide the bulk of the Crown's revenue. His notions of property may, too, have ignored altogether the property that a man has in his labour and hence the contribution of labour to both capital and landed wealth. But his purpose was to defend a class with the best arguments he could muster. He was not concerned with distributive justice. He took inequality of wealth for granted and considered how it might be perpetuated. His answer was to halt the progress towards greater and greater direct taxation and, as one of the means to that end, to exclude from Parliament the class which he believed was interested in placing all the burden of supplying the revenue from that source. 'The maxim that representation should follow taxation', he wrote, 'is one that nobody, least of all a Liberal, will dispute.'[60] Nor did the Liberals. They simply pointed out that payers of indirect taxation were also entitled to representation.

Cecil was rowing against the tide of English constitutional development and Victorian progressive sentiment. By what means did he hope to make headway? One tack was to argue the *political* advantages of indirect taxation. In fact, Cecil wished to hoodwink the taxpayer. Since uneducated men could not easily be brought to understand the necessity of high taxation, taxation always contained an element of political danger 'which it ought to be a statesman's constant study to lessen by every means at his command'. Whether it might be more statesmanlike to instruct and enlighten the people was not a question Cecil asked. The ruler who could not relieve the people of the burden of paying taxes 'was bound to relieve them to the utmost of his power from the bitterness and irritation which they are too apt to bring in their train'.

> Wherever political confusion has been the result of burdensome taxation, it has always been either an indirect tax on the bare necessities of life, or more commonly a direct demand upon the taxpayer, which has been the provocation to discontent. . . . Herein lies the political value of our system of indirect taxation. It can never excite to resistance, for, levied as it is upon luxuries, it is never a compulsory or an inevitable tax. . . . Nobody who does not wish to pay an indirect tax, need pay it, and it may therefore be fairly called a voluntary tax. It is a tax constructed with a safety-valve.[61]

Cecil's lack of sympathy with, or understanding of, the lives of the working-class poor revealed itself in a secondary recommendation which he listed as one of the political advantages of indirect taxation:

> The thrifty and frugal members of the community are far the most dangerous men to irritate, because they possess the strength of character which will enable them to give effect to their irritation. But it is precisely this class whom indirect taxation spares. On the

other hand, it extracts a very considerable revenue from the thriftless and the self-indulgent. But these are a class whose grievances receive little sympathy and whose habits are a fatal obstacle to the pursuit of any schemes of political disturbance. The fact that in 1859 we levied twenty-two millions and a half from the drinkers of intoxicating liquors alone shows what indirect taxation, properly levelled at the self-indulgent portion of the community, can do.[62]

After that, who will be surprised that the brewers voted Tory? But if there was meanness in Cecil's attitude and an abiding cruelty (in order that the revenue should be supplied a portion of the community was to remain in everlasting thriftless, uneducated, self-injuring indulgence), there was also a robust common sense, for increases in direct taxation are generally unpopular, while increases in indirect taxation go comparatively unnoticed.

Cecil, then, appealed not only to conservatives' acquisitiveness, but also to their desire for political tranquillity. It would therefore help if he could show that democracy engendered instability. At the very moment of the 'Conservative reaction' in England, the example to buttress his case was delivered, as he believed, into his hands: America, the crucible of democracy and the envy of Bright and his followers, fell into civil war. Between July 1861 and January 1865 Cecil published three long articles on the war, the first entitled 'Democracy on its Trial' and the last, 'The United States as an Example'. To Cecil the war proved that democracy had failed and the failure was a warning to stiffen the anti-democratic resolve of Englishmen. Like large numbers of his countrymen, especially Conservatives, Cecil gave his support to the Southern cause in the war, not because he connived at the institution of slavery, but because the hierarchical, agrarian social economy of the South and its anti-bourgeois, anti-capitalist mentality appealed to him. The test of any government, Cecil said, was whether it could maintain public order.

> Government is a defensive and remedial institution; its function is to maintain order and avert internal conflict, and it only succeeds when it does so. . . . If there were no such things as storms, sea-walls would be unnecessary. If you want to know whether your sea-wall is well or ill-constructed, the best way is to watch how it behaves on the occasion of a great storm. A knotty point

like slavery is the very touchstone to try the metal of a Government.[63]

By failing to preserve public order, democracy in America, the purest experiment in democracy in the world, had demonstrated its inadequacy as a form of government. The argument was unconvincing: as well might Cecil have argued that the French Revolution *proved* the inadequacy of monarchy as an institution. And less convincing still was the change of tack to argue, in the same essay, that Europe should pay attention to the South's hostility to democracy, especially since the institutions of the South did not lead him to qualify his characterisation of America as a 'pure democracy'.

> The really remarkable fact which is to be inferred from the conduct of the Southern States is, the genuine alarm with which they regarded the workings of democracy. Strictly speaking, they were not Democracies themselves. . . . But they were no mean judges of the working of a Democracy. They had acted in partnership with one for seventy years. They had watched it ripening year by year to the full development of mob supremacy, and they had enjoyed the fullest opportunity of judging of the temper and moderation with which it was likely to improve a triumph, or wield unfettered power over a conquered rival. We have seen what was the judgment that they formed. They deliberately decided that civil war, with all its horrors, and with all its peculiar risks to themselves as slaveowners, was a lighter evil than to be surrendered to the justice or clemency of a victorious Democracy. It is not for Europe to dispute the accuracy of their judgment.[64]

The war, in other words, did not signify the collapse of public order within a democratic state: liberal, capitalist democracy was at war with a rival system, the autarchical, seigneurial world view of the slavocracy.

That being so, it was essential for Cecil's case that the North should be defeated, and, in common with most foreign observers at the outset, he expected, or publicly said that he expected, the South to win its independence. 'There can be but one issue to the contest – the Southern States must form an independent nation. The hatred between the two parties is too deadly for reconciliation, and their warlike power is too nearly balanced for permanent conquest.'[65] As late as the beginning of 1865 he was still, albeit less confidently, asserting the inevitability of Southern nationhood. That belief and hope coloured his view of the North's conduct, which he argued was of a kind that betrayed the incapacity of democracy to nurture progress or defend freedom, the two causes with which its advocates consistently and fallaciously associated it. The United States was born by an act of rebellion against imperial overlordship; yet it refused to the South the right to secede. How, then, had America progressed from the darkness of earlier ages? The answer was, not at all.

The North is fighting for no sentimental cause – for no victory of a 'higher civilization'. It is fighting for a very ancient and vulgar object of war – for that which Russia has secured in Poland – that which Austria clings to in Venetia – that which Napoleon sought in Spain. It is a struggle for empire, conducted with a recklessness of human life which may have been paralleled in practice, but has never been avowed with equal cynicism. If any shame is left in the Americans, the first revision they will make in their constitution will be to repudiate formally the now exploded doctrine laid down in the Declaration of Independence, that 'Governments derive their just powers from the consent of the governed'.[66]

And if the object of the war was no sign of the devotion to progress which attended democracy, nor were the methods by which the war was waged. The reduction of whole towns, the raising of famine by fire in the countryside, the merciless murdering of civilians, all of which found their most cruel execution in Sherman's march through Georgia, marked a reversion to 'the old ruthless desolation of barbaric hordes'. 'A civilised government might fear that their good name would be tarnished by such a campaign; a civilised people might shrink from a partnership with such foul atrocities.'[67]

American democracy had forfeited its claim to be progressive. It had also failed to give sanctuary to freedom. Lincoln's war was no different from the one waged by the Tsar against Poland, whose national rising had been drenched in blood. The Tsar was cursed throughout the civilised world as the enemy of freedom; Lincoln was extolled as its champion. The methods by which Lincoln waged his imperialist war – imprisonment without trial, arbitrary power of conscription, a system of passports, unlimited discretion to declare martial law – were justified by democrats on the worthless ground that the authority for them came from the ballot box. They expressed the will of the majority. 'If one man imprisons you,' Cecil commented, 'that is tyranny; if two men, or a number of men imprison you, that is freedom.'[68]

Ever since Tocqueville published his critique of American democracy in the mid 1830s, European Conservatives had cited the American style of public life as a caution against experimenting with democratic institutions. Cecil was happy to use the civil war as a stick to beat Gladstone and Bright. (Would he have been so ready to grant Ireland secession on demand?) And America provided him the opportunity to elaborate a cherished theme: that democracy drove the natural leaders of a community from the field. Modern elections, with their loathsome canvassing, their canting speeches from the hustings, their implications of the 'mandate', all those things, in short, which Cecil called 'the lower forms of political warfare' and which conflicted with 'all the refining influences which are brought into play by an age of civilisation', were diminishing the appetite of men of intellect and honest character for politics.[69] In America the extreme had been reached. Office there was sought, not as a public duty, not even as the means to fulfil ambition, but for the 'journey-money' and the contracts. Candidates there were in abundance, but not such as were imbued with 'the higher forms of mental culture' or inspired by 'the higher instincts of patriotism and honour'. The result was that 'the electors of an American constituency are far more in the hands of their wire-pullers than the electors of an English county are in the hands of its landowners'.[70] Nor were the baneful aspects of American institutions remediable. They were genetic in democracy.

> Political equality is not merely a folly – it is a chimera. It is idle to discuss whether it ought to exist; for, as a matter of fact, it never does. Whatever may be the written text of a Constitution, the multitude always will have leaders among them, and those leaders not selected by themselves. They may set up the pretence of political equality, if they will, and delude themselves with a belief of its existence. But the only consequence will be, that they will have bad leaders instead of good. Every community has natural leaders, to whom, if they are not misled by the insane passion for equality, they will instinctively defer. Always wealth, in some countries birth, in all intellectual power and culture, mark out the men to whom, in a healthy state of feeling, a community looks to undertake its government. They have the leisure for the

task, and can give to it the close attention and the preparatory study which it needs. Fortune enables them to do it for the most part gratuitously, so that the struggles of ambition are not defiled by the taint of sordid greed. They occupy a position of sufficient prominence among their neighbours to feel that their course is closely watched, and they belong to a class among whom a failure in honour is mercilessly dealt with. . . . They are the aristocracy of a country in the original and best sense of the word. Whether a few of them are decorated by honorary titles or enjoy hereditary privileges, is a matter of secondary moment. The important point is, that the rulers of the country should be taken from among them, and that with them should be the political preponderance to which they have every right that superior fitness can confer.[71]

Cecil exposed the shallowness of Lincoln's 'war to preserve the Union' and uncovered the imperialist motive which he bequeathed to his country. As a critique of democracy, notwithstanding the justified, if unoriginal, alarm at the tyranny of the majority, the American essays were less successful. He was on safer ground when he left theoretical considerations out of the account and simply attempted to rouse the propertied classes to the plundering designs of Gladstonian Liberalism. That his warnings would be heeded he trusted to the good sense of the Whig aristocracy, who had been sustained in office by the Radicals for many years, but who were rapidly becoming the tail, not the head, of their party.

For some time the combination between the magnates and the mob seemed to carry all before it. Even now, when the war in America has blown the whole fabric of Democratic theory into the air, that combination is vigorous enough to make head against the strong flow of Conservative feeling which the last five or six years have witnessed. But it has the essential weakness, which no numerical preponderance can heal, of uniting, in one force, directly antagonistic interests. The owner of half a county, and the heir of a long pedigree, can never desire the same distribution of political power, or the same adjustment of taxation, as the artisans of a manufacturing town. The tenacious organisation of party, and the zeal of those to whose ambition it ministers, may for a long time induce the wealthy duke and the populous borough to throw their vote into the same scale even after their interests have diverged; but the time must come when the hollowness of the

alliance will betray itself. There are many things which the great
Revolution families have been willing to surrender for the sake of
retaining political power; but there is one thing that they will not
surrender, – and that is political power itself.[72]

To be successful, democratic agitation required one of two
circumstances: a centralised state vulnerable to a *coup de main* or the
co-operation of a large section of the class of property-owners. A
territorial aristocracy and the institutions of local authority, formal
and informal, protected England from the one; and therefore the
constitution was secure from revolutionary overthrow unless the
owners of property helped to undermine it. 'The danger of the
Constitution is not the discontent of those who have not the
franchise, or of their allies within its pale, but the apathy of the mass
who have it.'[73] The rabble-rousing of Bright and Co. actually did
good by reminding the governing classes of the need to be vigilant.
The Radicals discharged to the English upper and middle classes the
useful office which the flappers performed to the sages of Laputa,
and so long as they kept up their menacing speeches the
constitution was in no serious danger.[74]

In the spring of 1866 Cecil's essays bore the aspect of true
prophecy. The revolt of Robert Lowe and the Adullamites against
the Liberal Government's moderate reform bill appeared to
pressage that alliance between right-wing Whigs and Conservatives
which Cecil had called for as the necessary method of giving the
'Conservative reaction' in the country a parliamentary expression. It
was undone by Derby and Disraeli and all their followers who
pocketed their principles in order to dish the Whigs. Cecil resigned
his office in the Cabinet as Secretary of State for India in order to
fight against the Conservative Reform Bill of 1867. He failed; and the
'Conservative reaction' was swallowed up in household suffrage.
Perhaps Cecil had all along doubted any other outcome to the party
struggle. Perhaps the chirpy confidence of his journalism masked
his real understanding of the irresistible current of mid-Victorian
politics. 'I have for so many years entered a firm conviction that we
were going to the dogs', he wrote to Sir Henry Acland in February
1867, a week before Disraeli introduced the Government's reform
resolutions, 'that I have got to be quite accustomed to the
expectation.'[75] Defeat angered him and he rounded on his party's
leaders with a ferociousness that had not been seen in English
politics since Disraeli's excoriation of Peel in 1845 and 1846. But Cecil

loved the game of politics too deeply to die in a last ditch. Defeat wrung from him one of the finest statements of Conservative principle enunciated by an English politician. In the very essay in which he accused Disraeli of exhibiting recklessness, venality and cynicism on a scale unmatched since the days when Sunderland accepted favours from James II while negotiating the invasion of William of Orange, he reminded his readers of the proper behaviour of Conservative citizens in a parliamentary constitution. 'It is the duty of every Englishman, and of every English party, to accept a political defeat cordially, and to lend their best endeavours to secure the success, or to neutralise the evil, of the principles to which they have been forced to succumb.'[76]

NOTES

References to the papers of the third Marquis of Salisbury (earlier Lord Robert Cecil; Viscount Cranborne) in the Hatfield House Archive are prefixed 'HHM/3M' (Hatfield House Muniments, third Marquis).

1. 'The Church in her Relations to Political Parties', *Quarterly Review*, July 1865, p. 215. The essays which Cecil wrote for the periodical press are listed in full in Pinto-Duschinsky, *The Political Thought of Lord Salisbury, 1854–1868* (London, 1967) pp. 157–88.
2. Cecil to his father, 25 July 1859, in Lady Gwendolen Cecil, *Life of Robert Third Marquis of Salisbury*, i (London, 1921), 85–7.
3. 'The United States as an Example', *Quarterly Review*, Jan 1865, p. 266.
4. 'The Conservative Reaction', *Quarterly Review*, July 1860, pp. 280, 277.
5. 'Lord Salisbury and the Quarterly Review', *Quarterly Review*, Jan 1904, p. 298.
6. Knowsley Hall, Derby Papers, 158/10, Jolliffe to Derby, 3 Jan 1854.
7. 'Parliamentary Reform', *Quarterly Review*, 1865, p. 543.
8. HHM/3M/D/31/19, Cranborne to Carnarvon, 6 Mar 1868 (transcript).
9. 'The Past and Future of Conservative Policy', *Quarterly Review*, Oct 1869, pp. 545–6.
10. Ibid., p. 542.
11. 'The Faction-Fights', *Bentley's Quarterly Review*, July 1859, p. 348.
12. Ibid., p. 358.
13. 'English Politics and Parties', *Bentley's Quarterly Review*, Mar 1859, p. 13.
14. R. Taylor, *Lord Salisbury* (London, 1975) p. 15.
15. 'English Politics and Parties', *Bentley's Quarterly Review*, Mar 1859, pp. 1–5.
16. 'The Faction-Fights', *Bentley's Quarterly Review*, July 1859, p. 359.
17. Ibid., p. 360.
18. 'The Past and Future of Conservative Policy', *Quarterly Review*, Oct 1869, p. 542.

19. Cecil to Exeter, 24 July 1860, in Lady Gwendolen Cecil, *Life*, I, 95–6.
20. 'The Conservative Reaction', *Quarterly Review*, July 1860, pp. 290–2.
21. Somerset Record Office, Hylton Papers, DD/HY/Box 18/2, Derby to Jolliffe, 4 Mar 1857.
22. Stanley Diary, 19 Feb 1864 in *Disraeli, Derby and the Conservative Party: Journals and Memoirs of Edward Henry, Lord Stanley, 1849–1869*, ed. J. Vincent (Hassocks, Sussex, 1978), p. 208.
23. HHM/3M/E/Bentinck/1, Bentinck to Cranborne, 23 Dec 1866.
24. HHM/3M, Cecil to Exeter, 9 May 1858 (transcript).
25. Stanley Diary, 27 Nov 1861 in *Disraeli, Derby and the Conservative Party*, ed. Vincent, p. 179.
26. 'The Conservative Reaction', *Quarterly Review*, July 1860, p. 296.
27. 'The Theories of Parliamentary Reform', *Oxford Essays*, 1858, p. 52.
28. 'The Faction-Fights', *Bentley's Quarterly Review*, 7 July 1859, p. 344.
29. 'Parliamentary Reform', *Quarterly Review*, Apr 1865, p. 555.
30. HHM/3M/C/282–3, Salisbury to Canon Conybeare, 19 Sep 1881.
31. 'English Politics and Parties', *Bentley's Quarterly Review*, Mar 1859, p. 12.
32. Ibid., pp. 10, 6.
33. 'The Coming Session', *Quarterly Review*, Jan 1866, p. 260.
34. 'English Politics and Parties', *Bentley's Quarterly Review*, Mar 1859, p. 28.
35. 'The Budget and the Reform Bill', *Quarterly Review*, Apr 1860, p. 523.
36. 'The Past and Future of Conservative Policy', *Quarterly Review*, Oct 1869, pp. 539–40.
37. Ibid., p. 540.
38. Ibid.
39. Stanley Diary, 28 July 1863, in *Disraeli, Derby and the Conservative Party*, ed. Vincent, p. 200.
40. 'The Church in her Relations to Political parties', *Quarterly Review*, July 1865, pp. 207–8.
41. HHM/3M, Cecil to Mrs G. Renaud, Nov 1851 (transcript).
42. Ibid.
43. HHM/3M/D/7–4/182, Cecil to his mother [15 Aug 1853] (transcript).
44. Disraeli to Malmesbury, 22 Feb 1861 in Earl of Malmesbury, *Memoirs of an Ex-Minister* (London, 1884) II, 247.
45. 'The Church in her Relations to Political Parties', *Quarterly Review*, July 1865, p. 212.
46. Ibid., p. 215.
47. Ibid., p. 196.
48. 'The Conservative Reaction', *Quarterly Review*, July 1860, pp. 268–9.
49. 'The Bicentenary', *Quarterly Review*, July 1862, p. 255.
50. See D. M. Thompson, 'The Liberation Society, 1844–1868', in P. Hollis (ed.), *Pressure from Without in Early Victorian England* (London, 1974), p. 232.
51. 'Church Rates', *Quarterly Review*, Oct 1861, p. 563.
52. 'The House of Commons', *Quarterly Review*, July 1864, pp. 263–6.
53. Ibid., p. 258.
54. 'The Budget and the Reform Bill', *Quarterly Review*, Apr 1860, p. 524.
55. Ibid.
56. Ibid., p. 523.

57. 'The Income-Tax and its Rivals', *Quarterly Review*, Jan 1861, p. 230.
58. 'The Budget and the Reform Bill', *Quarterly Review*, Apr 1860, p. 523.
59. 'The House of Commons', *Quarterly Review*, July 1864, p. 266.
60. 'Church Rates', *Quarterly Review*, Oct 1861, p. 563.
61. 'The Income-Tax and its Rivals', *Quarterly Review*, Jan 1861, pp. 223–4.
62. Ibid., pp. 224–5.
63. 'Democracy on its Trial', *Quarterly Review*, July 1861, pp. 260–1.
64. Ibid., pp. 274–5.
65. 'The Confederate Struggle and Recognition', *Quarterly Review*, Oct 1862, p. 563.
66. 'The United States as an Example', *Quarterly Review*, Jan 1865, pp. 252–3.
67. Ibid., pp. 271, 274.
68. Ibid., p. 285.
69. 'The Church in her Relations to Political Parties', *Quarterly Review*, July 1865, p. 194.
70. 'The Confederate Struggle and Recognition', *Quarterly Review*, Oct 1862, p. 548.
71. Ibid., p. 547.
72. 'Parliamentary Reform', *Quarterly Review*, Apr 1865, pp. 542–3.
73. Ibid., p. 563.
74. Ibid., p. 564.
75. HHM/3M/D/1/2, Cranborne to Acland, 4 Feb 1867.
76. 'The Conservative Surrender', *Quarterly Review*, Oct 1867, pp. 534–5.

6
Salisbury at the India Office

E. D. STEELE

I

Lady Gwendolen Cecil described her father's time in the post of Secretary of State for India as 'scarcely . . . remunerative biographically'.[1] Her verdict has stood since it was pronounced, and can only be queried in a short essay. Salisbury's private letter-books while he was at the India Office in 1866–7 and 1874–8, on which she drew, are so bulky that a biographer preoccupied with the Prime Minister and Foreign Secretary could not have given their contents a quite disproportionate share of her attention. These volumes contain his regular letters to three viceroys and successive governors of Bombay and Madras, together with those to Sir Richard Temple[2] while he was still Lieutenant-Governor of Bengal, and to a few occasional correspondents. They do not contain his letters to politicians, officials and members of the Council of India in London. It was his habit to transact an unusual amount of business, for such an active minister, by word of mouth. If the detail is incomplete without reference to other sources, the substance of his policy is there and in the replies from India preserved among his papers. His ideas were only partly formed when he first became Secretary of State; but his intellectual confidence was undiminished in the course of the eight months to his resignation from Lord Derby's government on a question which had no direct connection with India. By the beginning of his second term, under Disraeli, he knew the limits of change in India, and made some adjustments to his broad objectives.

Accused of wishing to administer the sub-continent from home, he reasserted the final responsibility of the British Government, answerable to the House of Commons, for Indian affairs; and he did it so as not to leave a comfortable gap between constitutional theory and practice. The letter-books reveal how far he took his preference

116

for employing private correspondence to point viceroys and presidency governors in the direction he thought advisable on any of the significant matters raised from either side. Reminders of the Commons' supremacy carried the warning, spelt out now and again, that, subject to the will or whim of MPs, an overriding power of decision lay with the Cabinet and with him. As for his advisers at the India Office, he reorganised departmental procedures on his return in 1874 to enhance his independence of, and authority over, the Permanent Under-Secretary, while he relied rather more on the Council of India's political committee to inform his judgement. 'Salisbury', writes a historian of the department, 'undoubtedly wished to be a strong head of the . . . Office'.[3] His relations with the Council of India were not so smooth; unlike the bureaucracy under his hand, it existed to check and not only to serve him in the discharge of its mainly consultative functions. Its membership, eligible by distinction and Indian service, tended to regard Salisbury with an odd mixture of respect and apprehension: he, a Tory, was too radical for them. Although often Liberals in home politics, they were not, as a body, conditioned to undertake really fundamental reviews of their Indian experience and its lessons. 'Don't let yourself be guided by any one in the Office, for there is no one competent to guide you', he told his successor, Sir Stafford Northcote, in 1867, referring to officials and councillors alike.[4] He was more fortunate, more tolerant and better prepared during his second term, but essentially unchanged.

Salisbury was a compassionate, not a sentimental man; a difference that some minds find obscure. He did not deceive himself about the nature of the British presence in India; ultimately, it rested on force. Nor did he feel disposed to repeat his youthful criticism of Britain's imperial morality, which was characterised, he had said in 1855, by a 'process of aggression' and the 'repression of nationalities' in India and lesser conquests.[5] On the contrary, he thanked Disraeli, twenty years later, for his repudiation of 'the growing idea that England ought to pay tribute to India as a kind of apology for having conquered her'.[6] Salisbury's indulgence in such language arose from his impatience with those who would not abandon the pretence that liberalism – and, like other Tories, he was a liberal by the standards of Continental Europe – ought to direct imperial rule in India. His Indian policies did allow for very cautious liberalisation, and those on land and famine relief were ahead of their time; but his attitude to Indians did not differ from that of J. S.

Mill, who spent his working life rising through the East India House in the last forty years of Company rule. Mill's published belief in the unfitness of India's people for more than 'a limited and qualified freedom', and for that only if it went with 'much sterner powers of repression than elsewhere', dated from 1861, shortly after the Mutiny.[7] The memory of that upheaval was beginning to fade in Britain, but not in Salisbury's recollection. It strongly influenced his Indian foreign policy; he read the situation on the North-West frontier and the Russian threat in that quarter with the effect on internal security as his chief concern. His reputed partiality for the princely states of India masked a lively suspicion of the great princes as the centres of disaffection. These states had their uses; but the aspirations of their rulers were to be carefully watched and restrained. The whole problem of westernisation, in its economic and its political aspects, affected him similarly. He fought the battle of the cotton duties to affirm the primacy of Britain's interests when they conflicted with India's; and to avert the danger that protection of Indian against British industry would contribute to national self-assertion.

The duties he was resolved to abolish as tending to real protectionism had ardent champions in the Viceroy's Council under the Whig Lord Northbrook. This partisanship raised in an acute form the question of inter-governmental relations. Salisbury was always afraid of, and determined to curb, the growth of 'a sort of bastard Home Rule cry', started and encouraged by the British in India, administrators, businessmen and planters, but particularly by the first's senior ranks.[8] The economic case for doing away with the cotton duties, he told Northbrook, weighed less with him than did the thought of a future and grave agitation on the subject instigated by the white population. Few though they were in India, the innate desire of the British overseas and their racial superiority made them, he once stated, 'the only enemies who will ever seriously threaten England's power in India'.[9] If this conviction of Salisbury's is minimised or ignored, it distorts his entire policy. The peril was already manifest, it seemed to him, at the top of Anglo-Indian society, in the Viceroy's Council, members of which had succumbed to the 'illusion that it was a representative assembly defending popular rights against an alien despotism' – in London.[10] It followed that 'if England is to remain supreme she must . . . appeal to the coloured against the white as well as to the white against the coloured'.[11] The dilution of the Civil Service by natives, selected with an eye to loyalty rather than intellect, fitted into this strategy. He did not suppose that, in the event, the whites could retain control of many millions of Indians, but that they would probably inflict irreparable damage on Britain's will and ability to hold on to India.[12] He left Northbrook and Lord Lytton, the Tory who succeeded him, in no doubt that he expected them to dominate their advisers; and he would admit no conciliar claims faintly subversive of his authority derived from the House of Commons. For the House, while intermittent and unpredictable in giving its attention to India, was 'so peremptory a body',[13] conscious of what the latest expansion of the electorate had done for it. At the same time, Salisbury fully realised how the size, complexity and vulnerability of the Indian administration in almost every field protected it against too much interference from home, however desirable that might be.[14]

II

Salisbury looked beyond 'the . . . staple of Indian politics' that occupied a secretary of state – in Afghanistan, Burma and the more important princely states – to the peasant masses, 'depressed enough to be easily made desperate'.[15] Writing to Temple in 1875, who was alone among the regular correspondents in having spent his career in India, he was perturbed by the incidence of agrarian troubles involving land revenue assessments, the pressure of usury in the Deccan and Sind, European indigo planters in Bihar, and native landlords and tenants in Bengal. 'I confess I feel much more anxiety about these matters', he told Temple, 'than I do concerning . . . the vagaries of Cabul or . . . Ava, or the intrigues of Salar Jung, or . . . Dinkar Rao.'[16] Salisbury regarded the Punjab school of administrators, to which Sir Richard belonged, with aversion; he described one of its better-known figures as typical: 'half native in his principles, and wholly native in his slovenliness'.[17] Temple was not, however, a typical product, except in sympathising with the cultivator. Salisbury plied him with questions about the ryots' condition and prospects. During his second term at the India Office, he took up again an exhaustively discussed proposal and asked Northbrook to consider the implications of settling in perpetuity the amount of revenue exacted, directly or indirectly, from the ryot.[18] In 1866 he had viewed as unnecessary this suggested means of stimulating the expansion of the Indian economy, believing that 'in India every element of wealth is in a state of rapid growth'.[19] Little of his optimism survived into the 1870s. The Bengal famine of 1873–4, following that in Orissa seven years earlier, revealed the constant proximity of tragedy on a huge scale. Northbrook was a humane but unimaginative man, whose reaction was to liken India to pre-famine Ireland. Turning from such Whig conservatism to a man with a deserved reputation for activity and intelligence, though given to self-advertisement, Salisbury came out with an unsparing statement of the problem,' that a famine should find a population of ten millions destitute of all resource to meet it argues a grave social disease somewhere which is well worth your study'.[20]

In reply to this invitation, Temple could only convey the intractability of the problem and submit palliatives. He advocated strengthening tenant-right legislation; bringing wasteland into cultivation; and nervously criticised the indigo planters in the areas affected by famine for squeezing the ryot: 'I would not like to say this in public, nor in such a way as might annoy the large interests concerned.'[21] Salisbury posed two alternatives: a tenant-right that secured to the tenant the whole of any increase in the yield from his holding; or massive emigration. Without one or the other, he concluded, 'obviously the ryots cannot really flourish'.[22] This enlargement of the statutory tenant-right usual in British India was compatible with his continuing opposition to Irish demands for the three Fs: the legal rights enjoyed by landlords in Ireland prior to Gladstone's Act of 1870 did not exist under British administration in India, where absolute ownership of land was vested in government, as the successor of native rulers, and rarely alienated.[23] Temple would not commit himself to so sweeping a change at the expense of the native aristocracy and superior landholders; it was a political impossibility. If that direct route to it was blocked, greater productivity might be indirectly encouraged by an exodus to colonies with a pressing requirement for coolie labour. Salisbury's preference was for emigration, 'a quicker and more wholesome remedy', over an enlarged tenant-right. 'I look upon every emigrant as a prospective teacher of his fellow villagers', provided he was well treated 'and only so long'.[24] There was, however, no requirement for Indian immigration of the magnitude that Salisbury envisaged.

He had more success with his insistence on the gravity of peasant indebtedness: 'In the whole range of Indian politics there is no question on which greater issues hang', he told Sir Philip Wodehouse, the Governor of Bombay, in whose presidency the Deccan was the scene in 1875 of violent protests against the money-lenders, who were an integral part of native society.[25] The Secretary of State had previously raised with the Governor the feasibility of starting land banks to lend to the ryot at low rates of interest. He had the support of his predecessor, the Duke of Argyll, in proposing an experiment.[26] Wodehouse took six months to consider before demolishing the proposal. It was unworkable economically, so poor and irresponsible were the banks' potential clients, and politically unwise: 'Every possible lie would be disseminated by the native newspapers – and there would be a firm belief that you were attempting to get possession of all their lands.'[27] Salisbury 'reluctantly' dropped the idea of cheap credit to enhance productivity and deliver the cultivator from his bondage to the money-lender;[28] but the disturbances in the Deccan reinforced his conviction that some other solution must be found to a social evil calling for redress throughout India. The cultivators, he argued, must and could be protected only in one of two ways: either they should be treated as minors and incapable of contracting debts enforceable at law; or their creditors should be subject to a drastic statute of limitations, making debts irrecoverable after one year.[29] It had to be pointed out to Salisbury that the money-lender was indispensable in rural India, sustaining those who lived so close to the margin of existence even while he oppressed them.[30] Government could not replace the money-lender; but it was imperative to control him. Accepting him as 'an essential ingredient . . . in the country', Salisbury was at first apprehensive of widespread evictions, for which the Government would be popularly blamed: 'You cannot afford to allow large multitudes to be dispossessed . . . classes on whose contentment your empire depends.'[31] The Bombay Government's commission of inquiry into the disturbances, whose report reached home in May 1876, led him to emphasise suffering rather than revolt.

While the predominantly Hindu cultivators might be notable for their submissiveness, it was unsafe to leave them 'generation after generation in a condition of helplessness', he advised his friend Lytton after Northbrook had departed.[32] The North-West frontier and the Russians filled Lytton's thoughts: questions of 'less ultimate significance', Salisbury reminded him.[33] The ryot did not figure in the new Viceroy's ambitious schemes. Lytton based the defence of his procrastination on the money-lender's place in the countryside. Indian agriculturists, 'for good or ill', needed his help: 'Paralyze him, and you paralyze them.' Government intervention with his freedom promised to do far more harm than good, indeed to 'shake to its foundations the entire credit system of our empire'.[34] Salisbury hesitated to initiate official action from the India Office; but Lytton's attitude drove him to it. Not, though, before he had waited for over a year, knowing that the Viceroy, too, had the advantage of expert opinion. Salisbury did not underestimate the argument that, if indebtedness was a way of life, little could be expected of any efforts to change it. Nevertheless, he wished to try. In Temple there was now a governor of Bombay who would co-operate. Salisbury desired 'a strong equitable jurisdiction entitled to look behind acknowledgements of debt' and reduce both principal and interest, with the twin aims of keeping the occupier on his holding and out of virtual servitude to his creditor.[35] The idea of what Salisbury wanted was not original; but his letters to Temple show the way in which he brought Sir Richard, not the man to disappoint a secretary of state, to frame proposals, and to persevere with them: 'one way and another, your lordship may rely on my not letting the subject drop'.[36] The Governor was spurred on by being informed of Salisbury's intention to take up the question formally in London. In November 1877 he appointed a committee of the Council of India to hear evidence from witnesses familiar with the ryots in the Bombay presidency, and make recommendations.[37] Temple drafted his Bill before the committee had finished its work; and in his anxiety for legislation without further delay Salisbury sanctioned its introduction by telegraph, although not wholly satisfied with it. Without offering an explanation to Salisbury's successor at the India Office, Lord Cranbrook, Lytton and his Council chose instead to enact a law restricted to 'some minor points'. Cranbrook demanded, and got, 'a comprehensive measure', specifying that it should embody the method and the aims that Salisbury had put to Temple and which had been substantially reproduced in the latter's Bill.[38] The Deccan Agriculturists' Relief Act of 1879 helped to set a trend, and may be said to have owed much to Salisbury's vision and tenacity.[39]

In a long minute of April 1875 on the land revenue extracted from cultivators that was the mainstay of Indian finance, under the British as under those whom they had displaced, Salisbury aligned himself with 'the advocates of the ryot'. Humanity apart, it did not make economic sense to bleed the 'already feeble'. No sudden reform was possible: government could not afford it; higher returns as a result of the incentive provided by lower assessments would be very slow to materialise in Indian conditions. Nor could continuity of policy be guaranteed when secretaries of state came and went every two and a half years, on average, and the Anglo-Indian bureaucracy was generally unconvinced of the need for reform. All that Salisbury felt able to suggest was, he conceded, a 'mite': official opinion in India should be made aware that the authorities at home favoured leniency and regularity of assessment and frowned on abrupt revisions upwards to profit from rising agricultural prices. He distrusted, moreover, the enthusiasm of settlement officers for precision in their labours, for 'scientific refinements . . . which worry the ryot . . . and impose a costly machinery on the state'. It was his hope that in due course the bureaucratic mentality would accept 'our acts and language . . . as precedents'.[40] Salisbury's pessimism has been widely misunderstood in practically every context. He was not, as a rule, defeatist; but he did understand how little freedom of manoeuvre the politician might prudently assume. 'It is one of the most painful disenchantments of office', he observed to Lord Hobart, the idealistic Governor of Madras who died in 1875, 'to find how much of one's discretion has been mortgaged by one's predecessors'.[41]

The South Indian famine of 1876–8 intensified his desire to do something for the ryot. The proportions of the disaster in Madras moved him to urge agrarian reform on the Duke of Buckingham and Chandos, who succeeded Hobart: 'A population which does not accumulate can make very little fight against famine.'[42] Buckingham, a former cabinet colleague, leant heavily on his officials in that notoriously conservative presidency and returned singularly complacent answers to Salisbury's inquiries about debt and tenure. Hazarding the guess that the inhabitants of the United Kingdom were as prone to borrow from a variety of sources represented in India by the money-lender, he ignored the disparity between living standards and disposable incomes in the two countries. Later he admitted that many of the smaller occupiers holding land directly under government, as was usual in Madras, were really tenants of a money-lender. On the evidence presented to him, the ryot was no worse off than in previous generations; the extortion did not 'prejudice agriculture'. 'I doubt the actual impoverishment: I believe in a good deal of squeezing', he summed up.[43] The Duke was an honourable mediocrity surrounded by the abler men in his Council opposed to almost any departure from the most rigid administrative routine in India. Their combined ineptitude added considerably to the difficulties of famine relief.

III

Of the three famines with which Salisbury had to deal, the first made an ineradicable impression upon him. On the day he arrived at the India Office in 1866, Lord Ellenborough, the Tory who had both governed India and presided over the Board of Control, warned him to act on the approach of a terrible famine. The then Lord Cranborne trusted the Indian authorities to take the necessary steps: 'I did nothing for two months . . . and – it is said – a million people died.' If he had listened to Ellenborough, the mortality might have been less; the governments of Bengal and of India had taken no precautions 'I never could feel that I was free from all blame for the result.'[44] That Orissa famine permanently undermined his confidence in the Indian Civil Service. The enormity of its negligence was unforgettable, like his own sense of guilt. The civil servants' adherence in the circumstances to classical economics excited his scornful indignation. An unthinking belief in the efficacy of market forces played a grimly memorable part in Orissa; Salisbury referred bitterly to one administrator, subsequently promoted to high rank, whose 'sound education in political economy cost half a million lives'.[45] At the time he was first incredulous to learn how those immediately responsible behaved, who appeared to see the situation 'merely as a question of police'; then horrified to grasp the human cost of 'a very little neglect, or reluctance to believe in evil tidings', for doctrinal reasons and from administrative failure.[46] These comments were addressed to Sir John Lawrence, the only Indian civil servant to become viceroy, who as a national hero for his achievements in the Mutiny was immune from personal censure. Lawrence, the originator with his brother Henry and the epitome of the Punjab school, lost Salisbury's respect, with important consequences for other sectors of policy.[47] In the next great famine, of 1873–4, Salisbury adopted 'waste there must be if there is success' as his principle of relief, encountering some resistance from Northbrook but not Temple.[48] South India in 1876–8 caught him between 'the enthusiastic prodigality' of Madras, unable to respond flexibly, and the 'too pitiless political economy' of a new viceroy.[49] He suggested the recognition of famine as a contingency for which government in India should always be prepared, not only financially but administratively, 'so that when the emergency comes, the selected men, told off for their appointed tasks, ought to take up each his post . . . with as little doubt or confusion as sailors going into action'. The suggestion of what Lytton called 'a famine dictatorship' is an example of how Salisbury drew on the collective experience at his disposal in prompting the Government of India.[50]

Cranborne shared the current optimism about the pace of India's economic development in the 1860s.[51] He derived from the famine of 1866 a simplistic lesson: delaying the construction of railways and irrigation works meant 'the periodic loss of vast masses of human beings, and of all the productive power they represent'.[52] In 1874 that optimistic mood had given way to a sober realisation that the creation of wealth was not proceeding nearly fast enough to transform India. Salisbury was shocked at the tone of the Anglo-Indian press on the death toll in Bengal, which it depicted as a salutary cure for overpopulation. 'I have never seen in any other organs', he told Temple, '. . . anything so ghastly as the inhumanity which in one or two cases has been talked about the famine.'[53] The whole truth was even worse, according to Temple; behind the newspaper criticism of famine relief lay motives 'too sinister to find open expression'. The European community, business and official, resented the prospect of additional taxation to pay for relief measures; and the businessmen's hopes of extracting still higher profits from the stricken natives were being frustrated. Temple remarked wryly on the inconsistency between the self-admiring legend of British national character and the reality he discovered in so many of their countrymen in India.[54] His own performance during the crisis helped him to a baronetcy, an uncommon honour for an Indian civil servant. Salisbury warmly congratulated him on the quality of his organisation and personnel.[55] The effectiveness of timely, and more than adequate, relief in averting a catastrophe led to charges in Britain as well as India that the governments of Bengal and India had overreacted, this time. Northbrook thought it 'in the highest degree improbable' that another major regional famine would ever occur; there was no shortage of food in India, only a problem of distribution. The handling of 1873–4 should 'prove to the good folk at home that their Governments are to be trusted'.[56]

Within months of Northbrook's departure in 1876, severe and prolonged famine broke out in the South of the country, exposing the inability of British administration to keep the natives alive. 'I should like to hang and shoot a great many people in Southern India if it were allowable!' wrote Colonel O. T. Burne, Lytton's private secretary, in the course of a viceregal descent upon officialdom in the region.[57] Lytton did not hide, in private correspondence with the India Office, and with politicians of both parties at Westminster, his intolerance of 'humanitarian hysterics' about the fate of the starving ryot: if the British public wanted life saved, it ought to foot the bill for its 'cheap sentiment'. At the outset, in a letter to the Liberal MP Mountstuart Grant Duff, he welcomed the chance to establish the principle that the recurrence and scale of famine expenditure constituted too large a claim upon Indian finances for the Government to accept the responsibility of prevention of all starvation, the aim realised in 1873–4.[58] He had earmarked the revenues of India for other purposes. Salisbury knew that, on purely financial grounds, Lytton was right; but he still hoped to maintain the famine policy that had worked in Bengal, if it could be 'gently' divested of its 'philanthropy'.[59] The Duke of Buckingham and the Madras Government, however, administered relief with a comparative liberality which, Lytton claimed, would have bankrupted India but for his intervention. The Viceroy got the better of the argument with Madras about the presidency's relief operations by, he believed, acting before Salisbury had time to reach a contrary decision. 'The power of funk' reigned at the India Office, he asserted.[60] The dispute recalled Orissa. It was Lytton's contention that the teaching of political economy against state interference with private trade as a distortion of the market held good in India. 'In a longer or shorter time demand will attract supply but the longer time may be long enough to starve a population', Salisbury asked him not to forget. Such absolute dogmatism as Lytton professed was a mistake outside the sphere of religion, and he told him so.[61]

Salisbury's letters to the Viceroy and the Duke reflected his conflicting concerns. To the first he said, 'Public alms should be restricted to those who would die if they did not have them. Anything short of this we should not shrink from as inhuman.' Then, together with his Council, he was alarmed at the smallness of the food ration calculated on that basis.[62] Lytton yielded on details but prevailed on the main issue, exploiting the financial position: 'let the Duke and his Government alone, and how are we to deal with the danger to India?' he inquired.[63] Salisbury's Permanent Under-Secretary, Sir Louis Mallet, objected that the change of policy – giving up 'beyond certain limits' the endeavour to preserve life – should not have been left unannounced. The reply to this pertinent reminder was untypically evasive. Salisbury realised only too well the force of Mallet's remark: 'I doubt whether our public is prepared for this', and would have it that the policy had not changed; he blamed 'the physical conditions . . . so much against us', not lack of money, for the impossibility of adhering to it in full.[64] Those conditions, as Lytton described them in telling the Liberal elder statesman, Charles Villiers, how he had averted a 'social and financial catastrophe' by his firmness, were more favourable to relief than they had been in Bengal. A habitual cynic about others' motives, the Viceroy accused the Secretary of State of deferring to the clamour at home for 'cheap vicarious generosity'. Lytton did not really want the aid from the British Treasury which would have enabled him to spend more on famine relief and prevention.[65] He was rightly afraid of greater parliamentary and public interest in the running of the Indian Empire; it might lead to the diversion of more resources from his plans to tackle Afghanistan and Russia. The Government of India had consequently to provide against future visitations of famine if it was to stop Britain from interfering too much. 'Sensibility is a strong political force . . . now – just as honour used to be', was Salisbury's advice.[66] Indian budgets included from 1877–8 an element of famine insurance; while from the commission investigating these repeated calamities that reported in 1880 came a famine code such as Salisbury had adumbrated.[67]

IV

The best known feature of Salisbury's two periods as Secretary of State for India is his involvement with her foreign policy towards Afghanistan and Russia,[68] and the related question of reorganising the critical North-West frontier.[69] When every allowance had been made for the Government of India's special interests and expertise, its diplomacy was naturally subordinate to that of British ministers. Both Northbrook and Lytton sought to maintain their interpretation of policy in this field against Salisbury. Lytton was particularly outspoken, and tried to use India to dictate to the Cabinet. 'That the

Indian and therefore instructed view . . . is thwarted by the ignorant English view . . . is very far from being the aspect of affairs as we see it from here', Salisbury admonished an angry Viceroy.[70] The likely influence of Russian expansion in Central Asia on the Afghans was the cause of growing disagreement with Northbrook and, in his turn but for opposite reasons, with Lytton. In the tradition of Lawrence, the most influential of retired Anglo-Indians, Northbrook wanted to avoid renewing the attempt, so unsuccessful thirty years before, to set up an Afghan client state.[71] Lawrence and his school considered the Russian threat to Afghanistan and India to be grossly exaggerated, if not a bogey. Lytton was sent out with instructions from Disraeli and Salisbury to take a line which Northbrook had been loath to follow. 'We cannot conquer it; we cannot leave it alone. We can only spare to it our utmost vigilance',[72] was how Salisbury regarded Afghanistan in the mid 1870s. Repugnant for good historical reasons to a fiercely Moslem people, the permanent presence of a British envoy in the country seemed indispensable to him, and Anglo-Afghan relations hinged on this question. Lytton went much further than Salisbury, or Disraeli, intended. '. . . burning to distinguish himself in a great war', with Afghanistan or Russia, or both, the Viceroy was held in check until Cranbrook took over at the India Office. 'You are so strong, and I am so weak', Lytton confessed to Salisbury.[73]

In seeking to counter a possible Russian ascendancy over Afghanistan, Salisbury did not fear an invasion of India by the Tsar's armies from that quarter. The logistics, and Russia's financial weakness, precluded it. It was 'a chimera', he agreed with Northbrook. Two eventualities worried him. Russia, possessing 'all the Oriental aptitude for intrigue', might incite the Afghans to invade.[74] They were to be feared in conjunction with India's Moslems, in whom ever since the Mutiny the British had seen the greatest potential danger to their rule.[75] Moreover, Salisbury found the Government of India's posture towards Afghanistan undignified and subversive of its own security within and without. It acquiesced in the Afghans' obstinate refusal to admit a resident British envoy, and bought their goodwill with arms and money. '. . . if the Continental tale, "L'Angleterre donne en ventre" is believed in Asia . . . enemies will spring up on all sides', he said, arguing for a less compliant spirit on India's border, in dealing with Russia as well as Afghanistan, than Northbrook thought was wise.[76] In 1866–7 Cranborne (Salisbury) had been opposed to any such advance on the North-West frontier when the occupation of Quetta, giving control of the Baluchi tribes and turning the Afghan flank, was mentioned. 'I am not quite insane', he told the Foreign Secretary.[77] The approach of the Russians, and the obstinacy of the Afghans, altered his perspective. Lytton carried out what Northbrook resisted. 'The leading idea of our policy', Salisbury laid it down, 'is to keep the Beloch power with us if Cabul fails us.'[78] For him it was a precautionary move; he hoped the Viceroy would ensure that the occupation was not 'unnecessarily obtrusive', upsetting the Amir of Afghanistan, the Baluchi Khan of Kalat, in whose territory Quetta lay, the Lawrentians, Parliament and 'the world generally'.[79] The 'turbulent military' in India, avid for a war and its professional rewards, must not be permitted to set the frontier ablaze. Salisbury aspired to an 'increasing . . . diplomatic hold' on Afghanistan, and the ability to influence the succession of her rulers from Quetta. 'Armed action . . . actual or vicarious, we repudiate', he insisted, warning Lytton not to try setting the Turcomans on the Russians North of Afghanistan. The discussion of a resort to force in his letters to Lytton had been hypothetical, if not always dissuasive in tone.[80]

An ardent Turcophil, Lytton envisaged winning over the Afghans, at one point, by British support for an Islamic holy war against Russia to preserve the Ottoman Empire in its contemporary struggle for survival. Salisbury effectively killed this initiative, despite the Viceroy's best efforts: Indian Moslems 'might not distinguish with sufficient accuracy between the various species of *giaours*'.[81] He could restrain Lytton to the extent that he did in foreign policy because its main lines, unlike those of most other Indian policies, had been settled beforehand with the Viceroy-designate: 'as long as you do not step outside them, I should . . . embarrass you by interfering', Salisbury had occasion to tell him pleasantly soon after his arrival in India.[82] Lytton chafed furiously under a restraint which he declined to understand. In a specimen of his broadcast complaints, he alleged to Sir Garnet Wolseley, the general and currently a member of the Council of India, 'It is obvious that the pressure of Council, Parliament and press is stronger than the secretary of state's backbone.'[83] Salisbury was extraordinarily tolerant of the 'occasional bilious fit' with which he was familiar in an old friend and Hertfordshire neighbour.[84] 'I am close to the great democracy we all have to obey', said the defeated opponent of household suffrage to Lytton, who railed at the necessity.[85] As events confirmed after he had left the India Office, Salisbury judged the mood of Parliament and the public correctly from the indications that MPs and newspapers furnished. Even then his policy was not unnaturally confused with Lytton's deliberate indiscretions. For the minister was practically and personally obliged to shield the Viceroy from his many enemies. He failed to rescue Lytton's cherished scheme for taking the North-West frontier away from its Punjab administrators, imbued with Lawrence's ideas on the external menace, and putting it immediately under the Government of India. A substantial majority of Salisbury's Council rebelled; they did not trust Lytton, and could not prudently be overruled in the atmosphere the Viceroy had created. Salisbury assured members in vain that war was not in the offing if they approved the scheme. He was not sorry to let Lytton know, with underlying seriousness, of the councillors' 'incurable . . . suspicion . . . that you meditate annexing a continent or two to Her Majesty's Dominions whether she or her advisers like it or not'.[86]

V

The princely states comprised roughly two-fifths of the Indian Empire by area and a fifth of its population. Hyderabad, the biggest, and Mysore, the next most populous, constantly recur in Salisbury's correspondence. The first, under its Moslem dynasty and formidable minister, Sir Salar Jung, seemed 'a real danger'.[87] Cranborne, as he then was, opposed Hyderabad's recovery of the large territory of Berar, leased to the British before the Mutiny. Mysore had been administered by the British on behalf of its Hindu ruler since the 1830s, when disorder consequent upon misgovernment compelled them to intervene. Its eventual return to native rule was provisionally decided at cabinet level in 1867. The memorandum which Cranborne wrote for his colleagues on the subject examined the political value of Indian princes to the British. Their continued existence helped perpetuate the divisions that militated against Indian unity to overthrow 'the common enemy'. The Mutiny had strengthened this part of the case for their retention. They mostly showed little sympathy with the revolt. Cranborne attached more significance to his other points. Westernisation was being enforced through 'a gigantic engine of law on a purely European model', unsuited to the East by its rigidity and neglect of custom: but its operation did not extend to native states, including those in the position of Mysore, and ought not to do so until its impact was clearer. To Cranborne's mind, the peculiar advantage of retaining the rather less than semi-independent princes lay in the careers they offered to 'clever and pushing natives . . . energetic spirits . . . [who] will fret under our rule, as not merely an alien domination, but a personal injury to themselves'.[88] Speaking in the Commons, he emphasised this point: the good government of a native state 'raises . . . self respect . . . and forms an ideal'. The British official failings revealed by the Orissa famine, he said in the emotion of its immediate aftermath, were more terrible in their inhumanity than the misrule of princes and dewans. The latter had a positive role in the age 'of rapid transition' then apparent to Cranborne.[89] Nevertheless, he was not prepared, at that juncture, to restore the whole of Mysore to its maharajahs, nor, in practice, to withdraw British administrators from the undetermined area to be handed back. He drew a distinction between the major princes who were a latent threat, and the smaller ones who were not.[90] His attitude to both hardened in the interval between his periods of office.

Salisbury still believed in the princes' capability to harm the British, but he thought it was steadily declining, along with the potential for good that he had seen.[91] The deposition and replacement of the Gaekwar of Baroda, an important state, in 1875 after a complicated series of events, satisfied him that the British might remove a leading ruler with impunity. They were, he concluded, 'unfettered by . . . obligations or customary pledges' such as princes had relied on since Lord Canning set himself to gain their enduring confidence in the light of the Mutiny.[92] Northbrook treated the princes and their rights with more respect; he looked favourably on Hyderabad's claim to Berar. Salisbury dismissed the Viceroy's 'Chancery principles' in the matter, and argued in a radical fashion that alarmed him. The case for not returning Berar, like that for Britain's dominion in the sub-continent, should rest on the inhabitants' welfare. 'Speaking generally', wrote Salisbury, 'I am anxious to push forward the argument from the interests of the people more than . . . hitherto. . . . I consider it to be our true rôle and measure of action: and our observance of it the one justification for our presence.' He did not suppose that the British were really popular in the disputed territory, or anywhere else; no doubt Sir Salar Jung could win a plebiscite. The population's wishes, he assured Northbrook, were not to be confused with what was best for them.[93] Northbrook quoted Charles James Fox on the pervasive influence of British constitutionalism in India, even on 'the most absolute despotism'. At the same time the use of the phrase 'the interests of the people' disturbed him: it enunciated a dangerous principle in relation to the princely states, bound to call their legitimacy in question.[94] Salisbury accordingly consented to take the offending words out of his draft despatch on Berar.[95] It was all that he conceded.

Lytton's romantic enthusiasm for the princes, and for the native aristocracy in directly ruled territory, inspired his faulty political reasoning. Austria had lost her Italian provinces through a mistaken solicitude for the peasantry at the expense of a 'snubbed and repressed' nobility. Ireland's endemic unrest would be far more troublesome headed by 'a really powerful *national* aristocracy'. Supported by this questionable comparative analysis, he perceived in the Indian princes and nobles 'the most important problem now before us'. The ryots were 'an inert mass'.[96] Salisbury let the Viceroy have his way with the spectacular ceremonial of the Delhi Durbar in 1877; although he had misgivings lest it should attract the same dislike and ridicule at home as Disraeli's imperial gesture in styling Queen Victoria Empress of India. He was glad when Lytton's pageant was over: 'I . . . incautiously gave him too much encouragement', he reflected.[97] On the substance, as distinct from the show, of this policy of Lytton's, Salisbury was less encouraging from the start: 'it is worth trying', he said.[98] He opined to Disraeli that the policy, if carried through, would, at most, 'serve to hide to the eyes of our own people and perhaps of the growing literary class in India, the nakedness of the sword on which we . . . rely'.[99] A minute that he circulated to his Council, purporting to be in aid of Lytton, termed the princes 'glorified Lieutenant-Governors', reduced to that state by the tightening grip of the Government of India and its agents.[100]

His strongest objection to the Viceroy's main proposal, the erection of an Indian privy council for 'the biggest natives',[101] was the effect it could have on the European unofficial community. Although the privy council was only to be consultative, the whites might seek not equal but preferential treatment: elected representation on the Viceroy's Legislative Council.[102] Lytton trusted to the inveterate antagonism between the British in government service and the others, whom he called 'the residuum

. . . all of the most second-rate kind'. The latter did not compare with the whites of the American Confederacy, nor even with those in Jamaica recently divested of their colonial constitution.[103] What Lytton forgot, in his arrogance, was that the official and unofficial elements would make common cause, not for the first time, against a viceroy whose native policy offended them as a race.[104] Lytton's disparagement of the bureaucracy, 'a most unchoice one', raised up a host of envenomed foes.[105] Members of the Secretary of State's Council, who no longer needed to defer to viceroys, were nearly unanimous in condemning the idea of an Indian privy council, and everything it signified.[106] Lytton had ignored, to his cost, Salisbury's warning to remember the 'Puritan, middle-class mould' of Indian administrators.[107] In social origin they differed little from the businessmen and planters with whom they closed ranks. Salisbury was mindful of their related interests when discussing the restoration of Mysore to native government on conditions less restrictive than he had stipulated in 1867.[108]

As for Hyderabad and Berar, Sir Salar Jung's skilful lobbying of royalty and politicians in England made Salisbury think hard as he reaffirmed his opposition to the transfer: it was something on which he would be ready to resign. Not only was it 'no true kindness to hand back multitudes to the caprices of a native Court', but returning Berar would enhance the power of the princely state most to be feared and acutely embarrass the British all over India, 'for which of our titles is without a flaw!'[109]

VI

After he had been at the India Office in 1866–7 Cranborne declared that 'the impression produced on my mind . . . was that I was watching a vast country, as it were, in the act of creation'.[110] His letters to Sir John Lawrence during those few months are notable for sanguine expectations of economic change, which he was eager to promote through the major public works wholly or partly undertaken by government in India. Lawrence's financial caution, due largely to anxiety about the burden of taxation on the ryot, contrasted with the Secretary of State's outlook.[111] They were agreed on one urgent exception to economy – irrigation – but there was a perceptible difference between them on the benefits of railway construction. Cranborne endorsed uncritically the conventional

wisdom that railways held the key to India's economic development
at the speed he believed possible. He greeted as 'infallible proof of
the . . . rule' Lawrence's account of increased wages wherever the
railway penetrated.[112] Yet even before this short tenure of his post
ended, Cranborne was coming to understand that his hopes were
pitched too high. Farming much more for subsistence than for
profit, the ryots could not generate dramatic expansion simply
because the railway had reached them. A line to a thickly populated
and intensively cultivated part of Eastern India was 'financially
indefensible', he admitted. Significantly, it was to have opened
Orissa.[113] During his second period at the Office, Salisbury paid less
attention to economic development as such and more to eroding the
massive conservatism of Indian rural society. He thoroughly
approved of Temple's interest, as Lieutenant-Governor of Bengal, in
trying to foster elementary education: 'Nothing will be done either
for Christianity or for material progress unless the path can be made
a little wider for the advance of new ideas into the Hindoo brain.'[114]
Salisbury was never optimistic of converting India. Literacy, like
mobility stimulated by overseas emigration, was a prerequisite for
an economic awakening. It was also a visionary means, as he knew,
of counteracting a displeasing result of westernisation: the 'class of
newspaper contributors' writing in the vernacular or in English, and
turned out or influenced by the institutions of secondary and higher
education which the British had established.[115] Their unorganised
literary nationalism gave rise to concern; its fusion with popular, or
princely, discontent was an obvious, though exaggerated, risk. The
Government of India's Vernacular Press Act of 1877 had Salisbury's
wholehearted support: India was not ready for the freedom of the
press which he thought salutary at home. He did not, however,
overestimate the stirrings of Indian nationalism, except in so far as
they afforded an opportunity to Islamic reaction.[116] The cotton
duties question was of greater moment for the future and character
of westernisation.

Addressing the Commons in 1867, Cranborne observed that in
the last resort 'the welfare of the people of India' was decisive in his
policy: he took pleasure, it is clear, in teasing the Liberal opposition
with this parade of principle.[117] He acknowledged the frailty of
idealism, hoping that his country would not yield to the undeniably
powerful temptation to act 'rather for its own advantage than for its
own honour'.[118] After he had come to terms with the wide extension
of the franchise in the same year, his attitude changed. There was

conceivably no moral force in the suggestion that a rich Britain should make some economic sacrifice for a poor India. 'This . . . species of international communism' elicited from him the casuistical rejoinder that, if poverty were assessed in relative, and not absolute, terms, the lowest British working-class taxpayer was 'quite as poor as the poorest Indian taxpayer'.[119] The Lancashire cotton industry had never been reconciled to the levy of revenue duties on its exports to the sub-continent. Salisbury was not inclined to antagonise British and native millowners in India without good cause; he advised care to avoid disturbing their 'vested interests' when the introduction of factory legislation was contemplated.[120] Although the pressure on him in Britain could not easily have been withstood, he described it as 'far from a reinforcement' in his quarrel with the Indian Government. He did not want Manchester to rouse Bombay. His purpose in the 1870s was to secure complete free trade for Lancashire 'while there is time'.[121]

'They appear to imagine that England conquered India for their benefit', commented Salisbury of British business in India and its preference for a tax on Lancashire to any fiscal changes affecting itself.[122] He was not afraid of its vocal indignation at that stage of India's political evolution. He anticipated 'something more than [an] outcry' if free trade were not enforced and accepted before Indians absorbed, from this mainly European discontent among them, the idea that abolition of the cotton duties meant nothing more than exploitation for British domestic ends.[123] Northbrook and his Council took the view that India was being exploited by Manchester acting on the Government in London.[124] Their attitude only made Salisbury more determined to carry abolition. Concerned at 'the "Home Rule" tone' on this question in the Viceroy's Council, he asked Lytton, who was hesitating, to remember that 'England is much too democratically governed to forego her own interests for the alleged interests of India'.[125] Free trade had profited India, and would go on doing so, he had no doubt.[126] The Indian cotton industry proved him right by trebling the number of its mills in a decade and a half after it lost such protection as the duties gave. Lytton removed most of the duties in 1879, and a Liberal ministry and viceroy rounded off Salisbury's policy.[127] Not surprisingly, the Liberals' earlier attacks had lacked conviction.[128] To Salisbury as to so many others, free trade was an instrument of empire. This did not imply credulity about his countrymen's individual motives. He

reminded the Duke of Buckingham in Madras of 'a gloomy history
of City smoothness and official gullibility' in connection with the
financing of irrigation.[129] It seemed desirable to him that the
Government of India should exercise its option to purchase the East
Indian Railway linking Calcutta with the North; the Company was
'an *imperium in imperio* . . . wielding so vast a power'. The sometime
chairman of the Great Eastern in England did not expect the
directors of the East Indian Railway to do what was good for
India.[130] The natural superiority of private enterprise was 'one of
those dangerous platitudes', especially in the sub-continent.[131]

VII

The oversight of Indian policy by private correspondence between
secretary of state and viceroy was established practice, Salisbury
told Lytton when he replaced the aggrieved Northbrook.[132] He
differed from previous secretaries of state in his conception of what
that oversight involved. The failure of understanding with
Northbrook, of whom Salisbury said that he never learned anything
from his letters not to be found in the newspapers, added to his
distrust of Indian administrators who could so mislead a viceroy.[133]
Salisbury's correspondence with Lytton was not only intended to be
more fruitful than that with his predecessor: 'I do not see any other
way', he wrote, 'of avoiding conspiracies for thwarting our policy
among those . . . officially bound to assist you.'[134] Northbrook
could not be persuaded to embrace his doctrine that the transient
viceroy was alone deserving of the home government's full
confidence.[135] Salisbury was bent on reversing a process by which
the Viceroy's Council looked set to acquire 'something of
independent power'.[136] In this he succeeded, but not without
considerable friction which came into the open and was debated in
Parliament.[137] Salisbury imposed his view of the relationship
between the two governments because he saw himself, and was
seen, as the servant of the House of Commons, above all. One of his
first actions at the India Office in March 1874 was a despatch
instructing the Government of India to send legislative proposals
home for approval prior to their introduction into the Viceroy's
Council sitting with additional members, European and native, in a
law-making capacity. He announced this move to Northbrook as a
refinement of his statutory veto, presently 'very clumsy and

barbarous' and therefore difficult to employ.[138] The India Councils Bill of the same session created the post of public works member on Northbrook's Council against the wishes of viceroy and councillors. 'If they are offended with this . . . they have no skins left', remarked Salisbury.[139] The new post, whose holder would plan and regulate the heavy expenditure on railways and irrigation, was one that he had suggested to Lawrence in 1866; it met a demonstrable need.[140] The Indian Legislation Bill, which did not get through Parliament, for lack of time and because it was known that Northbrook's political friends were going to fight it, would have enabled the secretary of state to veto part of an Indian measure instead of having to sanction or disallow it in its entirety.[141] When Northbrook and his Council ignored the directive of March 1874 by passing in August 1875, without any reference to London, tariff legislation which preserved the cotton duties, Salisbury reacted strongly. The Viceroy's decision to resign followed in September, ostensibly on personal grounds.[142] After the cost of famine relief had forced a long delay, Lytton overruled a majority of his Council and acted on the duties. Thus Salisbury, by then at the Foreign Office, managed to defeat on this crucial issue the men whom he designated 'Anglo-Indian Butts' – an allusion to the founder and current leader of the Irish Home Rule party at Westminster.[143] However, Lytton himself clashed with Salisbury over foreign policy, and outdid Northbrook in his language defending the Government of India's claim to greater autonomy than it was being permitted.

Northbrook's closest adviser, and the moving spirit in his Council, was not an Indian civilian but the law member, Arthur Hobhouse. A Gladstonian Liberal, Hobhouse incited the Viceroy to see Salisbury's treatment of him and of India as arbitrary and unconstitutional. 'I take it to mean nothing else than that you have been worried and bullied out of office by Lord Salisbury', he wrote when Northbrook's resignation became generally known and invited speculation about the reasons.[144] He recalled his prediction that the steps Salisbury took in 1874 would lead to a collision between the British and Indian governments or reduce the latter to a 'nonentity'.[145] While Hobhouse's political animus was extreme, feeling certainly ran very high in the Viceroy's Council. The Government of India could not pretend, Northbrook conceded, that it had an absolute right to insist on consultation by the home authorities before they brought in legislation on their own initiative, as in the India Councils Act. In practice, it expected to be consulted, reasonably enough, about anything Indian, 'simply as a question of policy and of precedent'.[146] From this very early point, relations deteriorated. Northbrook, who liked to think 'huffiness' was not one of his failings, resented Salisbury's questioning of the way in which the deposition of the Gaekwar of Baroda had been managed: 'he ought to have known better than to interfere', complained the Viceroy to another Whig peer.[147] This was quite unjustifiable in the case of a major native ruler whose fate had exercised the Cabinet, interested the British press, and evoked signs of unrest in India requiring a sureness of touch on the part of government. Before Northbrook went, the Government of India counter-attacked. It sought practically to invert the aim of the legislative instructions of March 1874, which it had contravened in the budget that retained the cotton duties. In its exchanges with London on the Indian Legislation Bill, the Government represented that no bill on India should be brought into the British Parliament until it had been scrutinised, word for word, in India. Salisbury did not understand how someone of Northbrook's parliamentary experience could adopt such a position: 'Even if constitutionally tenable . . . it would be impossible'; steering a bill through Parliament needed 'incessant compromise', ruling out agreement with India to pass it 'in any assigned form'.[148] The truth was that Northbrook had not been consulted about the inclusion in the Bill of the secretary of state's power to veto Indian legislation in part, to which he, of course, objected.[149] He did not hide from politicians in Britain how 'very widely' he and Salisbury had come to disagree; how perilous he thought Salisbury's deliberate omission of 'customary and . . . indispensable' counsel with India was; and how 'highly improper' he considered the Secretary of State's public rebuke to the Government of India for exceeding the limits of its independent action on cotton duties.[150]

Lytton began with assurances that he intended to work with Salisbury and tame his Council.[151] It was not long before they were at odds; but friendship, political alliance and Lytton's inherent weakness saved an open rupture. A striking but volatile personality, the Tory Viceroy discovered that he could not hope to take advantage of Disraeli's predilection for him until there was a change at the India Office. 'Lord Salisbury is the strongest man in his cabinet', he told his zealous collaborator on the frontier, Captain Louis Cavagnari.[152] Salisbury calmly reproved him for raging against feebleness and division in the Cabinet that supposedly put

India in jeopardy; for refusing to grasp that 'to ask us to pursue a bold policy towards the military powers of Europe, when we have no conscription, is to ask us to make bricks without straw'; for a 'dangerous practice' in citing the Secretary of State from his private letters in an attack on the British Government's conduct of foreign affairs printed and circulated to individuals on both sides of politics; and for tendering advice to the Queen without going through the responsible minister.[153] Lytton remonstrated at his dependence 'in the most trivial details of . . . external policy' on the Cabinet, Parliament and public he despised and Salisbury served. His Council had been induced to share the Viceroy's enthusiasms in foreign policy; he forecast an intensification of its hostility to directives from home if the Government of India continued to be 'absolutely . . . controlled' and 'unable to lift a finger, speak a word, or move a man, without your . . . sanction'.[154] Stripped of the typical hyperbole, it was the same resentful protest as Northbrook had voiced.

Salisbury's judgement was more soundly based than either viceroy seems to have been willing to acknowledge. His most persistent critic on the Council of India, Sir Erskine Perry – christened 'Sir Irksome Verry' by the last secretary of state[155] – praised his 'great pains in administration' to Northbrook but added, 'he is rather a rusher' – by bureaucratic standards, that is.[156] Perry, whom Salisbury regarded as one of his ablest councillors, corresponded regularly with Northbrook and fought the trend, as he saw it, to make the viceroy 'a puppet'. He sketched, with grudging admiration, Salisbury's command of the Office and Council. If the 'useful conservative influence' of the Council was legitimately circumvented, secret matters kept from the full membership were routed through its political committee, to which Perry belonged and which Salisbury tended to dominate.[157] Salisbury made the councillors he valued work for him, while discouraging a revival of conciliar pretensions he rejected in 1867. Then he had gone over the heads of his Council in reaching a decision on Mysore. In a long letter to one of their number, he vigorously rebutted the claim, strongly put by Perry, that councillors should have been given the chance to vote on the question. He admitted to a breach of courtesy, but not of right, in neglecting to consult them. Only the monarch was entitled, he maintained, to come between a minister and the Commons. 'Personal responsibility', he said in the Commons, 'is the thing

requisite in the government of India'; that applied in London as well
as in the East. He set out in 1874 to disentangle the 'indistinct and
confused apportionment of responsibility and power' which he had
criticised seven years earlier.[158] By the time he moved to another
department in 1878, the secretary of state's position was better
defined and stronger, as, too, was the viceroy's under him. The
Council gave Salisbury some trouble towards the end, 'getting sore
at being left outside while all the real work is being done, and . . .
only called in to ratify', he reported. 'I may have to give way
occasionally in small matters.'[159] The councillor whose opinion he
rated most highly on political questions was, rather unexpectedly, a
representative figure of the Punjab school, Sir Robert Montgomery.
Salisbury's ability to secure the co-operation and esteem of such
'skilled Indians' on the Council, among whom he did not reckon his
usual allies Maine and Rawlinson, is impressive testimony to his
logic and flair.[160]

Salisbury had appointed eleven of the Council's fifteen members
by his last year; they were naturally more manageable than their
brethren in India.[161] The sorest point with the Civil Service there
was the inclination at home to suppose that British rule 'can be only
a temporary phenomenon . . . unless we . . . continue to make . . .
natives . . . the instruments'.[162] The service's impatience with
control from London did not predispose it to the admission of
Indians. The mood of British administrators, 'getting harder to
govern every year', made Salisbury reluctant to worsen it by
transferring to natives a sizeable minority of European posts. He felt
sure that the opening of such posts to Indians would lower the
standard of administration: but he resolved that 'the political
advantages of gradually effacing the line which separates them from
alien governors are . . . of great importance'.[163] The preferred
method of selection for natives was appointment without
competition, thus perpetuating the superiority of Europeans chosen
competitively and assured of monopolising the higher posts. Entry
by competition held in England remained possible for Indians.
Salisbury disliked the recruitment of well-educated natives: if their
very few successes by that avenue became more numerous, it should
be closed to them, 'which', he wrote, 'would be an indecent and
embarrassing necessity'. Lytton's reforms of 1879, as modified by
Cranbrook, reflected Salisbury's pragmatic thinking, although the
experiment was discontinued for want of candidates who were
both educationally inferior and administratively capable.[164]

Salisbury's pure theory of change was Burkean, like Gladstone's, only more so; as expounded in the minute on land revenue quoted above, it ran: 'I believe . . . all the enduring institutions which human societies have attained have been reached, not of the set design and forethought of some group of statesmen, but by that unbidden and unconscious convergence of many thoughts and wills in successive generations to which, as it obeys no single guiding hand, we may give the name of "drifting".'[165] His intellect and personality made 'drifting' a more positive activity than it sounded. He was incapable, like Gladstone again, of letting things go on exactly as before when the responsibility for ordering them better was, in a sense, his.

NOTES

I am grateful to the present Marquis of Salisbury and the India Office Library for allowing me to use the papers on which this essay is based. Robin Harcourt Williams at Hatfield gave me all the assistance I could have expected, and much more besides.

Papers of the third Marquis of Salisbury held at Hatfield House and classified HHM/3M (Hatfield House Muniments, third Marquis), are designated by the abbreviated prefix '3M'. Other abbreviations used are as follows: BL (British Library); IOL (India Office Library).

1. Lady Gwendolen Cecil, *Life of Robert Marquis of Salisbury*, 4 vols (London, 1921–32) II (1921), 65.
2. In the course of nearly two decades, Temple (1826–1902) administered the Central Provinces, Bengal and Bombay, with an interval of six years as finance member of the Viceroy's Council; on retirement, he entered British politics and sat as a Conservative MP between 1885 and 1895. He wrote extensively on India, his Indian service and Westminster as seen from the backbenches.
3. M. I. Moir, 'A Study of the History and Organization of the Political and Secret Departments of the East India Company, the Board of Control and the India Office, 1784–1919, with a Summary List of Records' (unpublished dissertation submitted in part requirement for the University of London Diploma in Archive Administration, 1966), pp. 159–63. I have consulted a copy available to readers in the IOL.
4. Iddesleigh papers, BL Add. MS 50019, Salisbury to Northcote, 22 Mar 1867.
5. 3 Hansard, CXXXVII, 1185–6 (26 Mar 1855).
6. 3M/D20, Salisbury to Disraeli, 16 July 1875.
7. J. S. Mill, *Considerations on Representative Government*, Everyman edn (London, 1954), p. 179.
8. 3M/C4, Salisbury to Lord Lytton, Viceroy of India, 1 Feb 1878.

9. 3M/C2, Salisbury to Lord Northbrook, Viceroy of India, 5 Nov 1875; 3M/C3, Salisbury to Lytton, 30 Aug 1876.

10. Ibid., Salisbury to Lytton, 31 Mar 1876.

11. Ibid., Salisbury to Lytton, 7 July 1876.

12. Ibid., Salisbury to Lytton, 13 July 1876.

13. 3M/C2, Salisbury to Northbrook, 10 Dec 1875.

14. Still the most useful account of the Indian Empire, in all its variety, during this period is Sir John Strachey's *India: Its Administration and Progress*, rev. edn (London, 1911). The author served for many years in the Viceroy's and Secretary of State's Council. Dharm Pal, *Administration of Sir John Lawrence in India (1864–1869)* (Simla, 1952); E. C. Moulton, *Lord Northbrook's Indian Administration, 1872–1876* (London, 1968); Lady Betty Balfour, *The History of Lord Lytton's Administration, 1876–1880* (London, 1899); and, above all, Sarvepalli Gopal, *British Policy in India, 1858–1905* (Cambridge, 1965) cover Salisbury's time at the India Office: the last three, and particularly Professor Gopal's book, depict Salisbury rather differently from this essay.

15. 3M/C2, Salisbury to Temple, 1 Sep 1875. M. H. Baden-Powell *The Land Systems of British India*, 3 vols (Oxford, 1892) remains authoritative in its complex field.

16. 3M/C2, Salisbury to Temple, 1 Sep 1875. Sir Dinkar Rao was a Hindu notable suspected of divided loyalties; for Sir Salar Jung see p. 130 above.

17. 3M/C2, Salisbury to Northbrook, 20 Sep 1875. Dislike of the Punjab school found vigorous expression in official India, as in John Beames, *Memoirs of a Bengal Civilian* (London, 1961).

18. 3M/C2, Salisbury to Northbrook, 2 Apr 1875.

19. IOL, Lawrence Papers, MSS Eur. F90/27, Salisbury to Sir John Lawrence, Viceroy of India, 3 Nov 1866.

20. 3M/E12, Northbrook to Salisbury, 30 Apr 1874; 3M/C2, Salisbury to Temple, 26 Feb 1875.

21. 3M/E171, Temple to Salisbury, 26 Mar and 16 Apr 1875.

22. 3M/C2, Salisbury to Temple, 19 Apr 1875.

23. Lady Gwendolen Cecil, *Life*, ii, 38–40; iii (1931) 42–3. For the situation in Ireland before and after the 1870 Act, see E. D. Steele *Irish Land and British Politics: Tenant-Right and Nationality, 1865–70* (Cambridge, 1974), ch. 1.

24. 3M/E171, Temple to Salisbury, 5 May and 13 June 1875; 3M/C2, Salisbury to Temple, 19 Apr and 20 Sep 1875; C. Kondapi, *Indians Overseas* (New Delhi, 1951) deals mainly with the experience of emigration.

25. 3M/C3, Salisbury to Wodehouse, 3 Feb 1876.

26. 3M/C2, Salisbury to Wodehouse, 9 Dec 1874.

27. 3M/E180, Wodehouse to Salisbury, 21 June 1875.

28. 3M/C2, Salisbury to Wodehouse, 29 July 1875.

29. Ibid.

30. 3M/E180, Wodehouse to Salisbury, 21 June 1875.

31. 3M/C3, Salisbury to Wodehouse, 18 Feb 1876.
32. Ibid., Salisbury to Lytton, 20 Mar 1877.
33. Ibid.
34. 3M/E116, Lytton to Salisbury, 12 Nov 1877.
35. 3M/C4, Salisbury to Temple, 20 July and 18 May 1877.
36. 3M/E171, Temple to Salisbury, 12 Nov 1877.
37. 3M/C4, Salisbury to Temple, 15 Oct 1877. The circumstances of the committee's appointment were recounted in an official despatch from the Secretary of State for India (Lord Cranbrook) to the Bombay Government, 26 Dec 1878, a copy of which is in the IOL, Sir Erskine Perry Papers, MSS Eur. D776.
38. 3M/E171, Temple to Salisbury, 18 Jan 1878; IOL, Sir Erskine Perry Papers, MSS Eur. D776, Secretary of State to the Bombay Government, 26 Dec 1878.
39. T. R. Metcalf, 'The British and the Moneylender in Nineteenth Century India', *Journal of Modern History* (1962), I. J. Catanach, *Rural Credit in Western India 1875–1930* (Berkeley and Los Angeles, 1970), ch. 1.
40. IOL, Council of India: Memoranda and Papers, C/138, Salisbury's minute on survey settlement in Madras, 20 Apr 1875.
41. 3M/C2, Salisbury to Hobart, 26 Feb 1875.
42. 3M/C4, Salisbury to Buckingham, 8 Feb 1878.
43. 3M/E80, Buckingham to Salisbury, 1 Dec 1877, 26 Jan and 9 Mar 1878.
44. 3M/C2, Salisbury to Northbrook, 29 Jan 1875; B. M. Bhatia, *Famines in India: A Study in Some Aspects of the Economic History of India, 1860–1965*, 2nd edn (London, 1967), is a standard work.
45. 3M/C4, Salisbury to Lytton, 11 Jan 1878.
46. IOL, Lawrence Papers, MSS Eur. F90/27, Cranborne to Lawrence, 16 Sep and 2 Oct 1866.
47. 3M/C2 Salisbury to Northbrook, 30 Apr 1875; 3M/C3, Salisbury to Northbrook, 10 Mar 1876.
48. 3M/C2, Salisbury to Temple, 3 July 1874; Moulton, *Lord Northbrook's Indian Administration*, pp. 101–3. Temple was charged with the supervision of famine relief several months before assuming the lieutenant-governorship.
49. 3M/C4, Salisbury to Lytton, 4 May 1877; Iddesleigh Papers, BL Add. MS 50019, Salisbury to Northcote, 26 Sep 1877.
50. 3M/C4, Salisbury to Sir John Strachey, finance member of the Viceroy's Council, 27 Aug 1877; 3M/E116, Lytton to Salisbury, 29 July 1877.
51. 'To keep peace, and to push on the public works – that is in brief the policy that we have to follow', 3 Hansard, CLXXXIV, 1091 (19 July 1866).
52. IOL, Lawrence Papers, MSS Eur. F90/27, Cranborne to Lawrence, 3 Nov 1866.
53. 3M/C2, Salisbury to Temple, 19 June 1874.
54. 3M/E171, Temple to Salisbury, 14 July and 2 Aug 1874.
55. 3M/C2, Salisbury to Temple, 2 Aug 1874.
56. IOL, Northbrook Papers, MSS Eur. C144/22, Northbrook to Sir Louis Mallet, Permanent Under-Secretary of State for India, 31 Aug 1874.

57. IOL, Lytton Papers, MSS. Eur. E218/48b, Burne to Mallet, 10 Sep 1877.
58. Ibid., E218/19, pt i, Lytton to Mallet, 11 Jan 1877; ibid., E218/18, Lytton to Grant Duff, 10 Dec 1876.
59. 3M/D45, Salisbury to Mallet, 11 Jan 1877.
60. IOL, Lytton Papers, MSS Eur. E218/19, pt iii, Lytton to Strachey, 24 Oct 1877 and to Charles Villiers MP, 22 Oct 1877.
61. 3M/C4, Salisbury to Lytton, 10 Aug and 13 Sep 1877.
62. 3M/C3, Salisbury to Lytton, 23 Feb 1877; 3M/C4, Salisbury to Lytton, 4 May 1877.
63. 3M/E116, Lytton to Salisbury, 29 July 1877.
64. 3M/E124, Mallet to Salisbury, 3 Sep 1877; 3M/D45, Salisbury to Mallet, 6 Sep 1877.
65. IOL, Lytton Papers, MSS Eur. E218/19, pt iii, Lytton to Villiers, 22 Oct 1877.
66. 3M/C3, Salisbury to Lytton, 16 Feb 1877.
67. Strachey, *India*, chs 14–15.
68. See D. Gillard, *The Struggle for Asia: A Study in British and Russian Imperialism, 1828–1914* (London, 1977); W. K. Fraser-Tytler, *A Study of Political Developments in Central and Southern Asia*, 3rd edn (London, 1967); and J. L. Duthie's two articles cited below, ch. 7, n. 2.
69. C. C. Davies, *The Problem of the North-West Frontier 1890–1908 with a Survey of Policy since 1844*, 2nd edn (London, 1975), esp. pp. 104–7.
70. 3M/C4, Salisbury to Lytton, 14 Aug 1877.
71. IOL, Northbrook Papers, MSS Eur. C144/23, Northbrook to Sir George Clerk, member of the Council of India, 11 Feb 1876: 'Why the Government are determined to meddle beats my comprehension.'
72. 3M/C2, Salisbury to Northbrook, 5 Mar 1875.
73. 3M/D72, Salisbury to the Earl of Derby, Foreign Secretary, 21 June 1877; 3M/E116, Lytton to Salisbury, 18 May 1876.
74. 3M/C2, Salisbury to Northbrook, 19 Feb 1875.
75. Ibid., Salisbury to Northbrook, 19 Nov 1875 (second letter of this date); 3M/C3, Salisbury to Buckingham, 24 Mar 1876.
76. 3M/C2, Salisbury to Northbrook, 6 Aug 1875.
77. 3M/D72, Cranborne to Lord Stanley (Derby), 7 Dec 1866.
78. 3M/C4, Salisbury to Lytton, 18 Oct 1877.
79. Ibid., Salisbury to Lytton, 18 and 26 Oct 1877.
80. Ibid., Salisbury to Lytton, 18 Oct and 14 Aug 1877; 3M/C3, Salisbury to Lytton, 22 Aug 1876.
81. 3M/C4, Salisbury to Lytton, 11 May 1877. A 'giaour' in Turkish was an infidel, and especially a Christian.
82. 3M/C3, Salisbury to Lytton, 7 July 1876.
83. Wolseley Papers, Leeds University microfilm 1670, reel 8, Lytton to Wolseley, 1 Sep 1877.
84. Hughenden Papers, B/XX/Ce, Salisbury to Disraeli, 13 Dec 1875. I have used a microfilm copy of the archive in the Cambridge University Library: reel 45, correspondence between Disraeli and Salisbury.
85. 3M/C4, Salisbury to Lytton, 2 Nov 1877.
86. Ibid., Salisbury to Lytton, 14 Aug, 9 and 16 Nov 1877.
87. 3M/C2, Salisbury to Northbrook, 29 May 1874. Sir W. Lee-Warner, *The*

Native States of India (London, 1910), esp. ch. 5, is standard for the princes prior to the Great War.

88. 3M/B5, Salisbury's memorandum on the Mysore question, n.d. but Jan 1867.
89. 3 Hansard, CLXXXV, 839–40 (22 Feb 1867); CLXXXVII, 1071–5 (24 May 1867).
90. 3M/B5, Salisbury's memorandum on the Mysore question [Jan 1867]; IOL, Lawrence Papers, MSS Eur. F90/27, Cranborne to Lawrence, 19 Nov 1866.
91. 3M/C2, Salisbury to Northbrook, 1 May 1874; 3M/C3, Salisbury to Northbrook, 30 Aug 1876.
92. Ibid., Salisbury to Northbrook, 30 July 1875.
93. Moulton, *Lord Northbrook's Indian Administration*, pp. 126–7, 3M/C2, Salisbury to Northbrook, 19 Nov 1875 (first letter of this date) and 25 Aug 1875.
94. 3M/E12, Northbrook to Salisbury, 30 Sep 1875.
95. 3M/C2, Salisbury to Northbrook, 19 Nov 1875 (first letter of this date).
96. 3M/E116, Lytton to Salisbury, 11 May 1876.
97. 3M/D45, Salisbury to Mallet, 11 Jan 1877.
98. 3M/C3, Salisbury to Lytton, 9 June 1876.
99. Hughenden Papers, B/XX/Ce (see above, n. 84), Salisbury to Disraeli, 7 June 1876.
100. IOL, Council of India: Memoranda and Papers, C/139, Salisbury's minute 2 Nov 1876 on secret letter from India no. 47.
101. 3M/E116, Lytton to Salisbury, 30 July 1876.
102. 3M/C3, Salisbury to Lytton, 30 Aug 1876.
103. 3M/E116, Lytton to Salisbury, 5 Aug 1876.
104. M. Maclagan, *Clemency Canning: Charles John 1st Earl Canning, Governor-General and Viceroy of India, 1856–1862* (London, 1962) ch. 7.
105. 3M/E116, Lytton to Salisbury, 5 Aug 1876.
106. 3M/C3, Salisbury to Lytton, 10 Nov 1876.
107. 3M/D40, Salisbury to Lytton, 20 Apr 1877.
108. 3M/C3, Salisbury to Lytton, 16 June 1876.
109. Ibid., Salisbury to Lytton, 27 Oct, 7 Apr and 16 Feb 1876.
110. 3 Hansard, CLXXXVII, 1075 (24 May 1867); B. B. Misra, *The Indian Middle Classes* (London, 1961), esp. ch. 12, and A. Seal, *The Emergence of Indian Nationalism: Competition and Collaboration in the later Nineteenth Century* (Cambridge, 1968) are indispensable for the whole subject of westernisation. A. K. Banerji, *Aspects of Indo-British Economic Relations 1858–1888* (Bombay, 1982) is a distinguished addition to the economic literature.
111. R. Bosworth Smith, *Life of Lord Lawrence*, 2 vols (London 1883) II, ch. 12.
112. IOL, Lawrence Papers, MSS Eur. F90/27, Cranborne to Lawrence, 3 Nov 1866.
113. Ibid., F90/28, Cranborne to Lawrence, 18 Feb 1867.
114. 3M/C2, Salisbury to Temple, 5 Feb 1875.
115. Ibid.

116. Ibid., Salisbury to Northbrook, 21 May 1875; Gopal, *British Policy in India*, pp. 118–20.
117. 3 Hansard, CLXXXV, 840 (22 Feb 1867).
118. Ibid.
119. 3M/C2, Salisbury to Sir B. Frere, member of the Council of India, 10 Dec 1875.
120. 3M/C3, Salisbury to Buckingham, 16 Aug 1876.
121. 3M/D45, Salisbury to Mallet, 4 Oct 1875; 3M/C3, Salisbury to Lytton, 24 Mar 1876; 3M/C2, Salisbury to Northbrook, 29 Sep 1875.
122. Ibid.
123. Ibid., Salisbury to Northbrook, 5 Nov 1875.
124. Moulton, *Lord Northbrook's Indian Administration*, ch. 6.
125. 3M/C2, Salisbury to Lytton, 20 April 1877.
126. Ibid.
127. Moulton, *Lord Northbrook's Indian Administration*, pp. 213–14; Strachey, *India*, p. 198; A. P. Kannangara, 'Indian Millowners and Indian Nationalism before 1914', *Past and Present*, (1968).
128. Moulton, *Lord Northbrook's Indian Administration*, pp. 213–14.
129. 3M/C3, Salisbury to Buckingham, 9 June 1876.
130. 3M/C4, Salisbury to Lieutenant-General Richard Strachey, member of the Council of India, 21 Feb 1878.
131. Ibid.
132. 3M/C3, Salisbury to Lytton, 24 Mar 1876. For the policy-making machinery, see A. B. Keith, *A Constitutional History of India, 1600–1935* (London, 1936); S. N. Singh, *The Secretary of State for India and his Council* (Delhi, 1962); and D. Williams, 'The Council of India and the Relationship between the Home and Supreme Governments, 1858–1870', *English Historical Review* (1966). Dr Agatha Ramm on 'Lord Salisbury and the Foreign Office' in R. Bullen (ed.), *The Foreign Office, 1782–1982* (Frederick, Md, 1984), shows how Salisbury mastered another department.
133. Hughenden Papers, B/XX/Ce (see above, n. 84), Salisbury to Disraeli, 13 May 1876.
134. 3M/C3, Salisbury to Lytton, 24 Mar 1876.
135. 3M/C2, Salisbury to Northbrook 10 July and 18 Dec 1874; 3M/E12, Northbrook to Salisbury, 20 Aug 1874: 'I should be sorry to see the form of government altered by giving more power to the Governor General.'
136. 3M/C2, Salisbury to Northbrook, 18 Dec 1874.
137. Salisbury put his case forcibly in speeches of 14 March and 4 August 1876: 3 Hansard, CCXXVII, 1960–76; CCXXX, 507–12. The official documents laid before Parliament are in Parliamentary Papers, 1876, LVI; 1878–9, LV.
138. 3M/C2, Salisbury to Northbrook, 6 Mar 1874.
139. 3M/D45, Salisbury to Mallet, 12 Aug 1874.
140. IOL, MSS Eur. F90/27, Cranborne to Lawrence, 19 Nov 1866.
141. 3M/C3, Salisbury to Lytton, 31 Mar and 30 Aug 1876.
142. But see IOL, Northbrook Papers, MSS Eur. C144/23, Northbrook to

Lord George Hamilton, Salisbury's Parliamentary Under-Secretary of State, 7 April 1876, cited above, p. 138 and n. 150.

143. 3M/C3, Salisbury to Lytton, 20 Apr 1877.
144. IOL, Northbrook Papers, MSS Eur. C144/18, Hobhouse to Northbrook, 5 Jan 1876. There are hostile references to the influence of Hobhouse in Salisbury's letters. J. L. Hammond and L. T. Hobhouse, *Lord Hobhouse: A Memoir* (London, 1905) minimise his political activities in India.
145. IOL, Northbrook Papers, MSS Eur. C144/18, Hobhouse to Northbrook, 5 Jan 1876.
146. 3M/E12, Northbrook to Salisbury, 2 June 1874.
147. IOL, Northbrook Papers, MSS Eur. C144/22, Northbrook to Clerk, 1 Aug 1874; ibid., C144/23, Northbrook to the Earl of Camperdown, 14 June 1875.
148. 3M/C3, Salisbury to Lytton, 31 Mar 1876.
149. IOL, Northbrook Papers, MSS Eur. C144/23, Northbrook to Hamilton, 17 Mar 1876.
150. Ibid., Northbrook to Hamilton, 7 Apr 1876.
151. 3M/E116, Lytton to Salisbury, 25 Apr 1876: 'Under the evil genius of Hobhouse my council seems to have a totally false conception of its function and position.'
152. IOL, Lytton Papers, MSS Eur. E218/219, pt. ii, Lytton to Cavagnari, 30 June 1877.
153. 3M/C4, Salisbury to Lytton, 14 Aug, 28 Sep and 8 Oct. 1877.
154. 3M/E116, Lytton to Salisbury, 16 July 1877.
155. Gladstone Papers, BL Add. MS 44101, the Duke of Argyll to W. E. Gladstone, 14 Sep 1869.
156. IOL, Northbrook papers, MSS Eur. C144/22, Perry to Northbrook 20 Mar 1874.
157. Ibid., C144/23, Perry to Northbrook, 9 July 1875.
158. 3M/E124, Cranborne to R. D. Mangles, member of the Council of India, 5 June 1867; 3 Hansard, CLXXXIX, 1382 (12 Aug 1867).
159. 3M/C4, Salisbury to Lytton, 25 May 1877.
160. 3M/C2, Salisbury to Northbrook, 30 Apr 1875.
161. While in opposition, Salisbury was responsible, with Lawrence's support, for the prospective abolition in 1869 of co-opted members on his Council under the Government of India Act 1858; the Gladstone ministry accepted this change in amending legislation. See Singh, *The Secretary of State for India*, pp. 24–8.
162. 3M/C2, Salisbury to Temple, 2 Apr 1875.
163. 3M/C4, Salisbury to Lytton, 2 Nov 1877.
164. 3M/C3, Salisbury to Lytton, 13 Apr 1877; Gopal, *British Policy in India*, pp. 117–19; Strachey, *India*, pp. 85–8.
165. IOL, Council of India: Memoranda and Papers, C/138, Salisbury's minute on survey settlement in Madras, 20 Apr 1875.

7
Lord Salisbury, Foreign Policy and Domestic Finance, 1860–1900

A. N. PORTER

The foreign policy of the third Marquis of Salisbury has received almost no critical attention now for some twenty years. While fresh biographies and other studies have done much for others who served at the Foreign Office, notably Palmerston and Aberdeen, Lord Salisbury has fared badly.[1] Articles looking closely at his career as Secretary of State for India (1874–8) only serve to highlight the recent neglect of his several spells of duty as the architect of Britain's diplomacy.[2] Thirteen years as Secretary of State for Foreign Affairs, with several more as a close and often influential observer in the Cabinet, are not to be lightly dismissed.[3] The intrinsic interest of the problems which faced Salisbury, in his attempts to contain the mounting challenges to Britain's mid-century pre-eminence, is considerable. It therefore seems appropriate to ask why there is this lack of scrutiny, and to explore the possibility that recent general writings on Britain's politics and diplomacy have suggested ways in which historians can once more move forward.

I

We must begin by looking briefly at the historiography. Neglect has been less a sign of failing enthusiasm or non-existent interest than a measure of the range and excellence of work done by historians since the 1930s, but especially in the 1950s and early 1960s. Lilian Penson's thirty years of research and writing culminated in her Creighton Lecture of 1960, published two years later as 'Foreign Affairs under the Third Marquess of Salisbury'. The major works of

R. E. Robinson and J. A. Gallagher, J. A. S. Grenville, Cedric Lowe and G. N. Sanderson soon followed.[4] It was hardly surprising that a biographer writing in 1973 and intent on revealing the lesser-known aspects of Salisbury's career should pay little attention to his diplomacy because of the 'extensive coverage' it had received.[5] A slightly later study of Salisbury's political career, notwithstanding the author's own extensive research, still drew very largely on the publications of the early sixties for its information on foreign affairs.[6]

At one level Salisbury's diplomacy was thus being taken for granted: a large measure of agreement had been established, about his methods as well as his preoccupations and priorities. His despatches were admired, by historians as they had been by contemporaries, for the clarity of their pronouncements, which reflected not only intellectual capacity of a high order, but also a perpetual concern lest he be misunderstood by those with whom Britain had dealings. His diplomatic style was unmistakable for its patience, willingness to take pains, preference for compromise, and subtle instinct for when to take a firm stand. The result was at its best a skilful patrician exercise, a diplomacy 'simply adjusting itself to new dangers in a cautious, empirical and uncommitted way'.[7]

New dangers were of course plentiful. From the moment of his arrival in the Foreign Office at a particularly anxious stage in the relations between Russia and Turkey, Salisbury, we have been told, never lost sight of the Eastern Question. By 1896 he had adjusted gradually to the impossibility either of defending Constantinople and the Straits, or of reviving the Ottoman Empire through internal reform. This departure from tradition was made easier by the intensification of Britain's grip on Egypt, an anxious and long-delayed process but one in the end both geographically convenient and temporarily reassuring. Britain's position in Egypt, however, was vulnerable in its turn, requiring protection not least to the south. Salisbury was compelled, not only by the 'condition of Egypt' question but also by the multiple fractures of societies in other parts of the continent, to address himself to the restoration of stability in other parts of Africa. The lengthy negotiation of Africa's partition, avoiding armed European conflict on the way, may fairly be regarded as Salisbury's 'chief diplomatic monument'.[8] By contrast, safeguarding India's defences in the borderlands of Persia or Afghanistan, and incidents still further east, were more manageable.

As the diplomatic picture was filled in, so an earlier set of expert judgements was laid aside. The view that the surviving written dispositions on policy by Salisbury were a poor guide to his thinking and activities was abandoned as the extent of the correspondence in his private papers became evident. Salisbury himself was cleared of the charge that he indulged in an extreme form of 'secret diplomacy', ignoring the Foreign Office and even the Cabinet in order to commit Britain to courses of action approved by none but himself. The 'splendid isolation' which he was supposed to favour was shown to be rhetorical rather than actual.[9] Diligent excavation and debate gave rise to the subtleties of academic consensus. 'His major objective, as we review the record of his action, was undoubtedly the maintenance of peace.' Penson's premise became Grenville's reflection: the one great object of his diplomacy was to avoid war.[10] It was an appropriate moment for many of Salisbury's characteristic analyses to be brought together in a collection of documents illustrating the development of Victorian foreign policy.[11]

Now that Salisbury was at last on show, there was perhaps less need to pay him direct attention. This feeling was reinforced by a shift taking place in the preoccupations of non-marxist students of foreign policy. Dissatisfaction with historical explanations which appeared to attribute too independent and creative a role to particular foreign secretaries was soon made felt. Representative here were, for example, the reviewers of Grenville's work who called for a greater attention to the context in which policy was worked out.[12] If diplomatic activity was to be properly understood, then it was important to know far more about subordinate officials and the departments of state in which they worked. The forging of alliances or collapse of good relations hinged, too, on broader structural or impersonal features, such as Britain's economic fortunes and strategic position of power relative to her rivals. Then, again, the political world of pressure groups, popular prejudices, party calculation and (however ill-defined) public opinion provided further determinants of policy. Dissections of individuals' perceptions and motives were felt to be inadequate without a fuller reconstruction of the environment which prompted and constrained them.

Of various works appearing in the last decade which have explored the context of Britain's nineteenth-century diplomacy, none are more grandly conceived than those by Paul Kennedy. With titles which reflect their author's enduring concern with the long-term patterns discernible in Britain's foreign relations,[13] they also share the widely observable preoccupation with the 'decline of Britain'.[14] Many would accept Kennedy's argument that Britain's diplomacy has broadly been that of a power anxious, if not to increase, at least to preserve as much as possible of the wealth and status which in the mid nineteenth century made her the strongest power in the world. This task has been inordinately difficult and, in the end, impossible, given 'the relative decline of Great Britain as an economic power', arguably 'the most critical conditioning element [of British diplomacy] . . . over the past hundred years'.[15] Resting on a worldwide network of commerce and finance, Britain's power and position were uniquely vulnerable to wars and rumours of wars. The cost of protecting this extended system against domestic challenges and external threats from economically expansive rivals rapidly grew to exceed Britain's own available resources. Domestic trends and external events not only had their own independent momentum but also reacted upon each other. 'Armaments policy and foreign policy and taxation policy and social policy all hung together.'[16] The result of this complicated interplay was a dominant diplomatic tradition of 'appeasement', according to which 'British governments from the mid-nineteenth century onwards' tended 'to favour a foreign policy which was, with rare exceptions . . . pragmatic, conciliatory and reasonable . . . predicated upon the assumption that, provided national interests were not too deleteriously affected, the peaceful settlement of disputes was much more to Britain's advantage than recourse to war'.[17] This was more often than not the instinctive approach of Conservative statesmen – Derby, Salisbury and Balfour. Liberals, while often inclined on principle to take a different line, usually finished by following suit.[18]

The diagnosis of such realities or 'background influences' does not, of course, resolve all the historian's problems of explanation. Even if it is necessary to state the truism that a country's international status and diplomacy are broadly determined by its changing material circumstances and cultural traditions, the matter cannot be left there. Historians must ask in what sense and to what degree did 'background determinants'[19] actually determine what happened? How much of a constraint on diplomatic freedom of choice were material circumstances? Did they provide a defined arena beyond which no diplomat could venture except at great risk but within which he often had a great deal of initiative and freedom to manoeuvre? Or did they provide a straitjacket which, notwithstanding the prisoner's occasional wriggle, prevented statesmen from affecting the course of events in any significant way? A further, related, question is, to what extent were the diplomats aware of these constraints or conscious of limits beyond which they could not go?

Kennedy's position is essentially the first of the above alternatives, and his *Anglo-German Antagonism* is a major attempt to reconcile the demands of structural analysis and the search for determinants with a detailed narrative of diplomatic exchanges between Britain and Germany. The second, largely determinist, view has more recently been developed by Bernard Porter in a provocative interpretation of Britain's relations with Europe since 1850.[20] Britain's fortunes were the result of 'fundamental, ineradicable and eventually fatal contradictions in her situation', which left 'little room for individual initiative or volition'. Statesmen were 'essentially ineffective, the prisoners of events rather than the authors of them'; it hardly ever mattered who conducted Britain's foreign affairs, and in thinking otherwise diplomatic historians have been deluded by the surviving profusion of Foreign Office paper.[21] A commercial economy, liberal values, island position and declining relative power presented inescapable constraints.

Such studies have been presented only as complementary to existing narratives of Britain's foreign affairs.[22] They are not intended by their authors to offer general re-evaluations of individual foreign secretaries, and in Lord Salisbury's case provide no more than occasional clues to either his perception of the 'background influences' or their influence on him. If we are to build on this work and integrate the findings of the two types of study, two questions present themselves. First, do the few specific observations made by these authors about Salisbury, limited though they are, nevertheless deepen our understanding of his approach to foreign relations? Secondly, does the current general concern with context hold out other promises of an enlargement of historians' perceptions either of Salisbury's vision and abilities, or of the dynamic behind his policies?

To the first the answer is 'Not really.' They accept the established view of Salisbury's approaches as cautious and pragmatic, and differ from earlier historians only in their tendency to attribute less to the touch of temperament and rather more to the objective difficulty of reconciling conflicting pressures.[23] Although these increased in the 1890s, such difficulties were perennial. There could be no question of Salisbury escaping from a diplomatic tradition of 'appeasement': 'Britain's fundamental national interests . . . the interests of political and economic liberalism . . . hardly changed at all . . . and so she was stuck too with a traditional foreign policy'.[24] Salisbury's well-known fears about democratic politics and the impact of an uncontrolled public opinion on diplomatic activity are referred to, and their effects recalled. They reinforced his public reticence, contributed to his feeling that the future was unpredictable, and confirmed his determination to avoid commitments to which, when the day came, Britain might be unable to adhere. Occasionally Salisbury felt it necessary to pay more specific heed to party divisions and opinion beyond Westminster, as for example in the years 1886–90.[25] Such points, however, do not add to the message of earlier discussions by historians often less concerned with problems of context.[26] Kennedy and Porter are agreed on the crucial importance of Britain's relative economic decline, but see 'no proper recognition' of its implications in the country at large at that time, and no discernible impact on foreign policy much before 1914.[27] It is the second and general question which therefore is of most interest and presents the greatest challenge.

There are those, it is true, who would reject this suggestion. They would argue, with good reason, that the studies published in the 1960s on which we still depend never saw Salisbury's (or indeed any) diplomacy as quite so cerebral an activity, or as detached from the domestic environment, as the contextualists seem to imply. Moreover, the operation of 'background determinants' is essentially general and pervasive: little or nothing is to be gained by looking for such influences in the day-to-day detail.[28] Therefore the gap between studies of the realities behind diplomacy and diplomatic history more traditionally conceived cannot be narrowed.

These objections might be conceded, and even added to, without accepting the conclusion. The organisation of late-nineteenth-century government frequently worked against any broad or systematic assessment of the factors bearing on British diplomacy. The absence of any machinery to cope with Cabinet business left members very much in the hands of the Secretary of State for Foreign Affairs, especially if, like Salisbury, he was also Prime Minister. Goschen was always a fussy, hypersensitive man, but

nevertheless had good grounds for expressing his unease during
the Portuguese crisis of 1891. Even as Chancellor of the Exchequer,
he avowed, 'I know so little. It is not right that we are kept so much
in the dark. . . . I don't see why we should not see Portuguese
despatches to and fro as we see Egypt, South East Europe and other
papers.'[29] Although Salisbury himself defended such reticence by
appealing to the difficulty of adapting policies to the views of
numerous ignorant Cabinet colleagues, it could be said that he was
nevertheless cut off as a result from other information and advice.
His isolation was increased by his further aversion to any
interference with other men's departmental affairs.[30] There was,
not surprisingly, a tendency at times for foreign policy and
defence-planning to diverge, each often lurching towards the other
once more in the aftermath of crises which exposed the lack of
co-ordination. Relations between the War Office and Admiralty
were distant, and co-ordinated planning almost non-existent until
after the South African war and the advent of the Committee of
Imperial Defence.[31] It has recently been suggested that only after
1900 were the comfortable but vague beliefs in the adequacy of
Britain's material resources, and of her traditional commitment to
free trade, for waging any war which might occur seriously
questioned.[32] In Salisbury's day there was neither the machinery
nor the carefully compiled information to hand which might have
made possible the accurate dovetailing of diplomacy to
circumstance and interest. Where so much clearly depended on the
instincts and idiosyncrasies of the Foreign Secretary and his
advisers, on accidents of memory and personal contacts, the
argument in favour of giving particular weight to narrowly defined
habits of 'the official mind' as the only consistent source of restraint
and order in policy is very strong. Other influences, it can often be
seen, were no more than contingent.

There are nevertheless some occasions or areas of policy which
reveal more consistent connections between the preoccupations of
individual statesmen, broader administrative assumptions, and
'background' circumstances. In an earlier work, I explored the
particular conjuncture of international relations and domestic
political conditions which crucially affected the handling of Britain's
diplomacy leading up to the South African war of 1899. This essay
provides an opportunity to suggest that Salisbury's career might
perhaps be looked at again for the light which it sheds on the
relationship between diplomacy and domestic finance. An

examination of this connection may provide one way of bridging the historiographical divide discussed above.

II

'Finance depends on policy, and the policy which affects it most is that regulating foreign affairs.'[33] This observation by Sydney Buxton reflects the most obvious view of the connection and was developed in his own work. Commenting, for example, on the events of the early 1880s, he noted how 'Foreign affairs played the principal part in the politics of the time, and it was, as usual, foreign policy and foreign complications, wars, and rumours of wars, which embarrassed our finances and injured our trade'.[34] Lord Salisbury, however, was well aware that the connection was frequently made in another way. Policy did not only generate demands for money: it was itself attuned to the possibilities or limitations of financial provision. 'Without money', he told the Queen, it was the fate of British diplomats 'to be always making bricks without straw'.[35]

Salisbury's suggestion may seem paradoxical. It can be argued that, as one of the richest and most powerful of nations, Britain suffered even at the end of the century no overall lack of financial resources. Although government expenditure rose very rapidly after 1870, above all as a result of increasing sums spent on defence, the nation's wealth also grew. Looking back over the financial record of forty years, Sir Robert Giffen argued that not only had this led to a substantial increase in government revenue, 'due exclusively to the larger yield of existing taxation, and not to any new burdens', but the tax burden per head of population had quite likely declined since the 1860s.[36] In other words, Britain's need to meet a rising civil expenditure and to match the armaments and preparations of foreign rivals – that 'stern and inevitable necessity' in Salisbury's opinion[37] – had been met without too much difficulty. Although Giffen agreed with the growing number of those who by 1902 believed that to meet rising expenditure a reconstruction of national finances was now required, he felt able at least to approve the financial management of the past.[38]

Salisbury, however, did not share this satisfaction. He had always been concerned less with the ability of the country as a whole to raise the funds required, than with the distribution and methods of taxation and with their results. Believing that levels of taxation should be kept as low as possible, and that indirect taxes were decidedly preferable to direct, he could only regard Britain's financial record after 1870 as disastrous. Not only did the annual estimates move constantly upwards, but direct taxation grew relatively more important and, he felt, landed property had to bear an increasingly disproportionate share of the tax burden. 'This question of the incidence of taxation is in truth the vital question of modern politics.'[39]

His views on taxation were developed in opposition to Gladstone's budgets of the early 1860s, and changed little thereafter. Even then, escalating defence costs seemed to present the most serious problem, and Salisbury saw little hope of reducing government spending while it remained possible only 'to preserve peace by preparing for war'.[40] At the same time, however, taxation 'of all kinds, and especially a high taxation always must involve an amount of political danger which it ought to be a statesman's constant aim to lessen by every means at his command'. A 'judicious system of indirect taxation' would provide the answer. Compared with direct taxes like the income tax, 'demoralizing, inquisitorial, intolerable . . . dangerous to the stability of the State if levied impartially over the whole nation, fatal to the rights of property if confined to the more wealthy few', indirect taxes were the least of evils. They attacked the improvident and the self-indulgent, and most people were hardly aware of them: as a result they excited little criticism and resistance. They were ultimately 'the only species of taxation which is capable, without political danger, of reaching the vast majority of the nation'.[41] In voicing this preference for indirect taxation, Salisbury was spelling out assumptions which many Conservatives warmly supported. Taxation should be imposed only for revenue purposes; all citizens had an equal responsibility to contribute, and no one class should be taxed simply for the benefit, support or relief of another. Exemptions from taxation or the principle of graduation were evils, likely to become instruments of oppression under a democratic system. Direct taxes, especially the income tax and, later, 'death duties', should be regarded only as a reserve to be tapped in time of emergency.[42] Salisbury reiterated these views while a member of Disraeli's Cabinet, and thirty years later the same principles inspired his attack on Harcourt's budget in 1894.[43]

By then, he was fighting what he well knew to be largely a rearguard action. Not only were the comparative simplicity of direct taxes and the low costs of collection powerful arguments in their favour. Successive governments had also abolished many indirect taxes, and the yield from the principal duties which remained – coffee, tea, sugar, beer – was becoming less elastic. Early in his second ministry, Salisbury declared his government's 'desire to introduce a more just system of levying the rates and taxes', because 'the interests of those who are connected with the land are more heavily burdened . . . than . . . what is called personal property, . . . property that is entirely separated from the land'.[44] Nevertheless, Conservative attempts, such as Goschen's wheel and van tax in 1888, to broaden the basis of taxation once more, were unsuccessful, and in the late 1890s Hicks Beach, fearing the political consequences of the charge that he was 'taxing the poor', abandoned such moves altogether.[45] Unable to reverse this trend in the distribution of taxation, Conservative chancellors adopted a policy of soothing their propertied and, especially after 1895, their rural landed supporters by subsidies from Exchequer revenues to local authorities and by adjustments in rating-policy.[46]

Not only was the drift of taxation policy unacceptable to Salisbury, but its impact was aggravated, so far as he could see, by the fact of agricultural depression. Those who were taxed most also had declining resources. In his public speeches he constantly returned to the theme that free trade had done immense damage to agriculture. Admittedly, there could be no question of abandoning the policy: it was, as it had always been, a political, not an economic, question, and unwise though 'many of the steps Mr. Gladstone induced us to take were . . . you very often cannot retrace your steps even when the direction in which they were originally taken is one which you ought not to have adopted'.[47] However, even if the past could rarely be untangled, it was important to recognise which parties had suffered most and needed to be spared further impositions. Salisbury felt there could be no argument but that free trade had brought falling prices, declining incomes and lack of investment in the land, a decided shift from arable farming to pasture, and everywhere a decline in rural employment. This in turn had had a seriously destructive impact on urban employment and welfare.[48]

In the late 1880s Salisbury saw fit to remind listeners that

the incomes of country gentlemen are not now obtained without difficulty or trouble, and there is no doubt that for some time to

come the possessors of land in this country will have to attend to
their own affairs very much more than they have in times past,
and probably therefore will be less prominent themselves in
attending to public affairs.[49]

Land, it seemed, was ceasing to provide such a ready support for
political careers, and was bringing only uncertain returns subject to
increasing fiscal burdens. Confronted with Harcourt's death duties,
Salisbury felt his continuing pessimism was justified: he attributed
to the growth of direct taxation not only declining investment in
land but also the flow of English capital abroad. The failure to tax
'personal property' equally with the land was demonstrable folly.
Where fixed assets were comparatively highly taxed, those with
freedom to choose avoided tying up their capital in land and
domestic production. Governments should not stand by when, as
happened only rarely, they had the power to reverse the process:
they should remove, not increase, the 'unjust burdens on the land',
and relieve wherever possible the hard-pressed ratepayer.
Governments should not watch capital go overseas: 'We want it
here. We cannot prosper without it.'[50]

Salisbury felt himself faced with a system of trade and taxation
which threatened the self-interest of his class, impoverished 'the
principal industry' of the country, encouraged financial
irresponsibility, acted as a disincentive to much productive
investment, and tied 'consumer and producer on English soil . . .
together in a common loss'.[51] Accepting that there was little he
could do to alter a set of practices which were rooted in delusion and
were rapidly creating their own vested interests, he derived a grim
satisfaction at times from setbacks to the extension of Treasury
claims.[52] Rather more positively, he saw the necessity these
tendencies created for a particular kind of diplomacy, one which
would not only avoid crises and the expenditure attendant upon
them, but also keep the general level of expenditure to a minimum.

This is not simply to call attention to Salisbury's well-known
preference for quiet, careful negotiation, or, as he put it, a Foreign
Office whose 'course is studiously unobtrusive'.[53] It is rather to
make the point that his predilection did not arise, as is often
thought, simply from calculations of party advantage or a
recognition that Britain's commerce was both very great and thrived
on peace, although he considered all these things. It rested rather on
his belief that the 'fabric of our prosperity is so artificial'; Britain had

created 'such a vast edifice of industry and manufacture and wealth within so narrow an area'[54] that, given the problems of her propertied classes, this made her doubly vulnerable. Not only would war or invasion easily shatter this industrial and commercial structure; it would also entail ever more direct taxation of an increasingly confiscatory kind levied above all on property-owners, many of whom could only meet the demand by forgoing productive investment. What was called for was a foreign and defence policy which would provide security for industry and commerce but at a price which land could afford to pay. Only if both needs were kept in view could one hope to maintain 'that confidence which induces capital to flow and insures that employment shall be general and wages shall be good'.[55]

III

The influence of financial considerations over the management of Britain's foreign affairs was not confined to the question of the sources – in Salisbury's view, limited – from which revenue could be drawn. There were also those financial restraints on his diplomacy arising from the power of the Treasury itself, a power which reflected the proverbial concern of Treasury officials with economy, and was derived from its position in part as arbiter between the spending departments. The Treasury's willingness to underwrite Foreign Office activities – salaries for a staff adequate to the efficient day-to-day running of the office, costs incurred by embassies and consular services, subsidies, loans and guarantees, funding for an adequate level of military and naval defence – varied not only from chancellor to chancellor but with the state of the parties and the weight of other departmental claims. The Treasury's power of veto, even of decision, was so considerable that the Permanent Under-Secretary, seeking to reconcile Lord Rosebery's preference for the foreign-secretaryship with the Liberal Party's need for a successor to Mr. Gladstone, claimed that Rosebery 'could dictate the foreign policy of a Government almost as well from the Treasury as from the FO.'[56]

Salisbury was well aware of this situation. Late in his career he set out the general problem in a letter to his Chancellor of the Exchequer:

That the Treasury should say that any expenditure is excessive or thriftless, in regard to the objects for which it is intended, is obviously within its functions. But in practice the Treasury goes much further. It acts as a Court of Appeal on other departments. Because any policy at every step requires money, the Treasury can veto everything and can do so on proposals which have nothing financial in their nature and pass judgement upon which it has no special qualifications . . . it is natural for a head of a department to feel annoyed if, by applying the financial brake, the Treasury hampers a policy in which it does not concur

and irritation was 'much more keenly felt if the interference of the Treasury wins, not at arresting a policy which it disapproves, but at securing sufficient delay to enable it to disapprove if it wishes'.[57] Such were the tactics of the Treasury in pursuit of its own departmental ambitions, and from time to time Salisbury's own highly critical, public outbursts showed that his awareness involved more than a detached intellectual acquaintance with the problems of colleagues. Particularly perhaps in the case of the defence departments, Salisbury was inclined to believe that 'the exaggerated control of the Treasury has done harm'.[58]

His experience of these financial curbs dated from his earliest days in the Foreign Office when, in the summer of 1878, he had failed to persuade Sir Stafford Northcote of the need for a financial agreement with Turkey and support for a railway from Alexandretta to Baghdad. Salisbury also lost this battle in the Cabinet.[59] From that experience two lessons were to be learned. Not only did a foreign secretary need the presence of at least a sympathetic chancellor at the Treasury; he had to be able to dominate the Cabinet when financial provision was at stake. In the years of Liberal government that followed, these lessons were reinforced. Gladstone was for a time both Prime Minister and Chancellor of the Exchequer, and, even when Childers took over the Treasury, always remained highly influential in financial questions. While the concentration of power attracted Gladstone, in Salisbury's view its effects on foreign and defence policy were wholly disastrous. The weakness of Granville at the Foreign Office was only in part evidence of his personal incapacity.

Here lies one explanation of Salisbury's willingness for most of his official life after 1885 to combine the offices of Prime Minister and Foreign Secretary, despite the immense personal labour involved.

The image of Salisbury as a reluctant premier, an emphasis on his personal enjoyment of diplomacy and high-minded preference for a pursuit at the Foreign Office 'far more genuinely truthful' than the debased bargaining of party politics, can be misleading.[60] They disguise the realities of political power and the necessary connections of domestic constraints with foreign policy. Foreign secretaries by themselves lacked enough power, knowledge and influence consistently to carry Cabinets with them. To conduct foreign policy as Prime Minister made all the difference to Salisbury between possible success and certain failure. The Foreign Office could be kept more fully in touch with domestic influences which might jeopardise Britain's foreign relations. It became possible for him to give effect to his conviction that defence was at least as much the preserve of the Foreign Office as of the War Office and Admiralty.[61] There was more hope of avoiding false economies which weakened necessary defences, as well as the chance to ensure that revenue was raised only after full discussion of the alternative sources. Above all, a foreign secretary who was prime minister had the constitutional power to select the Cabinet and to overrule the Treasury, powers of vital importance to the environment in which foreign policy was decided.

The problem of creating that favourable balance of power within the Cabinet, one which would hedge in the Chancellor and restrict the Treasury's capacity to upset a rational foreign policy, faced Salisbury most acutely during 1886–7. The European situation was very tense and unsettled between 1884 and 1890. Uncertain relations between Germany and Russia, the antics of Boulanger in France, upheavals in the Balkans and the international build-up of armaments made the danger of war seem very real. The Gladstone Government's achievement meanwhile had been to neglect Britain's own defences, to isolate the country completely from the Continent, and come close to war with Russia over Afghanistan. Salisbury was determined to reduce the danger and contribute to the easing of European tensions by repairing diplomatic bridges and restoring Britain's defensive capacity.[62] With this aim he combined the offices of Prime Minister and Foreign Secretary in his short-lived ministry of 1885, but it was not until his second term of office, and even then after some delay, that the prospect of progress really brightened.

That delay, from June 1886 to January 1887, when Salisbury reconstructed his ministry, is important. It not only reinforced the lessons of his earlier experience as to the connection between Cabinet construction, the power of the Treasury and foreign policy, but also gave prominence to the connection of diplomacy with domestic finance. It originated in Salisbury's inability in 1886 for party reasons either to reoccupy the Foreign Office or to avoid taking Lord Randolph Churchill as Chancellor of the Exchequer.[63] Even with the agreement that the Prime Minister would continue to take a special interest in his old department, Iddesleigh's handling of foreign affairs in the summer and autumn irritated his colleagues, above all Churchill. The Chancellor therefore began to formulate both an alternative diplomacy and a complementary budgetary strategy, reflecting his own uncompromising views as to the necessity for drastic economies in government expenditure. He interfered constantly with a view to bringing about closer ties with Germany; planned to encourage Austria in South-East Europe and cared little whether Russia kept away from Constantinople; and ignored Salisbury's interest both in Egypt and in better relations with France.[64] He worked for a broadly popular budget, one which relied significantly on savings of £1.3 million from the armed forces, and adopted the frequently voiced argument that, if forced to use limited resources more carefully, both the War Office and Admiralty would become far more efficient and effective than if provided with still more funds.[65]

From Salisbury's point of view Churchill's programme meant the worst of all possible worlds. Its diplomacy involved a level of commitment to another power which Salisbury genuinely felt no British government could give, and ignored the necessity of protecting Britain's position, especially in Egypt. The budget threatened to deprive diplomacy of a necessary support, for it promised serious restraints on British defences both at a time of acute international tension and when the first priority was to make good the effects of Gladstonian neglect.[66] Finally, the Chancellor's adjustment of the tax burden offended some of Salisbury's deepest prejudices by its proposals for graduated taxation, an increase in the death duties, and the failure of its local taxation plans to relieve the rural areas rather than the towns. 'The result (if I rightly understood your proposals)', Salisbury wrote, 'is that the ordinary country gentleman will have an extra burden of nine pence in the pound. . . .'[67] The further remission of indirect taxation in support of foolish economies and irresponsible diplomatic meddling, offering no prospect of improving either security or confidence, were hardly to the Prime Minister's taste.

The details of the Cabinet crisis which arose from the budget discussions and ended with Churchill's resignation are well known.[68] Undoubtedly Salisbury resented the challenge to his leadership which, in the face of persistent warnings, Churchill's behaviour over the past months had implied. Certainly, too, mounting irritation with the Chancellor among Cabinet colleagues, and Churchill's own miscalculations, made it easier for Salisbury to dispose of an awkward minister when, after resistance to his estimates and just before Christmas, Churchill incautiously offered his resignation. Salisbury's thinking, however, surely went further. There are strong grounds for suggesting that in his mind the budget was not largely a pretext, or merely the first convenient occasion for confronting Churchill;[69] nor, it may be suggested, was his decision to get rid of Churchill taken primarily with the Irish question in mind, whatever others may have thought.[70]

The task of the Conservative Government was to guard against a return of the Gladstonians. This was necessary primarily on account of their Irish policy, but also, particularly for a man with Salisbury's preoccupations, because of the damaging effects of the Liberal approach to defence, foreign affairs and finance. In vital respects Churchill's budget called into question some of the central purposes of a Conservative government as conceived by Salisbury, and thereby raised issues which went far beyond minor compromises over figures. Churchill knew this and reiterated the point in his final letters to Salisbury, in effect labouring the connection between foreign policy and finance: 'if the foreign policy of this country is conducted with skill and judgement, our present huge and increasing armaments are quite unnecessary, and the taxation which they involve perfectly unjustifiable'.[71] Two days later he again put starkly the case against large estimates. 'The foreign policy which is being adopted appears to me at once dangerous and methodless, but I take my stand upon expenditure and finance which involve and determine all other matters. . . .'[72] There was no way in which Salisbury could continue to work with a man who not only differed from him fundamentally on the direction of foreign policy, but was also both conscious of the power of the Treasury in that respect and prepared to use it in defiance of his colleagues.[73]

The resolution of this crisis was an uncommonly satisfactory one, given that the conflict between Salisbury and his chancellor was one in which the Prime Minister saw the conditions for the conduct of foreign policy as a major issue.[74] George Goschen, among Liberal Unionists the most sympathetic to Salisbury and above all 'anxious to stand up for the rights of property',[75] was recruited to the Exchequer. His ability added significantly to the Conservative front bench, and was a hopeful sign of future good relations between Conservatives and Liberal Unionists. Not only was he a ready convert to financial nostrums more in keeping with Salisbury's own, but to the eyes of his officials he seemed acutely concerned to avoid the slightest suggestion of favouritism towards the financial interests of the City of London which he had once known so well.[76] Salisbury once again took the Foreign Office. Although Iddesleigh's dismissal was requested by Goschen, it is hard to believe that Salisbury would again have given such a hostage to fortune. He now had a more sympathetic chancellor, and used his new power to insulate his diplomacy even from most Cabinet colleagues. This was done to a degree which Goschen found increasingly irksome; being a man who in the best of circumstances could find it hard to act decisively, he found the state and conduct of foreign affairs worrying for the uncertainty it gave to his financial planning.[77] It was only appropriate that Gladstone as an old Exchequer hand should regret how the tables had been turned. He complained to Edward Hamilton that the 'combined offices of Prime Minister and Foreign Secretary were not only incompatible but constitutionally wrong, because there was no check on the Foreign Secretary and the Prime Minister could over-rule the Treasury'.[78]

IV

It is not surprising that Lord Salisbury, critic of democratic finance as of democratic politics, should have done what he could to forge a government in which the power to conduct foreign affairs was strengthened at the expense of other departments. However, even the most favourably structured Cabinet could never be perfect; its behaviour inevitably remained uncertain in the face of the politically unpredictable. As Foreign Secretary, therefore, Salisbury was never able to feel free from financial worries. There is more to this observation than the obvious fact that Salisbury had his arguments with the Treasury over expenditure; neither is it intended to suggest that, where agreement existed, Salisbury's methods of Cabinet control had automatically prevailed.

There were naturally times when the Foreign Secretary and Chancellor were of a single economical mind. With whatever cost to the principles of free trade or in brushes with the Portuguese, both were pleased, while playing a part in 'what is called the partition of Africa', to have avoided the great cost of extensive administration. 'We have done it', said Salisbury, referring to the chartered enterprises of Rhodes and Goldie, 'in a characteristic way. We have done it by company'.[79] In other instances, the Treasury tactic of prolonged delay was sufficient to circumvent the Foreign Office's pressure for expenditure; although occasionally Goschen, for example, responded readily to requests for finance to underpin diplomatic initiatives, Salisbury more often found 'that Goschen is not in a subsidizing humour'.[80] Some campaigns by the Foreign Office were successful in overcoming Treasury resistance, but were nevertheless drawn out by parliamentary difficulties, as in the case of the Mombasa railway in East Africa.[81]

As with all departments, there were also quarrels over the Foreign Office's establishment. Occasionally these were bitter, as in 1888 when continual resistance to requests for more library staff pushed Salisbury's patience too far. Treasury behaviour was grossly irresponsible.

The number of unregistered letters must now be approaching one million. For . . . recent years there is no register or index . . . to give any sure information of the papers which exist, or where they may be found. The current business of the office depends entirely upon the memory, fortunately extensive, of Sir Edward Hertslet and his staff. It is naturally . . . not safe to rely on this resource.

From grave mishap in an emergency 'the Foreign Office are at present preserved, not by precaution, but by pure chance. . . . Lord Salisbury desires me to say that the responsibility for any accidents that may arise from the present state of things . . . must rest with the Treasury alone.'[82]

Salisbury attached weight to such matters from fear that failure to take care in little things might entail far greater loss or expenditure in the long run.[83] Yet, for all the sound and the fury, these costs were comparatively small, capable for the most part of being contained either by buoyant tax returns or at the expense of newcomers bidding for a share of the revenue. There was always an element of flexibility in Foreign Office budgetting when compared with that of many departments. Costs were often covered by exploiting Indian or Egyptian revenues, or the slave-trade vote; where chartered companies were unavailable, new protectorates could be accounted for as no more than temporary charges on the assumption of future self-sufficiency.[84] It was at another level of expenditure altogether that finance and diplomacy in Salisbury's view began seriously to affect one another, affecting distribution of the national tax burden and altering diplomatic strategies. Defence spending raised these issues most acutely, and Salisbury's attitude to the Naval Defence Act of 1889 is of particular interest.

The Naval Defence Act of 1889 (52 & 53 Vict. cap. 8) was sponsored by Salisbury's Cabinet in order to finance a five-year plan for naval construction.[85] It marked government response to the sporadic public campaign for naval expansion mounted since 1884 by both publicists and serving officials, and was widely supported. Many Liberals no less than Conservatives saw a building-programme as essential if Britain were to maintain her strength in the face of both recent Continental expansion, and technical changes in weaponry and ship construction. Salisbury was never one to be overawed by the claims of defence lobbies, and seems steadily to have maintained the view that defence spending was largely wasteful.[86] Nevertheless he fully recognised the inescapable necessity for naval spending in the late eighties.[87] Not only was it required for the protection of Britain's trade, the country's security from invasion and the maintenance of commercial confidence, but naval strength made possible Britain's diplomatic posture of friendly detachment from Europe as well as her claim to carry weight in the Continent's affairs.[88]

Recognising the need for expansion was only a first step. The programme also had to be paid for in the most politically acceptable manner. Funding expansion involved three distinct questions. How much of the Navy's needs for cruisers and battleships could be covered by the normal naval estimates, and so be met out of ordinary income? How large an additional sum would the Government need to borrow and over what period should it be repaid? And from what sources of taxation should repayment be met?

Liberals like Morley or Mundella who approved the outlay insisted that the cost should be met out of ordinary income,[89] in the normal peacetime fashion. Such suggestions, linked with Mundella's insistence that the Government should rely particularly upon private builders rather than its own yards, worried Salisbury. It raised for him the prospect that those benefiting most directly from the act – the shipping and commercial interests, among the most vociferous supporters of naval expansion – would have to meet little or none of the cost, and that others more easily taxed might be forced to bear the brunt. This was unjust, and entirely ignored the Liberal Party's share of responsibility for the state of the Navy. The naval programme was an extraordinary event and should be treated as such. 'Programmes are remedies when there has been neglect; but a healthy Admiralty ought not to require them.'[90]

These circumstances implied their own financial logic, and Salisbury explained his guiding principles clearly.

1. That this temporary exigency should not make a permanent change in our system of taxation.
2. That this financial operation should be kept separate not affecting the rest of the Budget.
3. That the burden should fall on the two interests mainly concerned in augmenting our navy – viz. the fixed property and the seagoing commerce of the country.[91]

Throughout the discussion his determination was to avoid 'the pernicious financial habit' of having 'the *whole* burden . . . upon realised property'.[92] The importance of making his position clear is illustrated by what is so far known of Goschen's reactions to Admiralty plans. Irked by the recent final rejection in Cabinet of his latest attempts to broaden the base of taxation (his wheel and van tax),[93] Goschen was in no mood to welcome greatly increased estimates or new ways of raising revenue. He had to give way on the broad question of expansion, but insisted in the interests of financial planning that Parliament should be committed to a defined programme over a fixed period.[94] This idea was a product largely of motives no higher than pique and Goschen's marked concern for his own financial reputation. But in the Chancellor's *amour propre* lay the makings of an accommodation with the Prime Minister, for the definition of a distinct plan made it easier to conceive of a separate scheme of funding.

During the spring of 1889 the building-plan was enlarged:[95]

Hamilton's plans of early January for twelve cruisers costing about £5 million were subsumed in a scheme to build seventy ships by 1894, including forty-two protected cruisers, at a total cost of £21.5 million. With these increases in size the case for separate financing grew stronger, and Goschen saw that in this way his ordinary financial strategy could be retained.[96] For Salisbury the gains were still more significant. The budget would be protected from radical change; the more dramatic the Navy's plans, the more acceptable or at least necessary was any new taxation likely to appear; and political damage would be minimised.[97]

Salisbury worked hard to reduce the financial and political dangers still further, preferring that nothing should be pushed across onto the ordinary annual naval estimates, and that the whole exercise should be paid for by government borrowing. If there was to be no simple addition to the National Debt, then repayment should be made over a long period, say thirteen years.[98] Here was the mind of the landowner at work, accustomed to mortgages and the long perspective, and, as his public speeches showed, impressed with the testimony to Britain's good credit provided by Goschen's highly successful conversion of the National Debt.[99]

However, the attractions of this idea to Salisbury, and the circumstances which made possible public borrowing at favourable rates, were precisely those which prompted orthodox Treasury men to throw up their hands in horror. Hamilton, who recorded in his diary only the most dramatic of his official activities, summarised there the 'remonstrance' he had written against government proposals to borrow: 'It will be the ruin of Mr. Goschen's financial reputation. There is absolutely no precedent for charging to capital account such expenditure when we are at peace with the world, when the income tax is at 6d in the £, when the revenue is on the rise, and when there is a general increase of prosperity and distinct signs of revival of trade.' Like Lord Salisbury, Hamilton saw the matter as having important implications for the future. 'Moreover a precedent set by a man of Mr. Goschen's financial authority is a most dangerous precedent, and one which heterodox financiers of the future, with whom we may very likely have to reckon, will not be slow to follow.'[100]

In the end, Salisbury gained many of his points. The Government placed a part of the programme on the ordinary ship-building vote, increasing the annual naval estimates by £600,000, but borrowed between £10 million and £11.5 million.[101] This was to be repaid over

seven years, from special taxes imposed for that precise purpose.
Where he had earlier criticised Goschen's idea of introducing new
death duties for ordinary expenditure,[102] Salisbury now accepted
such a temporary duty. He was not the only Cabinet member
concerned over this point: as he told the Chancellor,

> Beach was much troubled . . . by the idea that you had proposed
> the New Estates tax as a permanent addition to the taxing
> machinery of this country.
>
> I ventured to assure him that this was an entire
> misapprehension: and that . . . the tax should only last until the
> cost of the present addition to the Navy had been defrayed.[103]

This concession was the more easily made for two further
reasons. Salisbury's principle that the tax burden should be fairly
spread was fully met. Even if, despite some courting of the
commercial public, his ideas for a ship duty, or a tax on foreign
wines and spirits, were regarded as too politically dangerous, a
further tax on beer raised the required sum.[104] No wonder
supporters of temperance and peace movements often had much in
common! Finally, there was for Salisbury the satisfaction of a
notable constitutional victory: by this arrangement the House of
Commons' hands were tied in an unprecedented way. For a period
well into the life of the next parliament, with its possibility of a
Liberal ministry, a significant portion of the country's taxes were
firmly mortgaged to a specific end, and the possibility of popular
interference in naval provision was largely removed. Government
defenders of the Bill in the Commons were quite explicit as to their
intentions on this point, and a succession of Liberals angrily
condemned the 'new mode of voting supplies for the Navy, and . . .
of providing ways and means for meeting supplies'.[105]

The passage of the Act was no slight achievement. Salisbury
frankly admitted to the Lords that the scheme had been delayed by
the Government's 'utter dislike and reluctance to incur the
expenditure involved'.[106] From his own point of view, however, the
delay had been productive. The final measure helped to secure his
own diplomatic hand; its construction justified his approach to
Cabinet-making, and its provisions arguably reinforced his control
by restricting future parliamentary activity; its financial terms
represented a skilful compromise in the process of reconciling the
needs of foreign policy and security with the drift of 'democratic'

taxation and the defence of class interest. Although in the longer run
Hamilton was right to see in the 'Estate Duty . . . the thin end of the
wedge to a graduated system of taxation, which is pretty certain to
be expanded in future',[107] for the moment it was accepted as
limited, temporary and as giving good grounds for resisting further
impositions. That it rankled more than any other measures with Sir
Thomas Farrer in his critical review of Goschen's finance was one
indication of Salisbury's success.[108]

V

The argument of this essay conflicts at several points with other
recently expressed views of Salisbury's political career. Both Peter
Marsh and Colin Matthew, for example, seem agreed that Salisbury
abandoned all interest in the drift towards direct taxation, that he
ignored 'what was to be in the long run the ruin of his class'.[109] On
Marsh's evidence, it might be argued that this was so because
Salisbury, as Prime Minister and party-leader, rapidly learnt to
accept the necessities of party management in the immediate
interest of combating a wider radicalism and maintaining the Irish
union. Alternatively, in Matthew's view, dropping the issue was
the price Salisbury, Foreign Secretary as well as Prime Minister, saw
as essential to sustain the foreign and defence policy required by the
electoral mainstay of the late-century Conservative Party, 'villa
toryism and its stock-broking imperialism'.[110]

Evidently neither explanation is altogether satisfactory. At least
during his second ministry, Salisbury had neither abandoned his
interest in the taxation question nor ceased to try to control its
development. Marsh, in particular, runs the danger of focusing too
narrowly on domestic affairs and party leadership. While one may
agree with Matthew that 'Salisbury's external policy was not merely
a cerebral exercise unrelated to domestic developments',[111] it has to
be said that neither was it a reflex reaction to the interests of
suburban Tory voters. Salisbury's views were both broader and
more balanced than such interpretations suggest. Something of this
is conveyed in a speech he gave at Caernarvon in the spring of 1888:

> We have a population constantly growing in a limited island. We
> have all the difficulties of vicissitude in prosperity and adversity,

the increasing claims of the poor, the increasing difficulties of the rich. We have looming before us political questions such as were never presented to the world to settle before, the relations between capital and labour, and the like. All these things we have to do in the midst of other nations who are striving by our side, envying our Empire, occupying our markets, encroaching upon our sphere, and whose efforts unless we are wideawake and united and enterprising, will end in diminishing still further our means of supporting our vast industrial population.[112]

Britain's foreign relations held the key to the security of her interests at home and overseas, and as such were of at least equal importance with her more narrowly domestic problems. Salisbury began as Foreign Secretary, and, as we have seen, called the powers of the Prime Minister's office to his aid. In the later 1880s, the degree of international tension and the threats to Britain were such that external considerations inevitably established the order of priorities, above all the need for improved defence. That necessity was met, but in a way designed at the time to safeguard the domestic interests Salisbury held vital. If, as a result of party-leadership, Salisbury developed both a wider range of domestic preoccupations and a more mature sense of the possible, he did not abandon his long-standing concern for landed society and the financial threats to it. Class interest and national interest in a source of employment, welfare, investment and future prosperity forbade it. Salisbury demonstrated his continuing interest in the taxation question and contributed to the defence of landed property by conducting foreign affairs in a way which minimised the financial demands – prompted more than anything else by defence spending – likely to be made upon it.

There are various ways in which the persistence of these priorities into Salisbury's third ministry can be indicated. Again his Cabinet-making was significant.[113] He took the Foreign Office for himself, and, against a background of still-rising taxation, appointed to the Treasury Sir Michael Hicks Beach, that staunchest of agrarians whose fears in 1889 have been noted above. To the Admiralty there went no narrow-minded navalist or political weakling, but Goschen, well versed in both Treasury problems and foreign affairs. The Cecil family interest in the Cabinet was notoriously strong; it included Balfour, with his own special interest in defence, as First

Lord of the Treasury and Leader of the House of Commons, and also Selborne as Under-Secretary at the Colonial Office to keep an eye on Chamberlain.

The impact of this combination on a range of policies involving domestic expenditure has recently been thoroughly illuminated.[114] The Cabinet showed a strong and steadily growing partiality towards agrarian interests compared with those even of urban land-holders. The explanation for this more pronounced partisanship surely lies in the problems of rising overseas expenditure. The Cabinet's growing sense of embattlement, loss of control and unavoidable costs,[115] however much Beach and Salisbury might pare and scrape to find the cheapest option, led inevitably to hard choices and increasing favouritism as tax remissions looked ever more remote.

The Egyptian question, and, in particular the reconquest of the Sudan from 1896 to 1898, was as ever for the Foreign Secretary one of overriding importance which also raised domestic budgetary problems and serious political difficulties. Salisbury's correspondence with Beach and Cromer in the late 1890s shows the Cabinet's constant worry. The Foreign Secretary's warning to Baring in 1887 stood as a permanent caution:

> In considering the financial question you must not forget the extreme difficulty we have in persuading the House of Commons to incur any expense about Egypt. The pressure of taxation here is very heavy. Motions in the direction of economy will unite many who ordinarily vote apart, and the decision of the House on such points can not be confidently foretold.[116]

The feeling was strong in Britain that Egyptian officials regarded the 'British taxpayer as a legitimate "milch-cow" ' in their efforts to recover Egypt's solvency and prosperity,[117] and Salisbury was conscious of both the dangers of higher taxation *per se*, and a public resentment of increased costs in Egypt which might turn into an inconvenient demand for withdrawal. On the other hand, he was convinced of the importance to Britain of her hold on the Suez Canal, and wished to do everything possible to strengthen the hands of Baring and his assistants.

This dilemma was more acute than ever in 1896.[118] As British influence with the Turks weakened, as the Franco-Russian alliance made the possibility of naval intervention at Constantinople more remote, and relations with the Triple Alliance cooled, so Britain's position in Egypt grew in strategic importance. At the same time it was threatened not so much by internal unrest as by the Dervishes in the Sudan, the weakness of the Italians both against Abyssinia and at Kassala, and increasingly by the movement of the French towards the Nile's headwaters. The prospect of consolidating Britain's position by approaching the Nile through Uganda was still far off. It therefore seemed ever more necessary to tighten Britain's grip on Egypt by retaking the Sudan, at a pace fast enough to keep ahead of the French but at a cost which would strain neither British nor Egyptian budgets. Avoidance of setbacks on the way up the Nile was vital: in 1885 Gordon had not only died at Khartoum, but had cost Gladstone's government well over £4 million. Salisbury's government had committed itself in 1895 to build the Uganda railway,[119] and the prospect now of spending further sums and risking still more to achieve the same goal by another route was most unwelcome.

Suspicion of Egyptian officals' willingness to pass on the financial burdens of reconquest remained strong, and Salisbury's reluctance to advance was understandably acute. The decision to move was finally prompted in February 1896 largely by the difficulties of the Italians and fear of the consequences of their defeat.[120] However, from Dongola to Abu Hamed to Omdurman in September 1898 the next step was frequently in doubt. In mid 1897 the future was particularly uncertain. Salisbury pressed on Cromer his worry at the risks of an advance which seemed almost to have halted. Above all, 'my fear is that the pressure to send a British expedition to relieve you will become too strong to resist – especially as it will be pushed by every kind of royal and professional influence'.[121] The cost, financial as well as political, hardly bore contemplation.

At the Treasury there seemed a starker choice to be made: Egypt's resources had reached the point where either Cromer's development and irrigation policies could proceed or the Sudan could be retaken, but not both. Moreover, the cost 'could not . . . be defrayed by any assistance which under present conditions the taxpayers of the United Kingdom could properly be called upon to afford'.[122] Six months later the Treasury agreed that the development policy, essential to improving Egypt's own credit and ability to cover costs from the reoccupation, might proceed, but only 'on the understanding that after the capture of Khartoum no further military operations on a large scale or involving any considerable expense will be undertaken for the recovery of the provinces South of that place, and that Great Britain shall not be expected to give any financial assistance towards the expense of administering the reconquered districts'.[123] French pressure doubtless hastened this decision. Yet only when it had been taken was the advance on Omdurman authorised (26 January 1898), and the tendency in 1898 gradually to eliminate Egyptian claims to the Sudan was apparently stimulated by the need to obtain securities against British financial contributions to Egypt.[124]

There is a tendency in the writing of diplomatic history to assume that where necessities arise the financial means will always be found. Too often perhaps, as in the halting progress of Britain up the Nile after 1895, influences called on to explain the pattern ignore the financial constraints. Mentions of Cromer, Kitchener, the War and Foreign Offices, the influence of the French advance, overlook the difficulties in the way of finding finance, the persistent hope that circumstances might change altogether or that delay would reduce the scale of the problem, and the reluctance with which expenditure was finally approved. If in the Egyptian case Salisbury seemed sometimes more eager to advance than Beach, this should not lead to the automatic conclusion that he did not care about the cost. Wearing his Foreign Office hat, Salisbury knew that Beach could be relied on to put a strongly economical case, and that Chancellor and Prime Minister together would carry on the political battle to adjust the tax burdens as far as possible in favour of land. The financial load might in part be shifted away from the Imperial Government – onto the Egyptians, the Government of India, or Lord Rothschild and City shareholders[125] – thus lessening the weight of direct taxes.

All these possibilities were tried. Nevertheless, external pressures on Britain were multiplying in the late 1890s, and decisions as to where to advance and what to spend were becoming far more difficult. The handling even of questions of the utmost importance, such as Egypt and the Nile, was not immune from the effects of financial worry. Established strategies might still be broadly intact, but Salisbury's mounting gloom and conflicts within the Cabinet were evidence that they might not remain so for long as increasing costs reduced the possibilities for political and financial adjustment.

Space prevents more than the briefest reference to other aspects of Salisbury's work as Prime Minister and Foreign Secretary which undoubtedly either had direct budgetary implications or were important in reducing the likelihood of demands on the revenue.

His concern for the careful co-ordination of foreign policy with defence planning, and for the economical use of resources, was an enduring one. He was responsible for the setting up of the Cabinet Defence Committee, and for the establishment of the Hartington Commission. In 1889, he and his nephew Arthur Balfour considered at length with respect to the Army problems akin to those raised by the Naval Defence Act – the separation of ordinary from capital expenditure with distinct methods of financing for the latter. They took up the same questions almost as soon as they returned to office in 1895.[126] The Naval and Military Works Acts of 1895 to 1903 went on to develop the ideas of the late 1880s, financing military expenditure by the raising of government loans to the tune of £50 million. Criticisms heard in the earlier period were extensively developed, and the procedure was seen as enabling government to avoid the formal constraint of securing parliamentary approval for its expenditure plans.[127] Cabinet debate on these questions deserves investigation, bearing in mind Farrer's depiction of Goschen's and Salisbury's measures as the method by which 'the classes' transferred the burden of expenditure for their own enthusiasms to 'the masses' who did not share them.[128]

Ultimately Beach and Salisbury failed to stem the tide flowing against both the landed interest they represented and indirect taxation; but this was not for want of trying.[129] Salisbury's rearguard actions conducted from his base in the Foreign Office deserve recognition as much as Chamberlain's far more obvious attempt to shift the basis of British financial policy. Both contributed significantly to the reaction of 1906 and the subsequent Liberal reforms. As for the diplomacy of appeasement,[130] if that is indeed what Salisbury's was, in his case it was inspired far less by the needs of a liberal commercial society than by the instinct for survival of a landed elite. There are parallels here between the assumptions and activities of Lord Salisbury and those of continental statesmen which deserve notice; unfortunately they are often obscured by an undue preoccupation with Britain's commercial inheritance.

VI

At this point, it is necessary to return to the questions posed at the beginning of this essay, and to ask in what sense or to what degree financial considerations actually constrained Salisbury in his foreign policy. From the evidence examined above, his awareness that such limits existed would appear indisputable. Equally clearly, it arose less from any sense of the country's absolute inability to support expenditure than from consciousness of the damage to particular sectional interests which the incidence of increased taxation might cause. Salisbury's first concerns, therefore, were to minimise expenditure and to control its domestic financial impact.

Minimising expenditure with the intention of protecting the interests of landed property reinforced Salisbury's tendency to work hard and bargain long in pursuit of negotiated diplomatic agreements. It strengthened his scepticism of naval and military experts, contributed to his dislike of expanding armaments, and led him to rely on Britain's ability to shuttle ironclads between trouble spots rather than patrol an ever larger proportion of the seven seas. When expenses were unavoidable, Salisbury trusted to a combination of administrative reform and political skill to produce a more efficient use of resources and to ensure that those whom he particularly wished to protect were spared demands for payment.

There is little sign that financial constraints were decisive for Salisbury in matters more fundamental than those of style and means, which seems to suggest that both commercial and landed interests were for most of his time served by the same broad diplomatic strategy. On occasions when conflicts arose over Britain's general defence and diplomatic posture, as in the substantial commercial demand in the late 1880s for a more forward and aggressive stance, there was sufficient political and economic flexibility for acceptable compromises to be achieved. Salisbury perceived the financial limitations, but in the 1880s still felt he had room to manoeuvre.

This was, however, far less true for him in the late 1890s, as the Sudan crisis seems to show. A little later, the outbreak of war in South Africa was only one among the obvious signs that pressure on British resources was mounting still further; but Salisbury stuck to his last. His retirement from the Foreign Office in October 1900 was followed rapidly by the abandonment of major planks in his diplomatic platform, and by attempts to fashion a new financial dispensation.[131] The importance of financial considerations was fast changing from that of background influence to that of inescapable determinant.

The material presented here is drawn from a limited range of sources. However, it suggests that, while Salisbury was responding to the broad problems arising from international developments, and to the political necessity created by wide public concern, he was unlikely to adopt solutions indiscriminately. Where possible, when they had substantial financial implications, he worked to secure those least damaging to the interests of the land. There is little evidence that he abandoned this outlook later in his career. Although much work in this field remains to be done, nevertheless there seems good reason to think that the connections between foreign policy and domestic finance in the late nineteenth century are closer and more varied than historians have often thought. These connections perhaps offer one way in which the gulf between the traditional diplomatic historiography and the newer contextualism can be bridged; they certainly show that the career of the third Marquis of Salisbury remains a fruitful subject for study.

NOTES

I am most grateful to members of the Imperial History Seminar at the Institute of Historical Research, University of London, and especially to Robert Holland and Bernard Porter, for their comments on an early draft of this essay.

References to the papers of the third Marquis of Salisbury held at Hatfield House are prefixed 'HHM/3M' (Hatfield House Muniments, third Marquis). Other abbreviations used are as follows: BL (British Library); PRO (Public Records Office).

1. Kenneth Bourne, *Palmerston: The Early Years 1784–1841* (London, 1982); Muriel Chamberlain, *Lord Aberdeen: A Political Biography* (London, 1983).
2. J. L. Duthie, 'Some Further Insights into the Working of Mid-Victorian Imperialism: Lord Salisbury and Anglo-Afghan Relations: 1874–1878', *Journal of Imperial and Commonwealth History*, VIII, no. 3 (May 1980) 181–208, and 'Pragmatic Diplomacy or Imperial Encroachment? British Policy towards Afghanistan, 1874–79', *International History Review*, V, no. 4 (Nov 1983) 475–95; Richard Milman, *Britain and the Eastern Question 1875–1878* (Oxford, 1979).
3. Foreign Secretary April 1878 to April 1880; Prime Minister and Foreign Secretary June 1885 to January 1886; Prime Minister August 1886, and Foreign Secretary January 1887, to June 1892; Prime Minister and Foreign Secretary June 1895 to October 1900, finally retiring from the premiership, July 1902.
4. L. M. Penson, *Foreign Affairs under the Third Marquess of Salisbury* (London, 1962); R. E. Robinson and J. Gallagher, *Africa and the Victorians: The Official Mind of Imperialism* (London, 1961); J. A. S.

Grenville, *Lord Salisbury and Foreign Policy: The Close of the Nineteenth Century* (London, 1964; rev. edn 1970); G. N. Sanderson, *England, Europe and the Upper Nile, 1882–1899* (Edinburgh, 1965); C. J. Lowe, *The Reluctant Imperialists: British Foreign Policy 1878–1902*, 2 vols (London, 1967). See also the bibliography in K. Bourne, *The Foreign Policy of Victorian England 1830–1902* (Oxford, 1970).

5. Robert Taylor, *Lord Salisbury* (London, 1975), Preface, dated September 1973.

6. P. T. Marsh, *The Discipline of Popular Government: Lord Salisbury's Domestic Statecraft, 1881–1902* (Hassocks, Sussex, 1978).

7. Robinson and Gallagher, *Africa and the Victorians*, p. 255.

8. Ibid., p. 256.

9. See also C. H. D. Howard, *Splendid Isolation: A Study of Ideas concerning Britain's International Position and Foreign Policy during the Later Years of the Third Marquess of Salisbury* (London, 1967).

10. Penson, *Foreign Affairs*, p. 12; Grenville, *Lord Salisbury and Foreign Policy*, p. 6.

11. Bourne, *Foreign Policy*, documents 102–8, 114–19, 124–5, 127–8, 131, 136, 141.

12. F. V. Parsons, in *English Historical Review*, 81 (1966) 205–6; G. N. Sanderson, in *Journal of African History*, 7 (1966) 350–4; B. Semmel, in *Political Science Quarterly*, LXXX (1965) 640–2; Z. Steiner, in *Historical Journal*, VII (1964) 340–4. Steiner followed her own prescription in two books, *The Foreign Office and Foreign Policy 1898–1914* (Cambridge, 1969) and *Britain and the Origins of the First World War* (London, 1977).

13. P. M. Kennedy, *The Rise and Fall of British Naval Mastery* (London, 1976; 2nd edn 1983), *The Rise of the Anglo-German Antagonism 1860–1914* (London, 1980), *The Realities behind Diplomacy: Background Influences on British External Policy, 1865–1980* (London, 1981) and, most recently, his collected essays, *Strategy and Diplomacy 1870–1945* (Fontana, 1984).

14. This took hold as Britain's decolonisation was completed, and relations with the European Economic Community failed to blossom. For recent examples, see Tony Smith, *The Pattern of Imperialism: The United States, Great Britain, and the Late-Industrializing World since 1815* (Cambridge, 1981); and Bernard Porter, *The Lion's Share: A Short History of British Imperialism 1850–1970* (London 1975; 2nd edn 1984). Cf. B. R. Tomlinson, 'The Contraction of England: National Decline and the Loss of Empire', *Journal of Imperial and Commonwealth History*, XI, no. 1 (Oct 1982).

15. Kennedy, *Realities*, p. 21.

16. Ibid., pp. 49, 50. For the development of a similar equation after 1918, see John Gallagher, *The Decline, Revival and Fall of the British Empire* (Cambridge, 1982).

17. P. M. Kennedy, 'The Tradition of Appeasement in British Foreign Policy, 1865–1939', *British Journal of International Studies*, 2, no. 3 (1976) 195–215, repr. in *Strategy and Diplomacy*, pp. 15–39; cf. P. Schroeder, 'Munich and the British Tradition', *Historical Journal*, 19 (1976) 223–43.

18. Kennedy, *Realities*, pp. 40–1, 70–1.

19. The phrase is Kennedy's; see, for example, *Anglo-German Antagonism*, p. 435.
20. Bernard Porter, *Britain, Europe and the World 1850–1982; Delusions of Grandeur* (London, 1983).
21. Ibid., Preface and pp. 13–14, 16, 31, 65.
22. Kennedy, *Realities*, p. 11; Porter, *Britain, Europe and the World*, p. xiv.
23. Kennedy, *Strategy and Diplomacy*, p. 23, and *Realities*, p. 94; Porter, *Britain, Europe and the World*, pp. 72, 74.
24. Porter, *Britain, Europe and the World*, pp. 69–70; cf. Kennedy, *Anglo-German Antagonism*, p. 77, and *Realities*, p. 43.
25. Porter, *Britain, Europe and the World*, p. 50; Kennedy, *Anglo-German Antagonism*, pp. 191–4, 198–202, 207, 212, 220.
26. Lady Gwendolen Cecil, *Life of Robert Marquis of Salisbury*, 4 vols (London, 1921–32) iv (1932), 160–6, 320–1, 352, and *Biographical Studies of the Life and Political Character of Robert Third Marquis of Salisbury* (London, 1949) pp. 56–7; Grenville, *Lord Salisbury and Foreign Policy*, p. 17; C. J. Lowe, *Salisbury and the Mediterranean 1886–1896* (London, 1965) pp. 96, 98, 103–4.
27. Kennedy, *Realities*, pp. 25–6; Porter, *Britain, Europe and the World*, pp. 65, 71.
28. Cf. Porter, *Britain, Europe and the World*, p. 16.
29. See Viscount Chilston, *W. H. Smith* (London, 1965) pp. 343–4; and, most recently, M. J. Gilbert, 'The Malda Incident: A Study in Imperial Diplomacy, Local Agency and Indian Nationalism', *Journal of Imperial and Commonwealth History*, xiii, no. 2 (Jan 1985), 117–38.
30. Lady Gwendolen Cecil, *Life*, ii (1921) 145; iv, 3.
31. On these themes, see F. A. Johnson, *Defence by Committee* (London, 1960); W. S. Hamer, *The British Army: Civil–Military Relations 1885–1905* (Oxford, 1970) ch. 2 and *passim*.
32. David French, *British Economic and Strategic Planning 1905–15* (London, 1982).
33. S. C. Buxton, *Finance and Politics: An Historical Study, 1783–1885*, 2 vols (London, 1888) p. ix.
34. Ibid., ii, ch. 25 and pp. 235, 269.
35. Lady Gwendolen Cecil, *Life*, iv, 3.
36. Sir Robert Giffen, 'A Financial Retrospect, 1861–1901', *Journal of the Royal Statistical Society*, lxv (1902) 47–85.
37. Speech at the Guildhall, *The Times*, 10 Nov 1888, p. 10d.
38. Cf. C. F. Bastable, *Public Finance*, 3rd edn (London, 1903) Preface, pp. vi–vii.
39. 'The Budget and the Reform Bill', *Quarterly Review*, Apr 1860, repr. in *Lord Salisbury on Politics: A Selection from his Articles in the Quarterly Review, 1860–1883*, ed. Paul Smith (Cambridge, 1972) p. 124.
40. 'The Income Tax and its Rivals', *Quarterly Review*, Jan 1861, pp. 231–4. His views on the House of Lords were developed in the same period, and showed a similar persistence: see C. C. Weston, 'Salisbury and the Lords, 1868–1895', *Historical Journal*, xxv (1982) 103–29.
41. 'The Income Tax and its Rivals', *Quarterly Review*, Jan 1861, pp. 246,

223–4, 230; also his speeches in the House of Commons, 6 May 1861 and 7 April 1862, 3 Hansard, CLXII, 1576–83, and CLXVI, 679–83.

42. See H. V. Emy, 'The Impact of Financial Policy on English Party Politics before 1914', *Historical Journal*, XV (1972) 103–31; N. Blewett, 'Free Fooders, Balfourites, Whole Hoggers. Factionalism within the Unionist Party, 1906–10', *Historical Journal*, XI (1968) 95–124.

43. Speeches: to the Manchester Chamber of Commerce, *The Times*, 18 Oct 1879, p. 10; at St James's Hall, *The Times*, 9 June 1894, p. 11; and in the House of Lords, 30 July and 14 Aug 1894, 4 Hansard, XXVII, 1222–9, and XXVIII, 967.

44. Speech at Norwich, *The Times*, 28 July 1887, p. 7c.

45. For these developments, represented as the triumph of Peelite and Gladstonian principles, see H. C. G. Matthew, 'Disraeli, Gladstone, and the Politics of Mid-Victorian Budgets', *Historical Journal*, XXII (1979) 615–43, esp. pp. 636–41.

46. Avner Offer, *Property and Politics 1870–1914* (Cambridge, 1981) esp. chs 13–14.

47. Speech at Liverpool, *The Times*, 12 Jan 1888, p. 7b–d. See also House of Lords, 12 Mar 1888, 3 Hansard, CCCXXIII, 831.

48. Speeches: as President of the West Hertfordshire Agricultural Society, *The Times*, 10 Dec 1879, p. 10d; and at Brighton, *The Times*, 20 Nov 1895, p. 7a.

49. Speech at Caernarvon, *The Times*, 11 Apr 1888, p. 12a–e.

50. Speech at Trowbridge, *The Times*, 4 May 1894, p. 5c. See also House of Lords, 23 May 1898, 4 Hansard, LVIII, 286.

51. Speeches: at Norwich, *The Times*, 29 July 1887, p. 8a; and at Liverpool, *The Times*, 12 Jan 1888, p. 7b–d. Cf. House of Lords, 31 Jan 1893 and 5 Feb 1895, 4 Hansard, VIII, 19–25 and XXX, 28.

52. See his attitude to the case of *Attorney General* vs *Beech*, a revenue case – to quote Counsel for the Crown, 'of great importance, striking at the root of estate duty on settled estates' – but one which the Crown lost, both in the Court of Appeal and in the House of Lords: HHM/3M/ Beach 1897–8, fo. 92, Salisbury to Sir M. Hicks Beach, May 1898. For details of the case, see *The Times*, 29 July 1897, p. 7b; 2 May 1898, p. 3d–f; 6 Dec 1898, p. 14a; 7 Dec 1898, p. 13b.

53. Speech at Glasgow, *The Times*, 21 May 1891, p. 10a.

54. Evening speech at Bristol, *The Times*, 24 Apr 1889, pp. 6–7.

55. Lunchtime speech at Bristol, ibid.

56. Hamilton Papers, BL Add. MS 48646, fo. 21, Sir Edward Hamilton, Diary, 14 Apr 1887.

57. Salisbury to Hicks Beach, 18 Oct 1899, as quoted in Taylor, *Lord Salisbury*, pp. 162–3.

58. See his speeches of 14 Feb 1895 (on Uganda), 4 *Hansard*, XXX, 698–702, and 30 Jan 1900, 4 *Hansard*, LXXVIII, 26–34. The latter is discussed in Henry Roseveare, *The Treasury: The Evolution of a British Institution* (London, 1969) pp. 183–6, and the quotation is at p. 184.

59. See the correspondence between Salisbury and Northcote for August 1878, in HHM and the Iddesleigh Papers, BL Add. MS 50019; Lady Gwendolen Cecil, *Life*, II, 313.

60. Lady Gwendolen Cecil, *Biographical Studies*, pp. 44–6.
61. Speech in House of Lords, 14 May 1888, 3 Hansard, cccxxvii, 106–7.
62. Lady Gwendolen Cecil, *Life*, iii (1931) ch. 8, and iv, chs 1–3.
63. For illuminating accounts, see Marsh, *Discipline of Popular Government*, chs 3 and 4; and R. F. Foster, *Lord Randolph Churchill* (Oxford, 1981) chs 9 and 10.
64. Foster, *Churchill*, pp. 284–9, 295–7; also Robert Rhodes James, *Lord Randolph Churchill* (London, 1959) pp. 270–4.
65. For the debates on armaments, see Hamer, *The British Army*, *passim*; for Churchill at the Treasury, Foster, *Churchill*, pp. 289–93; and, for his budget, ibid., pp. 300–6.
66. Cf. Salisbury to Hicks Beach, 21 Dec 1886 cited in James, *Churchill*, pp. 290–1.
67. HHM/3M/D/15/Churchill, fo. 246, Salisbury to Churchill, 19 Dec 1886.
68. James, *Churchill*, ch. 10; Marsh, *Discipline of Popular Government*, pp. 96–102; Foster, *Churchill*, ch. 10.
69. James, *Churchill*, p. 309; cf. Foster, *Churchill*, p. 317.
70. Marsh, *Discipline of Popular Government*, p. 102.
71. Churchill to Salisbury 20 Dec 1886, cited in Foster, *Churchill*, p. 306, and James, *Churchill*, p. 287.
72. HHM/3M/D/15/Churchill, fo. 252, Churchill to Salisbury, 22 Dec 1886.
73. Even Hicks Beach, for example, was alarmed by Churchill's 'allusion to foreign policy', and felt his action involved more than 'a mere question of estimates' (cited in James, *Churchill*, p. 291); cf. the disputes over the reform of local government, where Churchill, according to Salisbury, 'would produce "all the obstacles his official position enables him to offer" ' (Foster, *Churchill*, p. 283).
74. Foster (ibid., p. 308) is inclined to see in Salisbury's emphasis on defence a political tactic, rather than evidence of real concern; it is more likely to have been both.
75. Marsh, *Discipline of Popular Government*, p. 117. See also Lady Gwendolen Cecil, *Life*, iv, 171–2.
76. Offer, *Property and Politics*, pp. 201–2 and ch. 13 ('Mr Goschen's Finance 1887–1892'); Hamilton Papers, BL Add. MS 48650, fos 48–9, Diary, 7 Feb 1889. For Goschen's background, see T. J. Spinner, *George Joachim Goschen: The Transformation of a Victorian Liberal* (Cambridge, 1973), and, for these years, ch. 9.
77. See, for example, Goschen to W. H. Smith 31 Mar 1891, cited in Chilston, *W. H. Smith*, pp. 343–4; Hamilton Papers, BL Add. MS 48651, fos 66–7, Diary, 5 Aug 1889, and *passim*.
78. Ibid., fos 35–6, Diary, 7 July 1889.
79. Speech at Glasgow, *The Times*, 21 May 1891, p. 10b.
80. For a study throwing light on Treasury–Foreign Office relations in the matter of shipping subsidies, see A. N. Porter, *Victorian Shipping, Business and Imperial Policy: Donald Currie, the Castle Line and Southern Africa* (R. H. S.: Woodbridge and New York, 1986). The quotation is from HHM/3M/D/IX/Holland, fo. 98, Salisbury to Holland, 26 Nov 1890, regarding a proposal to subsidise a Pacific line of steamers.
81. See J. S. Galbraith, *Mackinnon and East Africa 1878–1895* (Cambridge,

1972) pp. 200–7, 214–16. For an example of Salisbury's attempts to bring open public pressure to his aid, see his remarks on the railway and the Treasury in a speech at Glasgow, *The Times*, 21 May 1891, p. 10c.

82. PRO T1/8388B/20783/9449, Foreign Office to Treasury, 4 June 1888; cf. T1/9092A/17002/1896, minute by Ryder on 1557.

83. Lady Gwendolen Cecil, *Life*, IV, 172–7, where other examples are given. Eventually the complaints of Cabinet colleagues moved Goschen to anger with his own officials: see Hamilton Papers, BL Add. MS 48651, fo. 83, Diary, 23 Aug 1889.

84. See, for example, HHM/3M/Goschen 1891–4, fo. 23, Goschen to Salisbury, 15 Feb 1891. Treasury papers at the PRO contain a wealth of material on Egyptian finances, and would be well worth serious study.

85. For background and details, see Kennedy, *British Naval Mastery*, ch. 7 and pp. 178–9; also A. J. Marder, *The Anatomy of British Sea Power* (New York, 1940; repr. 1976) ch. 8.

86. See his responses to Lord Wolseley, 14 May and 29 June 1888, 3 Hansard, CCCXXVI, 106–7, and CCCXXVII, 1704–6; speech at Brighton, *The Times*, 20 Nov 1895, p. 7a.

87. Lady Gwendolen Cecil, *Life*, IV, 183–93.

88. Speeches at the Guildhall and at Bristol, *The Times*, 10 Nov 1888, p. 10d, and 24 Apr 1889, pp. 6–7; speech in the Lords moving the second reading of the Naval Defence Bill, 27 May 1889, 3 Hansard, CCCXXXVI, 1059–69; for Salisbury's contributions to Cabinet debates, see especially his memoranda during 1887–8, PRO CAB37/19/7, 37/21/14, 18, 37/22/32, 36, 37.

89. Hamilton Papers, BL Add. MS 48650, fos 24, 26, Diary, 11 Jan and 3 Feb 1889.

90. Salisbury in the House of Lords, 16 May 1893, 4 Hansard XII, 1035.

91. HHM/3M/D/VI/Goschen, fos 89–90, Salisbury to Goschen, 26 Jan 1889.

92. Salisbury to Goschen, 3 Mar 1889, cited in Lady Gwendolen Cecil, *Life*, IV, 191–2.

93. Hamilton Papers, BL Add. MS 48649, fo. 127, Diary, 29 Nov 1888.

94. Ibid., Add. MS 48650, fo. 6, Diary, 14 Dec 1888.

95. For the initial decision, see Salisbury to the Queen 11 Dec 1888, in *The Letters of Queen Victoria*, 3rd ser. ed. G. E. Buckle, 3 vols (London, 1930–2) I, 456.

96. It is important not to be misled by the importance contemporaries attached to balancing the annual budget into thinking that Victorian governments' financial planning was incurably short-sighted. Tasks such as Goschen's conversion of the National Debt in 1888 involved a continuing series of financial operations running on into 1890, and the timing of budgetary initiatives, such as police superannuation or Salisbury's 'assisted education', involved planning far in advance.

97. Salisbury had considered how to make Hamilton's January scheme more appealing, concluding a letter to Goschen, 'Without some such taking [telling?] programme I fear that G. H.'s proposals may seem unsatisfactory, and you would get lukewarm support for any new taxation' (HHM/3M/D/VI/Goschen, fos 85–6, 26 Jan 1889).

98. For one set of calculations, see HHM/3M/D/VI/Goschen, fo. 92, Salisbury to Goschen, 3 Mar 1889.
99. Speech at the Mansion House, *The Times*, 9 Aug 1888, p. 6b–c.
100. BL Add. MS, Hamilton Papers, 48650, fos 61–2, Diary, 24 Feb 1889.
101. See Salisbury's speech in the House of Lords, 27 May 1889, 3 Hansard, cccxxxvi, 1059–60.
102. HHM/3M/D/VI/Goschen, fo. 78, Salisbury to Goschen, 16 Nov 1888.
103. Ibid., fo. 96, Salisbury to Goschen, 24 Apr 1889.
104. See his public speeches, to the London Chamber of Commerce, and at Bristol, *The Times*, 28 Feb 1889, p. 10a–b, and 24 Apr 1889, p. 6a–f. For the arguments, see esp. HHM/3M/D/VI/Goschen, fo. 92, Salisbury to Goschen, 3 Mar 1889: part cited in Lady Gwendolen Cecil, *Life*, IV, 191–2. The Cabinet refused a levy on ground-rent landlords (Hamilton Papers, BL Add. MS 48650, fos 95, 99, Diary, 11 and 13 Apr 1889). For Goschen's defence of additional indirect taxation as essential, see Spinner, *Goschen*, pp. 141–2.
105. See Liberal criticisms in the second-reading debate, 6–7 May 1889, 3 Hansard, cccxxxv, 1329–37, 1374, 1377 (quotation from H. H. Fowler, col. 1329). Government speakers were Ashmead Bartlett and Lord George Hamilton (cols 1324–5, 1407–8). Edward Hamilton had anticipated considerable opposition on these grounds: see Hamilton Papers, BL Add. MS 48650, fos 68–9, 72, Diary, 5 Feb [error for Mar] and 9 Mar 1889.
106. Speech in Lords, 27 May 1889, 3 Hansard, cccxxxvi, 1065.
107. Hamilton Papers, BL Add. MS 48650, Diary, fos 110–12, 16 Apr 1889.
108. T. H. Farrer, 'The Imperial Finance of the last Four Years', *Contemporary Review*, 58 (Oct 1890) 481–500, esp. pp. 494–7.
109. Colin Matthew, reviewing Marsh, *Discipline of Popular Government*, in *Victorian Studies*, 23 (1979–80) 523.
110. Ibid.
111. Ibid.
112. *The Times*, 11 Apr 1888, p. 12a–e.
113. Most recently, Marsh, *Discipline of Popular Government*, pp. 243–5.
114. Offer, *Property and Politics*, ch. 14 ('Doles for Squire and Parson 1895–1902').
115. See esp. HHM/3M/Beach 1897–8, fos 47–8, Beach to Salisbury, 1 Nov 1897.
116. HHM/3M/A/55/5, Salisbury to Baring, 11 Feb 1887; also ibid., A/55/37, Salisbury to Baring, 28 Dec 1888.
117. Hamilton Papers, BL Add. MS 48645, fo. 107, Diary, 13 Feb 1887.
118. The best accounts are Robinson and Gallagher, *Africa and the Victorians*, ch. 12; Grenville, *Lord Salisbury and Foreign Policy*, chs 5 and 10; Sanderson, *England, Europe and the Upper Nile*, ch. 11. But cf. Keith M. Wilson, 'Constantinople or Cairo: Lord Salisbury and the Partition of the Ottoman Empire, 1886–1897', in Keith M. Wilson (ed.), *Imperialism and Nationalism in the Middle East: The Anglo-Egyptian Experience 1882–1982* (London, 1983) pp. 26–55.
119. Robinson and Gallagher, *Africa and the Victorians*, pp. 350–1.
120. HHM/3M/Beach, fo. 220 *et seq.*, Beach to Salisbury, 20 and 30 Mar 1896;

also fo. 264, 23 Oct 1896, and following to December. Grenville, *Lord Salisbury and Foreign Policy*, pp. 116–19; Sanderson, *England, Europe and the Upper Nile*, pp. 242–4.

121. HHM/3M/A/113/48, Salisbury to Cromer, 7 May 1897.
122. PRO T1/9154B/8699*, draft letter to Foreign Office, approved by Hicks Beach, 2 June 1897.
123. PRO T1/9244B/5395, Treasury to Foreign Office, 21 Jan 1898, and Foreign Office reply, 27 Jan.
124. Sanderson, *England, Europe and the Upper Nile*, pp. 266, n. 3, and 398.
125. Salisbury had plans to sell the railway built during the advance into the Sudan to private entrepreneurs, and enlisted Rothschild's aid: HHM/3M/A/113/59, 60–3, Salisbury to Cromer, 30 Nov 1897 *et seq.*
126. See, for example, Balfour Papers, BL Add. MS 49689, fo. 58, A. J. Balfour to Salisbury, 28 Jan 1889; PRO CAB/37/40/64, minutes by Balfour and Salisbury, Aug–Oct 1895.
127. Emy, in *Historical Journal*, xv, 115.
128. Farrer, in *Contemporary Review*, 58, pp. 494–7.
129. For figures giving the changing proportion of direct to indirect taxation, see Matthew, in *Historical Journal*, xxii, 638.
130. See above, p. 151.
131. In addition to Emy and Blewett (see above n. 42), see Alan Sykes, *Tariff Reform in British Politics 1903–1913* (Oxford, 1979); Bruce K. Murray, *The People's Budget 1909/10: Lloyd George and Liberal Politics* (Oxford, 1980); G. R. Monger, *The End of Isolation: British Foreign Policy 1900–1907* (London, 1963); S. Mahajan, 'The Defence of India and the End of Isolation. A Study in the Foreign Policy of the Conservative Government, 1900–1905', *Journal of Imperial and Commonwealth History*, x, no. 2 (Jan. 1982) 168–93.

8
Salisbury and the Church

E. D. STEELE

I

Salisbury's religious policy as Prime Minister was his highest priority; something not lost upon so secular-minded a historian as A. J. P. Taylor.[1] Salisbury had always been much less confident than Gladstone of the endurance and responsibility of the landed class to which they both belonged. The Tory built his policies around the view that the supremacy of a mass electorate – a recognised fact after 1867 – was only consistent with rational freedom and betterment while the influence of religion remained strong enough to contain and alleviate the tensions of an industrial and urban society. '. . . we are surrounded, crowded, embarrassed by . . . social questions . . . the sole hope of solving these great . . . problems is by the action of religion', he said in one of his regular speeches outside Parliament devoted to expounding the revised political philosophy of his later years.[2] His insight into the feared potential of socialism led him to emphasise that its spread would be as much a response to moral as to physical deprivation. It was imperative to treat the working class as 'Christian and reasonable beings'.[3] For their active participation in the political process was indispensable to 'prevent our democracy from sinking into a mechanical, wire-pulled democracy'. They must be educated for this role, he insisted, in order to defeat 'that fatal enemy of . . . progress – the professional politician', by which he meant the type of contemporary Liberal who played with fire in seeking short-term party gains.[4] Salisbury's decisive adoption of free elementary schooling, enacted in 1891, was inspired by the reflection that, 'in proportion as education has gone on, the Conservative cause has progressed in the greater urban centres of the country'.[5] In his traditional and forcefully enunciated view, there was 'no agency . . . so efficient . . . for this education . . . as the Church of Christ'.[6] The dogmatic teaching of institutional

185

Christianity, Anglican, Catholic and Wesleyan, in its schools provided a surer basis for class collaboration than 'the patent compressible religion'[7] of the Board Schools, which he thought must result in 'universal unbelief' with dire social consequences that did not need to be spelt out.[8]

Yet he was acutely conscious that the most serious threat to religion in his day came from within the Established Church. On its continuing strength the future of a Christian and conservative, not necessarily Tory, England depended. Writing to Disraeli and others in 1874, when ritualism was the target of impending legislation, and again in quieter times many years later to his kinsman Edward Talbot, then Vicar of Leeds, he referred to the same 'menacing if not imminent' fear of 'civil war' in the national church.[9] The mutual intolerance of High Churchmen and Evangelicals appalled him, with the intervention of Broad Churchmen like Archbishop Tait making matters worse. To this strife he ascribed a perceptible decline in the spiritual and intellectual quality of the Anglican clergy, 'due very much to the heated controversies which . . . have disgusted and alarmed sensitive and conscientious men'[10] Not long after this letter he astounded Archbishop Benson by throwing out the suggestion that 'Popery is going to prevail in another generation.'[11] It was not a possibility to which Salisbury looked forward with anything but foreboding and pain. He had a certain regard for English Catholics, and for Pope Leo XIII: but much of Catholic doctrine was abhorrent to him. To the highly politicised Catholicism of Ireland he was implacably opposed. If the disintegration of the Church of England benefited Catholicism, it would also stimulate a destructive hostility to religion familiar on the Continent but historically weak on this side of the Channel. His country's common Protestantism, for all the divisions inside the Church and between Church and Dissent, was a source of unity and pride. Salisbury expressed his own feeling as well as that of most of his compatriots when he declared without qualification in 1892, 'England is the Protestant nation of the world'.[12]

Salisbury himself was a High Churchman, whose experience of Tractarianism as an Oxford undergraduate shaped his religious life.[13] He was reluctantly obliged to take a leading part in defending his wing of the Church until he neared the premiership. At the centre of his faith lay a Catholic, but not Roman, understanding of the Eucharist, about which his daughter and biographer wrote movingly.[14] He was, however, impatient of ritual, even of that

introduced to give the Anglican Communion service a distinctively
Catholic interpretation. Ritualism, so called, was the supposedly
excessive, and sometimes illicit, introduction or revival of
ceremonial in Anglican worship under Tractarian influence. He told
a close friend, Lady John Manners, how much he disliked the
repeated sound of bells in the communion service: 'I detest those
three bells. They seem to say "Fight, Fight, Fight." They are simply
there to show that the ringer of them snaps his fingers at the
ultra-Protestants.'[15] He let it be known that he did not subscribe to
the *Guardian*, the High Church weekly; and he contributed to a fund
in aid of the proscribed ritualist, the Reverend H. A. Mackonochie
'*on the condition* that my name is suppressed. . . . I don't wish to see
Mackonochie crushed: but I disapprove of his follies far too strongly
to . . . appear publicly as his supporter.'[16] The practice of confession
by the extreme High Church elicited an uncompromisingly
Protestant, and English, reaction from him in the House of Lords.
Confession was not only 'unfavourable to Christian truth in its
results', but had been shown in other countries to be 'injurious to
the moral independence and virility of the nation to an extent to
which probably it had been given to no other institution to affect the
character of mankind'.[17] He spoke for the great majority of High
Churchmen, whose rediscovery of the Anglican Church's Catholic
heritage went with an appreciation of what one of their influential
figures called 'a healthy Teutonism'.[18] As the High Churchmen's
favourite politician, he tried to protect them from themselves, and
not merely from their enemies.

When he became Prime Minister, his recognised impartiality
between the rival factions in the Church enhanced his authority.
The Evangelicals complained that his allocation of ecclesiastical
patronage to them was not commensurate with their importance;
but they did so respectfully, even apologetically. From Churchmen
of every shade, there was more criticism of his care not to provoke
militant Dissent nor to irritate public opinion, which, although
averse to disestablishment, did not like governments that made too
much of the Church. The Tories were increasingly sensitive to the
suggestion that they favoured the Church at the expense of other
interests. Salisbury remarked to Lady John Manners in 1891 after a
difficult Cabinet on points affecting the maintenance of
denominational schools, 'I again acquired the sad conviction that
the Church is very weak with the present Conservative party.'[19] He
did his best for the Establishment in this political climate. His best

was often misunderstood, and particularly by E. W. Benson, who occupied the see of Canterbury during the greater part of Salisbury's tenure of power. 'I do not believe', wrote Benson in his diary for 1887, 'that S[alisbury] cares for anything but repartee. His friendship to the Church is purely selfish and political. . . .'[20] The truth was more complex than the Archbishop allowed himself to think on that and other occasions. Like many devout Christians, Salisbury distinguished sharply between the reverence owed to bishops or priests as such, and the freedom permitted to them. Benson was bitterly resentful of Salisbury's partial failure to consult him about episcopal appointments and legislation for the Church. No primate had been so treated, he claimed in respect of bishop-making, since the beginning of the eighteenth century.[21] Salisbury had little confidence in the Archbishop's judgement, or in that of the bishops collectively. They had not known how to deal with a 'deeply divided' Church, nor to prevent the emergence among the laity of a widespread preference for 'the elimination of all doctrine upon which anybody disagrees with anybody else'.[22]

II

Before he succeeded to the title and when Palmerston was Prime Minister, Salisbury had, as Lord Robert Cecil MP, strongly criticised that Liberal statesman's policy of judicious concession to isolate militant Dissent. Cecil took the Liberation Society in those years more seriously than did such of its friends in the Commons as Edward Baines, member for Leeds, and Sir John Trelawny, the Anglican baronet who sponsored a succession of its Church Rates Bills.[23] The young Tory persisted in seeing the thin end of the wedge in common-sense adjustments to the position of the Establishment. He did not, then, seem to grasp the implications of a point made by Trelawny in 1863; 'a large section of the Dissenting classes were highly favourable to the Church . . . and . . . they should be taken into account'.[24] On the other hand, Cecil was unimpressed by Disraeli's exploitation in the early 1860s of the ancient Tory cry of 'the Church in danger', to counter Palmerston's successful religious policy. Cecil dismissed this Disraelian initiative as 'a senseless affectation of Saxonism' on the part of an agnostic of Jewish origin: it was needlessly offensive to the Evangelicals, who approved and encouraged the Palmerstonian cultivation of Dissent.[25] After his breach with Disraeli over Parliamentary reform in 1867, his brief estrangement from a party that accepted 'A Jew adventurer'[26] as its leader in the following year, was ended by the demands of the threatened Anglican Church in Ireland on his conscience: 'If you support the Church, you must come forward and fight in the light, and not shelter yourselves behind ambiguous phrases and dilatory pleas', he said in March 1868,[27] anticipating his well-supported stand in the Lords on the Irish Church Bill when Disraeli gave place to Gladstone. It was a fight that Salisbury, as he had become, lost; but it taught him to apply in religious as in political questions a lesson which he had hitherto been inclined to treat as an uncongenial abstraction: 'Compromise is the very essence of English politics. . . .'[28]

On his reconciliation with Disraeli in 1874 he elicited assurances that his leader would withstand the temptation to discriminate against the High Church. At issue were both patronage and legislation, but more especially the latter, aimed at the ritualists in the atmosphere generated by their excesses. Salisbury's adherence to the Government turned on the second point. While he considered the ritualists 'idiots',[29] he understood why the High Church rallied to them in the face of a measure, the Public Worship Regulation Bill, designed to curb a small minority but capable of being construed more widely. Disraeli very quickly departed from the spirit, if not the letter, of the undertaking neither to introduce nor to support any such measure. The unpopularity of High Church clergy generally, and not only of ritualists, with many congregations was, for Salisbury and others, a conclusive objection to Archbishop Tait's opening proposals. These envisaged mixed clerical and lay panels of assessors, with laymen elected by diocesan churchwardens; their verdict on an incumbent who was the subject of complaint could, at episcopal discretion, result in the sequestration of his benefice.[30] On the formation of the ministry, Salisbury had warned Disraeli not to underestimate ritualism as a force; it was 'numerous enough if it goes against the Establishment to turn the scale . . . earnest to fanaticism . . . and if driven by any act of serious aggression will . . . bring the whole fabric of the Church down about our ears'.[31] He plainly exaggerated its numbers more than a little to make Disraeli hesitate. Its real strength lay, first, in the consciousness of more moderate High Churchmen that they, too, were vulnerable to the possible proscription of all recent changes in worship expressive of the doctrinal shift brought about by the Oxford Movement.

Secondly, even as introduced and as passed, the Bill appeared to subvert 'the moral and spiritual as well as the temporal status of the clergy'.[32] in the words of Salisbury's old Oxonian acquaintance, the historian, and later bishop, Stubbs. This apprehension was exactly what Salisbury predicted. It was eventually quietened when the essential limitations of the Act were realised. They were two; and Salisbury had worked to secure them: the appointment of an 'independent lay judge' to try ritual cases and an episcopal veto on the commencement of proceedings under the legislation.[33] As Salisbury hoped and expected all along, the working of the Act did little to clarify the legal situation. He told the Lords that, should Parliament seek to alter the balance of forces in the Church, 'you will . . . imperil the interests of the state itself'.[34]

For the 'desperate opposition' of the High Church he laid part of the blame on Archbishop Tait's 'vehement speeches' while the Bill was before the Upper House.[35] The emotional temperature went higher when Disraeli made his subsequent, opportunistic attack on ritualism in the Commons, alluding sarcastically to Salisbury's efforts to minimise the significance of the Bill.[36] 'Ritualist absurdities', Salisbury explained to his friend and appointee Robert Milman, the High Church Bishop of Calcutta, ruled out the erection by statute of new Indian bishoprics, to which he had intended to proceed as the responsible minister. Any extension of the Church's jurisdiction was temporarily suspect to a British public obsessed with the peril of crypto-Catholicism in the Establishment. 'My impression', Salisbury informed Milman, 'is that at this moment a bill for increasing the number of Bengal tigers would be received more patiently than a proposal to increase the number of bishops.'[37] The impact of the crisis may be judged by the division that arose between Gladstone and his party. He had gone to the aid of the High Church with fewer reservations than Salisbury, which was consistent with his religious outlook.[38] One member of his recent Cabinet, Lord Kimberley, anticipated that religious controversy would break up both political parties; and another, Lord Halifax, thought Gladstone's retirement from the Liberal leadership next year was explicable by the isolation in which his resistance to the anti-ritualist legislation had left him.[39] It required his later crusade against Ottoman misrule in the Balkans to win back the esteem of good Protestants.[40] Far less compromised by the events of 1874, Salisbury was able to demonstrate his moderation in ecclesiastical politics convincingly: the episcopal appointments he filled in India were a convenient means to that end.

The Anglican Establishment in the sub-continent existed primarily for the pastoral care of the British civilian and military population. The Crown – that is, the Secretary of State for India – nominated to bishoprics and chaplaincies; and Church factions in England watched the apportionment of patronage carefully.[41] For the see of Bombay Salisbury selected a High Churchman, with some misgivings because he was 'very stiff'. 'I hope he will be thawed into elasticity by the sun', he remarked to Milman.[42] The High Church at home, in the shape of a friend, Canon Liddon, who was one of its most influential personalities, thanked him warmly for this sign of confidence in an embattled body of the faithful.[43] In this decade he chose the saintly Thomas Valpy French and another Evangelical for Lahore and Rangoon. To Calcutta, the metropolitan see, he sent a moderate in succession to Milman.[44] The considerations that governed his choice of men for ecclesiastical promotion were tried out in the course of his two spells at the India Office. The longer of the two terms, from 1874 to 1878, and the coincidence of its start with the outbreak of religious warfare over the Public Worship Regulation Bill, formed his mind. Looking back on his experience of making bishops for India shortly before he arrived at the premiership, he wrote, 'I am still of opinion that while no school within the Church should have a monopoly of preferment, none . . . should be shut out from it.'[45] The political effects of factionalism inside the Church never ceased to worry him. Besides the larger question of the Establishment's survival in this country, there were the consequences for Toryism should its adherents let their High or Low sympathies run unchecked. 'If Conservatives cannot co-operate without interfering with each other upon these subjects,' the same letter continues, 'they had better not attempt to get together as a party at all.' The much more religiously divided Liberals, he pointed out, managed to combine in a way that the Tories should emulate.[46]

He wanted the Tory party to be comprehensive in its Anglicanism and after 1886 he was scrupulous not to offend the Nonconformist element in Liberal Unionism. His rise in Disraeli's Cabinet enabled him to defend the High Church more effectively at the same time as he endeavoured to restrain it. 'I will do what I can to keep High Church agitation quiet', replied Liddon on one occasion; 'but I am

not their commanding officer, and I should be sorry to answer for
their prudence.'[47] While the Canon's caution was justifiable, he
used his prestige to calm those who looked up to him. Turning to
Liddon's opponents, Salisbury responded to an approach from Tait
by urging the Archbishop not to persist with his active hostility to
ritualism; and he emphasised the unwisdom of invoking Parliament
again. Salisbury's advice was to respect settled congregational, not
clerical preferences, and to sanction them 'very clearly'. 'Ritualism is
too strong to be "put down": a serious attempt to do so would
simply shatter the Church', he argued. 'On the other hand, it is
odious to the majority of Churchmen. . . . If a fatal collision is to be
avoided, the only thing to be done is to get them into different
buildings.' The bishops should concert action on that basis; nothing
else 'would terminate or allay the strife which now exists'.[48] In fact,
the Church of England had already moved far in the suggested
direction. As for Disraeli, Salisbury found him comparatively easy
to deal with in ecclesiastical matters; by mutual consent their
disagreement over the legislation of 1874 was forgotten.[49] Despite
what he had said to gratify them, Disraeli had no stomach for
'Evangelical trash', as he echoed Queen Victoria in calling Low
Churchmen.[50] No fonder of the High Church, he ideally sought 'a
good sensible Churchman: not Low, but no nonsense', without
being very sure of his own meaning.[51] Salisbury had to remind him
not to forget the importance of the 'Right Centre', as he tactfully
designated the High Church.[52]

Disraeli's personal indifference to religion disposed him to give
way, or leave well alone, when standing up for the Church and her
concerns rendered the Government vulnerable in Parliament to
accusations of undue bias. Salisbury was furiously indignant with
him for dropping two clauses, intended to strengthen the Anglican
hold on grammar schools, from the Bill of 1874 which modified the
Liberals' Endowed Schools Act passed five years earlier.[53] Later, he
conceded that to have insisted on the clauses would have lent
credence to the idea, put about by the opposition, of 'a raid upon the
Dissenters'.[54] As he explained to Bishop Milman, the declared
enemies of the Church in the Commons were too few to impress on
a motion openly hostile to her, but not too few, when roused, to
thwart a ministerial Bill by employing the weapon of parliamentary
time, then a more formidable one than it is now.[55] Salisbury did,
however, have the satisfaction of keeping Disraeli, in an unanimous
Cabinet, to acceptance of a contentious amendment to the 1876

Education Bill. It was proposed to let ratepayers dissolve School Boards set up under the Act of 1870, where it could be shown that denominational schools met local needs. 'This is no "sacerdotal" movement', Salisbury told the Prime Minister. Ranged behind the amendment, which was not a substantial change but a demonstration, were the country gentlemen and clergy who resented the as yet limited intrusion of the Boards into their rural world. The clergy of every tendency, and their partisans on the Tory backbenches, would exact political vengeance were they to be disappointed over the amendment: 'Ecclesiastically-minded persons are proverbially unforgiving', he observed drily.[56] He did not hesitate to suggest that Disraeli merely wanted to appease the Liberal opposition. Such candour is evidence, not of revived antagonism between the two men, but of their 'very close' relations.[57]

A more significant success in the same year, 1876, was the initiation of further university reform under the aegis of the Tories: Salisbury had from the start of the ministry wished to pre-empt the Liberals from acting on their return to office in due course.[58] Anxious to improve the academic quality of Oxford and Cambridge, he wanted above all to preserve their Anglican character in the inevitable process of modernisation. He appreciated the difficulty of legislating for the ancient universities with these goals, which to others seemed conflicting. In an early sketch of what became his Bill, it was 'to provide sufficient security for religious trusts without mentioning the Church of England'; not that the Church could ever have been kept out of the debate on his proposals. It was a question of avoiding provocation. The instrument of change should be a statutory commission on the model of that in the Oxford University Act of the 1850s, and its carefully chosen membership 'sufficiently Conservative to be trusted with full powers', with a view to minimising parliamentary interference.[59] Salisbury brought forward the Bill; when it began to run out of time, he protested to Disraeli that the damage inflicted on the universities by its loss, if final, would be 'incalculable'.[60] Failure must exhibit their vulnerability to religious and secular critics and the Government's lukewarmness in their cause. Essentially the same Bill, enlarged to provide similarly for the sister university, went through next session. As the Chancellor, 'pledged . . . so deeply in this matter',[61] Salisbury's knowledge of Oxford enabled him to exploit an underlying alarm which he discerned there, and in Cambridge. The dons, Conservatives and Liberals, were more than willing to be sympathetically reformed by a Tory ministry if the alternative was to see a sizeable portion of their endowments appropriated for new seats of higher education in the North of England.[62]

Salisbury's solicitude for the Church and the two universities intimately linked with the Establishment did not conceal from him the disadvantages to religion and learning of comfortable incomes and lives to match. He wanted working fellows of colleges to be the rule; and said in Parliament, trenchantly, that collegiate funds should be diverted from the support of academic drones to the development of the physical sciences, in which he believed with a keenness reinforced by his amateur researches.[63] An opulent standard of living in a bishop he considered to be 'nowadays a direct detraction from his influence . . . by the apparent worldliness and waste'. Wealthy dioceses ought to help with the foundation of new ones. Archbishop Benson thought quite differently on the subject of 'the benefit of display' by the episcopate.[64] He reacted angrily to the proposed division of his see and sale of his country palace at Addington to raise money for the project. 'I, of course . . . am to be largely mulcted', he noted, criticising in the privacy of his diary the stupidity, and worse, of the prominent laymen and Tories concerned in the discussions: 'These blind men do not know . . . they are only guiding on the democracy to the House of Lords and [the] revenues of their own order.'[65] Whether ecclesiastical riches or scientific progress were in question, Salisbury had a vision of the Church nearer to reality than Benson's or that of the university reactionaries whom he displeased. An informed interest in science made Salisbury more, not less, hostile to those who used it to discredit Christianity: 'I think that even the indifferent part of the world is getting tired of the impudent pretensions of the Atheists', he commented to a regular scientific correspondent in 1883.[66]

But his finely tuned realism came between him and Benson from the outset of the latter's reign at Canterbury in 1882. When the Bill to legalise marriage with a deceased wife's sister, so often defeated in the Lords, seemed about to pass soon after Benson's elevation, Salisbury answered an appeal from the Archibishop with an analysis of his position; what he told Benson had a wider relevance. The Bill's repugnance to the institutional Church led Liberals to suppose that they were striving to get rid of a prohibition dictated by 'priestcraft'.[67] Then there was the social pressure exerted by the Prince of Wales and his brothers; Gladstone's private secretary commented that the reform they desired was 'a German idea'.[68] Finally, quite one third of the Tory peers had voted to give the Bill a majority in June 1883, subsequently reversed on the third reading. 'Party ties in a case of this kind have no power, Salisbury advised the Archbishop.[69] An authoritarian prelate, Benson constantly forgot the absolute requirement for delicacy and persuasion in handling religious issues. It was in spite of him and like-minded ecclesiastics that Salisbury contrived to put off this disputed revision of marriage law for so many years.[70] In other respects, he patiently obtained rather more, on the whole, than the minimum necessary for the Establishment to hold its ground. To do as much, he needed to pick men who would not impede the work.

III

As Prime Minister, Salisbury apportioned his patronage in the Church on a pattern similar to that of the Indian appointments he had made. His High Churchmanship, like Gladstone's, exposed him to hints of partiality from within the Cabinet, and charges from other quarters. In fact, he was less inclined than Gladstone to prefer High Churchmen. A reply from his private secretary to a member of the public towards the close of the ministry of 1886–92 listed recent selections to refute these complaints: Salisbury considered that Daniel Lloyd, Bishop of Bangor, and Mandell Creighton of Peterborough were definitely Broad Churchmen, Walsham How of Wakefield and W. C. Magee, Archbishop of York, Evangelicals, and Westcott of Durham more Evangelical than Broad.[71] The wording of the letter indicated the problem that faced Salisbury of identifying the ecclesiastical colour of individuals with precision. It was admittedly harder than it had been in his youth to draw a line between the Low and the Broad; but Salisbury's policy compounded the difficulty. He emphasised to Sir Michael Hicks Beach, the Cabinet minister most disposed to raise the claims of Evangelicals with him, that his choice normally fell on 'moderate men – neither ritualist nor ultra-Protestant: because I am convinced that the mass of English Churchmen are moderate men'. There was no absolute proscription of extremes: during the lifetime of that second government 'one Ritualist' had received a deanery and so, to balance him, had 'a very extreme Low Churchman'. Salisbury defended his preferment, lately, of a High Churchman to the see of

Chester by pointing to the recipient of Sodor and Man, an Evangelical who was more obviously a partisan.[72]

The two bishoprics were not comparable in prestige and size. Salisbury would not have given Chester to a pronounced Evangelical. The mention of one, enjoying a militant reputation, for the deanery of Bristol prompted him to declare: 'I look upon such men as curses to the Church'; but it was the man's pugnacity, rather than the character of his Evangelicalism, to which he objected. Hicks Beach agreed. Since the vacancy at Bristol had arisen on the death of a long-serving Whig dean unsympathetic to the High Church, Salisbury thought his successor should tend to be Low, while being, of course, 'a thoroughly moderate man'; to follow Dean Elliot with a High Churchman would be 'in the nature of a Russian bath'.[73] If the emphasis on moderation preserved the Church from more acute dissensions, it did not have an altogether healthy effect. Archbishop Benson had some reason for the frustration which caused him to lament that bishops were being 'reduced to the level of diocesan inspectorship'.[74] Salisbury returned to and developed a trend from which Gladstone had departed; his predecessor had picked, among others, the aggressively Evangelical J. C. Ryle as the first Bishop of Liverpool, and the advanced High Churchman, Edward King, for Lincoln. Neither Ryle nor King was an encouraging precedent: Liddon, who declined preferment for himself from Gladstone and Salisbury, remembered under the Tory 'the bitter and despairing feelings' of the High Church on Ryle's appointment.[75] King was prosecuted for ritualism by Benson in 1889–90, with a degree of success, in a theatrical exercise of his metropolitical authority which suggested a desire on the part of that otherwise less than High Church prelate to erect 'a Canterbury Papacy'.[76] It was safer for Salisbury to avoid stirring up the Church. At the same time he tried to prevent her from falling into the hands of Broad Churchmen through their occupation of the principal sees. It would look, to High and Low, as though 'rationalizing the Church' was the order of the day.[77]

Salisbury reminded the Queen's private secretary, Sir Henry Ponsonby, of a fact that he could not ignore. In the main, the Anglican clergy were High, and the laity Low, in their outlook.[78] Too many Broad Church bishops would alienate these predominant tendencies. E. H. Bickersteth, the Low Church Bishop of Exeter whom Gladstone had placed on the Bench, wrote to Salisbury in 1890 urging him not to neglect 'the strength of the Evangelical phalanx . . . far greater than many men suppose'; so powerful a force ought to be more Conservative in politics than it was. Instead, Evangelicals were saying that they stood to gain from the patronage of a Liberal ministry. Bickersteth was a Tory, which gave his remonstrance added weight.[79] Salisbury had been well aware of the Evangelicals' grievance before, telling a minister with quite different religious views in his first government that it was only fair to fill one out of three vacant bishoprics with 'a man leaning in their direction'.[80] Four years later, he sent a Cabinet colleague, Lord Cranbrook, to let the primate know of his anxiety to discover a good Evangelical for the next episcopal vacancy. 'Literally he cannot find one whom it would be decent to appoint', recorded Benson with a trace of malice, for he did not love Low Churchmen.[81] Salisbury revealingly asked Lord Harrowby, as representing the authentic Low Church in the Tory Party, to define 'a member of the flock' among several possible candidates for preferment.[82] He had already informed the Queen that the solidarity of the Unionist cause obliged him to conciliate the Evangelicals.[83] Appointments in the Church were closely observed by the Nonconformists, overwhelmingly Evangelical themselves and ready to sympathise with the Low Church. Resentment arising from the real or supposed exclusion of Evangelicals as each piece of preferment came up had, therefore, disturbing implications for Unionism; which Salisbury never forgot was an Anglican–Nonconformist alliance.[84] Moreover, as a High Churchman, he felt exposed to the public suspicion of his kind, memorably brought to the surface in 1874.

Nevertheless, he sounded out Liddon for a bishopric[85] several years after Lord Beauchamp, Harrowby's High Church equivalent, entered a strong plea for the Canon, his Gladstonian politics notwithstanding. Beauchamp contended that to leave Liddon unpromoted was to lengthen the odds against the Tories in the general election to which Salisbury's first administration, lacking a majority, had shortly to resort. The 'High Church Radicals' would use Liddon's 'ostracism' to win over clergy who thought, as he and they did, more of the Church's 'spiritual power' than of her 'temporal wealth'; and were accordingly less sensitive, compared with the rest of the Church, to the idea of disestablishment then being given a new prominence. Granting that Liddon's health was not what a bishop's should be, Beauchamp still argued for his preferment with the stress on it as 'a matter of electioneering'.[86] Salisbury admired Liddon for the personal faith they largely shared:

but did not have confidence in him as a leader of men.[87] It was, more than ever, undesirable to be publicly identified with a family friend and frequent visitor to Hatfield. When Liddon had been dead for nearly a dozen years, Salisbury, who was still Prime Minister, told his son Cranborne, an ardent High Churchman, that the Canon's portrait 'would seem strange and out of place' on the wall at Hatfield.[88] Liddon's expected refusal of a see may well have been a relief. Archbishop Benson observed this reluctance in the Prime Minister to make High Church bishops, and ascribed it to a purely political motive: 'Lord Salisbury is afraid of the working men's vote in the North, who will all vote against him if he names a High Churchman for Durham', stated Benson in his diary for February 1890.[89] The rigidity of High Churchmen like Liddon disturbed Salisbury equally. 'To believe in the Church of God is to deem it wrong to assist the *religious* life of those who remain outside her', the Canon had written, typically, to Edward Talbot, who differed from him on that crucial point.[90]

Salisbury attempted to persuade Talbot to commence his episcopal career in 1890, but not at Durham. He was eager to promote him, someone who revered Gladstone, because 'you have great influence with the High Churchmen – and are yet a man of peace, and of judgement'. He warned his cousin that when he and Gladstone ceased to head their respective parties, their probable successors were unlikely to prefer someone of Talbot's opinions, whose opportunity to do 'something to avert . . . Ecclesiastical Civil War' from the Bench of Bishops would be lost.[91] Talbot was his ideal of a Churchman. He disappointed Salisbury by declining; but his reasons and their presentation were unexceptionable. He would not leave his quasi-episcopal charge as Vicar of Leeds until he had spent longer in the provincial capital where he had gone after almost twenty years as the founding Warden of Keble: 'it is difficult perhaps from outside to see the importance . . . which attaches to the Vicarage . . . throughout all his countryside'. Admiring Gladstone though he did, Talbot recognised in Salisbury 'one who is not only prime minister, and a great Churchman, but to me something like a House Chief by the ties of two generations'.[92] Grandson of an earl on both sides, this *cadet de famille* had been sensibly brought up, in his mother's words, to carry into 'the *working-class* of gentry . . . whatever is really good and high-minded in the aristocracy';[93] a combination of modernity and tradition which Salisbury approved. The Liberal Talbot believed in the sincerity of Salisbury's politics; he knew the man well enough to assure Herbert Gladstone in 1880 that the Tory's attitude to diplomacy was perfectly serious for all his lightness of touch.[94]

Talbot's letters to Salisbury are those of a kindred spirit, indulging, at times, the same humour that so irritated Archbishop Benson in the statesman. Talbot recommended a candidate for an Indian bishopric as 'a fine, vigorous specimen of an *English* High Churchman. . . . He is six feet . . . and has a bonhomie and geniality characteristic of the larger animals.'[95] Theologically, he and Salisbury were very close. Talbot also shrank from 'the stronger dogmatisms about the manner of the Gift in the Eucharist', and had an inbred fear of 'the first beginnings of Mariolatry'.[96] His recommendations, usually of High Church clergymen, favoured the 'moderate and non-partisan'. Putting forward an intimate of Liddon's, he made it clear that he did so because the disciple had come to realise where the master was 'limited'.[97] The offer of Rochester to Talbot in 1895 came, and was accepted, without reference to the primate, who heard of it, to his intense mortification, from a bishop's wife. Benson relieved his feelings in his diary: 'Talbot must sign "Erastus Roffen". No appointments have been so Erastian in practice and manner as this.' He contrasted Salisbury's treatment of him with Gladstone's regular consultation, and described himself self-pityingly as a 'quantité négligeable' in the new bishop's eyes.[98] Inside the year the Archbishop experienced a fresh humiliation in the choice of a High Churchman for Newcastle: again, neither the Prime Minister nor the chosen candidate consulted him before, or informed him after, the event. Benson saw in the circumstances of these two selections the deliberate intention of Salisbury and the High Church to ignore him. A Liberal administration and a newly appointed Evangelical or Broad Church prelate would not have behaved thus, he wrote.[99]

Benson was certainly right in considering Erastianism to be far more characteristic of the Tories than of the Liberals in his time. He could not plausibly complain, however, that the Broad Church had suffered in its share of the patronage distributed under Salisbury. His own successor at Canterbury in 1896, Frederick Temple, was an outstanding figure in that school. The suggestions reaching Salisbury from Cabinet colleagues pointed to Broad Churchmen or to moderates hardly distinguishable from them. As a local landowner, W. H. Smith sought a bishop for Ely in 1885 who was 'a strong man . . . I care comparatively little as to the section of the

Church . . . but he ought to be a painstaking man of business' rather
than an eminent preacher or theologian.[100] He and Benson, who
was just such a man, got on well.[101] In 1891 Cross wanted a similar
bishop for Carlisle – 'as I am much interested in this diocese' – with
the injunction that 'a High Ritualist or a Low Evangelical would be a
disaster',[102] while in 1897 Hicks Beach, who had once remonstrated
at the neglect of Evangelicals, endorsed an earnest request from the
High Church Archdeacon of Bristol, where his constituency was
situated, for a prelate 'wide enough in his sympathies to hold
together both parties in the Church'.[103] To the pressure on Salisbury
to opt for Churchmen of this sort was added that of the Queen, who
would have given them a virtual monopoly of patronage if she had
had her way.[104] The party-political allegiance of bishops was a
factor; but the growing convention that they should abstain from
politics in their dioceses reduced its significance. The political
records of parochial clergy whose names members of the Cabinet
submitted for deaneries or canonries received more attention. The
convention affecting episcopal behaviour did not apply to them.
Hicks Beach's action in backing the leader of the *'very* High Church'
in Bristol for a deanery is an instance of politics taking first place.
The submission owed everything to the Conservatism of the
Reverend R. W. Randall, 'strong and fearless . . . on our side', and
to the size of his following in the city.[105]

IV

Launching his son Cranborne on a long political career in 1881,
Salisbury reminded him that 'Power is more and more leaving
Parliament and going to the platform.'[106] The effort to legislate for
the Church was particularly difficult because so much of what
urgently needed to be done did not lend itself to popular oratory. It
took the second Salisbury government nearly the whole of its term
to reform the law relating to tithe; one Bill after another unappealing
to the laity – squires, farmers and Nonconformists – failed through
obstruction, indifference and the doubts of those who managed
Government business in Parliament. Then there was the problem of
the parson's freehold. The abuses which flourished under its
protection called for 'a Church Reform Bill', no less, such as
Salisbury contemplated in 1885.[107] Its main features were
incorporated in the Clergy Discipline Act of 1892, finally passed in

co-operation with Gladstone, and the Benefices Act of 1898. Benson was a tireless advocate of these necessary changes, and bitterly critical of Salisbury personally for want of resolution in getting them through, in a modified form, without insufferable delay. Lastly, the future of denominational schools was a more tractable problem in that it could be discussed on the platform with advantage. The formidable opposition to the Church's involvement in education nevertheless imposed a caution which Salisbury was obliged to vindicate at some length to Bishop Talbot after the 1900 election had returned him to power with practically the same majority as in 1895. 'But we obtained not and have not any such majority on Church questions', insisted Salisbury. 'It is impossible to say beforehand whether on those subjects we have any majority at all'. His was a coalition government: four at least of the Cabinet remained Liberals in domestic policy. The two elections had been fought and won on Home Rule for Ireland and the South African War.[108] The situation had not altered since his earlier administrations between 1885 and 1892, when the Conservatives' ability to help the Church depended on the tolerance of Liberals and Liberal Unionists. Additionally there was the reluctance in his own party to do all that Salisbury achieved for the Church and her schools by persistence and 'wary walking'.[109]

The election of 1885 satisfied politicians that English disestablishment would not move into the centre of politics for many years to come. Salisbury's nephew and eventual successor in the premiership, A. J. Balfour, believed that if the radicals captured the Liberal Party they would be disposed to take on the landed class, 'as being easier', before the Church.[110] The distinct agitation for Welsh disestablishment continued to make progress and reached a high point as the Liberal Government of 1892–5 attempted to legislate in deference to the regional clamour.[111] On the one hand, Salisbury and the Church in England suffered no harm when they came under fire for resisting the Liberal Bills. 'Every cause and every person in England is stronger for being abused', he counselled Benson, to whom it had not occurred to regard Liberal censures and the hostility of Welsh Nonconformity in that light.[112] The effect was to unify the Church and to benefit both her and the Unionist alliance by the English unpopularity of the Welsh demand and its intemperate expression. On the other hand, it is doubtful whether Salisbury could have contrived to pass a Tithe Bill, after four years of trying, without the sense of urgency derived from the plight of the

Welsh Church. The Tithe Act of 1891 transferred the liability to tithe from the occupier to the owner of land. Harder hit than most by agricultural recession from the late 1870s, small farmers in Wales had protested, sometimes riotously, at having to pay this impost to the clergy of a minority church in the Principality; and it had been quite widely withheld. The severe hardship inflicted on clergy was reflected in Salisbury's correspondence.[113] Yet at the end of 1887, W. H. Smith, the Leader of the Commons, said that many Tories would oppose the reintroduction of the first Bill that had to be dropped. Smith alleged the inability of landlords to recover the tithe they would pay from their tenants in the middle of a depression.[114] But harassed by Irish nationalist and agrarian unrest, Salisbury shared the fear of an Ireland in Wales, should the protest against tithe there get out of hand. 'I feel like a Dutchman when he sees a little trickle of water running down a dyke', he remarked in discussing the question with Benson.[115]

The passing of the Tithe Act in 1891 cleared the way for much-needed legislation to facilitate the removal of criminal or scandalous clergymen. The Clergy Discipline Bill was originally Benson's. It made little headway until in 1891 Salisbury, 'looking more mountainous and solid than ever' in conference with the Archbishop and Sir Richard Webster, the Attorney-General, directed the law officer to make his wishes known to G. J. Goschen in the Commons. Goschen, the Liberal Unionist Chancellor of the Exchequer, who thought the Bill stood little chance of surviving, in all essentials, determined obstruction by a few, chiefly Welsh, Nonconformists, was to announce the Government's intention of proceeding with it next session. 'You may tell him', Salisbury instructed Webster, 'to say it *very strongly*'.[116] The primate was impatient for the measure, as he had been for the Tithe Bill, wanting a larger settlement of both questions than Salisbury and the Cabinet were prepared for. The Archbishop endeavoured to persuade W. H. Smith that the clergy were 'a worse class to *discontent* than any other'.[117] He repeatedly prophesied in his diary a separation between a neglected and offended Church and property, whose owners 'then . . . will . . . find that there is no class-right left defensible'.[118] But the diary also reveals the dread that Gladstone, belying his concern for the Church, meant to disestablish her in England.[119] For Benson was himself a Tory, and a nervous one; moderate Churchmen's political liberalism had diminished. Benson's exaggerated predictions did not convince. He became desperately anxious for the Clergy Discipline Bill, which only the Government could deliver: 'The scandals which cannot now be remedied . . . tend much more than anything to disestablishment'.[120] Despite Benson's suspicions of him Gladstone, whom the Conservatives had first approached a couple of years previously, intervened to help defeat the blocking tactics of the Nonconformist militants, who were beaten by resort to the closure.[121] The Prime Minister went up in the Archbishop's estimation. Next year he was writing appreciatively after a council of war on Liberal plans for the Welsh Church, 'Lord Salisbury admirable; he plays with big questions as a cat with a mouse. . . .'[122]

As a result of these legislative achievements in 1891–2, the Church expected more of the Conservatives. The use of the closure to pass the Clergy Discipline Bill was exceptional, Salisbury explained to the Archbishop, and had been acceptable to the opposition generally.[123] Otherwise, obstruction was bound to succeed, he told Dean Gregory of St Paul's, 'if the circumstances are such that the majority cannot be relied upon to attend'.[124] There was a limit to the amount of legislation for the Church which the Commons could be prevailed upon to digest in sessions that had to accommodate important bills on other topics, British and Irish. The Benefices Bill originated as the Church Patronage Bill in the mid-1880s. Benson brought it in to end the sale of the right of presentation to livings, and make arrangements for the elimination of clergy unfit to be incumbents but outside the scope of the Discipline Bill. Salisbury and Gladstone promised their support in 1887: yet in 1896 the former pleaded a shortage of parliamentary time in answer to a collective representation of all the bishops, with a single exception.[125] Benson, who died that year, was near to giving up hope for the Establishment in the long term: 'everyone admits that patronage is the grossest case for reform'. He imagined in his diary, as he was wont to do, what the clergy were saying among themselves. The attractions of disestablishment for them – not hitherto seriously felt outside a small circle of uncompromising High Churchmen – must grow: ' "Church principle cannot live in association with the modern English state. We work henceforth for its dissociation. It is now the only freedom." '[126] Yet he had been uncomfortable about the radicalism of the Bill in invading patrons' rights: 'I can't feel that as a bishop it is my place to . . . set an example of confiscation.'[127] The Bill nevertheless reached the statute-book under Salisbury. In his survey of political and social trends, at the end of the century, the historian and Unionist MP, W. E. H. Lecky disapproved of the Act's abolition without compensation of the sale of next presentations, in which there was a regular market. He compared the Conservatives' action unfavourably with Gladstone's in ensuring that patrons were compensated for the loss of their rights in the Irish Church Act of 1869.[128] The patronage of a living could still be sold under the Benefices Act, but with safeguards. Moreover, the diocesan was empowered to refuse institution for reasons of moral, mental and physical incapacity, debt or neglect of duty in a previous benefice.

Thus Salisbury had by the Clergy Discipline and Benefices Acts realised as far as possible his stated aim of dealing with 'criminous . . . and perhaps also . . . incompetent clergy'.[129] Education, viewed as inseparable from religion by the friends of the Church, overshadowed these purely ecclesiastical reforms. The maintenance of Church schools, and concern for the religious instruction of children in Board schools, weighed heavily on the working clergy, and in Salisbury they found their best friend.[130] Ironically, he increased their anxieties by the bold step he took in making elementary schooling free in the Assisted Education Act of 1891. The new government grant for this purpose applied to Voluntary schools already heavily dependent upon the state as to Board schools supported by the school rate; but the latter possessed in the rate an expanding source of revenue unmatched by the former's equivalent, the income from denominational subscriptions. Salisbury aspired by his even-handedness to rescue the Church's schools from their increasing difficulty in competing with better-funded rivals. 'It is very damping to fight for a system which has no expansion', wrote Talbot from Leeds. The grant was not enough to permit the Church to dispense with fees in all her schools. An amendment to the Bill enabled her to receive the grant for schools grouped together, and allocate it to end fee-paying in some while others continued to charge, augmenting church finances. 'Here . . .', Talbot told the Prime Minister, asking him to see that the change was made in the Bill, 'it was taken as almost the one ray of hope in the very dark situation. . . .' Free education was very much Salisbury's own initiative, sprung on his colleagues in a speech outside Parliament.[131] Cranbrook, under whom the Education Department came, objected to the 'great sacrifice of money . . . and parental duty, leading . . . to more of both'.[132] He was, besides, defeatist about the Church's prospects in this field, for all his public statements to the contrary. 'The liberty to build free schools is not liberty to be very active', he commented in his journal.[133] This attitude led to conflict with Salisbury, who accused him in Cabinet of being opposed to Voluntary schools. The Prime Minister took advice from and drafted amendments with Lord Sandford, a retired secretary of the Education Department who was devoted to the Church's interests.[134]

By 1895 the children in Board schools – nearly 2 million – slightly exceeded those who were being educated by the Church; although well over half a million others were in Catholic, Wesleyan and other Voluntary schools. The undenominational religious teaching under the School Boards varied quite widely. Salisbury endorsed 'a principle so righteous and so important that within the limits of practicability it ought to be pressed at all hazards and on all occasions'; namely, parental freedom to determine a child's religious education in school hours. He saw in the application of this principle the way to check the dechristianising influence of schools that were in an irreversibly strong position.[135] Temple, the Broad Church Bishop of London, with whom he was expostulating, had a different view. The Bishop did not believe that the majority of parents with children in those schools wanted teaching based 'on the authority of the Church or', he added, 'of one division of the Church'.[136] The last half-dozen words were a pointed reference to the High Churchmen on the capital's School Board, who had used Anglican control to take the offensive. Their moving spirit, Athelstan Riley, had said to Archbishop Benson when first elected 'I go on to the . . . Board to destroy it. Christians ought to destroy, not save it.'[137] Temple was content, acceptably to Nonconformists, with the New Testament as 'an authoritative textbook' in itself.[138] Salisbury appealed to the Bishop not to divide the Church's forces in the election of 1894 for the School Board.[139] After her 'in some respects . . . injudicious'[140] supporters had won, he persuaded one of his temporarily unemployed Cabinet ministers in that interval of Liberal government, the unwilling – 'my church views are broad' – Lord George Hamilton, to fill the chairmanship of the new Board.[141] 'He seemed to think that I had an inherent wet blanket element within me to damp down . . . the more violent of the protagonists', recalled Hamilton in his memoirs.[142] This instructive episode did not stop Salisbury from trying, once back in office, to give the principle of parental choice in Board school religious instruction a

statutory basis. The Conservatives' Education Bill of 1896, in which
the attempt was made, met with such criticism that it had to be
withdrawn. The 'limits of practicability' were too narrow.

It remained to save the Voluntary schools from what Talbot
termed 'killing competition'.[143] A bill providing financial help to
that end was carried the following session. Benson had rightly
sensed Salisbury's dilemma when listening to his reception of a big
deputation in 1895. His affection for the Church and desire to
succour her schools impressed those who heard him; but he ended
on a cautionary note: 'What we can do we must do quickly, and not
despair if it takes time to prepare the sinews of war.' The word
'despair' oppressed the Archbishop.[144] About three-quarters of the
money furnished by the Voluntary Schools Act of 1897 went on
raising the salaries of teachers, but not to the Board school level.[145]
Prelates begged Salisbury for the substantial assistance that was
necessary: 'This is not a case of "Wolf!" ' wrote Talbot.[146] If the
Liberal Unionists were unenthusiastic, there was considerable
hesitation among Tories. Balfour reported after the setback in 1896
that nearly all the metropolitan, Midland and West Country
Unionist MPs rejected the possibility of rate aid to Voluntary
schools.[147] It would be provocative to ratepayers, who greatly
outnumbered the voters paying income tax, and the Dissenting
activists disproportionately powerful in the constituencies. To this
unpopular solution, embracing both elementary and secondary
schools, Salisbury and his government were driven in the 1902
Education Act; educationally sound, its legacy of political ill-will
dogged the Unionists for years. To contemporaries the religious
aspect of the legislation was uppermost. It merited the appellation
of 'the Voluntary Schools Relief Bill', figuring as such in Liberal
polemic. The Church had cause for gratitude.[148]

V

The insularity of Salisbury's religious policy emerges from his
strictures on political Catholicism where it confronted him directly,
across the Irish Sea. He did not subscribe to Gladstone's obsessional
animosity against the Papacy. It was an institution which Salisbury,
drawing on his knowledge of France and French history, saw as a
barrier to the twin evils of irreligion and socialism on the Continent.
He was in favour of diplomatic relations with the Vatican, as an

abstract proposition: the certain domestic reaction excluded 'a perfectly harmless measure' in practice.[149] As he put it to his ambassador to Italy in 1889: 'The Pope is . . . to be looked upon in the light of a big gun – to be kept in good order, and turned the right way.'[150] Leo XIII had been distinctly helpful, in intention, with the Irish policy of British governments; and earned Salisbury's praise for his 'blameless attitude'.[151] The perceptible note of condescension calls for an explanation. As Archbishop Benson complained, Salisbury was close to being an Erastian. His fiercest assaults on the Irish Catholic hierarchy for its nationalist activity occurred after it had come to the fore in Irish politics on the split in Parnell's party. 'Can you', he asked an English audience, 'imagine the Archbishop of Canterbury summoning his suffragans and resolving that there should be a change in the leadership of the Conservative party?'[152] It was not simply a move to profit by the strife between Parnellite and anti-Parnellite. Salisbury took the opportunity to restate in public his philosophy of church and state. He held that 'ecclesiastical direction in secular affairs' inexorably corrupted Christianity, anywhere. 'One of the great arguments' for establishment was 'the considerable control' it imposed on the clergy, Catholic or Protestant.[153] Militant Dissenters in Britain were not guiltless, he remarked, of abusing religion for clearly political ends, but Catholic bishops in Ireland were much worse offenders and more dangerous. They had lately combined their spiritual force – the ordinary exercise of which was, he said, 'a tribute . . . to the Roman Catholic Church' – with blatant intimidation.[154] Salisbury wanted Britain to remain a religious country under the conditions proper to her. As for Ireland, he was fighting to prevent her from being turned into 'an ultra-clerical state under . . . Archbishops Croke and Walsh', the metropolitans of Cashel and Dublin, respectively.[155]

Naturally, he had no objection to clergymen in politics, so long as their participation involved a subordinate role. What he emphatically condemned was the employment of spiritual sanctions for purposes which he, from his English standpoint, thought illegitimate. English Catholics found his speeches unsettling, calculated to excite their fellow countrymen against them. Salisbury sent 'a confession of faith' in reply to the fifteenth Duke of Norfolk, the magnate who was their hereditary lay spokesman and a supporter of his. The offence of Irish Catholicism was 'almost as great an evil as lay domination in purely spiritual affairs'. He referred to Home Rule in his letter as the distortion of a 'purely . . . secular movement', which of course it was not and never had been in its previous incarnations. Salisbury promised the Duke 'to make it clear that I am only arraigning the men and not the order'.[156] For the Catholic laity in this country had long been predominantly of Irish birth or descent, as was a good proportion of the lower, but not the higher, clergy. Norfolk represented an ethnically and politically divided community, in which the native minority had a moral claim on the Unionists. Salisbury, therefore, emphasised that he was attacking Irish Catholicism as such. 'I utterly decline', he said to the Primrose League, 'to recognize the inhabitants of . . . Ireland as typical members of the Roman Catholic Church.'[157] The Pope had censured, with little effect, the 'immoral opinions' that inspired the upsurge of agrarian crime inseparable from the determined assertion of Irish nationality. Salisbury denounced the 'lamentably disciplined corps of Celtic priests, animated not by the spirit of their Church, but by . . . old traditional hatred'.[158]

It is true that he did not particularly like Ulster Protestants.[159] Their distinctive political growth, Orangeism, had spread on to the mainland where it put down deep roots in the industrial North-West of England and West of Scotland, areas of heavy Irish Catholic immigration.[160] His heir Cranborne won Darwen in Lancashire in 1885 and lost it seven years later. Salisbury advised him not to stand again for the constituency. The Catholic clergy were, as elsewhere, 'hopelessly slippery' when conflicting pressures were exerted upon them; while 'the Orange working man' was obstinate and demanding.[161] Cranborne found a more congenial seat in the South. But Salisbury did not equate Protestant Ulstermen, and their Orange brethren in England and Scotland, with Irish Catholics. Protestant Ulstermen were undeniably 'our brothers in race and religion',[162] whom it would be monstrous to 'sell into slavery' under Home Rule.[163] Moreover, with the political demise of the Irish landlords, which Salisbury had predicted on the passing of the first Gladstonian Land Act in 1870, it fell to the Northern Protestants to sustain a credible British presence in that country.[164] They faced in Archbishop Walsh and his lay satellites, as Salisbury persisted in regarding them, the 'ancient enemy' of Britain. 'The old charter printed in letters of blood in Irish history' licensed remorseless enmity to the settler because of his religion,[165] and because his ancestors planted in Ulster had responded to an appeal to help with 'the almost impossible task' of ruling Ireland.[166] The language of his speeches on the Irish question made a profound impression. The nationalists' power outside Ulster was such that he spoke in the early 1890s of 'the Irish republic' in the Southern provinces.[167] That 'republic' challenged Britain as an imperial and as *the* Protestant nation. The nationalists had achieved so much through their Church's perversion of the divine message and the sacraments entrusted to her. The Irish Catholic hierarchy and priesthood had perpetrated 'a breach of trust'. Consequently, Salisbury told Norfolk that he could not alter the 'essence' of what he had been saying to mass audiences, and proceeded to intensify his attacks on Irish Catholicism, as described.[168]

The situation of those like the Duke and J. L. Patterson, Catholic Bishop of Emmaus *in partibus*, was unenviable. Cranbrook, who encountered the Bishop at Salisbury's table, found him 'a good Tory full of blame for his co-religionist bishops in Ireland'.[169] A troubled Patterson begged Salisbury in 1891, on behalf of 'the *English* Catholic body', to revise his attitude to Gladstone's Roman Catholic Disabilities Bill, which would have opened to Catholics the Lord-Lieutenancy of Ireland and the Lord Chancellorship of England.[170] 'We must oppose . . . sentiment is strong even yet', Cranbrook had written.[171] No matter how loyal they were, English Catholics could not expect any concession, however small, that gave rise to uneasiness about Unionist resolution and Protestant integrity. Patterson protested that the Government were encouraging 'bigotry' by withholding support for Gladstone's Bill, while he anticipated the obvious answer: English Catholics, a minority in the Catholic Church in their own country, counted for too little politically.[172] Moreover, English bishops and priests had their predominantly Irish flock to consider; hence Salisbury's slighting allusion, in private, to their behaviour in places such as Darwen. Nor was their knowledge of Ireland and Irish prelates a reliable guide. The future cardinal, Vaughan, Bishop of Salford, suggested building 'a golden bridge of retreat' for the Irish hierarchy by educational concessions.[173]

For Salisbury the definition of a nationality fit to rule itself was very similar to J. S. Mill's. To begin with, it postulated 'a homogeneous people . . . who upon the deep questions that concern a community think with each other . . . have common interests . . . and are proud of common memories'.[174] These conditions did not exist in Ireland before partition. More important was the capacity to attain the qualifying level of civilisation for national freedom. The savage violence, and the threat of it, that disfigured the popular movement in Ireland proved her unfitness for self-rule: 'the tree is to be judged by its fruits, and . . . you have a bastard nationality before you', he said in 1887, sounding a theme of which he made a great deal in his speeches.[175] The indigenous Irish were a people 'unprogressive, all that is contrary to civilization and enlightenment'.[176] In arguing that the state of Ireland and the dark future he saw for her if she were ever allowed independence were directly related to the religion of the majority, Salisbury advertised an implacable Protestantism. There had always been that element in his creed, as in Gladstone's. It now stood him and the Unionists in very good stead. Gladstone and the Liberals were awkwardly placed in British politics by their alliance with Irish Catholic nationalism. Salisbury's religious policy, preoccupied with the Church of England, would have been more controversial if he had not appeared in front of the public as the champion of a common Protestantism bound up with British national feeling.

VI

Salisbury was the last devout Christian to be prime minister. His creed entered into all his policies, including Great Power diplomacy, where he endeavoured to reconcile 'the peace of Christendom' with British interests and aspirations.[177] He tried, with some success, to teach public opinion that 'complaisance and an accommodating spirit' were cause for pride in Britain's foreign policy.[178] A friend to missionaries, he warned them against becoming instruments of imperial expansion: 'They have a proverb in the East – first the missionary, then the consul, then the general.'[179] Not that he was opposed to the growth of empire, within reason, but he did not want Christianity discredited in the process. However, the scope for a Christian approach to international relations was severely circumscribed, in his view, by reality: the European war he dreaded could only be averted if the price of defeat under modern conditions were understood to be 'national annihilation'.[180]

At home, by contrast, religion seemed to him, as to so many others, vital to the working of late-Victorian institutions. Democracy was a fact in terms of voting power. Yet such was the conservatism, with a small 'c', of the mass electorate that the politicians set the pace of social reform from above, with Salisbury featuring it prominently in his popular oratory. The enacted reforms, embracing local government, allotments for agricultural labourers, housing, education, industrial conciliation and workers' compensation,[181] were substantial advances, by the standards of the day, and more were foreshadowed.[182] While Salisbury promoted 'social amelioration' through the statute book,[183] its purpose was to assist self-help, which he designated 'one of the most certain and remarkable fruits of the Christian religion'.[184] In saying this, he was uttering a commonplace, but with entire conviction: Christianising self-help was the recognised means of attempting to solve the contradictions between the values of religion and those of free-market economics. For the rest, contemporary industry and trade, he regularly reminded his audiences, depended on confidence, as did, therefore, hopes of greater prosperity to reduce the high unemployment of the 1880s and 1890s, which was 'a constant peril to the state', and to increase wage levels generally.[185] Confidence in turn depended on the good sense and restraint of the working-class[186] at a time when Salisbury thought it right to admit that 'we have . . . as far as we can, to make this country more pleasant to live in for the vast majority'.[187] It was at this point that the influence of religion was crucial to ensure that the legitimate socialism, so he considered it, of wider state intervention in support of self-help did not yield, in due course, to 'the socialism which is simply robbery'.[188] The moral authority of a political party was no substitute for that of organised religion, and especially of the Established Church.[189] Particularly for an Anglican in the Tractarian mould like Salisbury, the Church of England was first of all a spiritual entity, and not merely the accepted pastoral structure of some Broad Churchmen and Evangelicals. In the ritualist controversy, in his distribution of patronage, in the ecclesiastical reforms he took up, in legislating for universities and schools, Salisbury had the Church of his ideal in mind. He resisted the minimising tendency of belief towards the close of the century as incapable of providing spiritual sustenance and, consequently, of withstanding the secularisation of the age. Secularisation appeared to threaten society by the erosion of respect, founded on traditional Christian teaching, for the existing order. He exploited the threat when he fought hard for the Church and her schools. As for Unionism and Catholic Ireland, the former reflected ingrained religious and national attitudes, in vindication of which he spoke with such trenchancy.

To end on the main theme of this essay: the Tractarian Salisbury often and inevitably compromised to protect the Church, to the best of his ability, from dissension within and enemies without. He did so the more readily because he detested the unlovely results of partisanship in the practice of faith. The consciousness of fighting an uphill battle became stronger during his last years in the premiership: 'the Christian faith and the Christian Cross', he said sombrely, 'do not shine upon the peoples of the world with the unblemished splendour with which they shone in old times'.[190]

NOTES

I wish to thank the owners and custodians of the papers on which I have drawn: principally the present Marquis of Salisbury, the Master and Fellows of Trinity College, Cambridge and Lambeth Palace Library. I owe a very considerable debt of gratitude to Robin Harcourt Williams, the archivist at Hatfield House, for his unfailing helpfulness and patience.

Papers of the third Marquis of Salisbury (earlier Viscount Cranborne) held at Hatfield House and classified HHM/3M (Hatfield House Muniments, third Marquis) are designated by the abbreviated prefix '3M'. '4M' designates papers classified among those of the fourth Marquis. Other abbreviations used are as follows: BL (British Library); LPL (Lambeth Palace Library); NUCCA (National Union of Conservative and Constitutional Associations); TCC (Trinity College, Cambridge).

1. A. J. P. Taylor, *Essays in English History*, paperback edn (London, 1976), p. 126.
2. *The Times*, 10 July 1896, on the East London Church Fund.
3. Ibid., 11 May 1895, on the spiritual needs of East London.
4. Ibid., 22 May 1889, in London, on the Primrose League.
5. Ibid., 28 Nov 1889, at Nottingham during the NUCCA conference.
6. Ibid., 11 May 1895, on the spiritual needs of East London.
7. Ibid., 18 Oct 1893, at Preston.
8. Ibid., 23 Nov 1895, at Bradford.
9. Hughenden Papers, B/XX/Ce, Salisbury's memorandum of 2 Mar 1874 on Archbishop Tait's proposals for legislation against ritualism. I have used a microfilm copy in the Cambridge University Library: reel 45, correspondence between Disraeli and Salisbury. 3M/D80, Salisbury to the Rev. E. S. Talbot, 5 Mar 1890.
10. 3M/C7, Salisbury to J. H. Bailey, 30 July 1890. A. C. Tait (1811–82) was Archbishop of Canterbury from 1868 to his death.
11. TCC, Archbishop Benson Papers, letters 1893–6, Benson to Bishop Davidson of Winchester, June 1896. E. W. Benson, who died in 1896, held Canterbury from 1882; there is a substantial biography by his son, A. C. Benson, *The Life of Edward White Benson*, 2 vols (London, 1899).
12. *The Times*, 3 Feb 1892, at Exeter.

13. Lady Gwendolen Cecil, *Life of Robert Marquis of Salisbury*, 4 vols (London, 1921–32), I, ch. 4. The latest and one of the best studies of Tractarianism is G. Rowell, *The Vision Glorious: Themes and Personalities in the Catholic Revival in Anglicanism* (Oxford, 1983).
14. Lady Gwendolen Cecil, *Life*, I, 16, 120–1.
15. 3M/D48, Salisbury to Lady John Manners (from 1883 Duchess of Rutland), 11 May 1884.
16. 3M/D31, Cranborne to the Earl of Carnarvon, 22 Nov 1867; 3M/D78, Cranborne to J. A. Shaw Stewart, 2 June 1868.
17. 3 Hansard, CCIV, 283 (14 July 1873).
18. Dr Bright to an unnamed correspondent, 1 Jan 1897, in *Selected Letters of William Bright D. D.*, ed. B. J. Kidd (London, 1903).
19. 3M/D48, Salisbury to the Duchess of Rutland, 16 July 1891.
20. TCC Archbishop Benson Papers, Diary, 21 July 1887.
21. Ibid., 15 Aug 1895.
22. 4 Hansard, XII, 37–8 (4 May 1893). W. O. Chadwick, *The Victorian Church*, 2 vols (London, 1965–70) and F. W. Cornish, *History of the English Church in the Nineteenth Century*, 2 vols (London, 1910) are standard, as are, for the political background, Robert Blake, *The Conservative Party from Peel to Churchill* (London, 1970); J. R. Vincent, *The Formation of the Liberal Party, 1857–68* (London, 1965); and D. A. Hamer, *Liberal Politics in the Age of Gladstone and Rosebery* (Oxford, 1972).
23. Vincent, *The Formation of the Liberal Party*, pp. 65–76. For Edward Baines MP on the real nature of the Liberation Society, see his speech to its triennial conference, *The Nonconformist*, 9 June 1859. And compare Stewart, pp. 98, 100–3.
24. 3 Hansard, CLXX, 928 (29 Apr 1863).
25. Carnarvon Papers, BL Add. MS 60758, Cecil to Carnarvon, 18 Nov 1861. Robert Blake, *Disraeli* (London, 1966) takes a sympathetic but critical view of the man with whom Salisbury learnt to work.
26. 3M/DD, Salisbury to G. M. W. Sandford MP, 1 May 1868.
27. 3 Hansard, CXCI, 540 (30 Mar 1868).
28. Ibid., CXCVII, 93 (17 June 1869).
29. Salisbury to his wife, 15 Feb 1874, cited in Lady Gwendolen Cecil, *Life*, II (1921) 46–7.
30. J. Bentley, *Ritualism and Politics in Victorian Britain* (Oxford, 1978), ch. 3; P. T. Marsh, *The Victorian Church in Decline: Archbishop Tait and the Church of England 1868–1882* (London, 1968), ch. 7.
31. Hughenden Papers, B/XX/Ce, Salisbury to Disraeli, 22 Feb 1874.
32. 3M/H6, Salisbury to the Rev. William Stubbs, 20 June 1874.
33. 3M/D41, Salisbury to the Rev. Malcolm MacColl, 9 June 1874.
34. 3 Hansard, CCXIX, 56 (11 May 1874).
35. 3M/C2, Salisbury to Bishop Milman of Calcutta, 5 June 1874.
36. Lady Gwendolen Cecil in *Life*, II, 60–2, prints the immediately subsequent exchange of letters between the Prime Minister and Salisbury.
37. 3M/Lady Salisbury, Salisbury to Milman, 27 Mar 1874. At some time after Milman's death in 1876, a number of Salisbury's letters to him

were returned and are preserved with the correspondence of the Marchioness, his cousin.

38. J. Morley, *The Life of William Ewart Gladstone*, 2 vols (London, 1906) II, 109–10.

39. India Office Library, Northbrook Papers, MSS Eur. C144/22, Kimberley to Lord Northbrook, Viceroy of India, 9 Aug 1874; ibid., C144/23, Halifax to Northbrook, 21 Jan 1875.

40. R. T. Shannon, *Gladstone and the Bulgarian Agitation, 1876* (London, 1963).

41. C. J. Grimes, *Towards an Indian Church* (London, 1946), ch. 3.

42. 3M/Lady Salisbury, Salisbury to Milman, 15 Feb 1876.

43. 3M/H4, Canon H. P. Liddon to Salisbury, 7 Mar 1876. Liddon (1829–90) ranked with Dean R. W. Church (1815–90) and after E. B. Pusey (1800–82) in the later Victorian High Church.

44. 3M/E66, Salisbury to J. G. Fenwick, 26 Feb 1883.

45. Ibid.

46. Ibid.

47. 3M/H4, Liddon to Salisbury, 20 May 1879.

48. LPL, Archbishop Tait Papers, vol. 100, Salisbury to Tait, 5 Feb 1881.

49. Including the clash over the Endowed Schools Act Amendment Bill mentioned below. See Lady Gwendolen Cecil, *Life*, II, pp. 62–5, 202–5.

50. The Queen to Disraeli, 21 June 1875, and Disraeli to the Queen, 8 Dec 1875, in *The Letters of Queen Victoria*, 2nd ser., ed. G. E. Buckle, 3 vols (London, 1926–8) II, 370, 433.

51. 3M/E58, the Earl of Beaconsfield (Disraeli) to Salisbury, 17 Oct 1876.

52. 3M/D20, Salisbury to Beaconsfield, 20 Dec 1878.

53. Salisbury to Carnarvon, 23 and 24 July 1874, cited in Lady Gwendolen Cecil, *Life*, II, 62–4.

54. 3M/D20, Salisbury to Disraeli, 13 Oct 1874.

55. 3M/C2, Salisbury to Milman, 5 June 1874.

56. 3M/D20, Salisbury to Disraeli, 22 July 1876.

57. 3M/D38, Salisbury to Earl Beauchamp, 12 Nov 1886.

58. 3M/D20, Salisbury to Disraeli, 13 Oct 1874; W. R. Ward, *Victorian Oxford* (London, 1965), ch. 13.

59. 3M/D29, Salisbury to Gathorne Hardy, Secretary of State for War and MP for Oxford University, 12 Feb 1875.

60. 3M/D20, Salisbury to Disraeli, 24 June 1876.

61. Ibid.

62. Ibid., Salisbury to Disraeli, 2 Feb 1875.

63. Lady Gwendolen Cecil, *Life*, II, 64–5.

64. Cross Papers, BL Add. MS 51263, Salisbury to R. A. Cross, Home Secretary, 31 Oct 1874.

65. TCC, Archbishop Benson Papers, Diary, 9 Sep 1887.

66. 3M/D43, Salisbury to Professor Herbert McLeod, 18 Feb 1883.

67. LPL, Archbishop Benson Papers, vol. 22, Salisbury to Benson, 7 Dec 1883.

68. *The Diary of Sir Edward Walter Hamilton*, ed. D. W. R. Bahlman, 2 vols (Oxford, 1972) II, pp. 446–7 (11 June 1883).

69. LPL, Archbishop Benson Papers, vol. 22, Salisbury to Benson, 7 Dec 1883.
70. The Deceased Wife's Sister Marriage Act was passed in 1908.
71. 3M/D59, the Hon. Schomberg McDonnell to F. Perrott, 13 June 1891.
72. 3M/D9, Salisbury to Hicks Beach, 24 Oct 1889.
73. Ibid., Salisbury to Hicks Beach, 27 May 1891.
74. TCC, Archbishop Benson Papers, letters 1883–8, Benson to Dean Davidson of Windsor, 12 Mar 1888.
75. 3M/E114, Liddon to Earl Beauchamp, 19 July 1887.
76. Rowell, *The Vision Glorious*, p. 154, quoting a contemporary reaction.
77. The Queen to Benson, 1 Sep 1890, quoting Salisbury, *The Letters of Queen Victoria*, 3rd ser., ed. G. E. Buckle, 3 vols (London 1930–2), I, 634–5.
78. Salisbury to Ponsonby, 26 Jan 1890, cited in Lady Gwendolen Cecil, *Life*, IV, 209–10.
79. 3M/H1, Bickersteth to Salisbury, 17 Mar 1890.
80. 3M/D38, Salisbury to Beauchamp, 17 Dec 1885.
81. TCC Archbishop Benson Papers, Diary, 2 Dec 1889.
82. 3M/D66, Salisbury to the Earl of Harrowby, 27 Oct 1890.
83. Salisbury to the Queen, 3 Oct 1890, *The Letters of Queen Victoria*, 3rd ser., I, 644–5.
84. *The Times*, 1 Feb 1896, to the Nonconformist Unionist Association.
85. Liddon to Dr William Bright, 28 Jan and 7 Mar 1886, and to Salisbury, 25 Apr 1890, in J. O. Johnston, *Life and Letters of Henry Parry Liddon* (London, 1904), pp. 319–21 and 376–7.
86. 3M/E114, Beauchamp to Salisbury, 5 and 11 July, 25 and 27 Oct 1885 (quotations from 25 Oct).
87. 3M/D20, Salisbury to Beaconsfield, 20 Dec 1878.
88. 4M/387, Salisbury to Cranborne, 22 Mar 1901.
89. TCC, Archbishop Benson Papers, Diary, 2 Feb 1890.
90. G. Stephenson, *Edward Stuart Talbot, 1844–1934* (London, 1936), p. 38. In the context, 'with' in the unquoted part of Liddon's sentence should clearly read 'without'.
91. 3M/D80, Salisbury to Talbot, 5 Mar 1890.
92. 3M/H7, Talbot to Salisbury, 11 Mar 1890.
93. Stephenson, *Talbot*, pp. 7–8.
94. Ibid., p. 33.
95. 3M/H7, Talbot to Salisbury, 1 June 1876.
96. Ibid., Talbot to Salisbury, 29 July 1901.
97. Ibid., Talbot to Salisbury, 29 Oct 1891 and 13 Dec 1890.
98. TCC, Archbishop Benson Papers, Diary, 15 Aug 1895.
99. Ibid.
100. 3M/E160, W. H. Smith to Salisbury, 5 Nov 1885.
101. TCC, Archbishop Benson Papers, Diary, 21 July 1887.
102. 3M/E49, Viscount Cross to Salisbury, 27 Nov 1891.
103. 3M/E17, Hicks Beach to Salisbury, 27 Jan 1897, enclosing Archdeacon Robeson to Hicks Beach, 25 Jan.
104. This is implicit in a letter from her acting private secretary to Lord

Rosebery's private secretary during the Liberal Government of 1892–5: Lieutenant-Colonel Arthur Bigge to George Murray, 27 Apr 1895, *The Letters of Queen Victoria*, 3rd ser., II, 498–9.

105. 3M/E17, Hicks Beach to Salisbury, 7 Oct 1891.
106. 4M/387, Salisbury to Cranborne, 22 Feb 1881.
107. 3M/D15, Salisbury to Lord Randolph Churchill, 9 Dec 1885.
108. 3M/H7, Salisbury to Talbot, 7 Dec 1901.
109. 3M/H7, Salisbury to Churchill, 9 Dec 1885. P. T. Marsh, *The Discipline of Popular Government: Lord Salisbury's Domestic Statecraft, 1881–1902* (Hassocks, Sussex, 1978) is a good study of party and policy.
110. 3M/E8, Balfour to Salisbury, 24 July 1886.
111. P. M. H. Bell, *Disestablishment in Ireland and Wales* (London 1969).
112. TCC, Archbishop Benson Papers, Diary, 5 May 1894.
113. For example, 3M/H4, Bishop Hughes of St Asaph to Salisbury, 31 Jan 1888; 3M/H7, Archbishop Thomson of York to Salisbury, 28 Nov 1889.
114. TCC, Archbishop Benson Papers, Diary, 14 Dec 1887.
115. Ibid., 31 Jan 1887.
116. Ibid., 30 July 1891.
117. Ibid., 12 Sep 1887.
118. Ibid., 9 Sep 1887.
119. Ibid., 27 Nov 1885 and 12 Mar 1892.
120. TCC, Archbishop Benson Papers, letters 1889–92, Benson to George Cubitt MP, 2 Apr 1891.
121. Ibid., Diary, 25 July 1891 and 16 May 1892.
122. Ibid., 4 Mar 1893.
123. LPL, Archbishop Benson Papers, Salisbury to Benson, 6 June 1892.
124. 3M/C7, Salisbury to Gregory, 2 June 1892.
125. TCC, Archbishop Benson Papers, Diary, 12 Apr and 18 July 1887; LPL, Archbishop Benson Papers, Salisbury to Benson, 16 June 1896.
126. TCC, Archbishop Benson Papers, Diary, 10 July 1896.
127. Ibid., 23 July 1892.
128. W. E. H. Lecky, *Democracy and Liberty*, new edn, 2 vols (London, 1908), p. xix.
129. 3M/D15, Salisbury to Churchill, 9 Dec 1885.
130. The machinery of Victorian and Edwardian elementary education and its developments are very clearly described in A. L. Lowell's classic, *The Government of England*, 2 vols (London, 1908), II, ch. 47; for an example of Salisbury's eloquent sympathy with the clergy, see his speech in *The Times*, 22 Mar 1895, on Church schools.
131. 3M/H7, Talbot to Salisbury 19 July 1891; G. Sutherland, *Policy-Making in Elementary Education 1870–1895* (Oxford, 1973), ch. 10.
132. *The Diary of Gathorne Hardy, later Lord Cranbrook, 1866–1892*, ed. N. E. Johnson (Oxford, 1981), pp. 781–2 (8 Nov 1890); a valuable and meticulously edited source.
133. Ibid., p. 805 (18 July 1891).
134. Ibid. (16 July 1891).
135. 3M/H7, Salisbury to Frederick Temple, Bishop of London, 19 July 1894.
136. Ibid., Temple to Salisbury, 25 July 1894.

137. TCC, Archbishop Benson Papers, Diary, 23 Nov 1894.
138. 3M/H7, Temple to Salisbury, 25 July 1894.
139. Ibid., Salisbury to Temple, 19 July 1894.
140. Ibid. It was a narrow victory; the winners polled fewer votes overall than the losers (*The Times*, 24 Nov 1894).
141. 3M/E83, Hamilton to Salisbury, 26 Nov 1894.
142. Lord George Hamilton, *Parliamentary Reminiscences and Reflections, 1886–1906* (London, 1922), p. 233.
143. 3M/H7, Talbot to Salisbury, 7 Dec 1894.
144. TCC, Archbishop Benson Papers, Diary, 20 Nov 1895.
145. 3M/H5, Archbishop Maclagan of York to Salisbury, 18 Dec 1901.
146. 3M/H7, Talbot to Salisbury, 4 Dec 1901.
147. 3M/E8, Balfour to Salisbury, 18 Nov 1896.
148. Marsh, *Discipline of Popular Government*, pp. 314–19.
149. 3M/C7, Salisbury to W. Buchan, 20 Jan 1888.
150. 3M/D11, Salisbury to the Marquis of Dufferin and Ava, 15 Nov 1889.
151. 3M/E100, Salisbury to the Duke of Norfolk, 20 Nov 1891.
152. *The Times*, 22 Apr 1891, to the Primrose League. F. S. L. Lyons, *Charles Stewart Parnell* (London, 1977) and L. P. Curtis, *Coercion and Conciliation in Ireland, 1880–1892: A Study in Conservative Unionism* (Princeton, NJ, and London, 1963) are important for the nationalists and Salisbury, respectively.
153. *The Times*, 25 Nov 1891, at Birmingham to the NUCCA.
154. Ibid., 22 Apr 1891, to the Primrose League.
155. Ibid., 3 Feb 1892, at Exeter.
156. 3M/E100, Salisbury to Norfolk, 20 Nov 1891. His Home Secretary at the time, Henry Matthews, later Lord Llandaff, was in fact an English Catholic, the first to sit in a cabinet since the reign of James II.
157. *The Times*, 7 May 1892, to the Primrose League.
158. Ibid., 27 May 1893, at Londonderry.
159. A. B. Cooke and J. R. Vincent, *The Governing Passion: Cabinet Government and Party Politics in Britain, 1885–86* (Brighton, 1974), p. 160, quoting Salisbury to Churchill, 16 Nov 1885.
160. M. A. G. Ó Tuathaigh, 'The Irish in Nineteenth-Century Britain: Problems of Integration', *Transactions of the Royal Historical Society* (1981).
161. 4M/387, Salisbury to Cranborne, 13 Aug 1893.
162. *The Times*, 20 Dec 1887, at Derby.
163. Ibid., 7 May 1892, to the Primrose League.
164. 3 Hansard, ccii, 75–6 (14 June 1870); P. Buckland, *Irish Unionism and the Origin of Northern Ireland, 1886–1922* (Dublin, 1973).
165. *The Times*, 27 May 1893, at Londonderry.
166. Ibid., 25 May 1893, at Belfast.
167. Ibid., 3 Feb 1892, at Exeter.
168. 3M/E100, Salisbury to Norfolk, 20 Nov 1891.
169. *The Diary of Gathorne Hardy*, p. 673 (1 July 1887).
170. 3M/H6, Patterson to Salisbury, 6 Feb 1891.
171. *The Diary of Gathorne Hardy*, p. 789 (31 Jan 1891).
172. 3M/H6, Patterson to Salisbury, 6 Feb 1891.

173. 3M/H7, Vaughan to Salisbury, 14 Jan 1888.
174. *The Times*, 17 May 1886, to the NUCCA; J. S. Mill, *Considerations on Representative Government*, Everyman edn (London, 1954), ch. 16, and *England and Ireland* (London, 1868).
175. *The Times*, 20 Dec 1887, at Derby.
176. Ibid., 3 Feb 1892, at Exeter.
177. Ibid., 11 Nov 1895, at the Mansion House.
178. Ibid., 28 Feb 1889, to the London Chamber of Commerce.
179. Ibid., 20 June 1900, to the Society for the Propagation of the Gospel. The Bishop in Jerusalem, G. Popham Blyth, had been arguing that his activities were 'matters of political rather than religious consequence' – LPL, Archbishop Temple Papers, vol. 41, confidential print, Blyth to the Earl of Cromer, *de facto* ruler of Egypt, 15 Feb 1900, asking Cromer to lay his letter before the Prime Minister. See LPL, ibid., Salisbury to Temple, 14 Mar 1900.
180. *The Times*, 10 Nov 1888, at the Mansion House.
181. Most of these measures are discussed in Marsh, *Discipline of Popular Government*.
182. 3M/E39, Salisbury to Henry Chaplin, outgoing President of the Local Government Board, 20 Oct 1900.
183. *The Times*, 31 Oct 1895, at Watford.
184. Ibid., 10 July 1896, on the East London Church Fund.
185. Ibid., 24 Apr 1889, at Bristol on working-class Toryism.
186. Ibid., 27 Nov 1889, at the Nottingham Conference of the NUCCA.
187. Ibid., 31 Oct 1895, at Watford.
188. Ibid., 31 Oct 1894, at Edinburgh to the NUCCA.
189. Ibid., 11 May 1895, on the spiritual needs of East London.
190. Ibid., 20 June 1900, to the Society for the Propagation of the Gospel.

9
Salisbury and the Unionist Alliance

JOHN FRANCE

Lord Salisbury's most significant political achievement was to preside over the transformation of the Conservative Party into a party of government. Between 1846 and 1885 the Conservative Party held office for little more than ten years and formed a stable majority government only once (under Disraeli in 1874), whereas, from 1885, when Salisbury formed his first ministry, until 1902, when he retired, his party was in office for all but three years. Between them his predecessors, Derby and Disraeli, had led the party in eight general elections, losing seven of them; Salisbury led the Conservatives in five and 'lost' only two.[1] Such a dramatic change in fortunes owed something, no doubt, to subterranean shifts in the basis of Conservative electoral support,[2] but much the most important events occurred in the stratosphere of Westminster when, in 1886, the Liberal Party fractured. Conservative hegemony after 1886 was underpinned by the emergence of an anti-Gladstonian alliance at Westminster (and therefore also in the constituencies) and Conservative politics for the next decade were dominated by one theme – the formation of the Unionist alliance and the opportunities that this development offered for Conservative government. This essay will examine Salisbury's later political career, taking as its theme this most central achievement – the creation of the Unionist alliance. It will focus upon his relations with his political colleagues and in particular with the two leaders of Liberal Unionism, Hartington and Chamberlain; it will explore the tensions and, to some extent, the absence of tensions within the alliance. The methodological assumption underlying this mode of inquiry is that the behaviour of one politician can be explained to a very considerable extent by relating it to the behaviour of other politicians.

219

The realignment of political groupings at Westminster had been a recurring objective of Conservative statesmanship ever since Peel had wrecked the party in 1846. The 'democracy', which politicians regarded as a fact of political life after 1867, was thought to be unalterably Liberal in its natural orientation – a disturbing tendency which was likely to be accentuated by further extensions of the franchise, and few Conservatives believed there was a natural Conservative majority waiting to be 'discovered' within the electorate.

The assumption that the Conservative Party would not govern again without a realignment of political parties at Westminster was for many the dominant consideration in the choice of a successor to Beaconsfield as leader of the Conservative peers. One Conservative daily, the *St James's Gazette*, ran a series of leading articles expressing disbelief that 'any considerable section of the Conservative Party should think Lord Salisbury the most eligible' candidate.[3] The argument advanced is instructive. The problem about the 'rash, headstrong incautious, prejudiced' Salisbury was not only that he could justifiably be 'charged with a lack of straightforwardness' but that he was so evidently a bigger man than either of the other contenders, the Duke of Richmond and Lord Cairns, that he might eclipse Sir Stafford Northcote, the Conservative leader in the Commons, and establish a claim to the leadership of the Conservative Party in Parliament. Salisbury's inflexible resistance to parliamentary reform in 1867 led many to suppose that he lacked the qualities of tact, judgement and sensitivity necessary in a leader whose chief task would be to detach the moderate elements from Gladstone's Liberal Party.[4]

Misgivings about Salisbury's fitness for so delicate a mission were widespread and not confined to the liberal wing of the party. The Earl of Pembroke, a former junior minister and a staunch Conservative,[5] feared that if Salisbury became leader in the Lords 'the opportunities for reinforcement and reconstruction' that would arise on Gladstone's death or retirement would be 'thrown away'.[6] How much more plausible was a realignment if the Conservatives were led by Northcote – described in the moderate Liberal journal the *Spectator* as 'a sensible, cool, Whig of the old school'[7] – than under Salisbury, that 'reckless and defiant spirit' who was 'a menace to the constitution'.[8]

It should be remembered that Salisbury had to fight hard for recognition as Beaconsfield's successor. Even after Salisbury had assumed the lead in the Lords, Northcote (nicknamed 'the Goat' by the irreverent Fourth Party) still hoped to form the next Conservative ministry. Between 1881 and 1885 Salisbury gradually tightened his grip on the crown – though not without significant setbacks, notably on the Irish Land Bill (1881) and the Arrears Bill (1882). Salisbury's position in the party before 1884 was precarious indeed; thus one correspondent[9] wrote to Lord Randolph Churchill in 1882, 'The Country looks to *you* as the *coming man*. Lord Salisbury was the coming man – but he did *not come*', and nearly a year later Sir Henry Drummond Wolff described Salisbury as a 'broken reed' to be tolerated by the Fourth Party only because the alternative, Richmond, was 'too goaty and afraid'.[10]

Two episodes stand out as having enabled Salisbury to outstrip Northcote. The first was his decisive handling of the 1884–5 reform crisis, where Salisbury's quicker intellect, his grasp of the essentials, his flexibility and his natural political acumen combined to reveal Northcote for what he was – a 'born second-in-command'.[11] The second was the activity of the Fourth Party, which did so much to undermine Northcote's position in the Commons. By the beginning of 1885 the only people who believed Northcote had a future were Northcote himself and his son Henry, the 'little goat'.

Northcote's tactics as leader in the Commons had a damaging effect on Conservative morale. In his eagerness to demonstrate the common ground between Conservatives and moderate Liberals he was 'always jumping up and agreeing with the other side without first consulting his friends'[12] – an approach which angered Churchill, who likened Northcote's influence on the party to the 'influence of sewer gas on the human condition', which 'sickens, enfeebles, enervates and emasculates'.[13] There was, however, nothing very wrong with Northcote's avowed strategy of landing the moderate Liberals – nothing, that is, other than its failure. Few doubted its expediency, but many doubted the probability of its success and therefore grumbled about the price Northcote appeared to be willing to pay in advance of any Whig secessions. It was the overt, the shameless reliance that Northcote placed upon realignment rather than realignment as a stratagem which rankled with those Conservatives who demanded 'leadership'.

Salisbury was no less convinced than Northcote that such a junction was necessary. Indeed, his curious belief in the salience of class conflict led him to suppose that relationships at Westminster would, in time, reflect more exactly the fundamental struggle between the forces of property and those of spoliation.[14] During the manoeuvres which preceded the 1867 Reform Act he had looked in vain for a fusion of the Whigs and Derby and Disraeli's Conservatives into a party opposed to conceding predominance to 'mere numbers'. 'Pure "Squire" Conservatism', he told his recent ally Lord Carnarvon in 1868, was 'played out', and any Conservative Party of the future would depend for its success upon fusion with and under the leadership of the moderate Liberals.[15] His long-standing disposition towards fusion was accentuated by the electoral disaster of 1880; for, if proof were needed that pure, unalloyed Conservatism was insufficient for the purpose of sensible resistance, then this provided it amply. To his nephew Arthur Balfour he wrote with perplexed and gloomy relish,

> The hurricane that has swept us away is so strange and new a phenomenon that we shall not for some time understand its real meaning. I doubt if so much enthusiasm and such a general unity of action proceeds from any sentimental opinion, or from a mere academic judgement. It seems to me to be inspired by some definite desire for change; and means business. It may disappear as rapidly as it came, or it may be the beginning of a serious war of classes. Gladstone is doing all he can to give it the latter meaning.[16]

There was, however, a positive side to the electoral setback. If such a large Gladstonian majority posed problems for the party of resistance, might not its attendant Radical recklessness therefore provide an opportunity? When Balfour told his uncle of Wolff's suspicion that Northcote's hostility to the Fourth Party was 'owing to a scheme he is cherishing of forming eventually a junction with the Whigs', Salisbury was doubtful whether Northcote expected any coalition with the Whigs: 'He may hope by adopting a moderate attitude to lure one or two Whig rank and file to become Tories, and this, if Gladstone is violent is not unlikely to occur. I think his tactics so far are wise.'[17] Salisbury concurred in Northcote's strategy of enticing unhappy moderates into the Conservative camp while at the same time he was not sanguine about the immediate prospects of a large-scale realignment. This is important, for there persists a historiographical misconception about the disintegration of the Liberal Party according to which the Whigs and moderate Liberals are regarded as inevitably bent on abandoning an increasingly radicalised Liberal Party and finding salvation as the junior partners of the Unionist alliance. This misuse of hindsight does not aid our understanding of this episode. Certainly, many Conservatives supposed that if the Liberal Party did shatter, then it would do so along its abundantly clear fault line: that is, if Gladstonian Liberalism meant capitulation to Chamberlainite Radicalism, then more sober minds might be coaxed into the open arms of the Conservatives. But 'if' is the operative word here. Even as late as January 1886 it still seemed possible that the moderates would dominate Liberalism, or, failing that, that they would continue to be a very influential sect within the broad Liberal church.[18] What indeed was there to force them to abandon their mission to sabotage Radicalism from within the party of government, which had been their *raison d'être* of so many years? Moreover, what was there in Conservatism which might attract them? Certainly not the prospect of frequent office.

Once it is understood that the Tories needed the Whigs more urgently than the Whigs needed to escape the Liberal Party, other things fall into place. Northcote's tactics begin to make more sense – it was no use simply waiting for a split, some positive inducements were needed – and so does Salisbury's different approach to the same goal.

The orthodox view of the events of 1880–5, derived from the accounts of the Fourth Party, has obscured the important truth that Salisbury and Northcote were in agreement over the broad strategy of landing the Whigs and moderate Liberals. Where the two men differed was in tone and timing. Salisbury's tone had the merit of making the Tory Party seem much less helpless, and his appreciation of timing illustrated his awareness that a split within the Liberal ranks was not inevitable. Northcote staked everything on a successful fusion: Salisbury staked nothing but nevertheless pulled off the coup. In February 1882 the Lancashire Conservative J. W. Maclure[19] wrote imploring Salisbury to 'maintain a firm & decided action for the Conservative Party. Half hearted conduct will ruin us once & *for ever*. A policy which really brought the leading Whigs to the natural and *necessary* Guardians of their property would be a National and proper course but whilst we are weak-kneed they will never bow.'[20] And Salisbury never wavered in his adherence to this strategy until the schism within Liberalism became a *fait accompli* and the dissidents were quite unambiguously propping up the Conservative administration.

Salisbury's commitment to fusion was not unconditional. Throughout the 'caretaker' ministry of 1885 he poured cold water on Churchill's initiatives in this direction: 'the time for coalition has not come yet – nor will, so long as G. O. M. is to the fore'.[21] The personal element in this cannot be discounted. The chief beneficiaries of realignment in the autumn and winter of 1885 would have been Churchill and Hartington and certainly not Salisbury, who was thought to be too close to the diehard wing of the Conservative Party to be accommodated, especially as leader, within the only centre party which politicians were then capable of conceiving. It was not until the early summer of 1886 that fusion under Salisbury's leadership became a possibility.[22] Until then he was bound to oppose the formation of a new grouping the tone of which would be defined by Hartington or Churchill. In short, Salisbury wished to make Whigs into Tories and not the other way about, and this he quite reasonably supposed could only be accomplished under his auspices.

The emergence of the Unionist alliance was a gradual process which cannot be linked to any single event. The Hawarden Kite (17 December 1885); the electoral compact whereby sitting members who voted for the Union would not be opposed (April 1886); the vote on the second reading of the Home Rule Bill (8 June 1886); the general election which followed (July 1886); the formation of a Conservative ministry resting on Liberal Unionist support (July 1886); Churchill's resignation, which brought Goschen into the Cabinet in January 1887; the failure of the Round Table Conference (February 1887); and, finally, the formation of a Unionist coalition government (June 1895) – all these were important events in the long process of the formation of the Unionist alliance, but no single event may fairly be said to have marked its inception. The Unionist alliance was the product of the Liberal Party's failure to reunite: a failure which became so long-standing that Unionist politicians found that their temporary arrangement had become an enduring alliance. For some, like Salisbury, this was a welcome development; for others, like Chamberlain, it was not. Such was the basis of the long post-1885 Conservative hegemony.

The cornerstone of the Unionist alliance was the electoral compact whereby sitting Liberal MPs who voted against Gladstone's Home Rule Bill would not be opposed by Conservative candidates at the election. One recent authority has seen the electoral compact as weighted in favour of the Liberal Unionists[23] – a view which perhaps overlooks the limits of the pact and its operation at the general election. Salisbury took care to limit the guarantee of safe conduct to those Unionist Liberals whose seats would have been safe from Conservative attack had there been no split within the Liberal Party.[24] Thus, Conservative candidates fought sitting Liberal Unionist MPs in three seats. In fourteen more, seats which had been held by a Unionist Liberal at the dissolution were fought by Conservative candidates at the election. Sometimes this was because the Liberal Unionist member preferred to seek the Gladstonian nomination or to retire altogether rather than fight under the Liberal Unionist flag. Often, however, local Conservative associations simply announced their intention to put up their own candidates regardless of the leaders' pact. This left the sitting Unionist Liberal with neither Conservative nor Gladstonian support and with little alternative but to stand aside.[25]

There were short-term tactical advantages as well as long-term strategic objectives behind the electoral compact. Indeed, it made sense purely in terms of the 1886 election, for it meant that Conservative majorities would be swelled by additional Unionist votes which would make marginal Tory seats safe. In fact, Salisbury made only very minor concessions to Liberal Unionism at this time. First, the Conservatives gave up only one of their own seats to a Liberal Unionist, whereas the Liberal Unionists surrendered fourteen. Secondly, the Conservatives insisted on their right to contest seats where, if there had been no Liberal split, the Liberal MP would have been turned out at the next election. And, thirdly, Salisbury recommended that sitting Gladstonian MPs should be opposed 'by a Conservative if a Conservative has a fair chance of getting in'.[26] This effectively set a ceiling on the number of Liberal Unionist MPs at its 1886 pre-election maximum of ninety-five, for it was most unlikely that a Liberal Unionist organisation would exist, let alone one which was stronger than the Conservatives', if the constituency were not already represented by a Liberal Unionist MP. This meant that, if Liberal Unionism was to become strong, it would be entirely at the Gladstonians' expense and in seats where Conservatives had shown themselves to be weak.

The most compelling proof that Salisbury struck a very good bargain comes from the respective totals of Conservative and Liberal Unionist MPs returned in the elections from 1886 to 1900. In these four elections the Liberal Unionists never approached their 1886 pre-election total, and, more importantly, even in good years, like

1895 and 1900, they never equalled their 1886 election result; whereas the Conservatives bettered their 1885 total in all four subsequent elections and their 1886 total in 1895 and 1900.

Thus, in return for Hartington's albeit vague recommendation that Liberal voters who supported the Union should support Conservatives in the absence of a Liberal Unionist candidate (i.e. in the vast majority of constituencies) Salisbury had conceded in return no contest in seats which for the most part the Conservatives had no hope of winning. If the new alliance disintegrated, as many supposed it would, Salisbury would have at least gained a temporary electoral advantage for the Conservatives. If on the other hand it endured, he had ensured that fusion was not at the expense of the Conservative forces at Westminster.

It is a mistaken commonplace that Salisbury's offer of coalition in July 1886 was deliberately framed in such a manner that the Liberal Unionists would not accept it. The offending condition which it is supposed Hartington could not agree to was the exclusion of Chamberlain.[27] This misses two points. Chamberlain's inability to join a coalition *was* important, because Hartington could not look with equanimity on the division of the dissident Liberals. But the unwillingness of the Conservatives to countenance a coalition which included Chamberlain could not be a decisive factor, because in July 1886 Chamberlain himself was in no position to join with the Conservatives even had they been prepared to accept him.[28] Moreover, the Liberal Unionists were unanimously opposed to coalition with the Conservatives on any terms. Liberal Unionists at this stage maintained that they were the true church of Liberalism and that the schism would be healed on Gladstone's retirement. For most the 'mésalliance'[29] with the Conservatives was to be a temporary expedient rather than a step in the direction of fusion. Derby gave Hartington five reasons why coalition would be a dismal 'mistake':

(1) A coalition with Salisbury would make the breach between you and the Liberal party irreparable. As matters stand, it is temporary, and may be healed. (2) Chamberlain and you must be separated, as he could not join. But it is on your and his joint action that the political future of both of you depends. (3) The coalition would be one only in name. The leader of 300 must necessarily be more powerful than the leader of 60. You would be

really subordinate, even though nominally chief. (4) You would not be súre of your [?] faith. Once you had broken with the Liberal party, Salisbury might find or make any pretext to break up the concern, and remain in with his own people only. And he is just the sort of man who would do it. And in doing it he would have the sympathy of the Court, which since George the 3rd has never loved a Whig. (5) All coalitions are by their nature unpopular, and nine times out of ten they end in quarrels.[30]

The important decision against coalition in 1886 was made by the Liberal Unionists and not by the Conservatives.[31] Certainly there was opposition in Conservative circles to a Hartington premiership, but this should be distinguished from opposition to a Salisbury-led coalition government, which generally found favour. For many Conservatives the acid test of a coalition's acceptability was that their man should head it. When W. H. Smith[32] and Sir Michael Hicks Beach[33] agreed that the election results emphasised 'the absolute necessity of some kind of coalition with Hartington and his men'[34] they were thinking of a Salisbury-led government in which Hartington would lead in the Commons. Lord Cranborne reported this to his father:

> Smith & Beach had a conference today (I think) and determined they would in no way try to influence you – they only record their opinion that the Party would consent to be led by Hartington in the Commons if you thought it advisable; but this would only be endured if you were Chief.
> As to the advisability of this course Beach apparently thought that the leadership of Hartington in our House was impracticable but for his own part he would only be too glad, if it could be managed. Douglas[35] concurred, adding that to make Hartington absolutely Chief would 'break up the Conservative Party – they must be blooded they have regained the position they lost in 1880 & must occupy the first place' etc.
> The Unionists seem altogether opposed to a Coalition. . . .[36]

Hartington's refusal was received with regret rather than surprise by the Conservatives; Beach's comment 'some pears are rotten before they are ripe'[37] was characteristic. Salisbury formed a purely Conservative ministry, which, as Chamberlain had predicted, rested upon 'a definite and complete understanding with Hartington and an adequate though less complete understanding with me'.[38]

The events of July left the question of the future of the alliance unresolved. It became urgent once again when Churchill's resignation in December 1886 rocked the Conservative ministry and the question of coalition was revived. Churchill never intended to resign, but had his bluff called when Salisbury 'jumped at resignation like a dog at a bone'.[39] R. F. Foster would appear to be mistaken in his categorical assertion that at this point 'all (except Beach) advised against fusion with Hartington'.[40] In fact Beach was alone not in favouring coalition but in his insistence that the Conservatives should resign if this could not be achieved and in his ostensible belief that resignation would force Hartington's hand.[41] As in July 1886, a distinction should be made between a coalition led by Salisbury and one led by Hartington. To a Hartington premiership there was indeed opposition, as evidenced by this letter from Akers-Douglas, the Chief Whip, to Smith:

> I quite agree with you in approving Lord Salisbury's intention of working with Hartington if possible – Salisbury of course remaining Prime Minister.
> Hartington's lead in the H of Commons wd be followed by most of our men loyally – provided he was Lord Salisbury's lieutenant but I am not so certain as to their approval in the event of his being 1st Ld –
> I am sure however they wd prefer Beach or yourself.
> In any case and at all hazards a General Election *must* be avoided as we should certainly lose *many* seats.[42]

This letter does not support the contention that everyone but Beach opposed coalition: the position was the same as in July, when most Conservatives favoured coalition if satisfactory terms could be negotiated.

In the event Salisbury renewed his offer of the previous summer, and once again Hartington, after consulting with 'Goschen, Chamberlain, Courtney, H. Brand, Buckle, Ld Rothschild & heaps of others', declined. Hartington intimated to his mistress that but for the opposition among Conservatives 'it would have been a very difficult point indeed to decide on'.[43] A point which has escaped the attention of historians is that Hartington did not reject the overture categorically. According to Salisbury, what he said was that 'he could not, without losing all influence over Liberals in the Country either join in a Conservative Govt or form a Coalition Govt'. However, 'he might do this last to avoid a dissolution, or if the Conservatives by a resignation declared they were unable to carry on'. Salisbury, however, would 'not make on behalf of the Conservative Party a confession which would not be true and would be humiliating'[44] and determined to continue with few changes to his uninspiring frontbench – whom Churchill had referred to as 'Marshalls and Snelgroves': like that important London store, respectable but dowdy.[45]

If Salisbury's ideal was still fusion, and if he was prepared to serve under Hartington to secure this, his enthusiasm stopped far short of accepting Hartington's humiliating conditions and allowing the Liberal Unionists to cast themselves in the role of rescuers of a forlorn and wretched ministry. This was more than mere party pride, although that too was important; if Salisbury *resigned* to enable Hartington to form a government, he would lose control of the reins. Among Liberal Unionists even Goschen was reportedly in favour of a reconstruction under Hartington which would include not only Salisbury but also Churchill – a combination which Akers-Douglas was quite prepared to countenance.[46] This would have spelt utter humiliation for Salisbury and vindication for Churchill and it is hardly surprising that he resisted it. This also makes sense of Salisbury's attitude towards the man Randolph Churchill forgot. Salisbury was decisive in ensuring that Goschen joined only as Chancellor of the Exchequer and not as Leader of the House. This was partly out of deference to party feeling but it was also to do with Salisbury's shrewd calculation of the terms of a bargain. If the Liberal Unionists would not coalesce *en bloc*, then there was nothing to be gained by provoking Conservative discontent over the appointment of Goschen as leader in the Commons.

Talk of coalition surfaced from time to time after January 1887, but never again with quite the same plausibility until 1895. If Churchill's resignation could not be used to force a coalition, then it was most unlikely to occur until the political landscape had changed. Salisbury understood this and emphasised it in his correspondence with Alfred Austin,[47] who, though no fool, appreciated only the abstract logic of fusion. In February 1887 Salisbury explained that he had been 'so maltreated' in his last effort to promote a practical coalition that he must 'have a little rest in order to get well of [his] wounds'.[48] In June of the same year, justifying slight alterations to a piece of Austin's journalism because 'it is not desirable to quarrel with any category of your supporters – even the old Tories', he confided in Austin, 'I do not myself think that fusion will take place under the auspices of any names conspicuous now. A new name will be wanted – it might have been Randolph's if he had the most rudimentary common sense'.[49]

Salisbury was evidently not sanguine, and, while approving of Austin's propaganda, which was ardently pro-fusion, he often reminded his man on the *Standard* of the difficulties which any major reconstruction would involve: 'It is impossible to prophesy: but as far as I at present know, there will be no change in the Government before Parliament meets. Even if all other circumstances were propitious for such an operation, I doubt whether Hartington could keep his seat.'[50]

The realignment which Salisbury both worked for and sometimes seems to have thwarted occurred only very gradually. The Liberal Unionists supported the Conservative ministry until 1892 and in 1895 entered a coalition. It was not until 1911 that Liberal Unionists became eligible to join the Carlton, by which time the nominal distinction between a Liberal Unionist and a Conservative had lost its meaning.

Salisbury's dominant political reflexes were most often sceptical and libertarian. He tended instinctively to doubt the merits of any legislation, however 'worthy' its objective. 'Sobriety', he told one audience, 'is a very good thing and philanthropy is a very good thing, but freedom is better than either.'[51] The problem with legislation, particularly when promoted by Radicals, was that so often it undermined the rights of property upon which the stability, confidence and social cohesion of English life depended. In this state of 'bloodless civil war', Salisbury observed in a memorable sentence, 'to loot somebody or something is the common object under a thick varnish of pious phrases'.[52] When Churchill complained that Tories could 'govern & make war & increase taxation & expenditure "à Merveille" but legislation is not their province in a democratic constitution',[53] Salisbury replied with cynical and irresistible logic,

The Tory party is composed of very varying elements; and there is much trouble and vexation of spirit in trying to make them work together. I think the 'classes and dependents of class' are the strongest ingredients in our composition: but we have so to conduct our legislation that we shall give some satisfaction to both classes and masses. This is specially difficult with the classes – because all legislation is rather unwelcome to them, as tending to disturb a state of things with which they are satisfied. It is evident, therefore, that we must work at less speed and at a lower temperature, than our opponents. Our Bills must be tentative and cautious; not sweeping and dramatic.[54]

The same kind of principled cynicism can be found in Salisbury's frequently articulated belief that, as long as there was no fundamental redrawing of party lines at Westminster, the proper role of the Conservative Party was that of a strong minority party. Perpetual opposition was preferable to office if the latter could be purchased only by 'dishing legislation' on the lines of 1867. Hence, the duty of the honest Conservative opposition was to prevent the inevitable Liberal ministries from enacting Radical legislation.[55] Salisbury's contrasting achievement was to preside over three Conservative administrations[56] which enacted measures that might easily have originated in a Liberal Cabinet. There is irony as well as paradox in Salisbury's performance as Prime Minister. His government's policies, particularly those of the 1886 ministry, were characterised less by resistance than by recognition of the democratic imperative – policies which amounted, in the words of his son, to 'playing old Harry with Conservative principles'.[57]

There is a great temptation to resolve the paradox of Conservative policy by representing it as the outcome of a bargaining-process between the two partners to the alliance – the progressive Liberal Unionists extorting concessions from reactionary but acquiescent Conservatives. This explanation is open to serious objections. First, in terms of personnel, who among the Liberal Unionist leaders was likely to apply this progressive pressure? Certainly not Hartington, whose interest in legislation was non-existent and whose views, in so far as they can be ascertained at all, were conservative. Still less Goschen, whose legislative 'timidity' commended itself so much to Salisbury.[58] Even supposing that Chamberlain remained dangerously subversive after 1886, it is questionable whether he could overcome the overwhelming weight of opinion within the

alliance when it is recalled that the Conservatives were reconciled to
his eventual departure. The prospect of Chamberlain's disapproval
without Hartington's concurrence held no terror for Conservative
ministers, as evidenced by this observation from Beach: 'I do not see
why we are of necessity to do [Chamberlain's] bidding. When it
comes to the point, I think we have the whip hand of him, while
Gladstone is to the fore.'[59]

Liberal Unionist influence on Conservative policy has generally
been greatly exaggerated, no doubt because it provides such a tidy
explanation for the liberality of the Conservatives' measures.
Certainly there were occasions when the Liberal Unionists
influenced ministerial policy, but these were the exceptions rather
than the rule, and it would be mistaken to generalise from them.
Policy was more composite than such a model suggests; its final
shape was determined not by the static power relationship inherent
in the fact that the Conservative Government rested on Liberal
Unionist support, but by the outcome of a dynamic process of
statement, amendment, manoeuvre and compromise, involving
ministers, ex-ministers, Conservative backbenchers, Liberal
Unionist backbenchers, Liberal Unionist leaders, Gladstonians and
Irish Nationalists. The extent of Liberal Unionist influence was
situationally determined; it was neither constant in its intensity nor
straightforward in its objectives. Perhaps the most important aspect
of the relationship between Government policy and Liberal
Unionism was that the alliance gave Salisbury a ready-made excuse
for promoting broadly liberal legislation – legislation which there
were good reasons for promoting in any case. Needless to say,
Chamberlain was Salisbury's eager accomplice in his occasional
attempts to saddle the Liberal Unionists with the responsibility for
all this,[60] but the speciously attractive explanation of Conservative
social reform as Chamberlain's ransom must be doubted.

Although many Conservatives had serious misgivings about the
two most notable English measures passed by the second Salisbury
ministry, the creation of county councils (1888) and free education
(1891) – reforms which have often been explained in terms of Liberal
Unionist pressure – closer inspection reveals no decisive pattern of
Liberal Unionist influence. Thus, when Salisbury consulted with
Hartington in the autumn of 1886 about the details of the Local
Government Bill, he was delighted to find the Liberal Unionist
leader prepared to endorse a more reactionary settlement than the
Cabinet was itself proposing.[61]

Moreover, any persuasive power which Chamberlain exercised over the Cabinet diminished when Churchill resigned. Churchill's Liberal Unionist successor, Goschen, never attempted to exert a progressive influence on behalf of his party. Such consultations as there were on local government between the partners to the alliance were informal and irregular and there is no reason to suppose that the Liberal Unionists were other than confused and very often careless.

Similarly, free education cannot be explained in terms of Liberal Unionist pressure. While Chamberlain continued to press it in public, he did not seriously urge it upon his Conservative allies. Indeed, whenever the question arose his counsel was negative, because he understood that education was an issue upon which there could be no entirely happy compromise between Conservative and Radical 'Unionists'. Chamberlain confessed that he 'hardly [knew] what to say' about educational matters and referred to them only very 'gingerly', preferring to 'stand aloof' because he 'disliked taking any responsibility for any new educational and denominational endowment'.[62] Indeed, far from demanding legislative action Chamberlain had consistently 'urged that Free Education should be kept if possible to the last moment & then included, without the details of a Bill, in the programme for the dissolution'.[63] It was no fault of his that by Salisbury's unilateral policy declaration[64] the Conservative Government had recklessly committed itself too far to shelve the question decently until after the election. Bearing in mind that Chamberlain was unenthusiastic, it is not surprising to find that Hartington, who enthused about very little and who had opposed Chamberlain's free-schools cry in 1885, was not pressing this divisive programme upon the Conservative Government. His prognosis was that the difficulties would be too great and he 'rather apprehend[ed] a collapse'.[65] The simple truth is that the Liberal Unionists preferred to leave free education off the statute book, at least until the bribe had bought the alliance another term of office. The inspiration for this legislation came from another quarter.

A proper appreciation of the factors which shaped Conservative policy begins with an understanding that there was nothing quintessentially conservative in the policies of the Conservative governments in this period. There were attempts to devise programmes of legislation which, it was claimed, embodied or at least were consistent with truly Conservative principles (Churchill's

Tory Democracy outlined in the Dartford programme and Chamberlain's initiative of 1894 are examples), but these lacked conviction, for in legislative terms they seemed merely to plagiarise Liberalism. This was because Conservatives and Liberals shared the same political vision. It was an essentially one-dimensional perspective in which policy options were seen as appearing on a line between inaction, at one extreme, through Liberalism and Radicalism, leading on eventually to Socialism at the other. The argument among Conservatives was most often about what point on this line they should occupy, thereby defining the Conservative position, rather than about the merits or possibility of striking out in an entirely different direction. Between 1885 and 1903 the framework of political action is best understood in terms of degrees of Liberalism rather than in terms of wholly different and competing viewpoints. Some speech notes left behind by the Earl of Onslow articulate this with uncommon and shameless candour:

> Ever since the 'great Betrayal' was sprung upon England by Mr. Gladstone in 1885 . . . . the Conservative party – the old Tory party has ceased to exist.
>
>   In place of the Whigs and the Tories there now stand before the country two phases of Liberalism – the Liberalism which is traditional, and the Liberalism which is revolutionary. It is in support of traditional Liberalism that I claim your votes, of the Liberalism of Lord Palmerston, and of Mr. Gladstone before he put off the form of Dr. Jekyll to assume that of Mr. Hyde.[66]

The same point was made rather less happily by Salisbury's brother Lord Eustace Cecil, who wrote, 'As far as I can see Conservatism is dead and as powerless as the landed interest. Unionism is possible – but only by great concessions on the Conservative side – and a reconstruction in principles which must eventually be followed by a change of name. God help you through it all.'[67]

This is not to contend that conservatism and liberalism do not spring from quite different dispositions; undoubtedly they do. It is to assert, however, that in the world of practical policy options – as distinct from philosophical theorising or rhetoric – the parameters of political reality were set by Liberalism. Nor is it contended that this is always the case. Chamberlain and the Tariff Reformers challenged the established structure of Unionist politics so fundamentally after

1903 that it becomes possible for historians to speak of radical right which was quite evidently not on a continuum between inaction and Socialism but which gave rise to truly conservative positions in a different plane. However, the same cannot fairly be said of the period up to 1903 when the only alternative to 'degrees of Liberalism' was propounded by men like Wemyss and Henry Howorth, whose views had little purchase among the practitioners at Westminster.[68]

The keynote of the political agenda was set by the franchise reforms of 1867 and 1884–5 and all political questions in this period were seen very much in terms of the implications of the (irresistible) march of democracy in other spheres of English life – such as education, local government and the constitution. No leading Conservative had serious plans for such questions which had not been mapped out by the logic of democratic Liberalism working within an extended and extending franchise.

This is well illustrated by Lady Gwendolen Cecil's account of a conversation with the leader of the Tory squires, Henry Chaplin, about the Conservatives' Local Government Act of 1888, which 'dethroned the squirearchy' and set up popularly elected county councils. His 'ideal would have been to have kept Quarter Sessions, delegated to them all the powers, & given them all the money which are to be granted to the C.C.s'. This Lady Gwendolen considered an 'admirable measure for a Bismarck to carry out under a Prussian constitution', but not a realistic proposition for her father's Government. Chaplin declined to give an opinion on whether reform was necessary, but he agreed that if there was to be reform 'he did not see that we could have done anything else'.[69]

Concern about the requirements of 'the democracy' and the constraints which it imposed is usually only implicit in the correspondence between Conservative ministers; nevertheless it impregnated virtually everything they wrote and was certainly a critical element in their appreciation of political possibilities. 'I confess to much doubt', Beach lamented to Salisbury, 'whether the country *can* be governed now-a-days, by persons holding opinions which you & I should call even moderately Conservative.'[70] Salisbury, in common with most Conservatives, did not seriously believe that the policies which would honestly commend themselves to the Conservative mind were at all feasible under democratic conditions. When a disgruntled backbencher asked him why the magistrates' powers were being handed over to elected county councils, Salisbury, exhibiting this sense of Conservative paralysis in the face of the democratic *Zeitgeist*, replied that 'Representative bodies are the fashion of the day, & against a fashion it is almost impossible to argue.'[71]

Salisbury did not conceal his view that in an era of popular government his ministry's legislation would be shaped by Liberal rather than Conservative modes of thought. He looked upon this as the inevitable consequence of the unnecessary and ill-judged 'leap in the dark' which Disraeli had made in 1867; the equalisation of the borough and county franchise in 1884–5 followed logically and irresistibly. Explaining this metaphorically in a speech at Liverpool he remarked,

> I believe there is an amusement popular in Canada that is called tobogganing. When you begin to go down hill you must follow the course which those who started you designed for you, and you must follow it, though you may have the profoundest conviction that it was not the wisest course to select; and you must follow it; although you may reserve to yourselves abundant right to denounce with any amount of energy of language you please those who set you on that downward career.[72]

So, behind the electoral flattery of free education, elective county councils and smallholdings lay nothing so grand as a Conservative version of social reform or the promotion of an educated and participative property-owning democracy, but rather plain unease about the implications of, particularly, the 1884–5 reforms – an unease which appeared to be amply borne out by the party's poor performance in county seats at the 1885 elections. The propensity of voters, especially the newly enfranchised rural voters, to vote Liberal did not surprise Conservatives at all. 'If I were an ingenuous peasant,' mused Salisbury's daughter Maud, 'I am sure I should vote for the man who promised me all sorts of good things, rather than for the man who promised me nothing.'[73] Conservative reforms issued from a pragmatic appreciation of the requirements of electoral politics and this alone is an adequate explanation of the spectacle of Henry Chaplin clamouring for the introduction of a District Councils Bill in 1891 (which had no chance of passing), because rural members were 'quite distraught with eagerness to find something which the agricultural labourer will swallow'.[74]

This conception of the electorate gave Conservatives persuasive reasons for enacting moderate, but broadly liberal, reforms lest the Liberals once in office dealt with the same questions in a manner still more injurious to Conservative interests. The logic of this was difficult to challenge, but it had obvious drawbacks for the truly conservative. It might, as Gladstone complained, only accelerate the pace of change, because as Conservatives became liberalised so the Liberals were obliged to become radicalised. Moreover, it was tantamount to an admission that Conservatism can never find its true expression in office – a truth not lost on Salisbury, who once shrewdly observed that on some questions he could 'get better terms for property out of office than I can in office'.[75] Conservative ministers justified the 1891 Education Act on the grounds that, if the abolition of elementary-school fees was left to a future Liberal government, then Church schools were bound to suffer; whereas, if a Conservative ministry made education free without popular control, it would be difficult for the Liberals to legislate separately for this, as the resultant rise in rates would be unpopular. Many Conservatives who disliked the Bill were reluctantly persuaded by this 'lesser evil' argument.[76]

What was true of England was also true of Ireland, where policy was neither novel nor uniquely Conservative. Mythology has bulked so large in Irish historiography that it is difficult now to distinguish truth from half-truth. Orthodox (i.e. Liberal–Nationalist) explanations have centred on the essential difference between Gladstone's high-minded appreciation of the reality of Irish nationality and the Conservatives' contrasting emphasis on coercion and conciliation, later evolving into a policy of 'killing Home Rule with kindness'. There are strong objections to this analysis. First, it is naïve to suppose that either of the parties' leaders conceived of Irish politics except in a context of deep political calculation. Secondly, it implies a continuity which closer inspection shows to be a distortion of hindsight. Certainly, there were differences between typical Conservative and Liberal responses. No Liberal could have remarked, as Salisbury allegedly did, that he would enjoy taking part in an eviction,[77] but how meaningful were such differences of tone and sentiment when it came to policy-making? On the subject of Home Rule itself, Conservatives, including Salisbury, did not hold markedly different views from their opponents before 1886.[78] On the land question, it is true that the centrepiece of Gladstone's policy was the settlement of 1881, which conceded the three Fs and which in Gladstone's mind enshrined the interdependence of landlord and tenant,[79] whilst Conservatives regarded the 'dual ownership' as 'an abomination' and, if they thought at all about Irish land, they generally thought in terms of buying out landlords. Looked at more carefully, however, the distinction between Conservatives and Liberals becomes less clear. The differences between Conservatives and Liberals were of less consequence than those between Gladstone and the rest of the political world. By 1885 Gladstone was probably alone in his curiously English view that social harmony could be restored to Ireland by the active participation of the landlord class. Thus, while Radicals commonly complained that land purchase meant landlord relief, many of them (including Bright and Morley) had concluded that it was essential. By 1885 the principle of land purchase was embraced by Conservatives, Liberals and Parnellites alike – a consensus which allowed the Ashbourne Act to be passed quickly and with scarcely any opposition.

Salisbury's five land purchase Acts should not be regarded as an attempt to establish anything approaching a utopia in Ireland based on the conservative instincts of small property-owners. Neither he nor Balfour regarded purchase as a good thing in itself; indeed, Salisbury described it as 'only a remedy for worse evils'.[80] Moreover, it is quite wrong to see the two prongs of Balfour's attack – coercion and conciliation – as aimed at different aspects of the problem; that is, to see coercion as containing Ireland while purchase tackled the underlying problems. In reality they were both directed towards the containment rather than the profound solution of the Irish question. Certainly as far as Salisbury was concerned, the objects of the Balfour Purchase Act of 1891 were more modest than the wholesale conversion of tenants into proprietors. 'I do not in the least anticipate that it will put an end to the class of landlords', he wrote.

> But what we hope for from it is not that it will fill the country with peasant proprietors, but that it will establish them in greater or less numbers in various parts of the country, scattered all over it, so that the present uniformity of condition and feeling which enabled agitators to turn the whole political and social force of the occupiers against the landlords will be arrested and broken and will lose its formidable effect.[81]

Indeed, the object of Conservative policy had little to do with the establishment of the peasant proprietorship in Ireland, but was really, and more realistically, about removing one tier of landlordism – a fact not lost on Parnell, who calculated that 6 per cent of the owners whose estates had been purchased under the Ashbourne Act had carried off 57 per cent of the whole sum paid out. As few as nine men had taken over 40 per cent of the money advanced.[82]

Similarly, the claim that the Conservatives had a coherent strategy for Ireland which spanned the period from Ashbourne's Act in 1885 to Wyndham's in 1903 and was characterised by 'Constructive Unionism' cannot be sustained. Successive Conservative measures sprang more from immediate parliamentary and administrative exigencies than from any strategic application of a coherent and Conservative approach to Irish problems. There was little continuity in their approach to local government, for example – one aspect of the policy mistermed 'killing Home Rule by kindness'.[83] In 1892 Arthur Balfour introduced a Bill laden with safeguards and central control, whereas six years later his brother introduced an unfettered democratic franchise with devolved extensive local powers which resulted, to no one's great surprise, in the Nationalists taking nearly 75 per cent of the council seats at the elections. Far from being a calculated attempt to pre-empt Home Rule, the 1898 Act was no more than a way out of a parliamentary impasse that was holding up legislation; for, despite a majority of 150, the Government encountered serious problems arising from a combination of English apathy, Irish anger provoked by a report that Ireland contributed £2.75 million too much in terms of imperial taxation, and the failure of the Treasury to extend the agricultural-rating grant to Ireland. The terms of the 1888 English County Councils Act were adopted not because Ministers naïvely believed that local government would undercut the demand for Home Rule, but because the Lord Lieutenant had powers to apply to Ireland English legislation which had already passed through Parliament, thus avoiding the need to debate much of the new Bill. Until such a machinery of local government existed in Ireland, it would be impossible for the Treasury to subsidise agricultural rates as they had done in England. Notions of 'Constructive Unionism' were a very slight consideration in the extension of popular local government to Ireland.[84] Conservative ministers looked on Ireland as a continuing administrative problem to which no satisfactory political or legislative 'solution' was available Thus the Earl Cadogan remarked, 'Good government is more necessary here than good legislation.'[85] Arthur Balfour's popularity within the party stemmed not from the supposed profundity of his solution but from his unflinching defence of his vigorous administration. Unrepentant in the face of Nationalist abuse and Liberal didacticism, he appeared to demonstrate something very important to Conservative self-esteem – namely, that Conservative statesmanship was equal to the Irish question.

The survival of the alliance depended upon the harmonious co-operation of Salisbury, Hartington, Balfour and Chamberlain – the foursome properly described by Goschen as 'the "quartette" who control the destinies of the Unionist party'.[86] Even late in 1885 an alliance which embraced both Salisbury and Chamberlain would have been unthinkable. Their co-operation over a period of sixteen years depended upon the continued subordination of doctrine to the requirements of a shared appreciation of political reality and upon a preparedness to emphasise areas of agreement – initially 'the Union' and later foreign affairs. Their success demonstrates how even vigorously articulated and fundamental differences of outlook need be but small obstacles where there is a will to submerge such secondary considerations. It was eased considerably by Salisbury's generous (though not unlimited) acceptance of Chamberlain's continuing need to affirm his Radical intentions and by Chamberlain's equally clear recognition that, while he would not be humiliatingly contradicted by Salisbury, any attempt on his part to subvert Conservative policy would be emasculated by bland public utterances and private disregard.

In March 1886 Balfour warned Salisbury that they would 'find in him [Chamberlain], so long as he agrees with us, a very different kind of ally from the lukewarm and slippery Whig [Hartington] whom it is so difficult to differ from and so impossible to act with'.[87] Indeed, one important aspect of the Unionist alliance which has received curiously little recognition is that certainly until 1897 Hartington's behaviour presented more serious problems of alliance unity at the high political level than did Chamberlain's. Conservatives were less charitable towards Hartington when he failed to live up to their expectations – after all, he was not constrained by any past Radical utterances – and when he departed from the Conservative line he was regarded as either weak-kneed or devious. Though Salisbury smiled at Hartington's hedonistic, philistine lifestyle,[88] he certainly did not share posterity's misreading of the political character of the Whig leader. 'It's certainly true', recorded Lady Gwendolen, 'what S[alisbury] says, that in spite of his blunt manner & ungrammatical sentences there's no man who weighs his words more carefully than H[artington] or has more "intention" in what he says.'[89]

Conflict between the two leaders of the alliance reached its high point between 1892 and 1895. By then both men sat in the House of Lords,[90] which assumed a much greater importance when the Unionists were in opposition because it became the critical arena of debate and political action. The power of the Lords was justified by Salisbury in the quasi-democratic terms of the doctrine of the mandate. Salisbury had argued since 1868 that the House of Lords had a referendal role; its duty was to trigger a general election whenever there were reasonable grounds for believing that the House of Commons had no mandate for a particular Bill which it had passed up to the Lords.[91]

The assertion that the Lords would occasionally more truly reflect the will of the people than the Commons was most effectively demonstrated when the peers overwhelmingly rejected the second Home Rule Bill in 1893 and Gladstone failed to request a dissolution. Salisbury was only prepared to invoke the mandate theory and reject Liberal measures when the Unionist forces in both Houses were united. When Gladstone's government passed a deliberately offensive Parish Councils Bill up to the Lords, Salisbury's policy of resistance was successfully undermined by a series of statements from the Duke of Devonshire (as Hartington had now become) to the effect that the points at issue between the two houses were unimportant and he would not insist upon them. Hatfield took a very dim view of Devonshire's behaviour, which was attributed to electoral cowardice and a desire to 'exalt the Lib: Un: at the expense of the Conservatives'.[92] 'Did you ever know anything so disgraceful as the way the Duke [of Devonshire] has behaved,' asked Lady Salisbury, 'but we can expect nothing better from the man who betrayed Gordon.'[93] Lord Hugh Cecil told his brother Edward that their father's 'nervous exhaustion' (a medical condition apparently peculiar to Cecils) had been 'considerably increased by passionate indignation with the Lib: Un: party in general and with the Duke of Devonshire in particular . . . the inevitable inference is that he is not loyal – but what I call in my own mind (though the expression is perhaps too strong) a mean cur.'[94]

These differences had a significance beyond the immediate context of the Parish Councils Bill, for the question of the leadership of a future Unionist coalition government had yet to be settled and throughout these opposition years such speculation was a favourite subject of political gossip.[95] Some thought Salisbury would head such a government, while others supposed that Devonshire would take the first place; the important point is that there was general recognition that the Duke still had a claim which would have to be reckoned with. In the summer of 1894 Lily Harcourt and Mrs Gladstone discussed 'the future difficulties of the Unionist Party and the question as to the Salisbury or Hartington leadership':

> Mrs G. thinks Hartington most probable. Lily said she did not think Ldy Salisbury would allow the duchess the *pas*. Mrs. G. retorted 'Why you don't think she would be so *vulgar* as to wish her husband to be Prime Minister? Beside Ld. Salisbury is 60 and that is too old for a Prime Minister.' This from Mrs G. is quite delicious.[96]

Early in 1895 Chamberlain and Devonshire discussed the tactics they would employ when the Liberal ministry fell. Chamberlain reported the 'important conclusions' to Henry James: 'If asked to join a coalition the Duke will say "Aut Caesar aut Nullus". . . . As the L. U.'s will certainly hold the balance I do not think it possible for the Conservatives to form an Administration without our help.'[97] As events turned out, the Liberal Unionists did not hold the balance of power, and in any case Salisbury accepted the Queen's invitation to form a government instantly and before Parliament was dissolved. He did not renew the offers he had made in 1886 and 1887 to serve under the Liberal Unionist chief, and it is possible to read some significance into this. In 1895 Devonshire was better placed to accept such an offer than at any time before. Now that he was a peer he would be spared the problem of facing his constituents in a re-election. He had, moreover, ceased to see himself as the leader of a moderate majority Liberal Party purged of Home Rule. Most importantly, Liberal Unionist MPs had come to regard the alliance as a permanent feature of the political scene: the prospect of Devonshire leading a predominantly Conservative administration would not have aroused their misgivings in 1895 as it undoubtedly would have in 1886 or 1887.

As a member of the elected chamber, Chamberlain featured less in these controversies between the alliance leaders during the years of opposition. He was, however, beginning to think constructively once again, and in the autumn of 1894 he despatched lengthy letters and memoranda to Salisbury, Devonshire and Balfour which addressed the most fundamental questions of the future of Unionism.[98] Chamberlain recognised that the accession of Rosebery signified an attempt on the part of the Liberals to move away from the single-issue crusade for Home Rule towards a programme based appeal promising a range of popular and less popular measures – many of them 'confiscatory' and 'socialistic' – drawn together by the allegation that the House of Lords was an obstacle to legislative progression. Chamberlain argued that the Unionists needed to pre-empt this and establish a new framework of reference in the public mind. The polarities which he urged his colleagues to employ were simply these: the Liberal policy amounted to irrelevant constitutional meddling, whereas the Unionists offered a realistic programme of social reform. He even made the novel suggestion that the opposition should introduce Bills in the Lords to underline the point.[99] This Salisbury regarded as unnecessarily constructive: 'We are defending the House of Lords as a checking – not an originating – chamber. . . . I doubt whether we should impress its claim to be considered a good drag chain – by showing that on occasions it can pull on its own account.'[100]

Chamberlain's specific policy initiatives made some headway but only at the level of rhetoric. The Unionist Party fought the 1895 election on broadly, if only vaguely, Chamberlainite lines. In a speech at Edinburgh, Salisbury showed that he was prepared to adopt the essentials of Chamberlain's model even if he went on to strip it of all practical commitment:

> Mr. Chamberlain with whose general objects, I confess, I have the greatest sympathy, has been recently laying his views on the subject before the public. I do not know precisely the nature of the proposals which he recommends in these matters. Everything depends on details. But I am satisfied that there is not a taint of confiscation in anything that he has proposed, and I am sure that the general object he has in view will join with it the hearty concurrence of all sections of the Unionist party.[101]

This degree of consensus was sufficient unto the day, but its limitations became manifest when the new coalition ministry came to frame legislation. Paradoxically, the belief among Conservatives that the electorate demanded Liberal policies had acted as a cohesive force in Salisbury's first two ministries. It had lubricated the formation of the Unionist alliance and provided compelling reasons for legislating on moderately Liberal lines, occasionally, and where necessary, against the party's more visceral instincts. Towards the end of Salisbury's career this curious cohesion began to dissolve – partly because the Conservatives grew accustomed to office and electoral success. Thus, Chamberlain's 'solution' of a bold programme of social reform had less purchase as the problem of the compatibility of Conservatism and popular government appeared to recede. Whereas in 1892 Salisbury had lamented, 'I feel these social questions are destined to break up our party'[102] in 1898 he remarked with relief, 'Happily that [i.e. social legislation] seems to be at a discount.'[103]

Chamberlain's claim to have discovered the Unicorn – an extensive programme of social reforms acceptable to Conservatives – was shown to be fraudulent by the performance of Salisbury's third ministry. The Workmen's Compensation Act (1897) was the single big social measure passed by the ministry; and even this, while originating as a comprehensive measure which embodied Chamberlain's conception of social Unionism, ran into concerted Conservative opposition and Chamberlain's cherished principle of 'comprehensiveness' had to be abandoned. The problem of finding an acceptable form of old-age-pension provision, which Chamberlain had been advocating since the early 1890s, was scarcely nearer to solution when the unexpectedly high cost of the Boer War ruled it out altogether. The record of Salisbury's last government as far as domestic legislation was concerned was uninspiring and certainly not Chamberlainite in its intentions. For Salisbury, as for most Conservatives, if the prospects for resistance appeared a little better after 1895, there was still no alternative to 'degrees of Liberalism' on social questions. Chamberlain's claim to have invented a new kind of Unionism which was consistent with Conservative principle was regarded as casuistry which failed to conceal 'Radical principles of the deepest dye'.[104]

Salisbury's achievement was to nurse an understandably apprehensive Conservative party into era of popular politics and to make it, for the first time since Peel, a party of government. The critical factor in this accomplishment was the formation and the endurance of the Unionist alliance, which rested upon the co-operation of personalities with vastly different outlooks and commitments. The fact that neither Gladstone before him, nor Balfour afterwards, succeeded in working for any length of time with Hartington and Chamberlain is an illustration of the magnitude of Salisbury's achievement. Conservative government, however, is not synonymous with conservative policies, and the Unionist Party under Salisbury's leadership never offered a recognisably conservative alternative to Liberalism. This paradox finds its resolution in the interaction of Salisbury's cast of mind with his understanding of the constraints which acted upon Conservative government. Salisbury was deeply cynical about all political action – a cynicism which sprang from religious conviction allied with an incurably pessimistic frame of mind. He understood and took seriously all the intellectual positions on the political spectrum and showed himself quite able to employ any political argument which was expedient. Certainly there is, at the deepest level, a consistency between the Cranborne of the 1860s and the Salisbury of the 1880s and 1890s. But during the period of his pre-eminence he neither acted upon the narrow precepts which he had laid down in the 1850s and 1860s, nor sought to provide a conservative vision in opposition to the liberalism which saturated the English political mind.

NOTES

I wish to thank the following for co-operation in respect of copyright: Lord Chilston, Lord Derby, Lord Onslow, Lord Salisbury. For access to material in their possession or custody, I am grateful to the owners or custodians of the following manuscript collections: Austin Papers, Bristol University Library; Balfour Papers, Whittingehame House and British Library; Carnarvon Papers, British Library; Lady Gwendolen Cecil Papers, Hatfield House; Cecil-Maxse Papers, Kent Archives; Chamberlain Papers, Birmingham University; Churchill Papers, Churchill College, Cambridge; Cross Papers, British Library; Devonshire Papers, Chatsworth House; Hambleden Papers, Strand House; Hamilton Papers, British Library; Harcourt Papers, Bodleian Library; James Papers, Hereford and Worcester Record Office; Onslow Papers, Guildford Muniment Room; Salisbury Papers, Hatfield House; and Selborne Papers, Bodleian Library.

In the notes below, the locations of these collections are not repeated, except in the case of the Balfour Papers, where it is necessary to specify which source is cited; papers held at Hatfield House, where 'HHM'

(Hatfield House Muniments) identifies the source and 'GW' (Lady Gwendolen Cecil) and '3M' (third Marquis of Salisbury) the collections; and papers held at the British Library, cited by BL Add. MS no.

1. In 1885 and 1892. How the Conservatives would have fared in the elections after 1885 without their Liberal Unionist allies remains an imponderable question. It is noteworthy, however, that only once (1895) did they achieve a majority over Liberals, Liberal Unionists and Nationalists combined.
2. J. Cornford, in 'The Transformation of Conservatism in the Late Nineteenth Century', *Victorian Studies*, VII, no. 1 (Sep 1963) 35–66, has explained how the Third Reform Act accelerated a shift in the Conservative electoral base from the rural to the suburban. This coincided, it has been supposed, with the gravitation towards Conservatism of those who appreciated the dangers of a radicalised Liberalism.
3. *St James's Gazette*, 30 Apr 1881.
4. See *St James's Gazette*, 3, 5, 7 and 10 May 1881.
5. The thirteenth Earl of Pembroke; he had been, briefly, Under-Secretary of State for War in Disraeli's 1874 ministry, retiring because of ill-health in 1875.
6. Carnarvon Papers, BL Add. MS 60774 (no fos) Pembroke to the Earl of Carnarvon, 8 May 1881.
7. *Spectator*, 30 Apr 1881.
8. *The Times*, cited in R. Taylor, *Lord Salisbury* (London, 1975) p. 75.
9. George Bowyer.
10. Bowyer to Lord Randolph Churchill, 11 Nov 1882, and Sir Henry Drummond Wolff to Churchill, 28 Aug 1883, cited in A. Jones, *The Politics of Reform 1884* (Cambridge, 1972) pp. 55 and 72.
11. Robert Blake, *Disraeli* (London, 1966) p. 545.
12. Thynne's estimate, quoted in M. Egremont, *Balfour* (London, 1980) p. 57.
13. HHM/3M/E, Churchill to Salisbury, 28 Apr 1885.
14. The place of class conflict in Salisbury's outlook receives considerable attention in *Lord Salisbury on Politics: A Selection from his Articles in the Quarterly Review, 1860–1883*, ed. Paul Smith (Cambridge, 1972); see esp. p. 107.
15. Salisbury to Carnarvon, 24 Apr 1868, cited in Lady Gwendolen Cecil, *Life of Robert Marquis of Salisbury*, I (London, 1921) 294.
16. Salisbury to A. J. Balfour, 10 Apr 1880, cited in A. J. Balfour, *Chapters of Autobiography* (London, 1930) pp. 127–8.
17. Ibid., p. 48.
18. See, for example, *Spectator*, 30 Jan 1886, p. 138.
19. J. W. Maclure, Conservative MP for Stretford (Lancs) 1886–1901, a railway director and Honorary Secretary of the Lancashire Cotton Famine Fund.
20. HHM/3M/E, Maclure to Salisbury, 24 Feb 1882.
21. Churchill Papers, RCHL 1118b, Salisbury to Churchill, 30 Nov 1885.

22. See A. B. Cooke and J. R. Vincent, *The Governing Passion: Cabinet Government and Party Politics in Britain, 1885–86* (Brighton, 1974) p. 57.

23. P. T. Marsh, *The Discipline of Popular Government: Lord Salisbury's Domestic Statecraft 1881–1902* (Hassocks, Sussex, 1978) p. 111.

24. See Viscount Chilston, *Chief Whip: The Political Life and Times of Aretas Akers-Dougas 1st Viscount Chilston* (London 1961) p. 65.

25. A notable example was the case of H. Brand, the Hartingtonian whip who was forced to stand aside at Stroud because the local Conservatives insisted that they had made great progress with the working men of the district. See *The Times*, 17 June 1886.

26. HHM/3M/C6, Salisbury to D. Clarke, 11 June 1886 (copy).

27. This point is made in several works; most recently in R. F. Foster, *Lord Randolph Churchill* (Oxford, 1981) p. 272.

28. See Balfour's account of a conversation with Chamberlain in June: '[Balfour:] We may assume as almost certain that if Gladstone is beaten at the Election no single party will have an absolute majority in the House. Do you think under these circumstances that a Coalition Government could be formed? [Chamberlain:] So far as I am concerned it would be impossible for me to form part of such a Government and though I cannot of course speak for [Hartington] I doubt whether he would join one' – Balfour Papers, BL Add. MS 49688, fo. 114, Balfour to Salisbury [c. 13 June 1886].

29. 'Their view seems to be that in allying themselves with us they are contracting a mésalliance and though they are very affectionate in private they don't like showing us to their friends till they have had time to prepare them for the shock' – HHM/3M/D, Salisbury to Freston, 22 Apr 1886.

30. Devonshire Papers, 340.7019, Lord Derby to Lord Hartington, 12 July 1886. This was of course the fifteenth Earl of Derby, whom Salisbury had replaced as Foreign Secretary in 1878. After this Derby quickly moved over to the Liberals, holding office in Gladstone's second ministry. He became a Liberal Unionist in 1886.

31. C.f. R. F. Foster, *Churchill*, p. 272.

32. W. H. Smith, partner in the well-known firm of the same name; Financial Secretary to the Treasury 1874–7; First Lord of the Admiralty 1877; Secretary of State for War and, for a few days, Irish Secretary in the 1885 ministry; took the War Office again in 1886, becoming Leader of the Commons and First Lord of the Treasury on Churchill's resignation.

33. Sir Michael Hicks Beach held the posts of Irish Secretary and Colonial Secretary in Disraeli's 1874–8 ministry, and became Chancellor of the Exchequer and Leader of the House in the caretaker government of 1885. When the 1886 ministry was formed, he took the Irish Office, but poor eyesight forced him to stand aside for Balfour in 1887. He remained nominally in the Cabinet without a portfolio until February 1888, when, his health having improved, he took the Board of Trade. Beach was Chancellor of the Exchequer in the third Salisbury Ministry, retiring in 1902.

34. Cross Papers, BL Add. MS 51268, fo. 47, Smith to R. A. Cross, 17 July 1886.
35. Aretas Akers-Douglas, Conservative Chief Whip in the Commons.
36. HHM/3M/E, Cranborne to Salisbury, 15 July 1886. For corroboration see ibid., Smith to Salisbury, 19 July 1886; Hambleden Papers, PS9/156, Akers-Douglas to Smith, 17 July [1886]; and HHM/3M/D, Lord Cranbrook to Salisbury, 15 July 1886 (copy).
37. HHM/3M/E, Hicks Beach to Salisbury, 15 July 1886.
38. Balfour Papers, BL Add. MS 49688, fo. 114, Balfour to Salisbury [c. 13 June 1886].
39. Churchill's words related by Margot Asquith in *The Autobiography of Margot Asquith*, i (London, 1920) 62.
40. Foster, *Churchill*, p. 311.
41. At Hatfield Beach's refusal to take over the lead from Churchill was interpreted as a forcing-manoeuvre designed to bring about wide reconstruction under Hartington – 'a result which [Beach] had very much at heart.' HHM/3M/E, Lord Robert Cecil, memorandum, 19 Jan 1887.
42. Hambleden Papers, P59/205, Akers-Douglas to Smith, Christmas Day [1886]. See also HHM/3M/E, Smith to Salisbury, 31 Dec 1886: 'I am sorry to see by the papers that Hartington declines to join you. All these difficulties make one very sick of political life.'
43. Devonshire Papers (no fos), Hartington to Duchess of Manchester, 30 Dec 1886.
44. HHM/3M/D, Salisbury to Hicks Beach, telegram decypher, n.d. (copy). See also ibid., Salisbury to Cranbrook, 1 Jan 1887.
45. Hartington's scenario took insufficient account of constitutional convention. If Salisbury had resigned following a defeat in the Commons, the Queen would have sent not for Hartington but for Gladstone (the leader of the next largest party), who would have been entitled to request a dissolution, the Parliament having expressed no confidence in two governments.
46. 'Goschen seemed last night much in favour of a coalition with Hartington at its head Randolph & yourself members – if everything else fails this might work & wd prevent what I should fear in a coalition without R. C. namely his presence below Gangway' – HHM/3M/E, Akers-Douglas to Salisbury [c. 1 Jan 1887].
47. Alfred Austin, poet, journalist and Conservative apologist, who was the inspiration behind the Conservative periodical the *National Review*.
48. Austin Papers (no folios), Salisbury to Austin, 19 Feb 1887.
49. HHM/3M/D, Salisbury to Austin, 5 June 1887 (copy).
50. Ibid., Salisbury to Austin, 11 Oct 1887 (copy). Hartington's majority in Rossendale in 1886 was a surprisingly healthy 1450, but on his elevation to the Lords it reverted to the Liberals.
51. Quoted in Marsh, *Discipline of Popular Government*, p. 128.
52. Hambleden Papers, PS14/11, Salisbury to Smith, 5 Feb 1889.
53. HHM/3M/E, Churchill to Salisbury, 6 Nov 1886.
54. Churchill Papers, RCHL 1991, Salisbury to Churchill, 7 Nov 1886.

55. See, for instance, Salisbury's article in the *Quarterly Review*, cxxxiii (1872) 592–3.
56. Adherents of constitutional rectitude would insist there were four, because of the accession of a new sovereign in 1901.
57. Whittingehame House, Balfour Papers, bundle 28, Cranborne to Gerald Balfour, 3 Aug 1887.
58. See B. E. Dugdale, *Arthur James Balfour*, cheap edn (London, 1939) I, 92.
59. HHM/3M/E, Hicks Beach to Salisbury, 21 Dec 1886.
60. See, for instance, Salisbury's speech at Liverpool reported in *The Times*, 13 Jan 1888.
61. HHM/3M/D, Salisbury to Hicks Beach, 26 Nov 1886 (copy).
62. Chamberlain Papers, JC5/22/144, Joseph Chamberlain to Hartington, 3 Sep 1889 (copy).
63. Ibid., JC5/22/150, Chamberlain to Hartington, 21 Nov 1890 (copy).
64. In a speech at Nottingham reported in *The Times*, 27 Nov 1889.
65. Chamberlain Papers, JC5/22/52, Hartington to Chamberlain, 20 Nov 1890.
66. Onslow Papers, 173/7/2, the Earl of Onslow's speech notes [c. 1892?]. Churchill put the same point more directly when he wrote to Fitzgibbon, 'The work is practically done, the Tory party will be turned into the Liberal party' – cited in Lord Rosebery, *Lord Randolph Churchill* (London, 1906) p. 161.
67. HHM/3M/E, Lord Eustace Cecil to Salisbury, 12 Aug 1887. The contention that old Toryism was dead was, understandably, particularly prevalent in Liberal Unionist writings. In 1895 Dicey wrote, 'The various electoral, economical and social influences which have transformed the conditions of party warfare so as to render it nowadays a contest between the partisans of the Constitution and the advocates of revolutionary changes must tend to render the policy of the Unionist party more and more the policy of moderate Liberalism as represented by the Liberal Unionists?' ('The Case for Fusion', *Nineteenth Century*, June 1895, pp. 918–25).
68. Wemyss, who had no time for the Conservatives, was the leading light of the Liberty and Property Defence League, which promoted a doctrine of resistance to state interference and confiscation. H. H. Howorth was the Conservative MP for Salford between 1886 and 1900. One of the only ten to vote against the abolition of school fees in 1891, Howorth's experience as a wire-puller in Lancashire convinced him that Conservatism could be a vital political creed without resorting to policies which imitated Liberalism. He was a forthright critic of Liberal Unionism and particularly of Chamberlain.
69. HHM/GW, Lady Gwendolen Cecil, Diary, 22 Mar 1888.
70. HHM/3M/C6, Salisbury to Sir John Dorington, 18 Aug 1886 (copy).
72. 12 Jan 1888. Salisbury speech at Liverpool.
73. Selborne Papers, adds 1/76, Maud Wolmer to Lord Wolmer, 25 Sep 1885.
74. HHM/3M/E, C. T. Ritchie to Salisbury, 30 Dec 1891.

75. Balfour Papers, BL Add. MS 49690, fo. 3, Salisbury to Balfour, 28 Jan 1892.
76. For instance, Cranborne: 3 Hansard, CCCLIV, 1218–20 (23 June 1891).
77. See A. B. Cooke's introduction to the *The Ashbourne Papers 1869–1913* (Belfast, 1974), p. ix.
78. Salisbury's caretaker ministry never came close to granting an elected Irish legislature. The furthest Salisbury himself went in this direction was in discussion with Carnarvon, when he 'said he individually was prepared to go the extent of provincial councils in Ireland but not a central one' (Carnarvon Papers, BL Add. MS 60925, facing fo. 3, Carnarvon Journal, 6 July 1885).
79. See A. Warren, 'Gladstone, Land and Social Reconstruction in Ireland 1881–1887', *Parliamentary History*, 23 (1983) pp. 153–73.
80. HHM/3M/C7, Salisbury to Colonel T. Waring, 2 May 1890 (copy).
81. Ibid.
82. 3 Hansard, CCXLII, 982–9 (24 Mar 1890).
83. The phrase originates from a speech delivered by Gerald Balfour to his constituents in October 1895.
84. This analysis is based upon A. Gailey, 'Unionist Rhetoric and Irish Local Government Reform 1895–9', *Irish Historical Studies*, XXIV, no. 93 (May 1984) 52–68.
85. Ibid., p. 68.
86. Balfour Papers, BL Add. MS 49706, fo. 158, G. J. Goschen to Balfour, 21 Jan 1895.
87. Ibid., Add. MS 49688, fo. 88, Balfour to Salisbury, 24 Mar 1886 (copy).
88. 'Hartington is at Newmarket & all political arrangements have to be hung up till some quadruped has run faster than some other quadruped' (ibid., Add. MS 49689, fo. 141, Salisbury to Balfour, 15 Oct 1891).
89. HHM/GW, Diary, 15 Mar 1888.
90. Hartington acceded to his father's dukedom in 1891. Henceforth he will be referred to as 'Devonshire'.
91. On the mandate theory see Corinne C. Weston, 'Salisbury and the Lords, 1868–1895', *Historical Journal*, XXV, no. 1 (1982) 103–29; and V. Bogdanor, *The People and the Party System* (Cambridge, 1981) pts I–III.
92. Cecil-Maxse Papers, U1599 C714/16, Hugh Cecil to Edward Cecil, 25–7 Feb 1894.
93. Harcourt Papers, dep. 403, Lewis Harcourt, Journal, 28 Feb 1894.
94. Cecil-Maxse Papers, U1599 C714/16, Hugh Cecil to Edward Cecil, 25–7 Feb 1894.
95. See Hamilton Papers, BL Add. MSS 48659–65, Edward Hamilton, Journal, 6 Nov 1892, 1 Jan 1893 and 25 Mar, 12 Aug, 3 Nov and 11 Dec 1894; and Harcourt Papers, deps 390–419, Journal, 8 Feb 1893, 11 Jan and 24 July 1894, and 11 June 1895.
96. Harcourt Papers, dep. 410, Journal, 24 July 1894.
97. James Papers, M45/1747, Chamberlain to Henry James, 9 Jan 1895 (copy).
98. Devonshire Papers, 340.2588, Chamberlain to Devonshire,

memorandum, 13 Nov 1894; Balfour Papers, BL Add. MS 49773, fo. 67, Chamberlain to Balfour 8 Dec 1894; Chamberlain Papers, JC5/67/21, Chamberlain to Salisbury, 29 Oct 1894.

99. Ibid., JC5/74/23, Chamberlain to Wolmer, 12 Oct 1894 (copy).
100. Ibid., JC5/67/22–3, Salisbury to Chamberlain, 9 Nov 1894.
101. Speech at Edinburgh reported in *The Times*, 31 Oct 1894.
102. Balfour Papers, BL Add. MS 49690, fo. 65, Salisbury to Balfour, 26 July 1892.
103. Salisbury to Balfour, 22 Aug 1898, cited in Marsh, *Discipline of Popular Government*, p. 269.
104. The Marquis of Londonderry's words, cited ibid., p. 266.

10
Private Property and Public Policy

F. M. L. THOMPSON

All prime ministers before Asquith were members of landed families, usually the heads of such families, or like Disraeli had landed status hastily manufactured for them as a necessary preparation for a frontbench career. Since Asquith only Churchill, Eden, Macmillan and Home, among twentieth-century prime ministers, have been members of landed families, by descent or marriage; of these Home was the only one actually at the head of a long-established landowning dynasty, of whom it could be argued that his hereditary title and estates were an essential ingredient of political success. His appointment in 1963 was widely regarded at the time as an intriguing, but quaint, anachronism. The *fin de siècle* premierships of the third Marquis of Salisbury and the fifth Earl of Rosebery in effect marked the end of an era in which great landowners with hereditary titles frequently held the highest office and in which it was possible to govern the country from the House of Lords. The great patrician landowners did not, of course, abruptly drop all the reins of power in 1902 when Salisbury resigned or in 1905 when his nephew Balfour followed suit. They remained, and in some respects still remain, important, influential and powerful people in their localities and at the centre. Heirs to titles, and younger sons, remain attractive candidates for many rural, and some urban, constituencies in which the traditions or memories of family connections and property are strong; while hereditary access to the House of Lords creates an opening for a career for a peer with a taste for politics, provided he inherits before old age has already set in. Patricians remained extremely important in the inner counsels of both major political parties until 1914, and were close to the heart of the Conservative Party at least until 1979, indispensable in Cabinet-making and highly influential in the selection of party leaders. Nevertheless, from 1902, or at the latest from 1911, when Balfour was forced out of the leadership of the Conservative Party, the patricians were edged away from the centre of the stage and from the leading roles, a reflection of the relative decline in the weight of inherited landed position in the political nation.

This decline was one facet, arguably the most prominent facet, of a vast and complex secular movement towards a more popular, national and bureaucratised – some would say, democratic – form of politics in place of the traditional restricted, local, personal and informal politics in which landed estates with their many dependants and their role in local administration and Church affairs had been the dominant foci of power. It would be idle to suppose that a single individual case study can throw any light on this process, whose general causes in population growth, the rise of urban society and the spread of industry, and whose progress in terms of successive Reform Acts and developments in communications, are not susceptible of verification or refutation on the strength of a single instance. Historians have often argued, however, that the decline in the political authority of the landed elite from the 1880s onwards was not simply a consequence of the growth in the wealth, education, professionalism and voting-power of other sections of society, but was also a result of a positive decline in the income and wealth of the landed magnates themselves brought on by the great agricultural depression that began about 1874.[1] To be sure, the character and the very existence of the 'agricultural depression' can be doubted, and regional differences associated with different types of farming were such that some areas of dairying and market gardening were buoyant and prosperous in the 1880s and 1890s.[2] Hertfordshire, however, where the Salisbury heartland lay, was characterised by barley-and-sheep mixed arable farming, which in these decades was afflicted by falling prices only slightly less severely than wheat farming, and farm rents in the county fell by a fifth in the twenty years after 1874.[3] The individual case study can, therefore, address the question of whether falling income, by making the costs of high political life harder to bear, contributed in any way to making Lord Salisbury's the last patrician premiership.

First, however, it must be made clear that there was no necessary and automatic connection between great landed wealth and political or social eminence at any time in the nineteenth century, either before or after the onset of agricultural depression. The second, third and fourth dukes of Cleveland (1842–91), for example, like the fifth and sixth dukes of Portland (1854–1947) and the third Marquis of Bute (1848–1900), made no impact on high politics, were virtually unknown in high society, and are remembered, if at all, for their eccentricities: the fifth Duke of Portland, disliking daylight, tunnelled his way into Welbeck Abbey, and was alleged to have burrowed about in his London property off Baker Street, while the third Marquis of Bute poured millions into his ceaseless building operations at Cardiff Castle, Castell Coch, Falkland Palace in Fife, Mount Stuart on the Isle of Bute, and elsewhere. Yet all of these peers enjoyed incomes of £100,000 a year or more from their estates. Enormously wealthy landowners could, and did, contract out of politics and society. It was equally true that, for those who did choose to go into politics, great wealth, personal or parental, was no guarantee of success. The families of the dukes of Northumberland, Sutherland and Westminster, of the marquises of Londonderry, of the earls of Dudley and the earls Fitzwilliam, all of whom may be ranked as super-wealthy landowners, all produced a fair sprinkling of Victorian politicians, but none made any particular mark. Wealth, and the springboard offered by an assured social position and a renowned family name, were indeed invaluable assets for an aspiring patrician politician and could give him much more than a head start over self-made men – who generally could not hope to enter politics until middle-age – or career politicians of no lineage. They were not, however, indispensable conditions for entry into public life by patricians, let alone sufficient conditions for reaching the top. That depended on the merits of the individual, on a particular combination of talents, character, experience, good fortune and ambition which enabled a patrician to take advantage of the opportunities conferred by his birth.

The personal qualities which brought the third Marquis of Salisbury to the top in a political career which lasted just short of fifty years, during which he was leader of the Conservative Party for seventeen years, Prime Minister for thirteen and a half years, and Foreign Secretary for thirteen years, have been analysed and illustrated in earlier chapters. When all is said, Salisbury was still a representative of his order, that of the old landed aristocracy, as well as a remarkable individual and astute minister in charge of the affairs of an urban and industrial nation. The most representative traditionally conservative political action of his career was when, as Lord Cranborne, he resigned from the Cabinet in 1867, outraged by

the dangerously democratic tendencies of the draft Second Reform
Bill. It was at this period that he referred to Disraeli as 'a mere
political gamester', and was widely regarded as the last refuge and
rallying-point for diehard Conservatism and repudiation of the
unprincipled politics of playing to the gallery.[4] Thereafter he rapidly
learnt the wisdom of flexibility in politics, and he was the first to see
the electoral potential of 'villa Toryism' in middle-class suburbia.[5]
By the 1880s he was a skilful exponent of the Disraelian brand of
tactical politics, shorn of the master's rhetoric and the flamboyance
of Tory democracy, it is true, but still pursuing the general aim of
preserving stability and protecting the interests of property by
means of abandoning traditional positions when they became
untenable, and compromising with former opponents when there
was a chance of enlisting their support. Sometimes regarded as
hidebound and reactionary in relation to domestic policy, the
Salisbury of the 1880s and 1890s was in fact more of a cynic and
sceptic, almost an amused onlooker, both disinclined to resist
changes and reluctant to press reforms, because he doubted the
ability of government or legislation to make things better, but quite
content for departmental ministers to press ahead with their own
schemes. His stance was far removed from that of a narrow-minded
defender of the landed interest who viewed every issue from the
standpoint of the harm or good it might do to the aristocracy, or who
regarded the sectional interests of landowners and agriculture as
rightfully the prime concerns of the state. Nevertheless, Hatfield
House was his political base, the centre and powerhouse of his
political network, the ultimate source of his authority. He was
emphatically a large landowner in politics.

All was not as it seemed on the surface. The image of the Cecils as
great landed magnates, owning one of the largest and most famous
country houses in the land and wielding great influence in the
county and nationally by virtue of their broad acres, was indeed a
powerful one. The third Marquis's father ran true to form: he
regarded himself as primarily a great country landowner in the
aristocratic tradition, and busied himself with country pursuits and
with the duties and obligations of a landowner concerned with farm
tenants and rural labourers.[6] Hatfield House and its surrounding
Hertfordshire estate of some 13,000 acres was not, however, the
ultimate source or even the main source of the Cecil fortunes by the
late nineteenth century. By the 1880s it is fair to say that well over
half of the third Marquis's total income came from urban property,

not from agricultural rents, and the proportion was steadily increasing. When allowance is made for the fact that a fair proportion of the receipts from farm rents was ploughed back into the management, upkeep and improvement of the estate – somewhere between a quarter and a third – while there was little expenditure on the urban properties, it is apparent that a very large fraction of the Marquis's disposable income, perhaps as much as threequarters, came from non-agricultural sources. In a narrowly financial sense, therefore, the third Marquis was far from a plain country landowner. Someone like Henry Chaplin of Blankney Hall, Sleaford, master of 23,000 Lincolnshire acres, tireless if unimaginative advocate of the sectional interests of agricultural landowners and of farming, filled that role. Salisbury made him Chancellor of the Duchy of Lancaster in 1885, and then in 1889 appointed him as the first president of the newly formed Board of Agriculture, while he joined Salisbury's third Cabinet as President of the Local Government Board in 1895. He was not a great success in office; known in the House as 'the squire' he was regarded as a throwback to the pre-1832 generations of MPs. Walter Long, an altogether more weighty politician than Chaplin, who was Salisbury's second President of the Board of Agriculture, from 1895 to 1900, and who was a serious candidate to succeed Balfour as leader of the Conservative Party in 1911, also liked to pretend that he was a plain country landowner from Wiltshire, hard hit by the relentless pressure of agricultural depression, and, by 1911, the 'confiscatory' legislation of the Liberals.[7] Appearances were deceptive. In the 1890s Long was a director of the Great Western Railway and of at least four other companies, and was making regular investments in Stock Exchange securities, particularly in Canadian stocks, so that by the time he died in 1924 a third of his assets were in stocks and shares.[8] 'Pure' landowners, after Chaplin, were distinctly scarce on the frontbench.

No consolidated accounts have been found which bring together all the different sources of Salisbury's income. In effect there must have been separate accounting-procedures for the London estate, the two different parts of the Gascoyne estate, the Cranborne estate and the main block of the Hertfordshire estate. The only one which appears to have survived is the last of these. It is possible to construct estimates of the total of income from all the estates, but these have some margin of error. Also, some of the receipts, for example from the Essex property, came in the form of capital payments and seem to have been invested in Stock Exchange securities, which then in turn yielded an income whose origins lay in the property. In the light of all this, a comparison between the rental simply of the Hertfordshire estate in 1868 and in 1902 would be very misleading as an indication of Salisbury's real financial position. Very roughly, his gross income in 1868 would seem to have been of the order of £53,000 a year, and in 1902 of the order of £60,000 a year, there having been in the interval a sharp rise in income from the urban properties and a sharp fall in agricultural rentals. Figures of this kind would still not place him among the top fifty or so great landowners in terms of gross annual income, but, one suspects, would place him somewhere in the second fifty.

Whether Salisbury's general outlook, his political beliefs, policies and conduct were in any way influenced, let alone determined, by his hybrid character as both an urban and a rural landowner and by his lack of dependence on agricultural rents is another question. The probability is that his own personal experiences, perhaps particularly while he was the second son and before he unexpectedly became heir to the title and estates in 1865, were much more decisive influences. Even so, the nature and condition of property assets could be sensitive, possibly vulnerable, areas for someone in public life, while they frequently furnished the opportunities and the framework for political activity. His early career certainly taught Salisbury how to live thriftily on a small income, and how to earn his own living, in ways unusually tough for a member of a wealthy landed family. This sprang from his marriage to Georgina Alderson in 1857, a match greatly disliked by his father because, although she was the daughter of a baron of the exchequer, she had no fortune and no lineage. He disapproved so strongly that he declined to attend the wedding, and declined to increase his son's annual allowance of £100. Admittedly the future Salisbury also had about £300 a year from a trust secured on part of his mother's estate, but there was no way in which he could bring up a family, already grown to five children by 1864, on that kind of income. Accordingly, he took to living on political journalism, writing regularly, trenchantly and provocatively for the *Saturday Review* and the *Quarterly Review* from 1858 onwards, thereby also establishing his reputation as an intelligent anti-liberal of the thinking classes, who was against equality and democracy and also against humbug, affectation and the bumbledom of petty administrators.[9] He also took to dabbling on the Stock Exchange in speculative ventures, with rather less happy results. Having had experience in Australia during the gold rush of the 1850s, it was understandable that he should become involved in Australian ventures, but he had a sticky time in 1864 when the abortive Adelaide (North Arm) Railway Company folded up, and as one of the directors he found himself liable for a share of the initial promotion and advertising costs. By 1866 he was one of the original subscribers to the National Provincial Aerated Bread Company, and was rather more seriously involved in Charles Lafitte and Company, merchant bankers, and Overend and Gurney, the discount house. The Overend and Gurney crash found him in an exposed position, and he had to write to his father asking to be bailed out: 'This smash in the City has hit me hard. . . . I am terribly "locked up" . . . the sum I need will I fear be 5000 or 6000 [but] I have no reason to fear ultimate loss.'[10]

By this time his elder brother was dead, and as Lord Cranborne with an assured inheritance his financial standing was secure enough for him to weather the 1866 crisis. Shortly after this, but probably more because he was out of office, in opposition, and estranged from Disraeli, than because he was still short of money, he allowed himself to be persuaded by that great railway manipulator, Sir Edward Watkin, to become Chairman of the Great Eastern Railway. In the event he succeeded to the marquisate within three months of joining the Great Eastern, so that the fee of £700 a year which he received as Chairman from 1868 to 1872 was of no moment, and he was able to take a lofty attitude towards those railway directors and chairmen who milked their companies of extravagant fees. What remained was the opportunity of useful employment with the challenge of matching his abilities to the needs of top management. Enlisted chiefly in the hope that his name would restore shareholders' and public confidence in a railway which was nearly bankrupt and unable to pay any dividends, Salisbury in practice rapidly mastered the essentials of railway operation, acted as a decision-making chairman well informed on details, and was far from being an aristocratic figurehead. He was no doubt fortunate in that his period of office coincided with a rapid recovery and expansion of the economy, and of railway traffic and receipts in its train, leading up to the great boom of the early 1870s. All the same, he was a great business success as Chairman and deserved the credit he received for the return of the Great Eastern to tolerable health, and to declaring dividends.[11]

How did his early career and his business experience influence his attitude to the family estates which he inherited in 1868? There are three main directions in which this influence may be detected. First, although he was only thirty-eight when he inherited, which was considerably younger than normal for landed inheritance, he had spent his first thirty-five years as a younger son forced to fend for himself, and by the time he became first the heir and then the Marquis it was too late for him to develop a 'vocational enthusiasm' or effortless aptitude for the role of running a great estate, the more so since he had rebelled against a father who placed these things among his most cherished ideals.[12] The result was that he never cared greatly for chatting to his tenants, cultivating his neighbours or professing interest in or understanding of the state of farming. Rather unusually, he left most of the running of his town and country houses and their stables to his wife – though he did take a close interest in the gardens – remarking, 'it has taken me years to know the difference between a horse and a cow, please do not expect me to do anything more'.[13] Second, he had a well-developed appetite for accounts, and delighted in such exercises as an annual calculation of the average daily cost of keeping persons and horses at Hatfield, mastering the details of the administrative structure and investigating the possibilities of new domestic technology.[14] Already by 1871 Hatfield House had electric bells, some twenty years before they became at all common. Salisbury was experimenting with electric lights, unsuccessfully, in 1870, a good ten years before Hatfield and Cragside engaged in a race to be the first large house to be effectively lit by electricity. In 1877 he was intrigued by telephones, writing that 'nothing would give me greater pleasure than to infringe Professor Bell's patent by manufacturing my own telephone. But I am in the condition of the Irish groom, who being asked by his confessor whether he ever greased the teeth of his master's horses, replied "No your Reverence – will you tell me how? and I'll do it next time." Pray, how do you make a telephone?'[15] The essence of top management, however, consisted in his view of having a thorough understanding of the work of each department, having a clear chain of responsibility, accountability and reporting, and then leaving the departmental heads and subordinates to get on with it. This practice would in any case have been necessitated by his continuous involvement at the centre of high politics for the rest of his life after 1874, but the successful blend of supervision and delegation may well have derived from his experience in business.

Third, and the foremost element for understanding the interplay between private and personal circumstances, and public politics, he had a profound distrust of government or authority meddling in the affairs of individuals or trespassing on the territory of private enterprise, distrust which was pragmatically sceptical more than ideologically hostile. This he combined with a strongly paternalist sense of the obligations of large landowners and large employers towards their dependants and their workers. The combination was philosophically awkward, although Salisbury never showed any signs of being troubled by a conflict of ideals. It worked well enough in practice, and if pressed he would no doubt have argued that the paternalistic obligations were limited to the provision of the physical framework within which individual lives were led, particularly housing, and did not legitimately extend to any interference with the moral or social content of those lives. If environmentalism meant anything – and sanitary and housing reformers were committed to the view that it did – this was logically a distinction without a difference; and Salisbury sometimes tied himself in knots, both publicly and over estate affairs, with the inherent inconsistency between his positions, though few were so ungentlemanly as to point this out at the time. It is tempting to say that his respect for the dignity, independence and beliefs of the individual, and his attachment to private enterprise and market forces, derived from his early experience and knowledge of the business world, while his concept of a paternalism that was implicitly a denial of market-place ethics came from the traditional ethos of his landed inheritance. In reality, however, individualist and *laissez-faire* attitudes were the common frame of reference of educated mid Victorians, and business experience was not an essential preparation for holding them. Salisbury's best-publicised act of private liberalism, indeed, when in the 1880s he offered the Methodists a site for a chapel in Hatfield, although as a strong Churchman he had previously caused considerable ill-feeling by referring to chapels as 'objectionable buildings', was a declaration of toleration and, if a matter of calculation at all, of a political, not a business, nature. It is true that he was then criticised for trying to tuck the Methodists away out of sight of his town, but his reply was withering:

it is untrue that the site which he offered to the Wesleyan body was a mile from the town, with no house in sight except a workhouse; it was twenty yards from the most thickly populated part of the town. It is true that it is about the same distance from the workhouse, but he is not aware that the neighbourhood of a workhouse is prejudicial to a religious building. A chapel recently erected in the same locality by Lord Salisbury for the Church of England is still nearer to the workhouse.[16]

Housing was another matter, where philanthropy or paternalism tangled with business principles.

It also tangled with politics. The private affairs of people in public life had been politically sensitive at least since the 1830s, when Tory radicals started slinging mud at mill-owners and Radicals retaliated in kind against landowners. The way in which one handled one's property, whether it was a factory with women and children in the workforce or a landed estate with tenants and labourers, was very visible to critical outside eyes, and could not be discreetly concealed as could the potentially far more dangerous private affairs of any who flouted the moral conventions. Most wounding of all was the chance that opponents might find a stick with which to belabour some prominent man by discovering that private practice contradicted his public stance. When he inherited the family estates in Dorset in 1851, Lord Shaftesbury was mortified to discover the appalling state of affairs there. 'Surely I am the most perplexed of men', he wrote. 'I have passed my life in rating others for allowing rotten houses and immoral, unhealthy dwellings; and now I come into an estate rife with abominations! Why, there are things here to make one's flesh creep; and I have not a farthing to set them right.' 'Shocking state of cottages,' he recorded, 'stuffed like figs in a drum.' 'Rural and lovely scenery,' he said of a visit to Hinton Martel, 'but what a cottage – what a domicile for men and Christians I found in that village. Yet, what can I do?' Such was his constant refrain: 'inspected a few cottages' in Cranborne, where his seat of St Giles lay, 'filthy, close, indecent, unwholesome. But what can I do? I am half pauperised: the debts are endless; no money is payable for a whole year, and I am not a young man. Every sixpence I expend – and spend I must on many things – is borrowed.' The short-term face-saving solution was that his sister, Lady Caroline Neeld, who had a little spare money, built him four cottages in the village: 'the world will now, at least, see our good intentions,' he commented, 'and that is of high importance where, like me, a party has been a great professor'. Neither did he neglect, in accordance with his known principles, to take immediate steps to set up a school and appoint a scripture-reader. In the longer term he economised by shutting up St Giles for several years, channelling most of the spare income from the estate into a programme of cottage-building which within twenty years had removed all the worst blackspots.[17]

Salisbury was a great deal more fortunate than Shaftesbury. He did not inherit a debt-ridden estate, and he did not bring with him a reputation as a scourge of bad and negligent landlords. He did, however, inherit at the very time that the Assistant Commissioners of the Royal Commission on the Employment of Women and Children in Agriculture were touring the country and reporting on the living-conditions of the rural population and of agricultural labourers in particular. Lord Salisbury and the Hatfield estate were not specifically mentioned, but the absence of his name from the list of some score of large landowners who were singled out as 'setting a noble example of their consciousness of responsibility in respect of the dwellings of labourers' was not particularly reassuring. More disturbing was the conclusion of the Assistant Commissioner who investigated Hertfordshire, George Culley. 'What I said, for instance, of the Duke of Bedford's estate in Bedfordshire', he reported in 1869, 'I might repeat of Mr Abel Smith's in Herts; no expense has been spared in providing for the comfort of everybody connected with it. With the exception, however, of Mr Abel Smith's, I know of no large estate in the part of the county to which my inquiries were confined where the cottages are, either in quality or quantity, what the owner would like to see them.'[18] The parts of the county visited included the Hatfield and Hitchin Unions, which covered most of the Salisbury estate. Of Hatfield the relieving-officer of the Union stated, 'there are some good and some very bad cottages; on the whole I cannot report favourably on them'. The Vice-Chairman of the Board of Guardians echoed this opinion, adding, 'in the town of Hatfield there are many cottages deficient in ventilation and in water supply. The town cottages certainly not well situated with respect to the farms. I do not believe the cottages to be overcrowded. There is a considerable amount of drunkenness and some immorality, but this I attribute to the congregation of cottages rather than to overcrowding of inhabitants.'[19] Culley was therefore simply corroborating local views when he concluded, 'I do not remember visiting any town or large village in Herts, with the exception of Watton [Abel Smith's home village], where I did not see some very bad cottages inhabited by farm labourers. As bad as any a man need to occupy may be found in Hatfield, St Alban's, Harpenden, Hitchin and Stevenage.'[20]

None of this pointed a finger directly at Salisbury, and there were crumbs of local consolation to be gathered from the even worse conditions described in neighbouring places. J. B. Lawes, of Rothamsted, said flatly of Harpenden that 'the cottages are bad and insufficient for the wants of the labourers', while it was reported of Redbourn that 'the condition of the cottages is very bad, particularly those connected with farms'. The very worst cottages were said to be 'in the back lanes of towns such as Baldock and Hitchin', but there were also wretched specimens in, for example, Clothall, where the Salisbury estate had a farm.[21] Hatfield, however, was clearly the sore point, the sensitive area. However much Lord Salisbury might emphasise that he did not own more than one third of Hatfield town, and that the worst conditions there were the typical 'open parish' result of small property-owners running up small and shoddy cottages on speculation and ensuring that they were overcrowded by exacting exorbitant rents, it was virtually impossible to dispel the popular impression that it was 'his' town. He was inevitably regarded as the patron and benefactor of the town, and, in so far as it was more than a large village housing agricultural labourers, the great house was its major source of employment and custom. In any case, while it remained true until the early 1880s that Salisbury was only a minority landlord in the town as it then existed, he controlled practically all the surrounding land, so that fresh sites had to be on Cecil land. Improvement and development meant that Hatfield became more like a Cecil town by the end of the century than it had ever been before.

In the following thirty years or so Salisbury improved himself out of the situation of 1869 with a sustained effort of investment and of personal involvement that the most insistent demands of high politics could not deflect. His personal concern that the common labourers should have decent housing, with enough rooms to separate the sleeping sexes and discourage sin, and with adequate sanitation and reasonable comfort and convenience, was undoubted. So also was his keenness to provide this as economically as possible, to keep building-costs low by eschewing ornamentation, frills or fancy designs in favour of plain utility, on the principle that good sound cottages should also pay a market rate of return. But so too was a desire to raise Hatfield in particular above the level of possible reproach or criticism, a thread that can be seen running consistently through all the years of his building operations. Some great landowners lavished cosmetic treatment on the immediately visible surroundings of their country seats and neglected the condition of the rest of their estates which were safely out of sight. Salisbury most certainly did not do this. The building-accounts for parts of the family estates outside the Hatfield district have not all survived, so that it is not possible to give a precise picture of the geographical distribution of activity over the entire period of Salisbury's lordship, but sufficient occasional references do survive to indicate that outlying and detached estates did receive a fair share of attention. Thus, in the ten years after 1892 it was noted that twenty-one cottages were built on the Cranborne estate in Dorset and forty-eight on his farms in Hertfordshire, a proportion which positively discriminated in favour of Dorset, as Cranborne was less than a quarter the size of the Hatfield estate.[22] The discrimination was not altogether surprising, since in 1868 Cranborne had been singled out as one of the particularly black spots in a county which as a whole had the dismal reputation of having the worst cottage accommodation in England. 'In Cranborne [the cottages] are improving. Lord Salisbury has built and is building', it was stated in 1868. But this was merely some mitigation of the Assistant Commissioner's general remarks:

> The estate of Lord Rivers, having been long held by life tenants, is notorious for its bad cottages. And such villages as Bere Regis, Fordington, Winfrith, Cranbourne, or Charminster (in which there is an average of 7 persons to a house), . . . are a disgrace to the owners of the land, and contain many cottages unfit for human habitation. Nor can this condemnation be confined to large open villages.[23]

Farms and properties in Hertfordshire which were detached from the Hatfield heartland – Clothall, Hertford Heath, the Hadhams, Hoddesdon or Meesden, and North and South Mimms close by in Middlesex – were also not neglected, while a stray reference to the fact that only £24 was spent on buildings and repairs on the Essex estate in 1870, compared to £15,910 spent on the Hertfordshire estate, is probably very misleading.[24] There were only half a dozen small farms in Essex – at Clavering and Nazeing, and on the

Gascoyne inheritance in Barking, Dagenham and Hornchurch – and it would be unreasonable to expect the expenditure of a single, random, year to be representative of their normal treatment; in any case a large proportion of the Hertfordshire expenditure for 1870 was on a new dairy and new gardens for Hatfield House. Nevertheless, in the ten years when forty-eight cottages were built on Salisbury farms in Hertfordshire, no fewer than 218 were built in Hatfield.[25] Lord Salisbury was a good landlord throughout his territories; but, judged simply in terms of quantity, he was a better one immediately outside his own park gates.

The park gates themselves were new, symbol of Lord Salisbury's combination of aristocratic tradition and practical business sense. A new drive to Hatfield House, complete with appropriate gates and lodge to match, was constructed in 1876–9 to give direct access to Hatfield railway station.[26] This involved turning the whole house round, the old front facing towards the turnpike to London becoming the back, and the old back becoming the main entrance for rail-borne (and latterly car-borne) family and visitors. Eminently practical, the rearrangement was typical of Salisbury's pursuit of the convenient and indifference to the aesthetic. It was typical, also, of the conventional character of Salisbury's behaviour as a landlord during his first ten years: conscientious, unexceptionable by the standards of the day, in no way distinctive or unusual. The pattern of expenditure on building-works tells the story. Half the total expenditure of the ten years to 1877 was devoted to Hatfield House and its gardens, park, out-buildings, and lodges; one fifth went on farm buildings and another fifth on cottages, which were mostly built in pairs on individual farms, and a new school was provided for Hatfield town.[27] This was normal for a well-managed estate which was not burdened by debts and which had a healthy annual surplus available for investment in improvements. Farm buildings were being cared for and modernised; farm labourers were being decently rehoused in isolated cottages where the farmers wanted them, close to their work; a landlord's social obligation to look after the education of his dependents was being discharged; and all the rest was quite properly being used to improve the comfort, convenience and utility of the owner's own residence. There was nothing here to put Salisbury in the class who were earning glowing reputations at the time as exceptionally good landlords – the dukes of Bedford, Northumberland, Grafton and Richmond, the Earl of Leicester, or plain Mr Abel Smith, for example – and equally there was nothing to put him in the negligent class. Estate management, which was adequate while leaving ample room for personal indulgence, carries the mark of a routine carried on by the agent and clerk of works from his father's day, with Salisbury's personal interest and intervention being focused on the House.

This was not entirely true. Lady Salisbury set about visiting the estate cottages very soon after 1868, and was much concerned about their sanitation and water supply, giving precise instructions for installing guttering and pipes to catch rainwater. Lord Salisbury was much interested by the experiment which his father had started in the early 1860s by building both concrete cottages and mud cottages (wattle and daub, or cob) at Hatfield Hyde in order to compare costs and serviceability. From 1873 he added a third type to the comparison, Richmond cottages, probably called after the design used on the Duke of Richmond's Sussex estate, the Duke being a close friend. The Richmond cottages, uncharacteristically, required fancy imported French ornamental tiles. They did not win outright, for, while mud and concrete cottages sank without trace and Richmond cottages survived to be used in special situations until the late 1880s, the bulk of subsequent cottage-building settled on an estate design, which owed much to Lady Salisbury and later to Lady Gwendolen.[28] It was plain, sanitary and moral, intended to be economical not attractive. Standard cottages had a living-room and a scullery, and two bedrooms; some had three bedrooms. They were generally built in pairs, but in the town some were in rows. In the 1890s the installation of earth closets in place of cesspools or no separate privies was still being counted as an important improvement, although in the better houses in Hatfield and in several of the farmhouses water closets were being introduced at the time. Luxuries were beyond the means of labourers and their families; any attempts at architectural effects were reserved for the lodges, including those at the entrances to the more important farms, larger houses for senior estate officials, and public buildings. This did not prevent the labourers' cottages of the late nineteenth century becoming highly desirable residences for commuters in the late twentieth century.

Lady Gwendolen recalled that on succeeding to the estates her father 'found the mass of his cottage property unsatisfactory. He declined to delegate reform in this matter to agents. He and Lady Salisbury carried out a prolonged inspection and entered gradually upon a campaign of demolition and reconstruction.'[29] This is

approximately accurate, except that the records show nothing much
happening before 1879; in the earlier years, to which Lady
Gwendolen's recollection might be taken to apply, she would have
been a child of ten. 1879, indeed, with the first order for the
demolition of tumbledown cottages in Hatfield and their
replacement by three new ones, seems to have marked a turning-
point in policy, the inauguration both of more active personal
control and of a definite cottage campaign.[30] The explanation of this
change in direction is unclear. It was not associated with any notable
public developments or any fresh general publicity for the
wretchedness of rural cottages, which had last attracted wide
attention in 1868–9. It may have been purely the result of the time it
took Salisbury to survey the condition of his inheritance and mature
his plans; and it may reflect the waning influence and reliability of
the head agent inherited from his father's time, who was to retire in
1885. The change itself was clear enough. Initially a switch in the
directions of expenditure, not a change in the overall level, apart
from a tailing-off in what was spent on Hatfield House; the great
surge in total expenditure did not get under way until 1887. From
1879 onwards, however, activity on farm buildings and the building
of isolated cottages on farms was greatly reduced, cottage-building
and rebuilding was more and more concentrated on Hatfield and
Hatfield Hyde, and more, and more varied, attention was paid to
the needs of Hatfield as a community. In part this was a negative
response to agricultural depression, whose effects were being felt by
tenant farmers on the estate by 1879; the response was to curtail
expenditure on the farms, while reducing rents, and to cease
pandering to the farmers' pronounced preference for housing their
labourers on the farm, under their close control.[31] The relative
decline in this farm-based expenditure was undoubted; but the
increase on the village or town-based side was not simply a rebound
effect; it reflected positive policy decisions.

Lady Gwendolen recalled that her father 'resisted the farmers'
constant pressure for tied cottages, and kept their letting resolutely
in his own hands.' He may well have objected to tied cottages,
holding that the tyranny of farmers over labourers through the fear
of eviction and homelessness was heartless and unjust. But where
the system already existed on his estate Salisbury was either
unwilling, or unable, to alter it; cottages that lay out on the farms,
including the new ones built in the early 1870s and the few pairs
which were built at the end of the 1890s, chiefly on outlying farms,

invariably continued to be let with the farms, to the tenant farmer, throughout his time.[32] Salisbury only became a direct landlord of his labourers in the village and town setting. This alternative to the tied-cottage system chanced to coincide with the reported preference of Hertfordshire farm labourers for living in villages, rather than on isolated farms, although this preference may itself have been essentially an antipathy to tied cottages rather than to social isolation as such. 'It is said to be a Hertfordshire custom to love a village and hate solitude,' it was stated in the 1890s, 'but there is also a strong dislike to being tied to an employer by occupying his cottage.'[33] The chance for Salisbury to back the alternative came with the weakening position of farmers after 1879, and their contracting demand for labour.

Farm labourers, working for Salisbury tenant farmers, were among the beneficiaries of the new policy, and their good fortune in living in rows of well-built, three-bedroom Hatfield cottages was singled out for comment by Rider Haggard when conducting his tour of English farming in 1901.[34] They were not, however, the only, nor probably the most numerous, of the beneficiaries. There were large numbers of estate workers employed in the gardens, Park and Home Farm of Hatfield House: twenty to thirty gardeners, workers in the estate sawmill and carpenter's shop, building, repair and maintenance men, dynamo men (after 1881), farm and dairy workers, most of the stable staff – all these lived outside the grounds.[35] In addition the responsible officials, head agent, clerk of the works, surveyor, manager of the sawmill, head gardener, head gamekeeper, bailiff of the Home Farm and foreman of estate workers, all customarily lived in superior estate houses; vicar and doctor, although not exactly estate employees, might well occupy similar estate houses, while the socially inferior schoolteachers could expect something better than the most humble cottage. These, along with others such as tradesmen and small-town craftsmen who had at most only indirect connections with the estate, probably formed the majority of the inhabitants of Hatfield. There is no sign that Salisbury set out to benefit only 'his people' in his building policy, and indeed, contrary to the common practice, he charged the same cottage rents to employees and non-employees alike, with a couple of trifling exceptions.[36] He was embarked on the policy of being a rural-housing landlord, not simply a landlord whose responsibilities were confined to his own tenants and workers.

This did not happen all at once. For several years after 1879 activities in Hatfield were limited to replacing the worst cottages and improving those that were worth saving. This was a comparatively modest programme, a matter of a couple of cottages in Fore Street, a few more in Back Street and a pair near to Countess Anne's school. The major effort of this period was the building of the Temperance Hotel, a measure aimed at improving the moral balance in Hatfield rather than at routing the demon drink, since neither on personal nor on political grounds had Salisbury any desire to pose as a temperance advocate. 'It is quite true that we are building a small club and coffee-palace here', he explained to Lady Janetta Manners, one of his favourite correspondents, who was a strong teetotaller; 'the plans have just been settled. I have no wish to extirpate beer – but we have about a dozen public houses in this little village, and no coffee house: so that the balance is not quite fair.'[37] New cottages which were not simply replacements but made an addition to the supply of accommodation were concentrated, at this period, at Hatfield Hyde. This lay some two miles north of Hatfield, and at the beginning of the 1860s was a tiny hamlet of no more than half-a-dozen cottages and a farmhouse. Its development began in Salisbury's father's time, coinciding with the 1865 Union Chargeability Act and perhaps a response to it, as the Act removed the incentive on large landowners to keep down the poor-rates in parishes that they controlled by restricting the number of cottages and hence inhabitants. Salisbury continued this expansion so that by the 1870s Hatfield Hyde had grown into a rather motley estate village, ungracious with its assortment of cottage types but large enough for people to begin to call it Hatfield Newtown. Nothing now survives of Hatfield Hyde, and it is preserved only as the name of one of the districts of Welwyn Garden city, a fate which may have been preordained by its evident shortcomings as a new town. These seem to have stemmed from its character as a single-class, labourers', village, with no resident moral influences. In the troublesome case of the thirteen gardeners who left work an hour early, the agent's investigations uncovered Grovestock and Scales as the ringleaders, who 'live at New Town where possibly they may have heard nothing to their advantage. . . . I hope we shall hear no more in future about strikes here, as I gave them a good rowing.'[38]

A fear that he was creating a nest of disaffected and insubordinate labourers who might become radicals, on his own estate, may have induced Salisbury to alter course. Alternatively, he may have reached the conclusion that the way to tackle the problem of the bad conditions in the two thirds of Hatfield which he did not own was to increase the share in his ownership by new development, trusting that the competition of his superior cottages at reasonable rents would drive the bad petty landlords out of existence: they would either have to improve and become good landlords, or they would be forced out of business.[39] Whatever the cause, the third phase of Lord Salisbury's building operations began in 1887, with the building of a block of thirty-seven new cottages in Hatfield, the Primrose Cottages. Other similar ventures followed, so that by 1902 over a hundred new cottages had been added to Hatfield, enough to house about 500 people and to raise the fraction of the town owned by Lord Salisbury from one third to well over half. At the same time this third phase saw Salisbury providing the town with an expensive waterworks and water supply, a cottage hospital, a hall for the Church Army, a new post office, a shed for the sanitary inspector, a house for the schoolmaster, and, crowning glory of his last years, a new boys' school and technical institute, which cost over twice as much as the 1870 school and almost as much as had been spent on the new drive to the station. A third leg to this Hatfield programme, besides the cottages and the public buildings, was to provide for the social and moral order of the town, in case the simple proximity of the great house was not sufficient, by building or extending at least nine superior and dignified town houses, including a fine new vicarage for his second son, Lord William, an outstanding vicar whose kindliness no less than his eccentricity passed into folk memory. The outlay on these nine houses fell little short of the cost of a hundred cottages.[40] All in all, Hatfield was transformed in these closing years of the nineteenth century, becoming much more of a Salisbury town that it had ever been before.

This image of increasing dependence on a rising flow of paternal benevolence was not what Salisbury had set out to achieve, and did not sit too comfortably beside his views of a modernised Conservative politics distancing itself from taunts about the 'feudal' behaviour of its grandees. He had, in effect, set out to practice 'five per cent philanthropy'. The essence of this doctrine was that, provided the supplier was not grasping, it was perfectly possible to provide adequate, well-built dwellings at reasonable rents and obtain a fair rate of return on the investment; all that was needed, the theory continued, was for a few philanthropic individuals or associations to finance practical examples of this on the ground, and then ordinary commercial builders would imitate the example and before very long bad housing would be only a fading memory. The theory also implied civic independence and non-interference by the philanthropists. The demonstration effect failed to work for Salisbury, just as it failed to work for the much larger philanthropic housing efforts of Peabody, Waterlow and others in London. It failed for the very simple reason that the sums were wrong and commercial builders could not afford to follow such extravagant examples. Either the rents were too high, excluding a large proportion of the lower-waged workers, who could only afford much cheaper and poorer accommodation, or the rate of return on the capital was too low, acceptable only to charitable feelings, not to the market place; frequently both. Rents which yielded a return of 5 per cent gross on the building cost, with the landlord paying the rates, and with no allowance for the value of the land, for the costs of management, for maintenance and repairs or for depreciation, were pitifully inadequate and totally unattractive to the market. The usual calculation was that the least grasping and most altruistic builder or housing-landlord needed a rental income of at least 8 or 9 per cent on the building cost to be able to stay in business and avoid making a loss. Salisbury could not escape from this financial logic except by subsidising his estate housing for philanthropic and social reasons, but he deluded himself into believing that he had succeeded in getting rid of 'the system of eleemosynary rents, traditional on most large estates', and was behaving in accordance with strict business principles.[41]

Lord Salisbury was resolute, methodical and efficient: he reached the target he had set himself. For 133 cottages built between 1887 and 1900, for which both the building costs and the rents are known, the rents were producing, in 1902, an average rate of return on the capital of 5.25 per cent, with a range from 3.9 to 5.9 per cent.[42] It was a triumph of the will; it was not a great social achievement. In the later nineteenth century there was much discussion of cottage-building as a profitable investment, and the general opinion was that farm labourers could not afford to pay more than 2s. a week in rent, at which level cottages had to be constructed at less than £85 each or they would be loss-making.[43] The Duke of Bedford, probably the best-known and best-respected cottage-building landowner of the day, published detailed accounts of some of his activities in Bedfordshire: they showed that he charged rents of 1s. 6d. a week on cottages costing £135 and £158 each, representing gross yields of just over 2 per cent and net yields, after deducting the expenses of rates, repairs, and management, of 1 per cent in the first case and 0.3 per cent in the second. He had deliberately abandoned 'the ruthlessness of the commercial system' and accepted considerable financial loss on his cottage property, because he knew 'of no more satisfactory form of philanthropy possible for the owner of a great estate than the provision of good cottages', and that it was impossible to provide good cottages without generous subsidies.[44] This was typical of the experience of most great landowners, except that some did not choose to be philanthropic and simply did not build cottages in any number. It was also confirmed by large-scale inquiry that 1s. 6d. a week was the most usual cottage rent throughout England, in the 1890s, and in Hertfordshire rents of 1s. and 1s. 3d. were not uncommon.[45] How then, did Salisbury contrive to flout the experience of his peers?

The answer is that he did not. He certainly favoured economical building, without frills, and one batch of ten cottages cost only £86 each; but these can scarcely have come up to his own standards, since the average cost of the 133 cottages was £180, with one large group running up to £249. The strikingly high rate of return on capital was produced not by low building costs, but by high rents. These averaged 3s. 6d. a week; no more than twenty cottages had rents as low as 1s. 9d. and 2s., and the highest, for over fifty cottages, were 5s. 3d. Such rents were beyond the reach of farm labourers, whose earnings at this time were 14s. to 16s. a week. The great majority of his cottages were suited to better-off workers with earnings of 24s. to 36s. a week, a bracket which would have included the more skilled among his own estate workers, and could only have been occupied by farm labourers' families if they took in a lodger, a practice of which he strongly disapproved. In effect he had succeeded in demonstrating on the small stage of Hatfield what the model-dwelling companies had already demonstrated in the metropolis, that if a return of 5 per cent on outlay was required, then adequate housing of reasonable quality could only be provided for the superior and better-paid sections of the working classes. The achievement should not be derided: it brought greatly improved health, welfare and comfort to the beneficiaries. But it was a limited achievement, of little direct relevance to the labourers. For them it was necessary to build down to the level of rents they could afford, which meant inadequate accommodation and facilities and flimsy construction; or to do as the Duke of Bedford did, build well and subsidise rents by as much as the urgings of humanitarian feelings or enlightened self-interest required. Since the gross return of 5 per cent was in itself commercially inadequate, because out of it Salisbury had to pay for rates, repairs and management, he was effectively practising an attenuated or parsimonious philanthropy for the benefit of the better-off, a paradoxical result for his liberality.

Curiously enough, Lord Salisbury was well aware of all this, at the general level, when he made his dramatic entry into the public debate on housing with his famous article 'Labourers' and Artisans' Dwellings' in the *National Review* of November 1883. Reviewing the work of the Peabody Trust and other housing agencies in London, he found that, 'in spite of the lowness of the interest they accept, they have not been able to reduce their rent sufficiently to meet the wants of the class for whom help is most sorely needed'. He concluded that 'a considerable number of the better-paid workmen have been housed; and they have ceased to add to the pressure by competing with the poorest class for the accommodation that exists. But beyond this, nothing has been done for the housing of this poorest class, whose need is the greatest, and who furnish most of the terrible cases of overcrowding'. He drew virtually the same conclusion about rural housing. 'The cost of a healthy cottage at present prices may be put at an average of £150', he stated. 'To pay four per cent interest on this sum, and to lay by two per cent for repairs and replacement of capital, the rent must be not less than £9 a year, or three and sixpence a week – a sum which is beyond the ordinary means of an agricultural labourer'. He saw very clearly that in both town and country low wages were the root of the problem. 'The difficulty in their case,' he said of the poorest class in London, 'as in that of the agricultural labourer, is their poverty. Until their wages rise they cannot pay for the bare cost of decent lodgings'. He had no policies to offer for raising wages, leaving it to be inferred that he held that wages were determined by economic laws with which it was dangerous and useless to tamper. But, for rural cottages at least, he warmly approved of the housing-subsidies provided by 'a class of landowners sufficiently at ease to disregard exact considerations of profit and loss', who 'have been generally impelled, partly by their own interest, partly by other considerations, to provide suitable lodging for those who cultivate their land.' Among the solutions which he suggested for the housing problem, his favourite seems to have been a wide extension of low-rent employer housing of this kind. 'Many employers of labour would find, if not a profit, at all events a convenience which would be indirectly profitable, as well as a satisfaction for their benevolent feelings, in the provision of decent lodging for the poorer class of those whom they employ, at a price within their means.' His further proposal that the state should give a lead in this, by providing low-rent housing for its lowest-paid employees in the post office, the police and the revenue service, was highly controversial with its implications of state socialism and the creation of a gigantic system of tied cottages. Not surprisingly, no more was heard of this idea when Salisbury was in power. The justification, and indeed the necessity, of private employers, including private landowners, providing below-cost housing for their low-paid workers remained.[46]

There remained also the contrast between what Salisbury the politician advocated and what Salisbury the landowner practised. It is true that the 133 Hatfield cottages whose economics have been analysed did not include any examples of the detached pairs of cottages built on farm holdings at some distance from any village. Information on their rents is not available since they were tied cottages, and it is quite possible that they were let at non-economic rents; in the case of some of them, which cost more than £250, and where a full rent on Salisbury's own principles would have had to be 5s. 9d. or 6s. a week, this is virtually certain. No more than a dozen such cottages on farms, however, were built in his time; the total labour force of the farms of the Hatfield estate, on the normal contemporary estimate of two cottages for every 100 cultivated acres, would have required at least 250 cottages.[47] The conclusion is inescapable that to a substantial extent he chose not to act as an open-handed benefactor in the way in which he suggested the natural leaders of rural and industrial communities ought to act. When it came to the management of his own estate, it seems that his sense of the rectitude of business principles was stronger than his sense of humanitarian or paternalist obligations.

When Lord Salisbury captured the leading position as a housing-reformer with his 1883 article, and continued to make the running on the housing question with speeches in the Lords, membership of the Royal Commission on the Housing of the Working Classes of 1884–5, and a prime role in the passing of the 1885 Housing of the Working Classes Act, his critics did not notice this discrepancy.[48] They were alarmed and angry that he was dishing the liberals and stealing their clothing in best Disraelian manner, confident that on housing he could be exposed as a mere political opportunist, and less interested in conducting rational argument than in the chance that Salisbury might turn out to have feet of clay. While Joseph Chamberlain was preparing his counterblast for the *Fortnightly Review*, in which he coupled his alternative housing policy with somewhat ineffective criticism of Salisbury as an unwitting advocate of nationalisation of the land, he and that journal's editor, T. H. S. Escott, were concocting a scheme to destroy Salisbury's credibility by exposing him as a bad landlord.[49] A reporter was commissioned to investigate Salisbury's cottage property in Hatfield, who at once came up with lurid descriptions of filthy, noisome hovels as the basis for a blistering and sensational attack. Before publishing this, Escott prudently decided to send a second reporter down to Hatfield to check the facts. He found that the first account was grossly exaggerated, where it was not just a complete fabrication: Lord Salisbury's cottages, he reported, were in fact very good ones, and disreputable and neglected cottages all belonged to other people. The exposure was withdrawn from publication, and Chamberlain backed away from using sensational journalism as a political weapon, saved by the skin of his teeth from making a fool of himself. The following year Escott, in the course of an extremely critical profile of Lord Salisbury, had the grace to present the Hatfield cottage matter in its true light. 'How comes it', he asked, 'that a peer who is so studiously courteous in his private demeanour, who, whatever may be the condition of his Dorchester [*sic*] estate – which is more remote from him and does not therefore come within his personal purview – is so excellent a landlord as the condition of his Hatfield property shows him to be, can thus trample upon the tenderest sentiments and deepest convictions of those who presume to dissent from his political opinions, or whom nature has made his inferiors in the social scale?'[50]

Chamberlain was not the only one who thought the condition of an opponent's property might be used to trip him up. In November 1883, only a couple of weeks after the false Hatfield report, Salisbury wrote to H. J. B. Manners, 'I see Chamberlain is at the great landowners again. Is it not time we went to the great screw-owners? I think they ought to set to work at the Central Office to find out how the Chamberlain firm lodge their hands and how they treat them.'[51] He clearly had second thoughts about the wisdom, or the feasibility, of doing this, and nothing more was heard of such a tit-for-tat. Possibly prudence and instinct for self-protection were at work. On his Hatfield flank Salisbury was secure from exposure, for, although his major improvements there still lay in the future in 1883, he had already accomplished much in removing the blackspots on his property, amply sufficient to convince any outside observer that he was a good landlord. He was, however, not so secure on his urban flank, and very likely did not want to risk being pilloried as a slum landlord, which was certain to happen in any serious muck-raking contest with Chamberlain.

The precise boundaries of Salisbury's property in central London were not public knowledge at the time, and in any case it was difficult to discover what control, if any, Salisbury as ground landlord had over the condition and use of buildings that might be in the possession of long leaseholders or their sub-lessess. It was because of this uncertainty that Chamberlain and Escott called off their sleuth, who had contemplated a devastating survey of both the Salisbury and the Bedford London estates.[51] Nevertheless, he had been rummaging in the right area, near St Martin's Lane; and there was enough rumour and gossip for Salisbury to make a denial. 'It should not be forgotten that everything that bore his name did not belong to him,' he was reported to have told a deputation of the Amalgamated Society of Riverside Workmen and other trade unionists, 'and he might say that streets which were called Salisbury St. and Cranbourne St. should not be supposed to be his property. It was true they belonged to his family some 200 years ago, but as some of his ancestors were thriftless, the property had passed into other hands. His property in London was very small, and not in any one of the districts where these unsanitary, overcrowded dwellings existed.'[53] This was said at a private meeting at his Arlington Street house, and Salisbury was angry that a report had been leaked to *The Times*: 'they have altered the language in which I spoke of my own property', he complained to Manners.[54] He did not say in what way it had been altered: perhaps he actually said that he did not own every bit of Salisbury Street, for he certainly did own most of it. In any case the denial was disingenuous. He indisputably did own Cecil Court, and Cecil Court was a well-known little slum of crowded tenements in a narrow alley running between St Martin's Lane and the present Charing Cross Road. He was also aware that Cecil Court was a slum, for his London agent had virtually told him so in 1880.[55]

The two rather unsavoury Courts which he owned, Cecil and the adjoining St Martin's, did not make Salisbury a slum landlord in a big way: together they can hardly have had much more than a couple of hundred residents. His degree of responsibility for their condition was in any case far from clear. He was the ground landlord, and the buildings themselves were let on long leases, the leaseholders being the people who decided how the buildings were occupied and what should be their state of disrepair. On the other hand he, or the Salisbury estate, could not disclaim all responsibility, since all the original building leases had fallen in at some stage in the recent past, at which point both building and ground had been in Salisbury's possession and it would have been possible to use the landlord's powers to end overcrowding. Instead the decision was made to issue new long leases, at greatly enhanced rents which necessarily encouraged and perpetuated the tenementing of the buildings: a typical situation was that of 30 St Martin's Court, let on a long lease for £60 a year, which the absentee leaseholder sub-let in tenements to perhaps seven weekly tenants – whether single lodgers, or families, is not clear – from whom if he was lucky he collected £91 a year.[56] Rescue from this embarrassing position was, however, at hand. The construction of Charing Cross Road, authorised in 1877 and under way by the early 1880s, opened up this district to commercially attractive redevelopment. One harbinger of this was Salisbury's lease to Quintin Hogg in 1880 of a frontage in St Martin's Lane and several back-houses in Cecil and St Martin's Courts, which were to be demolished; a minimum of £6,000 was to be spent on the redevelopment, possibly as a theatre, and Hogg took a lease for eighty years at a rent of £200.[57] In this fashion Salisbury's slums were improved out of existence by market forces. The slum-dwellers presumably moved elsewhere and became someone else's problem as their dwellings were demolished.

It certainly did not occur to Salisbury that he could have any responsibility for rehousing displaced people on the other segment of his London property, Cecil Street and Salisbury Street on the south side of the Strand. These streets, recently deprived of their wharf on the Thames by the completion of the Embankment, were the remnant of the seventeenth-century Cecil House, laid out on its site at the beginning of the next century. The houses, in the 1880s, were still comfortable and fairly superior middle-class residences, on annual rents of £55–85. The original building-leases had long since fallen in, and indeed further cycles of succeeding long leases had also been completed. By 1880 the policy was to restrict all leases in the two streets to annual tenancies, a necessary preparation for selling off the entire site, which was accomplished in 1888. Salisbury, according to the public report, received £200,000 for the 2–3 acres in question, and the developers intended 'to clear the site for the erection of several blocks of new buildings . . . including hotels facing the Embankment, one or more theatres, clubs, and residential chambers.'[58] In the 1890s the Hotel Cecil, rising provocatively above the neighbouring Savoy, duly appeared.[59]

The function of the London property was to produce money, not to display personal benevolence or paternalist concern. In the 1870s and 1880s it produced about £20,000 a year, net, the landlord's expenditures on the property being very small.[60] Much the same could be said of Lord Salisbury's other properties, the inheritance of the Gascoyne heiress who had been his father's first wife, and his mother. It is not that these estates were not well-managed: Salisbury almost certainly gave more sustained personal attention to the detail of their administration than is revealed by the fragmentary records that have survived, and these themselves indicate no more than the occasional instances of inefficiencies and mishaps that can be expected on any estate. It is rather that there is no sign of personal identification with these detached estates, or of social concern for their inhabitants. On learning that the elderly manager of the Childwall (Liverpool) gas works, estate-owned, had embezzled £300, Salisbury wrote 'that he must not be employed any more but in view of his age (76) and long service I would not take away his pension and house.'[61] The benevolence of a landowner to estate servants clearly extended far from Hatfield and was not dimmed by detachment; but there is no evidence that it extended into providing amenities for the growing population on that estate who were not estate servants.

The Childwall estate, on the north-eastern edge of Liverpool, had been the original seat of the Gascoyne family; a country house and some 1800 acres of surrounding farm land in the early nineteenth century. While Fanny, the Gascoyne heiress, was alive, the Salisburys made quite frequent use of Childwall Hall, as an autumn residence, but in 1836 as an economy measure it was let, and no Salisburys even lived there again.[62] The attachment, and presence, of a family residence on the estate, even a holiday residence, was thus absent; and the tenant, though of gentry rank, did not perform as a substitute squire. The tide of building development reached the edges of the Childwall estate, in Everton and West Derby, in 1843, and from then onwards the estate administration was continuously engaged in approving the laying out of streets – though not in actually making or paying for them – and in negotiating building agreements, on leases at first for seventy-five years and later for ninety-nine years. By 1852 the ground rents, from 380 separate leases and agreements, were bringing in £3624 a year, at a time when the farm land, held in seventeen middling to small farms, yielded £5693 in rents.[63] By 1868 the ground rents had grown to over £6000 a year, by 1889 to over £10,000; since one or two farms in Wavertree had disappeared, as well as several fields in Everton and West Derby which had been accommodation land, the farm rents can be presumed to have fallen by several hundred pounds. There were more than 2000 houses on the Childwall estate by 1889 – a small fraction of the total in the Liverpool conurbation, but in themselves the equivalent of a large outer suburb.[64]

Salisbury certainly showed lively curiosity about the commercial arrangements for the development of the estate, and on his succession took pains to see that he was fully informed. In particular he was puzzled by the practice, which was apparently the general custom on leasehold building estates in Liverpool, under which the ground landlord made sizable advances to the builder, amounting to half the cost of construction, at various distinct stages in the course of construction of each house. Such a system was not familiar in Southern experience, where the channels of credit for speculative builders were more developed and more specialised. It meant that Salisbury had loans outstanding to the builders at work on his estate amounting to upwards of £20,000 at any one time. Nevertheless, such loans were expected by all the builders in the district, and it was necessary to continue the practice if building land was to be let on leases. Some of the large building estates in Liverpool, those of the Earl of Derby, the Earl of Sefton and the Blundells, were also being developed on leases, but freehold building land was readily available and possibly was more common than leasehold. This competition could have serious effects on the leasehold estates. 'The explanation of the delay in taking up leases', Salisbury was told in December 1870, 'is that in consequence of the very depressed state of the money market in Liverpool builders find it very difficult to effect mortgages upon leasehold properties; freehold properties can be readily dealt with but at present there exists a great prejudice against leasehold property.'[65]

The upshot was that Salisbury continued with the practices and routines established in his father's time, with no changes in development policy, a regime punctuated by occasional progresses round the estate, accompanied by his London solicitor, to see for himself what was going on.[66] What was happening was unremarkable: development with terraced cottages for the working classes on the inner edge closest to central Liverpool, with conversions to shops and pubs every now and then as settlement grew denser, and further out some better-class semi-detached and detached houses – a few, alongside Sefton Park, set in large grounds – most of which were themselves destined to be overwhelmed by the advance of more close-packed housing within a generation.[67] The only remarkable feature was that Salisbury, unlike several other aristocrats who became considerable urban landlords, appears to have made no attempt to cultivate a political interest, either local, municipal or parliamentary, in his newly peopled ground. The one recorded attempt to capitalise on the Cecil interest, a very half-hearted attempt since Lord Salisbury seems to have played a completely passive part in it, was a complete flop. At the 1893 by-election for the West Derby constituency his eldest son, Lord Cranborne, was considered as a possible candidate by the local Conservative association: he received one vote, against the winner Walter Long's thirteen, eleven for C. T. Ritchie, the President of the Local Government Board before 1892, and ten for the local man, J. de B. Adam, past Lord Mayor of Liverpool.[68] The explanation of the indifference, no doubt, was that Salisbury saw no point in even starting to foster a local interest, with all the extra effort and expenditure that entailed, when it could never hope to rival or even augment significantly the towering presence of the Derbys, the uncrowned kings of Liverpool.

This meant that in relation to his Childwall estate Salisbury was simply a rentier, albeit a mildly active managerial rentier. In relation to the Bifrons estate, Barking, even the managerial bit seems to have been missing. This was the Bamber part of the Bamber-Gascoyne inheritance, some 500 or so acres around Barking Creek with a house, Bifrons, which was always let from 1801 onwards.[69] In the surviving records at Hatfield there is no mention of Salisbury visiting the Bifrons estate, neither is the estate ever mentioned by his chief London agent. This is not conclusive, but the impression is created that this property was left alone to look after itself until in due season it should become ripe for building development. It is not even certain when that was. The estate surfaces briefly in some sale particulars of 1889 of building plots, and then again disappears from view. The particulars describe this as being a sale of the first portion of the Gascoigne [*sic*] estate; on the other hand, the accompanying map shows that Gascoigne Road, the central road of this chunk of development, was already formed and partly built up, implying earlier building activity. Small as it is, this scrap of evidence does suggest that in the handling of this portion of the Bifrons estate Lord Salisbury was practising what he preached and doing his bit as a private landowner to implement one of the remedies for London's overcrowded slums which he had proposed in his 1883 *National Review* article. The building plots were all small, with 15-foot frontages, but with depths of 80–90 feet would have afforded comparatively large gardens; they were advertised as being 'especially adapted for the erection of workmen's dwellings'; the conditions of sale imposed a minimum value of only £100 for each house to be erected, considerably less than the cost of a Hatfield cottage; and stress was laid on the frequent cheap workmen's trains to London being run by the London, Tilbury and Southend Railway. All this fitted perfectly Salisbury's advocacy in 1883 of decanting workers to outer suburbs, provided that cheap transport was available. Further, in 1889 the plots were sold freehold, in contrast with the ordinary leasing policy in central London and in Liverpool. It is possible that this was because Salisbury was not a dominant landowner in Barking, able to dictate his own terms, and was conforming to local custom, if indeed that custom was one of freehold building tenures. It is equally possible that, with agitation against leasehold building tenures and in favour of leasehold enfranchisement at its height in 1889, he was taking out political insurance against the risk of anti-ground-landlord publicity.[70] Gascoigne Road was shortly followed by Cecil, Cranborne and Salisbury Roads, Bifrons Street and many others bearing names without family associations, until finally all the Barking, Dagenham and Hornchurch property was built over. As the Salisbury estate shed itself of the building land, and its stake in the district dwindled, so the purchase money flowed in; the amounts are unrecorded, but it would be surprising if building land in this area did not fetch over £1000 an acre in the late nineteenth century.

Except conceivably in the last instance, Lord Salisbury as an urban landowner behaved much like any other conventional, honest and competent Victorian urban landlord. Interested in maximising the financial returns from his property, without countenancing shady practices or tolerating jerry builders, he was largely indifferent to the new communities appearing on his estates: he was not one of that small class of great urban landowners who nursed and nurtured the new towns or suburbs which they created. Even the explicit encouragement of workmen's dwellings at Barking was most likely due less to a personal decision than to the influence of the existing surrounding environment of jute works, workshops and workers' cottages, which made any other kind of development unattractive to the speculative builders who would carry it out. As a rural landowner, by contrast, Lord Salisbury was a paternalist of the Victorian-modified school, acknowledging moral obligations and social responsibilities for his tenantry, servants and dependants, while conscious of the damaging effects of excessive or indiscriminate charity; he tried to practice businesslike philanthropy, a doctrine intended to avoid demoralising the recipients and destroying their independence. The property structure and estate administration were the link between the two worlds, and in the final analysis the person of Lord Salisbury himself provided the pipeline which carried the flow of resources from urban rents and the town-dwellers who generated them, to the country and the country-dwellers who benefited from their expenditure.

The expenditure on the Hatfield estate was effectively financed by the urban income, as was Salisbury's way of living, itself made specially expensive by the nature of his political life. The urban income also insulated Salisbury from the financial effects of agricultural depression and falling agricultural rents. It did not, of course, prevent his tenant farmers from experiencing the depression, and he had to become a reluctant farmer himself when several Hatfield tenants were ruined and their farms fell in hand. Publicly he expressed some enthusiasm for this, angrily denying suggestions made by some local Conservative farmers that his farms in hand were out of cultivation and growing nothing but weeds and thistles, and anxious to provide a demonstration that it was possible to go on farming properly, and economically, even with the low prices of the 1880s.[71] But his heart was not in it. His private thoughts were revealed to Lady Janetta Manners. In 1881 he told her, 'like all landowners, I find tenants just now are a weariness to the flesh. How pleasant it must be to have nothing but Consols.' And again in 1888, further anticipating Lady Bracknell, he wrote to Lady Janetta, recently become Duchess of Rutland, 'I should have been more inclined to condole with you on the unbounded nuisance of having to look after a landed property – an evil which seems quite imaginary to those who are not suffering it. I wish all property was in Consols – an ideal Consols, never liable to be converted.'[72] He was a great landowner because birth and circumstance decreed it, and he was prepared to make the most of his not unenviable lot. It is hard to avoid thinking, however, that what he really enjoyed being was not a landowner, not a party-leader, not even an eminent statesman, but an intellectual conservative poking fun at some of the 'modern' institutions and progressive ideas of Victorian Britain.

The marriage market he had satirised in the *Saturday Review* in his youth. 'The market is absolutely glutted with unsaleable young ladies', he wrote in 1861. 'Heiresses, of course, are still brisk, and something is doing in pretty orphans. . . . The majority of fashionable mothers appear to have studied with envy the accomplishments of the pretty horse-breakers, and to have conceived of the ingenious plans of entrapping men to make wives of their daughters by fitting them to be their mistresses.'[73] In his maturity he ridiculed, inconsistently, the craze for higher education for women, saying of the ladies' colleges at Oxford and Cambridge,

> from all I hear the young ladies do not become very amiable or attractive members of society. Speaking of them generally, these colleges are decidedly free-thinking. . . . On Sunday morning they discuss all conceivable forms of unbelief. I dare say these colleges are useful in furnishing a diploma to ladies who wish to be governesses: but for any other purpose I should do my utmost to dissuade any female relation over whom I had any influence from going there. I have heard several instances of young ladies suffering permanently in health in consequence of attempting to study like men at an age when men can do it safely but they cannot.[74]

Another great craze of his time, the urge to extend the machinery of elective and representative institutions into local government, he found equally laughable. If applied to country villages, he told the Marquis of Bath, 'the best man would not stand on canvass, and we should ever be in danger of seeing itinerant orators returned.' As it was, on the existing Boards of Guardians 'half are generally the best men in the place, the other half the nominees of the rabble.'[75] He returned to the point in 1886, telling Lord Cranbrook that entrusting the administration of the poor-law to an electorate that included potential recipients of poor relief would be, 'it seems to me, look at it how you will, rather like leaving the cat in charge of the cream jug.'[76] When it came to proposing parish councils he said in a public speech, 'If, among the many duties the modern state undertakes, the duty of amusing the rural population should be included, I should rather recommend a circus or something of that kind. As far as I have had the opportunity of attending vestries, I am bound to say that amusement is not the feature to be remarked upon as most prominent in them.' However much he tried to maintain, in view of the furore this created, that he 'never made such a statement as that "Circuses would do just as well for the labourer as Parish Councils"; nor did he ever make any observation to which that interpretation could reasonably be affixed', it did indeed express his true sentiments.[77]

Parish councils and other high matters of state were treated no more lightly than his domestic arrangements. Replying to a newspaper story that he had employed an Italian Jesuit priest as his majordomo, he remarked, 'I am surprised that so foolish a story should have attracted any attention. . . . Italian priests do not accept positions as butlers, which they would probably be incompetent to fill, and I have never had an Italian, whether priest or layman, in my service as butler.'[78] Household, estates, politics – all these were to be taken seriously, but not too seriously. At the end of the day Lord Salisbury's aim was to survive, without too many uncomfortable changes, fending off unpleasant or unworkable ideas with mockery, not courting disaster by opposing the irresistible, and not sacrificing compassion. This he achieved.

NOTES

All the research in the Hatfield House Archive, and much of that in the Liverpool Public Library, was done by my wife, Anne, whose help and encouragement were indispensable.

References to papers held at Hatfield House are prefixed 'HHM' (Hatfield House Muniments). The papers of the third Marquis of Salisbury are classified '3M'. PP = Parliamentary Papers.

1. Most recently by Lawrence Stone and Jeanne Fawtier Stone in *An Open Elite? England, 1540–1880* (Oxford, 1984) pp. 30–1, 280, 424–5.
2. For different interpretations of the great agricultural depression, see P. J. Perry, *British Farming in the Great Depression, 1870–1914* (Newton

Abbott, 1974); and F. M. L. Thompson, 'Free Trade and the Land', in G. E. Mingay (ed.), *The Victorian Countryside* (London, 1981) I, 103–17.

3. Schedule B rent assessments, *Reports of the Commissioners of Inland Revenue*, PP, 1884–5, XXII, and 1896, XLIX.

4. Robert Blake, *The Conservative Party from Peel to Churchill* (London, 1970) p. 109.

5. J. Cornford, 'The Transformation of Conservatism in the Late Nineteenth Century', *Victorian Studies*, VII, no. 1 (Sep 1963).

6. Lady Gwendolen Cecil, *Life of Robert Marquis of Salisbury*, II (London, 1921) 3.

7. F. M. L. Thompson, *English Landed Society in the Nineteenth Century* (London, 1963), pp. 322–3; Avner Offer, *Property and Politics, 1870–1914* (Cambridge, 1981) p. 362.

8. Geoffrey Channon, 'G. W. R. Gentlemen and Company Directors' (forthcoming) p. 19.

9. Lord David Cecil, *The Cecils of Hatfield House* (London 1973) pp. 225–9; J. F. A. Mason, 'The Third Marquess of Salisbury in the *Saturday Review*', *Bulletin of the Institute of Historical Research*, XXXIV (1961); *Lord Salisbury on Politics: A Selection from his Articles in the Quarterly Review, 1860–1883*, ed. Paul Smith (Cambridge, 1972).

10. HHM/3M/L, Nicholson and Herbert, solicitors, to Lord Robert Cecil, 2 Oct 1861, Oct 1864, Dec 1866 and 17 May 1867; T. C. Barker, 'Lord Salisbury, Chairman of the Great Eastern Railway, 1868–72', in Sheila Marriner (ed.), *Business and Businessmen* (Liverpool, 1978), which quotes the letter, Cranborne to Salisbury, 14 May 1866.

11. Barker, in Marriner, *Business and Businessmen*.

12. Lady Gwendolen Cecil, *Life*, II, 3.

13. Lord David Cecil, *The Cecils of Hatfield House*, p. 249.

14. HHM/Abstracts of accounts. In 1891–2, for example, 23,709 individuals (family, visitors and servants) or an average of sixty-five every day, were lodged at Hatfield, consuming 15.5 oz of bread per head per day and 1 lb 14.8 oz of meat, at an average cost of 11s. 2.1d. per head per day. In 1894–5, 8837 horses and donkeys were fed in the Hatfield stables, at a cost of 1s. 5.2d. per head per day, and 719 in the London stables at 1s. 11.5d. per head per day.

15. HHM/3M/D43, Salisbury to Professor M'Leod, Indian Civil Service College, 29 Dec 1870, 16 Jan 1871, 4 Dec 1877 and 19 Apr 1881. Mark Girouard, in *The Victorian Country House* (London, 1979) p. 25, places electric bells in the 1890s.

16. HHM/3M/C7, to W. Laycock, Ilkley, 8 Aug 1888; ibid., press-cuttings book, 1899, p. 17.

17. E. Hodder, *The Life and Work of the Seventh Earl of Shaftesbury* (London, 1887) pp. 448–50.

18. *Royal Commission on the Employment of Women and Children in Agriculture*, PP, 1868–9, XIII, report of Assistant Commissioner George Culley, J2, para. 116.

19. Ibid., minutes of evidence, Hatfield Union, paras 16–20; Hitchin Union, paras 28–9.

20. Ibid., Culley, J2, p. 116.

21. Ibid., minutes of evidence, paras 23a, 24, 29.
22. HHM/New buildings account 1883–1943, note on index page.
23. *Royal Commission on the Employment of Women and Children in Agriculture*, PP, 1868–9, XIII report of Assistant Commissioner the Hon. Edward Stanhope, G18, and evidence collected by him, p. 30. It is interesting that it was reported of the cottages in St Giles, 'Belong to Lord Shaftesbury and are excellent. All have large gardens and allotments. Rents 1s.' – a terse but satisfactory recognition of his efforts since 1851.
24. HHM/Abstracts of accounts, repair account, new buildings section, note on account for 1870.
25. HHM/New buildings account 1883–1943, note on index page.
26. HHM/Abstracts of accounts, 1876–9.
27. HHM/Abstracts of accounts, 1868–77. The distribution of building-expenditure on the Hatfield estate, 1868–1902, can be tabulated as follows:

| | Total expenditure £ | Percentages of total expenditure | | | | | | |
| | | | Cottages | | Hatfield town | Farm buildings | Hertford, Essendon, etc. | Hatfield House and Park |
		Total	Hatfield	Hatfield Hyde				
1863–7[a]	4,006	17.5	–	10	–	19	–	63
1868–77	23,519	20	2	7	8	21	–	50
1878–87	14,951	40	27	3	18	9	–	33
1888–97	43,243	40	35	4	41	7	1.5	10
1897–1902	19,320	46	25	13	32	9	9.5	3
1903–12[b]	45,994	32	14.5	5.5	40	19	2.5	7

[a] Second Marquis.
[b] Fourth Marquis.

28. HHM/Abstracts of account, 1864–73; HHM/3M/L, Clerk of Works, H. T. Shillito, to Salisbury, 17 Nov and 6 Dec 1873, 8 June 1875 and (for later Richmond cottages) 4 May 1880 and 6 Apr 1888. The Earl of Leicester was experimenting with concrete cottages at Holkham at much the same time: Susanna Wade Martins, *A Great Estate at Work* (Cambridge, 1980) pp 228–9. The results were equally unsatisfactory.
29. Lady Gwendolen Cecil, *Life*, II, 3–4.
30. HHM/3M/L, Shillito to Salisbury's secretary, R. T. Gunton, 17 Apr 1879.
31. Ibid., F. Dagg to Salisbury, 24 Aug 1879 and 22 Aug 1881. Farm rents were reduced, selectively, by up to 30 per cent.
32. Lady Gwendolen Cecil, *Life*, II, 4. Newly built, as well as existing, cottages are recorded as being let with the farms (HHM/Rent books, 1875–1901, *passim*). The well-known cottage-builders who, nevertheless, did manage to abolish tied cottages on their estates and to let directly to farm labourers included the Duke of Grafton, the Marquis of Bristol, the Earl Cadogan, the Earl of Leicester and Lord Walsingham: *Royal Commission on Labour*, PP 1893–4, XXXVII, pt II, General Report by William Little, Senior Assistant, p. 115.

33. *R.C. on Labour*, PP 1893–4, xxxv, Report of Assistant Commissioner Cecil M. Chapman, para. 66.
34. H. Rider Haggard, 'Back to the Land: Farming about Hatfield', 26 July 1901, in HHM/Press cuttings.
35. In 1873 it was a matter of relief that only thirteen gardeners had left work early, at 5 p.m. instead of 6 p.m. on a Saturday, and this was a small proportion which did not imply mass insubordination: HHM/3M/L, Dagg to Salisbury, 5 Apr 1873. Some of the estate workers had cottages at nominal or peppercorn rents, in some cases as little as 6d. a year.
36. The only differential rents charged were for Primrose Cottages, Hatfield (3s. 3d. weekly to employees, 3s. 9d. to non-employees), and St Peter's Cottages, Hatfield (2s. 9d. weekly to employees, 3s. to non-employees): HHM/New Buildings account, 1883–1943, cost of erecting certain cottages since 1887, 12 Mar 1902 (unbound memorandum).
37. HHM/3M/D48, to Lady Janetta Manners, 29 May 1884. Countess Anne was the wife of the early-eighteenth-century fifth Earl of Salisbury.
38. HHM/3M/L, Dagg to Salisbury, 5 Mar 1873. The two gardeners were dismissed. Another, who had worked in the gardens since a boy, was simply suspended for a month.
39. The second explanation is that favoured by Lady Gwendolen Cecil (*Life*, II 3–4).
40. HHM/New Buildings account, 1883–1943. For 1888–1902 expenditure on the large houses in Hatfield totalled £15,600, on public buildings and works £14,700, and on cottages £19,900.
41. For Salisbury's views on the pernicious nature of eleemosynary rents, see Lady Gwendolen Cecil, *Life*, II 3–4. The standard, somewhat uncritical, work on philanthropic housing is J. N. Tarn, *Five per cent Philanthropy* (London, 1973).
42. Calculated from memorandum on cost of erecting certain cottages since 1887, 12 Mar 1902 (HHM/New Buildings account, 1883–1943).
43. Martins, *A Great Estate at Work*, pp. 244–5, provides a summary of this discussion.
44. Duke of Bedford, *A Great Agricultural Estate*, (London 1897) pp. 81–99. The cottages of other notable builders, the Marquis of Cholmondeley and the Earl of Leicester, in Norfolk, cost £120 and £115 in the 1860s, rising to £300 in the 1890s, and returned 2½ per cent or less in rents (Martins, *A Great Estate at Work*, pp. 224–5, 240–1, 245). Salisbury was aware that '2s. 6d. house rent would only be true in a district where the wages ran up to 15s.', but was in danger of ignoring this on his own estate (HHM/3M/D48, to Lady Janetta Manners, 3 June 1886).
45. *Royal Commission on Labour*, PP 1893–4,, xxv, Assistant Commissioner Chapman, para. 77; ibid., xxxvII, pt. II, General Report by William Little, p. 116.
46. Lord Salisbury, 'Labourers' and Artisans' Dwellings', *National Review*, II (1883) esp. pp. 304, 309, 313, 315; rep. in A. S. Wohl (ed.), *Mearns's Bitter Cry of Outcast London* (New York, 1970) pp. 111–33. See Neil Kunze, 'Lord Salisbury's Ideas on Housing Reform, 1883–85', *Canadian*

Journal of History, VIII (1973), for an emphasis on Salisbury's support for government intervention in housing.

47. Costs, but not rents, of farm cottages are in HHM/Abstracts of accounts, 1868–1902. See Martins, *A Great Estate at Work*, p. 241, for ratio of cottages to cultivated area.
48. A. S. Wohl, *The Eternal Slum* (London, 1977) pp. 227–48.
49. Joseph Chamberlain, 'Labourers' and Artisans' Dwellings', *Fortnightly Review*, XXXV (1883). For the story of the Chamberlain–Escott plot I am indebted to N. Kunze, 'The Late Victorian Press and Politics: Frank Harris and Lord Salisbury's Cottages' (forthcoming), which gives a full account.
50. 'The Marquis of Salisbury, KG', *Fortnightly Review*, XXXVI (1884) 157–8. Escott's authorship is established by Kunze, in *Canadian Journal of History*, VIII, 254, n. 28.
51. HHM/3M/D47, to H. J. B. Manners (later 8th Duke of Rutland), 26 Nov 1883.
50. Kunze, 'The Late Victorian Press and Politics'.
53. *The Times*, 6 Dec 1883, p. 10.
54. HHM/3M/D47, to J. J. B. Manners, 6 Dec 1883.
55. HHM/3M/L, Nicholson and Herbert, solicitors, to Salisbury, 16 Nov 1880. In 1888 the *Star* revived the accounts of Salisbury as owner of the Cecil Court slum, apparently without any political impact: Wohl, *The Eternal Slum*, p. 228, n. 18. Cecil Court and the adjoining St Martin's Court, also owned by Salisbury, were marked as pockets of mixed character, containing some very poor and some comfortable residents, on Charles Booth's Map of London Poverty, 1889, accompanying *Life and Labour in London*. Priscilla Metcalf adds Ryder's Court, north-east of Leicester Square and between Cranbourn Street and Newport Street, as another Salisbury slum: *Victorian London* (London 1972) p. 147.
56. HHM/3M/L, Nicholson and Herbert to Salisbury, 16 Nov 1880.
57. Ibid.
58. Ibid. The sale was reported in *The Times*, 7 May 1888, p. 8.
59. Metcalf, *Victorian London*, p. 153. The Hotel Cecil, a 'mansarded monster', with twin domes, bore no relation to Lord Salisbury's French residence at Puys, which he sometimes referred to as the Hotel Cecil.
60. HHM/3M/L, Nicholson and Herbert to Salisbury, 11 and 14 July 1868. The estate was given a gross annual value of £22,730 in the early 1890s, in a valuation that was probably a few years out of date: Peter H. Lindert, 'Who Owned Victorian England?' (Davis, Calif., 1983) Appendix B3, p. 28, no. 2690A (the identification with Salisbury is mine).
61. HHM/3M, Salisbury's notebook, 24 Nov 1880.
62. Carola Oman, *The Gascoyne Heiress* (London, 1968) p. 178.
63. Liverpool Public Library, Local History Collection, 920 SAL, 14/35, Leasehold rental, 1851–2; 14/38, Farm rental, 1853–4.
64. Ibid., 14/35, Leasehold rentals 1867–8 and 1888–9.
65. Ibid., 17/12, memorandum on building advances by C. Spencely, solicitor, and G. R. Isborn, surveyor, of Liverpool, 25 Oct 1869; memorandum by Isborn on building-advances account, 15 Dec 1870.

66. HHM/3M/L, Nicholson and Herbert to Salisbury, 13 Nov 1880, referring to their recent visit to the Liverpool property.
67. Liverpool Public Library, 920 SAL, 17/12, Advertisement of Salisbury building-land to let in Everton, Wavertree Road, Green Bank, Broad Green and Childwall, Mosley Hill and Woolton, 1869; HHM/3M/L, Nicholson and Herbert to Salisbury, 13 Nov 1880, discussing Walton Breck Road, Salisbury Road, Wavertree, and Chichester Street, Wavertree.
68. P. J. Waller, *Democracy and Sectarianism: A Political and Social History of Liverpool, 1868–1939* (Liverpool, 1981) p. 139. For other urban landlords who did develop municipal or parliamentary interests, see David Cannadine (ed.), *Patricians, Power and Politics in Nineteenth-Century Towns* (Leicester, 1982); and David Cannadine, *Lords and Landlords* (Leicester, 1980) esp. ch. 2.
69. Oman, *The Gascoyne Heiress*, p. 31.
70. Essex Record Office, Sage Collection Sale Catalogues, vol. 12, Freehold Building Land, Gascoigne Estate, Barking, 1889.
71. HHM/3M/01, random letters to Lord Salisbury, from J. W. Salisbury, Harpenden, 12 Oct 1885, and Lord Salisbury's reply.
72. HHM/3M/D48, to Lady Janetta Manners, 6 Mar 1881, 1 Apr 1888.
73. 'The Marriage Market and Belgravian Intelligence', *Saturday Review*, XII (1861) 9.
74. HHM/3M/D48, to Lady Janetta Manners, 7 Oct 1883.
75. HHM/3M/D82, to Marquis of Bath, 13 Feb 1874.
76. HHM/3M/D29, to Lord Cranbrook, 25 Nov 1886.
77. HHM/3M/C7, Secretary's notebook, to H. S. Foster, South Kensington, 9 May 1892. See Lady Gwendolen Cecil, *Life*, II, 399, for Salisbury's Birmingham speech of 1 Nov 1891.
78. HHM/3M/C7, to W. H. Reynolds, Wolverhampton, 3 Dec 1891.

Reading List

For other relevant – and no less important – material on Salisbury's career, readers should consult the notes elsewhere in this book.

Biographical

David Cecil, *The Cecils of Hatfield House* (London, 1973).

Lady Gwendolen Cecil, *Life of Robert, Marquis of Salisbury*, 4 vols (London, 1921–32).

Lady Gwendolen Cecil, *Biographical Studies of the Life and Political Career of Robert, Third Marquis of Salisbury* (London, 1949).

Judith M. Hughes, *Emotion and High Politics: Personal Relations at the Summit in Late Nineteenth-Century Britain and Germany* (University of California, 1983).

Robert Taylor, *Lord Salisbury* (London, 1975).

Domestic and Irish Politics

J. P. Cornford, 'The Parliamentary Foundations of the Hotel Cecil', in Robert Robson (ed.), *Ideas and Institutions of Victorian Britain* (London, 1967).

Maurice Cowling (ed.), *Conservative Essays* (London, 1978).

L. P. Curtis, *Coercion and Conciliation in Ireland, 1880–1892: A Study in Conservative Unionism* (Princeton and London, 1963).

P. T. Marsh, *The Discipline of Popular Government: Lord Salisbury's Domestic Statecraft, 1881–1902* (Hassocks, Sussex, 1978).

Foreign Affairs

J. A. S. Grenville, *Lord Salisbury and Foreign Policy: The Close of the Nineteenth Century* (London, 1964; rev. edn, 1970).

C. H. D. Howard, *Splendid Isolation: A Study of Ideas Concerning Britain's International Position and Foreign Policy during the Later Years of the Third Marquess of Salisbury* (London, 1967).

C. J. Lowe, *Salisbury and the Mediterranean 1886–1896* (London, 1965).

L. M. Penson, *Foreign Affairs under the Third Marquess of Salisbury* (London, 1962).

Agatha Ramm, 'Lord Salisbury and the Foreign Office', in R. Bullen (ed.), *The Foreign Office, 1782–1982* (Frederick, Md., 1984).

Political Ideas

Elie Kedourie, 'Lord Salisbury and Politics', in *The Crossman Confessions and Other Essays in Politics, History and Religion* (London, 1984).

Michael Pinto-Duchinsky, *The Political Thought of Lord Salisbury, 1854–1868* (London, 1967).

Essays by the Late Marquess of Salisbury K. G.: Biographical (London, 1905).

Paul Smith (ed.), *Lord Salisbury on Politics: A Selection from his Articles in the Quarterly Review, 1860–1883* (Cambridge, 1972).

Index